THE BEST
OF
ROBERT MORLEY

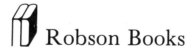 Robson Books

Publisher's note

The material in this volume has been selected by the
author from his four previously published collections:
A Musing Morley (1974), Morley Marvels (1976),
More Morley (1978), Morley Matters (1980).

THIS COLLECTION FIRST PUBLISHED
IN GREAT BRITAIN IN 1981 BY ROBSON
BOOKS LTD., BOLSOVER HOUSE
5—6 CLIPSTONE STREET LONDON W1P 7EB
COPYRIGHT © ROBERT MORLEY

Morley, Robert
   The best of Robert Morley.
   1.   Actors – Great Britain – Biography
   I.   Title
   792'. 028092'4   PN2598. M67
   ISBN 0 86051 146 4

Printed in Hungary

Contents

The Root of All Evil

Flights of Fancy

Morley at Large

Family Album

Dedicated to my wife who has, over the years, lovingly and with conspicuous heroism made *The Best of Robert Morley.*

Preface

I grew up determined to be Basil Loder. I never wanted to drive a train, captain England or write a book. Basil Loder was an officer in the guards who was obliged to resign his commission when he married an actress friend of Sir Gerald Du Maurier's.

We're going back through the years, gentle reader, to the days of the West End theatre. The stalls were somewhere to sit between dinner and supper and in those days they were called Imperial Fauteuils'. 'I have,' people would remark, 'two Imperial Fauteuils for Gerald Du Maurier's new play.' Whether they went on to admit that they were looking forward to catching a glimpse of Basil Loder at the same time is unlikely, but Basil would almost certainly have been there: somewhere, perhaps, towards the end of the first act when excitement was mounting there would be time for a dramatic pause and he would appear dressed for tennis, polo, croquet or in grey flannels and a blazer waiting for his tea. 'Meet you on the course,' he would say, 'in a quarter of an hour'; or 'I put the guns in the car. We really should be on our way'; or 'Monica and I thought of going to the dairy.'

Basil's life off-stage was suggested rather than stated. He could have been a Queen's messenger, a big-game hunter or a golf club secretary. When planning his productions, Du Maurier must have arranged that at least once an act he should be joined on-stage by Basil who might or might not offer him a cigarette, pour him a drink, or pat him gently on the back and indicate where he could be contacted during the next hour or so. He seldom remained on stage for more than a minute or so before sauntering off to the billiard-room, the conservatory or the stables. Sometimes, alas, never to return. As I relived the play after the performance I would suddenly realize that Basil was still taking a bath.

I had the inestimable advantage, therefore, of growing up knowing exactly what I wished to do in life. I wanted to go straight through the looking-glass and join Basil Loder on the other side; but by the time I'd gone through the glass he was no longer there. 'I think I'll just go and get myself buried,' he must have murmured and exited quietly forever. I did, however, get to know his brother Eric, a superb example of the looking-glass man, married to all that was best in the Canadian Pacific Railway. He once confided to me that he and his wife could not conveniently spend their income.

To go through the looking-glass is not, of course, to break it. The glass is intact – it is you who have split yourself in two and now, from the other side, must continually be peering backwards, waiting for the one you left behind to catch up. It is wiser to emulate the antics of those trained in mirror mime if you don't want to leave half of yourself too far behind. It is this conscious desire on my own part to catch up with my image that has created the Robert Morley I have come to know and love: the actor, the writer, the chat show performer and, above all, the chief spokesman for British Airways in America and Heinz soup in Australia. I owe it all to my alter ego. I am mindful when I pause to admire myself in the glass that there are two of us at it. I am by no means the sole culprit yet why this feeling of guilt? Time and time again our mastery of mirror mime has paid off. Together we've succeeded where, had there been only one of us, he must surely have failed. It's only recently that I have begun to have doubts about whither we're both headed. No, that's not strictly true: I know where I'm headed. I am set in my ways. I am stuck in the country. I am happy at my desk, the days filming, the evening chat show, the family lunch on Sunday. Nothing comes amiss. But the other one, the other me, is a shade impatient. What did it mean the other morning when he had already finished shaving while there was still lather on my chin? Will he turn one day and hurry away and will I ever be able to catch him up?

'Which way has he gone?' I will ask. 'What's he up to now? I must know his plans.'

'Lie down old fellow,' they will tell me. 'His plans don't matter anymore. We've sent for the doctor and unless we're very much mistaken, you're the one that's gone on ahead.'

R. M. 1981

A
LIFE
CROWDED
WITH
INCIDENT

Adventures of a Card-Carrying Diner

Every now and again something catches my eye. This morning it was the turn of the spheroid weight clock. The idea, originally conceived in 1670, is for a timepiece relying on spheres or balls as a driving force. A plan to recreate exactly one thousand of them by bringing together brass sheets, steel pins and mature wood through the rare skills of practised craftsmen is now afoot and my application to secure one is keenly anticipated. I am urged not to delay and assured that, as usual, orders will be dealt with in strict rotation.

I am, I must confess, sorely tempted. Only the knowledge that the mechanism requires my attention at thirty-six-hour intervals and that the cost is just over £300, including VAT, makes me hesitate to complete the order form.

Meanwhile, and on another page, an executive credit card wallet is obviously more in tune with my mood, for only yesterday I snapped my Diner's Club card by inadvertently sitting down on it. The problem posed by the executive-type credit card wallet is that there are compartments for four cards and I only possess one, or rather one that I care to support. If I can think what to put in the empty pockets I shall certainly write for one, if only to avoid a repetition of the trauma of yesterday.

I had been invited to luncheon with the Foreign Secretary, a comparatively rare—why should I lie?—a unique happening, and judged I had time enough beforehand to call at the head offices of Diner's Club to secure a fresh talisman.

The foyer of the head office in Oxford Street is just as I had hoped —thick carpets, pretty receptionists, and the sort of helpful, cheerful atmosphere that used years ago, but alas no longer, to distinguish the American Embassy.

I explained at some length that I needed a replacement but that

I had only a few minutes to snatch from my busy life and would perfectly understand if there were other tasks occupying the committee at this time and they would prefer to post me my new card. I was anxious, of course, not to be late for luncheon and, as always when I have more than one task in hand, tended to overstate. Obviously, damaged Diner's Club shields are an everyday occurrence in Oxford Street. I was urged to sit down, not to fuss, and assured that the process would take at the outside two minutes. I was wondering, I told the young lady who now held the two pieces of my card in her hand while she talked into the phone, whether, as my time was nearly up, I might extend my credit for a further period. She frowned slightly and warned that that might take a little longer. Obviously, although she didn't say so, enquiries as to my past conduct would have to be considered at another level. Don't bother, I begged, it was of no consequence. I knew they'd send me a replacement in due course.

For the next ten minutes I sat uneasily, wondering how bad the traffic might be outside and whether I was wise to tarry another moment. Suddenly a young man appeared through one of the many doors which led from the foyer. 'Mr Morley,' he said, 'how nice to see you here. What can we do for you?' Back to square one, I exhibited my divided card, which he took from me. They gave me, he said, the wrong number. I told him I was a little pressed for time. 'This won't take a minute,' he replied. 'Did you want the period extended?' Would it take longer? I asked. He thought it might, and disappeared.

After another ten minutes the picture of the Foreign Secretary impatiently pacing the carpet brought me to my senses. He already had the Cod War on his hands. I had no wish to add to his anxiety. I think, I told the girl, it would be best for all concerned if I were to leave now and they posted the card.

'Hold on,' said the young lady, 'it's on its way.'

Sure enough, through a glass door I espied another approaching with several documents. The new girl greeted me with great cordiality, assured me of the pleasure my visit afforded and invited me to sign first a receipt for the new card and then the card itself. Hastily I complied. 'Sorry to dash off,' I told her, and was about to pick up the card when she herself regained possession. 'We shall need,' she said, 'one more thing . . . identification. Have you a driving licence or a cheque book?' Neither, I assured her, 'but you have my identity card.' 'True,' she said, 'but I have just given you that.'

'What about the old one?' I queried.

'Unfortunately,' she told me, 'I had to destroy that before I could issue this.'

'Look,' I told her, 'this is me. It has been me for years. I have always looked like this.'

'I am afraid,' she said sternly, 'I must call Security.'

My nerve cracked. I had visions of guard dogs snuffling at my heels, of men with mine-detectors, of patient interrogation with lights shining in my eyes. I had visions of disappointing the Cabinet.

Suddenly I snatched the card from her, turned on my heel, ran down the corridor. A lift was waiting. I pressed the button to descend and was immediately whisked to the top of the building. This is it, I told myself. In a moment the bells would start ringing.

The door opened on the top floor. No dogs, no guard, no one. I pressed the button again and reached the ground level. I walked slowly out of the building and down Oxford Street, anticipating the tap on my shoulder.

The annoying thing is that I should have been in plenty of time for luncheon at Marlborough House but when I drove up, proudly displaying the government hospitality sticker on my windscreen, it was to find the gates locked. For a moment I thought the sentry was coming to open them but he turned away, stamping his feet. I left the car and hurried round to the back. There was as yet not much sign of jollification. Perhaps, after all, the Foreign Secretary and I were lunching *vis-à-vis, à deux*, but the invitation had read: to meet the Vice-Premier of New Zealand.

The porter at the door looked a shade bleak. 'Which way for the Kiwis?' I asked. I find it better to establish informal relations as soon as possible with custodians. He looked surprised. 'What would you be wanting?' he asked. I showed him the invitation. 'This is Lancaster House,' he told me . . .

I felt like an American tourist with the right seats for the wrong play. I remembered all the times I had pointed out to Americans the one-time residence of the late Queen Mary.

At least I had my Diner's Club card. Not that I was asked for it.

Accustomed as I am to Public Speaking...

'How would you like,' they ask, 'a trip to Acapulco to give away the awards to the International Balloonists' Association?'

'Very much,' you tell them, and wait expectantly.

'A round trip ticket – first class, naturally – for two?'

'For two!'

'And hotel accommodation and a solatium?'

Once it has been decided to have a conjuror it is always a problem to fix the fee. 'How much would you think was reasonable?' they ask. With balloonists the sky is the limit, you imagine. They laugh uneasily. A figure is broached. You're up and away. It's as simple as that.

At the other end of the scale is the Christmas Bazaar – a humble affair miles from Acapulco, miles from anywhere – on the way to Friern Barnet. No solatium, only the vague hope you will be doing your bit for the Retired Lighthouse-Keepers' Fund. They need that little extra at Christmas now they've left the lighthouse and no helicopter ferries in the turkey and plum pudding.

I never really enjoy opening bazaars; if people decide to support the cause they leave it till later, round about three. Bazaars are opened sharp at two – just the stall-holders, the lady who rang you up last August and her husband playing the Mr. Thatcher role and anxious for you to know he is usually busy in the afternoons. I tell everyone that it's great to be asked on this great day to help this great cause. And that I haven't had to do all the hard work (that bit's true, at least), and I'm not going to detain them a moment longer from spending their money. Then I progress round the stalls spending my own. A cake here, a duster there, and home-made chutney. At least you are sure of the chutney . . . it is impossible to have a failure with chutney; there's nothing to set and no ingredient barred. As I leave the public starts to arrive. Do they realise they've missed me? Have they missed me? If so, they are putting a brave face on it; at this sort of function you need a brave face right through the afternoon.

Acapulco, of course, is more fun – more rewarding too. The vast junket is sponsored by the people who make the balloons, who bottle the gas, who construct the baskets. There are any number of side-shows besides myself. The town is full of conventioneers wearing perspex identity labels; if they were all struck dumb or suffered heart attacks or lost their memories they could be instantly packaged and returned to Washington, Wyoming, Hot Springs. My badge is usually a little more elaborate than theirs – the rosette larger . . . should one wear it at all? It's like announcing one's own name on TV commercials – if they don't know who you are, to hell with them. But of course a lot of them don't know who you are and never will. You can see their lips moving as they spell out the label – at least it's printed clearly. When you give them an autograph you leave them trying to make out who the devil Rob Mosspy thinks he is.

Your part in the ceremonial parade may take only a few moments; once you've made your speech, given away the prizes, you are no longer an employee; you sign for the steak dinner; in an altogether more lordly manner you accept congratulation, your ticket home and your solatium. You tell everyone how much you've enjoyed it and are promised, by a slightly optimistic PRO, a return date next year. You never quite know what to do with the shrunken head they gave you on that last evening. Could it have been a hint? But surely you were asked to show off? Only when you learn that next year's guest is to be Alice Faye do you dispose of it.

Between Acapulco and Friern Barnet come the public luncheons, the banquets, the Brains Trusts, the debates, the invitations to drop in and draw the lucky number out of the tombola. It is never wise to arrive early at any of these functions; once the organisers have got it into their heads that you are going to let them down and not show, they are extravagantly grateful when you finally do turn up. The gin fairly splashes into the glass – it is easy for you to play the hand outstretched. 'But you couldn't really believe I'd forget this was the day? I've been looking forward to it for weeks. Tell me who everyone is.' My trouble is, I can never remember who they are for ten seconds. I confuse the Chair. with the Sec. and mistake last year's Pres. for this year's Treas. Luckily, there are a few simple and abiding guide lines. Everyone works hard at an extraordinarily difficult job, finds immense satisfaction in their task, can be persuaded to tell you at some length how they came to join the organisation, who came to the party last year, and whether or not they've seen *Billy* at Drury Lane.

At luncheon it is always much more difficult to talk to men than women. Although I have a sneaky admiration for their love of punishment

I personally find the Rotarians something of a trial. For one thing, they usually ask me to speak-about the theatre – about which they have a very limited knowledge and interest – and for another the food is always terrible. I think food is important, obviously, but never more so than shortly before you are due to be spoken to – or should it be at?

Years ago I campaigned in Australia for a higher standard of public nosh. After I had been asked out on at least fifty occasions and invariably complained about the quality of the cold ham, I was bidden to a special banquet and invited to choose the menu. I suppose I went to town, but on this occasion I was the only one to be served with caviare, sole and a partridge – everyone else ate ham as usual. I think I was supposed to feel ashamed, but I didn't – just not as hungry as usual.

Nearly everyone who rises to propose a toast begins by depreciating himself or herself, saying how unfit they are for the task and how worried their spouse or child is at this moment in time. The battle is lost before it's begun but you can't stop them going on trying to fight it. Hence the nightly torture inflicted on all good men foolish enough to come to the aid of the party.

There is another side of the business I haven't touched on but which provides a golden retirement to a host of charming and unobtrusive busybodies who flit from Angmering to Broadstairs and back to Luton, speaking at Ladies' Luncheon Clubs on everything under the sun from cleaning the Crown Jewels to keeping bees in the Holy Land. Such activity is organised by professional matchmakers who have an encyclopaedic knowledge of their clients' depth of interests and purses, who select from their catalogue of playmates the one most likely to succeed at a party of culture vultures in Basingstoke and who will leave their listeners a little wiser and better briefed on the loves of the late Lord Byron. It is not knowledge which will stay with them. There is no danger that next week their thoughts will still be on Marathon when they are finding out exactly what to do to get a reasonable brass rubbing when they've forgotten the blanco. Knowledge comes and goes, and there is no lack of speakers. One of the really nice things about talking to the girls is that you get the fee immediately afterwards in a plain envelope.

Cold Comfort

There are people apparently who never have a cold, and I am grateful not to be one of them. Every now and then I need a cold in the head and every now and then, thanks to the bounty of nature, I get one. I am one who welcomes the early warning system going into action. That prickling at the back of the throat, the sudden but unmistakeable urge to halt awhile, to take stock of one's symptoms and to plan ahead. 'I think,' I announce, 'I may be starting a cold.' I find it helpful to make an early announcement, not so much to alert others, but to alert myself. Having decided thus to have a cold, there is a good deal to be decided. Where, for instance, do I intend to have my cold? I dream naturally of bed, to go to bed with a cold, to climb between crisp, clean sheets at about half past eleven in the morning, to arrange the radio on the bedside table, to get others to carry the television up to the bedroom and place it at the foot of the bed. To put out the aspirins and the lemon cordial, to satisfy oneself that there is plenty of whisky in the bottle, and then to close one's eyes and doze fitfully, waking only occasionally to manage a little lunch or tea, or to summon one of the family to enquire bravely what they've been up to and whether it's still raining. To feel a little better and then a little worse, to be not absolutely certain the whole thing isn't going to my chest. Tomorrow, I tell myself, I'll go to bed tomorrow, better still I won't even get up. It's no good walking around and giving everyone else my cold. I find a cold improves my character enormously. I develop what is for me an altogether unnatural concern for others. 'I won't kiss you,' I tell comparative strangers whom indeed I have never kissed before, 'I won't kiss you because I have a little bit of a cold.' They must know as I do how ill I really am, and admire as I do, my own courage and fortitude.

As a child I was put to bed with a cold and although I specialised in bilious attacks, I was always glad of the few extra days' respite from the horrors of childhood. People were nicer to me when I was in bed. I needed people to be nicer to me. I still do, which is why when I am getting a cold, even if I only think I may be getting one, I tell as many people as possible. If I am in a play, the first person I tell is my understudy. I like to see the emotions I have aroused. He rather enjoys playing my part. On the other hand, he quite obviously has no desire to step to stardom over my dead body. 'If I'm not better, I think I shall stay off tomorrow,' I tell him. On the morrow my cold is worse, and I insist on playing.

My cold wakes me in the night. At other times I sleep in a great gulp of unconsciousness, but to put on the light and grope for a handkerchief, and then for my watch, to realise at five in the morning how much of the night still remains for slumber is a luxury usually denied me. It is surprising how well I feel, except for my cold. Deafness no longer worries me. The onslaught of writer's cramp appears to have receded, my digestion is back to square one. In another week my cold will be gone, and I shall have other things to think about, other people to enquire after, but just at the moment I am concentrating all my resources, all my reserves of courage on that most faithful and loyal confidant, myself. I want him to get better, and he usually does.

My life, like most people's lives, has a terrible monotony. That is why nature invented the cold, and why it has been such a success over the years. It provides man with an opportunity to break out, to desert the canteen at lunchtime and visit the chemist's to shop around for some wonder drug without the benefit of skilled medical interference. His cold provides him with a topic of conversation and perhaps a few days' holiday. He will return, having got over his cold − note the phrase − he has surmounted yet another obstacle in the long march to the grave. The common cold is the rainbow in the medical history of a man's life, a sign that he will get better this time. He will get ill again, of course, but this time he will recover.

Waste Not, Want Not

Each morning I pad down to the kitchen and while my wife lays up the breakfast tray, I pick up the mail from the floor and tear open the envelopes. On an average half of their contents go, after a moment's hesitation, into the dustbin outside, although for some reason I am usually left with the envelopes. I realise that a good deal of time, effort and thought has gone into the task of contacting me in favour of the *Reader's Digest's* special offer of *The Tale of Two Cities*, or to alert me that a limited number of medals are now available (but won't apparently be so for long) with Churchill's face on the obverse. I don't, of course, believe that just because *I* don't rise to the bait, no fish are caught that particular morning. It's true I have never seen a Churchill medal on the lapel of any of my neighbours, but we are an unostentatious lot around this neck of the Thames Valley. It is not for me to estimate how much it costs someone to employ the vast army of executives, market experts, typists, designers and even postal sorters to mount these operations, but it must pay, and life would be immeasurably duller if people like me were not apprised daily of an entirely new scheme which would cut out death duties, or of another which will enable us to make a profitable living on the racecourse in future.

I only mention all this because on my desk at this moment there lies an order form for an article of six hundred words on Waste, numbered Job No. 062J503, and promising a reward. I should have been annoyed if it had found its way into the dustbin.

When chided that I am wasting time, money or breath, I am fairly certain to be enjoying myself. I am not so much a waster as a recylist. I recycle money at speed, in at one pocket, out the other is my practice. No one knows how long the stuff will last; the trick surely is not to be caught holding any of the bread when you are picked up for the last time. I wasn't even holding any when I was picked up for the first time, unless you count one or two pre-birth rattles and a small sum payable on my twenty-first birthday, a legacy from a defunct grandparent. Even when you are a baby it is never wise to count on anything promised from living relatives. Where there's a will, there is often a change.

Spending and money are synonymous – like moment and time. I am not saying it's a waste of breath to utter such phrases, because some people enjoy using redundancies, and the whole idea of saving one's breath is ludicrous. The quickest way to die is to hold your breath, or get someone to hold it for you. I suppose if someone really bores you, you might ask him to recycle his breath a little more slowly, but it probably wouldn't help in the long run, which brings us to the third imponderable, Time itself. Nearly everyone resents the other fellow's work rate. The man in the Jaguar will honk at the roadmender, brewing up; the housewife chivvy and complain of the plumber who is taking time out for a fag. The housewife genuinely believes it's her time because she is paying for it. Victorian tyranny subscribed to the theory of time being bought and sold. A twelve-fifteen hour day was not uncommon. Later ten, and now eight hours is regarded as the acceptable norm. Doctor Brudski, the celebrated Polish economist (who resides, naturally, in London) recently opined that a four-hour day would soon be mandatory if the economy was to recover equilibrium, and I go along with the doctor. Personally, I enjoyed the recent three-day week. I didn't work it, actually, because I wasn't employed at the time, but I know a lot of people who did. Thursday to Monday makes a nice break. '*You* may have enjoyed it,' my business friends tell me, 'but we lost a hell of a lot of motor cars and pocket computers.'

Pocket computers are the new growth industry, apparently. I bought mine in the transit lounge in Bahrein, because all the sales staff were using them avidly. It now lies in a drawer of my desk, along with tape recorders, pocket barometers, desk sets, electric erasers, complimentary money clips, jumbo-size fountain pens, eight rulers and three travellers' cheques for twenty pounds each. I think I shall probably throw away a ruler one day soon, but I don't imagine even then it will be wasted. Some fool is sure to unearth it eventually on the rubbish heap, and take it home. 'Look what I've found,' he'll tell them, 'a perfectly good ruler.'

It's easy to get rid of money and time and breath, and typing paper, come to think of it, but rubbish clings to one. If all the cardboard boxes containing old lampshades were collected and piled on top of each other, and a man climbed to the summit of the heap, he could look down on Everest.

The Collector

From time to time I have wandered into Sotheby's, playing at being a connoisseur. I have purchased a catalogue at the door and stared at the paintings on the walls. I have never actually plucked up sufficient courage to ask to hold an object of vertu in my hand, but I have examined the folly of Fabergé at a respectful distance. In one of the many houses I shared with my parents years ago, we had a specimen table, a small oval affair on which the objects displayed were protected by a glass top. There were one or two miniatures, a silver coach, a Victorian châtelaine and a parasol handle by the master himself, but not much else. In Sotheby's I have a special expression I adopt when I think anyone is watching. Only I know whether this Vermeer is genuine and no one is going to call my hand, it says.

In the sale-room itself I am circumspect and motionless, always apprehensive lest by some involuntary movement I acquire a porcelain horse or a commode. I am happy in Sotheby's because there is little I want and seldom anything I could afford. Not having bought Lot 185 for seventy-five pounds I am, I argue, seventy-five pounds better off. It must be terrible to be a collector, to go round the world seeking pieces of milk glass and finding them, at a price. In point of fact I do collect silver donkeys, but find my enthusiasm impaired. I am beginning to think I shan't ever buy another. In my youth I once owned a stamp album, but I was and still am extremely clumsy and impatient with inanimate objects, and I soon tired of sticking in the stamps on the wrong pages and trying to detach them again without tearing them.

With an hour to kill in a strange town I, like everyone else, search out the antique shop, unless the pub is open. There must be something about living with sixteen cupboards at the same time that induces resignation. All antique dealers share this curious detachment, or is it I who have the same effect on each of them? They don't seem to expect me to buy anything. My arrival interrupts them apparently, but from what task?

They seem to have just stepped out of old-fashioned motor cars and not yet had time to undo the cords that bind the refectory table to the roof. Like racehorse trainers, they are always on the move.

In inspecting the stock, I ignore the goods on display; hidden in a dark corner, I tell myself, is the treasure I seek, but how will I recognise it? I know the dialogue once I have done so, of course.

'That old lamp, how much would you want for that?'

'I didn't even know I had it. Take if for fifty pence. It's no use to me.'

After that I only have to carry it ouside and rub. But to rub what? Ah, there's the rub. Would I recognise a Renoir or a sixteenth-century wassail cup? Unlikely; more than unlikely – unthinkable. Why then do I waste my time? Why do I pause, once over the threshold, and listen with such pleasure to the jangling of the bell and the footsteps of the approaching proprietor? Why do I long to be confronted with age in a cardigan? When I come face to face with anyone young and obviously on the ball, I cut short my visit. What I am really looking for is a victim. If there is to be a wide boy, it's got to be me.

Of course, it's different if you're selling something, as I was the other morning. I arrived early. Sotheby's had hired the gold chairs and the television set. The catalogues were over two pounds, but I had brought the one they had already posted to me. One of the perks is not having to pay for a catalogue. You also get a chair reserved, but I didn't sit on mine. I perched at the back on a table. I thought some dealer might be made a shade more comfortable, might even stay longer and bid for my lot, which came on at the end, more or less. My lot was a Utrillo. I had bought it casually one day out of a window in Bond Street when I had decided to turn myself into a company. In those days it was a fashionable tax ploy. It didn't work, of course; no tax ploy ever really works. If it did it would mean the end for chartered accountants. If there was a Golden Mean, a guaranteed panacea against tax, how simple life would be, and how happy. I bought the picture for my boardroom, not so well furnished as some, being just a shack in the garden. I didn't hang it there. I was always hoping to hold our annual general meetings in the drawing-room, where we could all admire my attempt to emulate Onassis. But the annual general meeting for some reason was invariably held at my accountants; and on the day when they wound up the company they asked about the picture, and it was suggested that I ought to sell it and give the proceeds to the Revenue. I didn't feel particularly aggrieved. I had looked at the picture for twenty years and was a bit sick of it.

In course of time, Sotheby's sent an expert to look at it himself. He didn't think it was the best Utrillo he had ever seen, but he did think it would fetch a good deal more than I had paid for it. I felt strangely proud. For once my art appreciation had been vindicated. Flushed with triumph I showed him another picture I had bought at about the same time, but lightning, it seemed, had as usual not struck twice.

On the appointed day I delivered the picture to Sotheby's and they took it into their custody with the casual sangfroid which distinguishes the firm. I left it propped against a door, along with its betters, waiting to have its photograph taken for the catalogue. The latter, when it arrived, was impressive. On the cover was a list of the vendors. I was delighted at my own billing. This is the sort of cast I have always dreamed of appearing with. The Viscount Astor, The Edward James Foundation, Mrs. Bernard Van Custem, Monsieur Clement Rouart of Paris, The Estate of the late Hugo Cassirer, and Me.

The best pictures of all, however, seldom disclosed the owner's name. The Provenance stopped just short of that. Who, for instance, was selling the Renoir? As it turned out, no one. It was bought in for just under three hundred thousand pounds, but most of the others sold, though not as well as had been expected. There were four Pissarros which went as one lot for two hundred and twenty thousand. The auctioneer gave no indication of whether the price was a triumph or a disaster. Neither, I suppose; just about average. How often, I wondered, did they sell four Pissarros on the same morning and all together, in one minute flat?

I suppose it's only money, after all. From the back it was difficult to tell where the bidding came from. Sometimes the buyer's name was announced, but as often as not, Mr. Wilson merely looked in someone's direction and nodded. Half way through the sale I dropped the top of my felt pen. For a good ten minutes I concentrated on recovering it. I was convinced it had rolled some distance and pursued it under everyone's feet. I didn't bob up too quickly, lest I should be mistaken for a bidder. While Manets and Degas were disposed of above my head, I crawled around unheeding. I needed the top, I told myself, needed it more than an Impressionist picture at that moment. Suddenly I found it on the pen itself. It hadn't rolled away after all. Something else must have dropped, but what it was I never found out. By the time my picture came under the hammer I was late for lunch. It fetched almost exactly what the expert had predicted.

I haven't the slightest idea who bought it. I don't miss it. I hope the Revenue will spend the money sensibly and are grateful that all those years ago I walked down Bond Street with an eye for a bargain.

Let Your Fingers Do the Aching

Our village now boasts a medical centre. No longer are we permitted to pay a personal call on our medicos, to trudge up the garden path and, passing through a side door, enter the old homestead, catching a glimpse through the window of the doctor's brood hatching round the swimming pool or returning, kitted up, from a brisk winter toboggan ride. How healthy they always seem, plenty of fresh air, nourishing food and instant correctives at hand for any childish irregularities.

But is this so, I wonder? While health may be the perquisite of Master Dose, the doctor's son, it becomes increasingly obvious that Mr Dose has by no means had his fair share of it. Far from it.

The other morning, suffering from a severely strained finger, I made my way to the new premises, where chairs are arranged in a small airline hangar or conference chamber and patients wait like passengers in transit for their papers to be shuffled and a summons to be issued by the processing dispenser. Gone are the posters urging forward hesitant blood donors and chill warnings on smoking and breast cancer. Even the' well-thumbed periodicals seem to have disappeared.

There were in fact no other customers present; it was after hours and I had accepted an invitation to attend when more urgent cases had been already prescribed for and were e'en now hurrying home to bed, or the armchair in front of the telly, carrying magic potions and certificates of inability to work.

My own doctor was still discussing the day's happenings with his locum—possibly the last but by no means the least Latin word still in use by the Profession. Always delighted with a second stethoscope, I exhibited my finger and explained that a Mr George Cole, with whom I was currently acting, had damaged it by falling clumsily into my arms one evening in the previous week and that it still hurt.

'It would do,' said my doctor, 'and eventually it may thicken up like mine.' He held up his finger with every appearance of pride.

'That,' remarked the locum, 'was where he was bitten by a patient.'

I am, I trust, never slow to see a joke. Moreover I have always encouraged the medical profession to try and look on the bright side. Too often they appear downcast about their own pay packets or when discussing euthanasia and kindred topics on television. I therefore gave a chuckle of appreciation and enquired whether, in my case, the digit was actually broken. My doctor re-examined it, rotated it gently and decided it wasn't.

'What shall I do about it?' I asked.

'Nothing,' he told me. 'There's nothing you can do with a finger.' He studied his own with apparent satisfaction. There seemed little left for me to do on this occasion but wish them both the compliments of the season and tell myself I am lucky to have a doctor so patently aware of the limitations of medical skill.

Over Christmas my finger became increasingly painful. The day after Boxing Day was, I estimated, a permissible date once more to engage their attention. The premises were now decorated with a sprig of holly.

'Has,' I enquired of the dispenser, 'medical knowledge made any significant advance over Christmas, at least where sprained fingers are concerned?'

The dispenser is an old and valued friend who, having presided for many years over the appointment book and the drug cupboard, has perforce the task of alerting the medico as to what actually ails the patients. She can tell whooping cough a mile off, and from a slightly closer distance distinguish chicken pox from measles. Naturally she rows in with the modern conception that the physician and his staff have healed, or at least treated, themselves for every imaginable complaint to which flesh is heir, and is herself the president of our local Weight Watchers. I never meet her without remembering how, years ago, I and a bunch of fellow-actors inspected the wards of the Liverpool General Hospital, an enormous Gothic building in which we started our tour with the prematures and concluded with the stiffs where we were encouraged to admire the post-mortem stitching—a dying craft, apparently. I cannot now remember the purpose of our visit. Could we have been contemplating a Repertory production of *The Doctor's Dilemma*? While being revived by Matron after the ordeal, I fell to questioning her over the sherry as to what extraordinary ailments she had encountered during her professional life.

'Only the other day,' she confided, 'we had a patient here with a skin rash which seemed to trouble him, and certainly the doctors, who tried a variety of treatments on him without success. One day a junior intern was leaning against the porter's desk when the patient looked in to have his hand redressed. "How," said the ancient custodian, "is your leprosy case getting on?" Of course he was right —that's what it was. Leprosy. We hadn't seen a case here for years.'

'Were you able to cure him?' I asked.

'I think we shipped him back to India,' Matron replied.

But to get back to my finger. This time the locum was on his own. 'What seems to be the trouble?' he asked. I reminded him of my earlier visit. 'Ah, yes,' he told me. 'I remember perfectly. It's been paining you, has it? Let's have a look. My goodness, it's quite swollen. What you have done here,' he informed me, 'is to release some latent rheumatism.'

'I haven't got rheumatism,' I assured him.

'You have now,' he replied. 'Let me tell you of my own experience. I was drawing up a bucket from an old well when unaccountably my hand slipped on the winch. The handle rotated sharply and, as far as I was concerned, unexpectedly, in an obverse direction and I experienced a sharp pain in my second digital joint. In other words, exactly as you have done—I sprained it. I remember I was in considerable pain or at least discomfort for five or six weeks. Eventually, however, I made a complete recovery.'

'No thickening?' I asked.

'Absolutely not.' He held his finger aloft.

'So you think,' I said, 'that the pain will continue for five weeks and then everything will be hunky-dory?'

'Ah,' he said, 'all cases are different. There is no hard and fast rule with fingers, alas.'

I forbore to ask him why in that case he had told me about his own symptoms. I knew already.

The medical profession has made a dramatic switch from witch doctors to trade unionists. Juju is out, differentials are in. As part of the campaign to create a different image, the doctor has not only come down to earth, he is already at least readying a plot of the stuff for his own use. We are all human, he tells his patients, subject to all the illnesses of man, and we shall eventually and inevitably succumb to one or other of them. Let me tell you of the ones I have suffered, indeed from which I am still suffering. I, too, have had hernias, gall-bladders, lassa fever, mumps, shingles and of course triennial diverticulosis, which is now troubling your good self. Nowadays it is impossible to find an illness from which your medical practitioner hasn't made at least a partial recovery. You name it, he's had it.

When I left the surgery it was with a bottle of pills. 'It seems strange to take pills for a sprained finger,' I remarked to a colleague at the theatre that evening who himself walks with a pronounced limp.

'Indolid,' he told me, 'we're all on that.'

I do not care for an ailment of mine, still less a panacea, to be dismissed lightly. 'Do you happen to know whether,' I asked, 'it's habit-forming? Are there any side effects I should know about? Will it make me drowsy?'

'Not more than usual,' he opined, 'but you want to be careful how you pick up things. The purpose of the drug is to relax the muscles. You can easily strain a finger, and not realise it at the time.'

Show Me the Way to Go Home

I am always surprised by a good map. Like life itself it assumes it knows better than I where the pieces fit in. It is the ultimate in the finished jigsaw and constantly surprises.

Once, in Russia, gazing at the wide open spaces of Siberia and not wishing to be thought by the Intourist guide to have entirely lost my bearings, I remarked that in Britain the sea is usually blue, at least on the map. So it is here, she assured me. No, white, I told her. All that ocean is white, unless the map has faded. Removing my index finger sternly from the middle of China, she explained that China had been thereabouts ever since she could remember.

I was taught Geography at school but never took to it. Just as now my mind becomes a blank when introducing person to person, so in those days I failed to recall the necessary seven seaside towns beginning with the letter P or the names of the tributaries running into the Humber. Equally, at school I was unable to satisfy my inquisitors by producing a map which bore any relation to the shape of the country, let alone the size. On my page there was never room for Scapa Flow, which is probably why I still haven't been there.

I suspect that I am not the only one who still can't work out on a map where I am, in full global context. I accept that were I to go round and round I would end up in the same place from where I started, but at the age of four, when I seemed to have peaked as far as awareness was concerned, I had it all explained to me by a nurse on Folkestone Shingle and immediately started digging furiously to reach Australia, which Nannie assured me was at my feet. Alas, I was interrupted, and Australia had to wait quite a time before they first cheered me in soup commercials.

Nevertheless, I am never discouraged by my inability to map-read and seldom get into a car without enquiring whether I can act as route-finder. 'Give it me in any case,' I tell them, 'I like to know where I'm going.'

It always takes me several minutes to pinpoint our point of departure by which time, unless I manage to delay the start on some pretext, we've moved on. I usually find that a complication now arises. Our route is invariably in reverse to that indicated. Thus, although travelling from Bognor Regis to Epping, say, the cartographer has assumed I wish to proceed backwards. It is quite fatal to reverse the map, as although by so doing you can tell right from left, you cannot, unless dyslexia plays its part in your vision, read the place names.

On the other hand, holding the map correctly I find it virtually impossible to twist my neck sufficiently to read any but the largest cities marked on our route and these, naturally, I would wish to avoid. On a journey as tortuous and convoluted as I describe, and if the vehicle is travelling at speed, I find I am off the page, still unprepared to turn the sheet music; the car is now in the middle of the third movement, I am either still on the second or, even worse, already embarked on the fourth.

The average motoring map is not structured for continuity unless one proceeds straight down the middle of the land and this often involves vast fuel expenditure. Once, one could obtain from friendly, if profligate motoring associations, route maps which were tailored to your need. Thus, driving even in the reverse direction from that indicated was comparatively simple, you could read the map from top to bottom as if it were Chinese and understand it a good deal better. True, in order to obtain them you had to belong to a club and display a badge on the bonnet and, in earlier days, men were deployed at cross-roads to stand and salute as you passed by. I remember so well the pleasure of those salutes and how perfectly I acknowledged them with a brief smile and nod. A wave would have been overdoing it. The legend was that when the scout failed to salute, it was not because he was bored or had the sun in his eyes, but that a little further on a policeman was hiding in the ditch with a stop-watch at the ready, while further on still his colleague waited to flag you down for exceeding the speed limit.

Although as I write I am continually worsted by maps, I still enjoy the encounter and can never resist helpful comments and the occasional expression of surprise. 'I should have thought,' I tell the driver, 'that it would have been quicker to have taken the Lyme Regis route, it certainly looks more direct, but I expect you know best.' I like to suggest that, were it not for the fact he needs both feet for the controls, my companion ought to be kicking himself at this point.

In the days when I toured Britain by rail in search of theatres sufficiently unsophisticated to permit me to perform in them, I used to sit opposite a very old actor whose sole contribution to any conversation was to announce the name of the station at which we had stopped but were not planning to alight. He had for every town in England a comment connected with an earlier struggle. Thus, on reaching Widnes he would recall a landlady there once tried to charge him extra for coal, or on halting at Leamington Spa he remembered for our delight how he had been badly poisoned by a meat pie which he had purchased the day before in Darlington. We never, unfortunately, stopped long enough in Darlington to enable him to carry out his threat of personal violence towards the vendor.

Similarly, when we toured by motor I frequently had resources to a gazetteer, now alas mislaid, which enlivened the journeys for my companions when I was able to read aloud the delights of the villages through which we passed. 'Osterly,' I would tell them, 'here there is an interesting Norman church with a perp. tower and tomb of a crusader, while further along the road we shall come to Connis Grange, the seat of the Mountjoy family but not, alas, open to the public.'

I enjoy the maps provided by airlines, following as best I can the ruled lines of the routes so neatly drawn across the world. We must, I tell myself after a long, intricate calculation, surely be in the middle of Iran and, if I look down, I should be able to manage to pinpoint Isfahan. 'In a few minutes,' announces the Captain at this moment, 'passengers on the left of the plane will be able to see the lights of Tbilisi.' Either he is lost, or we have not been travelling at the proper speed.

On the rare occasions when I know which country we are crossing I am constantly surprised by the terrain as it appears beneath. Countries which I believed populated seem comparatively deserted, whilst others, such as Greenland, appear to me at any rate to teem with life. 'How extraordinary,' I remember remarking to a companion, 'that so many houses around these parts appear to have swimming pools.' The fellow seemed surprised. 'What houses?' he asked. 'What swimming pools?' I pointed at the sparkling reflections beneath. 'Those are icebergs,' he told me.

I cannot forbear to mention, although I fear I may have done so before, my finest hour as a map-reader, when I sat beside David Tomlinson in an attempt to cross the English Channel in a small plane manifestly underpowered and in dense fog. David, impatient of my inability to follow the route, seized the map, looked at it briefly, referred to the instrument panel and jotted a calculation down while still grasping the joy-stick.

'As I thought,' he announced, 'we are about to land at Lydd.'

At that moment the fog lifted momentarily to disclose us dead on course for Lancing Chapel spire. 'I see they moved that, then,' was all I said. It was the bravest thing I ever said.

Rather to my surprise, it was not to prove the last.

Myself and I

What pride we fatties take in shedding a few pounds; how we love to be able to button our coats once more and enquire of our friends whether they have noticed anything about us. 'Lost a bit, haven't you?' 'Yes,' we tell them, adding as reassurance that this is not a wasting disease, but sheer will power. My present pathetic attempt to join the ranks of the sightly was triggered off by a paperback I picked up in Deauville after a particularly unsuccessful evening at the tables.

The morning after is for me a time of resolution. I wake early and lie in bed cursing my folly. I am not a good loser. I read once that all gamblers are ugly, and on such mornings I recall the faces around the table and compare my own in the mirror of the hotel bedroom. 'So that's why I gamble,' I tell myself, 'because I am not beautiful.' From now on, I decide, everything will be different. No more lunatic forays to the green baize. But good resolution does not end there. My whole way of life must in future be purposeful and to begin with I must change my image. Remorse and diet complement each other. Having shed the weight I can begin to search afresh for the treasure which lies just beneath the surface of my mind. I will write a play, or better still a novel, and sell the film rights for a fortune. It would be simpler and quicker probably to win the money on the football pools, but that way lies not redemption. Banning myself from casinos and racetracks I vow never again to fill in a football coupon. It doesn't last, naturally, but while it does I am proud of the fact that I am no longer myself. I pass up the rolls and butter, disdainfully regard the plates of others, and when the call for luncheon comes, sit on at my desk, admiring the waistline which is to come. One meal a day is enough for anyone, even a dog.

My paperback tells me that there is scarcely a man or woman in America or western Europe who isn't, like myself, overweight. We are all, it seems, dying of over-eating. The world is no longer divided between the fat and the thin, but between the very fat and the fairly fat. Why this theory should help keep me on a diet I don't know, but it does — at the moment. I shall soon be back, I suppose, to the old sweet trolley, the spinning ball, toast and butter and baccarat, but meanwhile I don't plan to join Gamblers' Anonymous or the Weightwatchers. I don't want to belong to a group. It's just possible that there are people as silly as I, or even sillier, but I don't particularly want to know them. Above all I don't want to know myself. Not because I don't love myself, I do, passionately, but because I am fascinated by my unpredictability. What, I wonder, am I going to think next, let alone do? All the years I have known myself still leave me totally unprepared for my next thought or action. There are patterns, of course, of a sort. I know, for instance, that so many times a day I shall stop whatever I am doing and play myself one or two games of Box-O. For ignorant readers, perhaps I should explain that this game consists of throwing dice into a small tray and endeavouring to cancel out exactly the digits one to nine by throwing the right numbers. I play myself for enormous stakes, often a million pounds, and on occasions my life. I also take omens. A favourable result will secure me a film or at least a successful medical.

Normally a cautious sort of fellow, there seems no limit to my recklessness when I am with myself. I will sit in a hotel lobby or on a park bench, one leg crossed over the other, and the toe of my shoe pointing at a hall porter or a tree, waiting for the seventeenth to breast the tape. The seventeenth person is the one whom I have promised myself I am to marry, or exchange worldly wealth or age or health, or, if it is a particularly slack afternoon and neither of us is inclined for larger stakes, a head of hair. The seventeenth having passed, I am seldom content with my fate, petitioning myself for three more lives, and promising that if, at the end of this borrowed time I am still not suited, I will cheerfully submit to the death penalty.

What purpose is there in all this, you ask, and why tell us about it? Be patient, gentle reader. How would you have liked to have lived with absurdity all your life? How would you like never to be able to go for a gentle stroll without suddenly being interrupted and dared to reach the pillarbox ahead of the lady with the Pekinese, or the postman on his bicycle, or merely the next bus? I know only too well that if I shrug off the challenge I shall die before I reach the age of seventy-four. Even more difficult are the contests not to arrive ahead of, but to pass at precisely the same moment. I am no judge of pace, and have long ago given up driving a car. Besides, for some reason or other I am not allowed to run. Years ago, when we were both children, and by far the easiest way to avoid the cracks on the pavement was to do so on tiptoe, I was sternly forbidden. Flat-foot or nothing was the rule. It's no wonder, really, that I take so little exercise.

All in all I suppose I am more fortunate than most; as I have already observed I genuinely like myself, and have no reason to believe that the feeling is not reciprocated. There is little of what used to be called jobbing back; both of us realising that we are capable of mischief has kept us out of trouble. Only on very rare occasions do we despair simultaneously. Worse things happen at sea has been our favourite proverb. I like to humour myself. In the final analysis he is the only one on whom I can rely. We were born and we shall die quite alone, save for each other.

The Man of Leisure

All characters are imaginary, with the possible exception of my father, and bear no relation to any living member of my family or their friends.

We had a house once in the grounds of Wellington College, and my father decided to build a pool in the garden, in which he could keep goldfish, and even dug a few spadefuls before the jobbing gardener took over. When the time came to lay the concrete, we all weighed in. My father was not, strictly speaking, a do-it-yourself man. Something went wrong with the mix and the goldfish were always waking in the night, gasping for water. My father's design for the pool, like its construction, could be faulted, its proportions resembling a washbasin which had become detached from its pedestal. A year after it was completed, my father's marriage broke up along with his folly. No great harm was done by either event and it was simple to lift the pieces of concrete off the damp, beaten-down earth and hope the slugs would find a new home.

It was some forty years later that I was in a position to build a pool of my own, an altogether larger affair in which we could all swim. Up to that time I had taken my young to swim at my neighbour's. Rumour had it that he didn't like children, but I ignored the *canard*. He was a generous fellow, a man of the utmost good humour, and married into the bargain. If there was a cloven hoof concealed by the white flannels he habitually sported, I failed to observe it, indeed would have taken pains not to do so. It was inconceivable to me that he didn't look forward to our arrival to splash happily about in his elegant pseudo-Grecian folly. It is true he only heated the water at weekends and missed the brouhaha during the week when he was working away in town to earn the bread to buy the coke, for his was an old-fashioned boiler designed some years before the war, but Friday to Sunday we were in clover at a temperature of eighty and better.

As I say, I simply didn't believe he didn't like children, although sometimes I would admonish my chicks not to be quite so scream-happy. 'Mr. Neighbour,' I would tell them, 'doesn't really like . . .' – I couldn't bring myself to betray him completely – '. . . doesn't like children screaming,' I would finish lamely, as I threw their water wings onto the back seat and slammed the door.

It is the noise of the door slamming that I have come to dread in my turn, now I am older and wiser, disturbing the afternoon siesta beside my own water-hole. It could be the butcher's car in the drive or the postman's (mysteriously, we still rate two deliveries a day), or it could be my wife back from shopping, only I know she hasn't gone shopping. I close my eyes for the last ten seconds of bliss and open them, aware of the advance of the Pool Men. They come armed with flippers and rings and inflatable rubber monsters. Some of them even bring aqualungs and snorkel tubes. Some of them are already in swimming costumes, others disappear briefly into the house in search of a changing-room and a loo. The mothers, the au pairs, the house guests bring up the rear carrying baskets of food and clothes. Even if one doesn't have to rise to greet the children, it's a brave man who doesn't bestir when the grown ups start introducing each other.

'We've come to swim. I do hope you don't mind. This is Mrs. Armitage who's staying with us, and you know Bertha from Stockholm. George, say good afternoon to Mr. Morley, and Prudence, and this is their friend, Simon, and his friend Tiger, at least we call him Tiger.'

The children approach warily, anxious to have done with formality. They hurry away to dip their hands in the water and look reproachfully at me.

'It's colder than yesterday. Much colder.'

'It's been raining,' I tell them apologetically. Why the hell do I have to apologise for the rainfall?

The largest child always jumps in beside me.

'Not to splash,' comes a split second after the soaking.

'I am not sure whether Tiger swims or not,' says one of the mums cheerfully, 'but no doubt we shall find out.'

The mums don't swim, at least not right away. They like to talk and cover themselves with oil. One or two of them bring pencils and *The Times* crossword. The children demand an audience. 'Watch me, Mummy, watch me,' they shout and Mummy not only watches, but shouts back. She knows Sylvia can't hear under her bathing cap, so she shouts first to indicate that she wishes to communicate, and the second time, when Sylvia has temporarily disengaged her cap from her ear, because everyone else is shouting too.

I am a man who scoffs at those who wash their cars on Sundays in their drives, yet am a compulsive pool-cleaner myself. I really worry about the band-aids and elastoplast e'en now sinking to the bottom. I don't even like the way the children suck up the water and then expel it. When one of them complains that his eyes are stinging, I make a mental note to increase the algymycin as soon as the opportunity presents itself. After a few minutes the withdrawal symptoms start. Some of the young begin to shiver violently, some of the mothers to try and get their loved ones out of the water and into a towel. The exchanges begin with cajolery and finish in violent confrontation.

'Mummy says out, Roger. Daphne dear, I think you have been in long enough.' No child ever agrees. It is a point of honour to demand another few minutes, a last float to see who is shivering most. 'If you don't come out now I shan't bring you again.' Oh, if only I could believe it, if only Henry believed it, if only Mother herself believed it. 'If you don't come out now there'll be no television for a *week*.' The threats are empty. They always were, even in my own childhood. When the bathing finally stops, the children begin to think of things for me to do. 'Uncle Robert, will you get the croquet mallets? Mr. Morley, will you put up the swing? Can we see the skull which laughs? Where's the cat?'

'You are not to bother Mr. Morley,' the mothers insist. 'It's time for tea. I wonder if you have such a thing as a knife. We don't seem to have remembered to bring one for the cake.'

On my way back from the kitchen I observe the little groups picnicking on the grass. I am filled with remorse at my own inhospitality. 'There's food in the house,' I tell them, 'and chocolate biscuits and Coca Cola, and I can boil a kettle. It's no trouble.' Before I know what I'm saying we are all in the front garden. Only then do I discover I have already eaten the last Bath Oliver and we're out of bread.

When it's time to go home, everyone comes and thanks me and I beg them to come again whenever they would like to. I even urge the parents to make a plan for tomorrow, insist next time they bring even more of their friends and neighbours. Why, why? Of course the real reason I no longer swim myself is that I, too, am growing a cloven hoof.

Sartorial Collapse of a Stout Party

I am not a great one for observing other men's wardrobes. Back-stage at the Savoy recently, I noticed a fellow wearing a safety-pin in his ear.

'Don't look now,' I told Julian Orchard, a fellow busker on this occasion, 'but one of the stage-hands is wearing a safety-pin in his lobe.'

'He's been wearing it ever since we opened,' Julian informed me, 'and that was six months ago.'

On the whole I am a sloppy dresser myself and tend to be wary of men who wear matching collars and ties and, above all, matching handkerchiefs. My generation continues to take the first one on the pile in the drawer, just as when young we were taught to take the cake which was nearest, if not necessarily dearest. Boys were not encouraged to take an interest in clothes. We were as a rule kept short of trouser-length and pocket money. Our hair was trimmed. If we had returned to school at the end of the holidays with it styled, we would have certainly been sent home again for good, branded as moral lepers.

True, the school tarts did sometimes use brilliantine. Everyone else resorted to a white glue substance and usually forgot to comb it in properly. Boys were not encouraged to look pretty, or girls either for that matter. 'There will be plenty of time for that sort of thing when you've done your sums,' we were told.

But, of course, there wasn't. Dress-sense has to be instilled, like road safety, which is why my generation never dressed properly all their lives and the world was a great deal duller. Recently in Leningrad, I thought how much more cheerful everything seemed than when I visited it last. It's the children, I told myself. The Russians are dressing up the kids, and so they are. Hopefully, the new commissars will look a good deal less forbidding. No, in my day, girls wore tweeds and a rope of Tecla pearls and if Bob was their uncle, he might take them to a matinée.

Accepting a film engagement recently, I thought I must do something to vary my performance and experimented with a single earring; clip-on, of course. I am not one to suffer pain for the cause of art. I was surprised, sitting in Asprey's, trying the thing on and trying to persuade the salesman I was only prepared to pay for one of a pair, that no one seemed startled. I had thought my lot might rush home to their wives and start to pack for Rhodesia. 'The rot has started,' I could hear them telling each other. 'That cad Morley has gone over to the other side. Let's get out of here, pronto.'

In the end, no one noticed the earring or, if they did, never remarked on it. It is difficult to shock these days—in the cinema or even in somewhere like Asprey's.

The temptation to become a snappy dresser, in my own case, is not so much resisted as thwarted. When I see a shirt with red, white and blue stripes, it is never in my size. Twelve-inch socks always come in plain colours. To lighten the general effect, I have to rely on that mad hatter, H..b..t.. J..n..n, and even then the fellow usually snatches back the pink velour with which I am about to sally forth, and plonks the regulation dun felt over my ears.

This very morning I cogitated in my bath as to what I should wear to support a fellow thespian on TV later in the day, for a brief appearance on *This Is Your Life*. Not blue, I told the taps. Everyone wears blue on TV. It's supposed to help the eyes if you have blue ones. I am not sure what happens if you have brown eyes. *This Is Your Life* is a programme conducted with maniacal secrecy. If he had his way, the producer would like you to stay overnight in a hotel in Bloomsbury, so as not to alert the proposed victim, who is encouraged to sleep innocently in Chelsea. A note on the confidential instructions indicated that there would be plenty of time and facilities for changing after the run-through. The best people don't normally go to the runs-through, which are usually a good deal more hilarious than the programmes. Anna Neagle, for instance, traditionally doesn't attend. Her part is taken by the studio floor manager and very good he usually is in the role. He reads out her script and, before we have time to ask each other whether she is really going to tell that story, he is away and back again as the Lord Olivier. When Mike Yarwood retires, there will always be a niche for him. If there is one programme that won't retire, it's this one.

I fear I have kept you all waiting on tenterhooks for my final decision. I opted for my brown DB (20/7/71). It is not the latest fashion but it had just come back from the cleaners. With it I wore my yellow waistcoat (undated) and a rather pretty home-woven tie my sister gave me a few Christmases ago and which was still unused and consequently unspotted. There would, of course, be no question of changing into anything but pyjamas a good deal later in the day.

When I arrived it was to find it had been snowing recently so the star of the programme, the subject's headmaster, was marooned in Somerset and we had to make do with a school friend. I can't pretend that there was any attempt at sartorial sensation either at the rehearsal or the performance, and the only two people who bothered to change were the subject's mother, who wore gold, and an Italian opera star who rehearsed in a polo-neck and sported a beautiful silk suit and Gucci tie on transmission.

If it is elegance you are after, I am afraid it's still Rome—much as I hate to admit it. I cannot bear overcoats draped over the shoulders, but wish sometimes I had the nerve to carry a handbag. It takes so much longer to empty out pockets in search of the missing theatre tickets. Those two inside breast-pockets are the real killers, particularly the one on the left, which no one ever uses unless they are left-handed or unless the coat is on the hanger, in which case I pop a passport inside and it disappears or, to be more accurate, it is some time till I think of looking there for it.

It must be twenty years since I did a cabaret at the Café de Paris and ordered a shot-silk smoking jacket from my tailor. I didn't exactly choose the roll of silk but when I told him I wanted something to catch the eye he produced, with pride and, I imagine, considerable relief, a swatch which he had obtained for a South American millionaire who had subsequently disappeared up the Amazon without paying for it. It wasn't exactly the thing for the Amazon. I was never sure it was the thing for the Café, but it has stood me in good stead ever since for those one-night compère stands at the charity galas and the occasional university debate.

Normally, I don't trust a man in a smoking jacket. In my book, he is trying too hard. I never accept a script in which the playwright insists my character should be wearing one, knowing he will prove tiresome, failed and epigrammatic. Years ago, of course, he was also a queer.

I suppose the real reason I try not to notice what the young are wearing is that it makes me nervous. It's not only that they all seem to have lost their shirts, they seem to be on the verge of unprovoked assault. They can only be dressed like that, surely, because they are contemplating attending a football match. Just as, years ago, the front parlour was never used, so today the suits of the young, along with their shoes and socks, are kept in the locked cupboard. They sally forth in plimsolls and army surplus anoraks. They gather menacingly at street corners to discuss mugging and I am surely their potential victim.

Only the other afternoon, climbing up from the Underground, I found the staircase barred by the menacing, bearded face of a destitute giant who, as a preliminary to a karate chop, held out his hand. I backed nervously away. This is it, I told myself. Another moment, and I shall be somersaulting backwards to lie supine on the concrete while my pockets are rifled and my head bloodied. Nothing of the kind occurred. The giant turned out to be the brainiest of my godchildren, who, at an early age, had taken every conceivable honour at Sussex University and become a top government adviser on nuclear physics, and had flown backwards and forwards to Washington to consult with the President himself—or so his proud parent used to tell me. He had left nuclear physics behind and taken up a professorship at London University where he was now researching worms.

I wished him well and continued my journey. Next time I may well be less fortunate.

By Appointment

Her Majesty Queen Elizabeth II, Defender of the Faith and a good deal
more besides, is arguably the most expert monarch who has ever sat on
the throne of Britain. I am not one of those who think that a throne is an
uncomfortable seat, or that the life of a Queen isn't on the whole more
rewarding and enjoyable than most. It must be bliss never to have to carry
money and yet to be able to afford almost anything.

I have met her, I suppose, on half a dozen occasions in real life, and
more often in my dreams. In the latter I am invariably the host and she
appears to be in need of – or at any rate to welcome – advice. I awake with
the pleasant but ephemeral sensation that I have put matters to rights once
again in her country and mine. To listen to her on a more formal occasion,
opening a school, or, less frequently these days, alas, launching a liner, one
is conscious that she is not the girl to fling her bonnet over the windmill,
she subdues the high spirits and the ready laugh, her smile is watchful, her
demeanour purposeful, she is there to do the job she has been asked to do
and she does no more and no less than the 'happening' warrants.

On less formal occasions she is altogether more approachable and a
great deal jollier. She has a curiously reassuring and hearty laugh; she
speaks her mind, I suppose, without the fear of contradiction. It may not
be a remarkable mind, but there is no gainsaying that it belongs to a most
remarkable and dedicated woman with whom it is a pleasure to take tea
once a year at one of her Royal Garden Parties. I am not, of course, Her
Majesty's sole guest on such occasions. She asks upwards of five
thousand others, and most of them come. The invitations arrive in plenty
of time to get propped up on the mantelpiece. Friends then know that we
are busy on that particular afternoon and don't waste time asking us to tea
with them. I am curiously forgetful about removing the elegantly-
engraved card once the function is over. It is often still in place when it's
time to put up the Christmas cards. With it come small admission tickets,
a sticker for the car and directions for parking. The sticker has an X on it

so that on the day you can leave the car almost anywhere. We chose the Mall this year, driving boldly up onto the footpath; another surge and we would have been in Green Park.

I am a lifelong opponent of the morning coat and grey topper, and although others sport them on these occasions, I and most of the Mayors wear civilian dress – in my case without a chain of office. Mayors and their wives go to Buckingham Palace Garden Parties in droves; so do Red Cross Officials, Embassy Staffs, County Councillors, Welfare Workers, Probation Officers and actors; anyone, in fact, who has led a decent, industrious and sober life working in and for the community and hasn't got a great deal to show for it except the engraved invitation, the car park badge and the tickets which have to be surrendered at the gate. There is a choice of gates but most prefer The Grand Entrance, which takes you into the Palace itself and out again pretty quickly, with just time to glimpse the china in the glass case, the portraits of some long-forgotten relatives, and the damask on the sofas. Bold spirits even sit down momentarily on the latter pretending to tie a shoe lace, but verysoon Palace Life is over for the year (unless you decide to return the same way) and you are out through the French windows, to be confronted with the tents, the bandstands and the Gentlemen Ushers.

Impeccable is the word for the latter, though the tents in blue and white look pretty enough. The Gentlemen Ushers are distinguished by their umbrellas, which become ceremonial wands for the afternoon. It is their task to prevent a crush around the members of the family who are now about to essay singly, or in pairs, the two hundred yards' stroll across the turf which separates the terrace from the Royal tea tent, the enclosure within the enclosure, where they, too, will partake presently of tea, iced coffee, miniature éclairs, chocolate cake, and bridge rolls.

This is the walkabout originally introduced by Alfred the Great, and ever since refined and perfected by generations of Palace Guards trained to a ferrule. Their task at three–thirty when the gates open and the guests arrive, is to find in the throng exactly the right people, and more important, exactly the right amount of the right people to ensure a smooth passage of their charges across the sward. Too many, and the princess is impeded, too few and they face the chop. The ideal is a few steps forward, a pause while a bishop is greeted and polite chit-chat exchanged, a gracious dismissal of the gratified cleric and on to greet a privileged couple from the Guildford or Reading Chamber of Commerce. Royalty has to think fast, but the Ushers even faster. Inside their hats are the lists of those they hope to find in the crush. Each one must be approachedn discreetly tapped on the shoulder (not, alas, with a sword, but with the brolly), and invited to stand still or move a little to the right and await the presentation. Gratified but self-conscious, the sheep await further instructions from the sheep dog. Others may move where they wish, secure an early cup of iced coffee, go listen to the band, even take a sortie around the lake and peer into the summerhouse, where the slide and the other toys are put away, but the chosen stand rooted in pleasure and anticipation, and presently the Royal Family comes out onto the terrace, the bands play 'God Save the Queen', and the various members are off, spreading themselves for our delight.

The Monarch has the lion's share of the crowd, naturally, and those waiting to be presented to her need considerable stamina and determination not to be nudged off course. They themselves have temporarily become part of the charmed circle – they stand their ground, smiling compulsively no matter how often their toes are stepped on. The tone is set by the officials who bend over backwards to ask the smallest favour. 'I wonder if you could possibly move back just six inches, or possibly nine, it would be most awfully kind? Thank you so much, that's perfect.' Elsewhere the crowds, standing on tiptoe – and one year, regrettably, even on chairs – to catch a glimpse of those they normally only meet on the television, are not quite so large. There is a little more time for the chat show, sometimes even too much, but Royalty is never at a loss and flatters outrageously.

'How nice of you to come, how lucky I am to meet you in this crowd. I envy you so much living at Burnham–on–Crouch. How sensible of you to choose to retire there.'

Circumstances and weather permitting, we stand, hat in hand, smiling inanely in the direction in which we think Her Majesty is probably moving, before going off to get our share of the cake. It may be only a small slice, and some of us have done a good deal more than the others to deserve it, but we all enjoy it. Afterwards, when it is over and the Queen has walked, briskly this time, back to the Palace, I like to linger beside those who are waiting for cars to pick them up. The loud speaker booms out all the way to Admiralty Arch . . . The Lord Mayor of Liverpool and Mrs. Brady, His Excellency the Dutch Ambassador, American Embassy Car Number Twenty, The Dowager Duchess of Builth, Mr. Bagbody. It is always Mr. Bagbody who intrigues. Why is he asked, who can he be? One of Her Majesty's Inspectors of Taxes, The Head of the Secret Service, a tramway employee from Blackpool completing a stint of twenty-five years' driving past the illuminations, a bird watcher from the Fens, a bank manager who has spent his leisure moments auditing the funds of a Society which protects windmills? Mr. Bagbody could be anyone as he stands there in his top hat and tails or his neat blue suit, his proud lady on his arm. It is 6.30 p.m. but in a moment he will be driven out of the Palace Gates; for him and for us, midnight is already striking.

As Chance Would Have It

I wish I understood Providence. We do not meet, alas, as often as I would wish, and always so unexpectedly.

The other evening at Doncaster, for instance. Five nights earlier we had missed each other at Wolverhampton. I can quite understand Providence not showing at Wolverhampton. In the days when I was on tour in the provinces most of the year, Monday to Saturday twice nightly at the Grand Theatre, Wolverhampton, was enough for me. If there was a midnight train after the performance, I was on it.

I only visit the city peripherally these days to inspect the race track. Even so, disaster usually strikes. It is not an easy track to find. Nearby, the notorious Spaghetti Junction lies in wait for victims. So awesome is this complex of motorways, so complicated its maze, that a driver can become entangled in the web and, with tears blurring his vision, and his windscreen wipers at full tilt, he has to wait to be rescued by expert trackers and seldom drives again. Although we reached the races on the occasion of which I write, the effort was in vain as the horse I was hoping to run had forgotten her passport and was turned back at the starting gate. But at Doncaster, leading from start to finish, she won an auction plate by some six lengths and four hundred pounds for me.

Money counts, I am not the man to pretend it doesn't. But it is difficult to describe the ecstasy of seeing one's horse win a race. It is a pleasure to be savoured not only because of its rarity but because one has done nothing whatever to deserve the prize.

One hasn't bred it or broken it, trained it or ridden it, and only bought it because no one else would. Suddenly you stand beside it in the winners' enclosure avoiding its hooves and basking in its reflected glory. Your horse has run before, probably more than once, and all sorts of excuses have been put forward and accepted as to why it finished where it did. She hadn't liked the starter's assistant, she had been put off by a bumpy journey, possibly a bumpy race. She isn't the sort that likes going round bends or being too far in front, which she never was, or too far behind, which is why she nearly stopped altogether. You drive home from the track questioning the prudence in keeping such a sad ugly duckling and then, suddenly, on a summer evening in Doncaster, with the crowd roaring and champagne corks beginning to pop, she turns into a swan.

There are two sorts of rewards in life: those that come through effort and concentration and dedication and hard work, and those that come out of the blue heaven, which surprise you at the actual prize-giving but which later, on sober reflection, you expected all the time. Providence is on my side, you tell yourself. I never doubted it, and stride on once more, a giant refreshed by sheer luck.

The second time I remember Providence actually taking a hand where I was concerned, was at school. When sitting one day in my usual black despair and almost unable to swallow the Wednesday mince, my housemaster summoned me to his side and announced he was sending me home for the rest of the term. I went home for the rest of my life. But why? Why did the lightning strike that particular afternoon? Why, an hour later, was I standing on the platform of Wellington College station, my playbox secured, my ticket in my pocket, gazing fearfully along the track lest I woke up before the engine arrived?

I have never discovered. But I have never forgotten one moment of the day's happenings, or ceased to believe, like Logan Pearsall Smith, that I am on occasions, and for strictly limited periods, God's Ewe Lamb.

I was a good deal older on the third occasion. I was a small-part actor with a good deal of spare time on my hands and I had, like most actors, written a play. And although it had been turned down by everyone who read it, it was suddenly accepted by a great West End star who I can only think hadn't read it at all because she subsequently insisted on my re-writing practically every line. But accept it she did, and asked me to luncheon and gave me a cheque for a hundred pounds with the coffee. And I walked out of her house on air and collided heavily with a pillar box. Once again, I expected to wake up and found I had already done so and was still clutching the cheque. The house disappeared in the war, along with my benefactor, but the pillar box is still there, a private shrine which I never fail to touch in reverence and gratitude each time I pass it.

Once Providence had got me married and arranged the family, I don't pretend that I was on my own exactly, but his sudden appearances became rather a thing of the past. True, there was the curious case of Joan Tetzel, whom I used to work with in radio in New York before the war. One day, twenty years later, I read the script of a play called *The Little*

Hut and told the producer that if he could find her again I would do the play.

'But she's gone,' I warned him. 'Vanished into American thin air.'

'Not at all, she was in my office this morning, wondering what on earth had happened to you,' he told me.

Then, twenty years later again, almost to the day, the same thing happened. I conjured up her name at luncheon with my agent and met her an hour later in a picture gallery. Neither of us had heard or thought of each other in the meantime.

That sort of thing doesn't require much effort on the part of Providence, I imagine, but I am always setting him greater challenges. Every so often I receive mysterious letters from unknown Irish publicans inviting me to buy sweepstake tickets, and I fill out the coupons, copy the address, add the five pounds, stick down the envelope and hold it up for Providence in case he's watching. He never seems to be. Then, too, I sometimes tempt Providence to meet me in a fun spot – Las Vegas, Monte Carlo, or nearer home. You'll find me, I tell him, at the second table on the right, just at the back of the 'Dorch'. I suppose, like me, he leads a busy life.

But if I ever think myself neglected, I do well to remember the first time we met on a summer afternoon in Folkestone, Kent. As usual in those days, I didn't know what on earth to do with myself, only that I didn't want to play cricket, and I somehow managed to slip away unnoticed from the dreaded sound of bat and ball and my hated companions. I walked in no particular direction (or so I thought), past the bandstand and the lifts which moved surprisingly down the cliff face to the pier and the roller skating rink beneath, and I turned my back on the sea and my face towards the shops, planning to buy myself a half pound of chocolate biscuits of which I was, even in those days, extravagantly fond. But when I reached the grocery shop it was closed. Next door to it stood the Pleasure Gardens Theatre and a poster advertising Charles Macdonald's production of Shaw's *The Doctor's Dilemma*, with Esmé Percy, and across it a sticker announcing EXTRA MATINEE TODAY. Providence reached in my pocket for the shilling I had saved for the biscuits and in a moment I was at the back of the gallery.

The Theatre had the strangest smell and, although I had never experienced it before and this was my first visit to a play, I recognised the scent of pleasure. There was a string orchestra already playing in the pit and the bottom of the curtain was lit by the footlights. I wondered what on earth lay on the other side. How was I to know, until it rose, that it was home?

Eurovision Swansong

'Well, that's it then,' I told my wife as I put down the *Daily Mail*. 'We're off at last. I simply cannot stay in this country longer than it will take to unload the property on some friendly Arab and get the ritual permission from the Foreign Exchange Commission.'

'I don't think it's called that,' she said, 'and where will we go?'

'The Dordogne, of course; isn't that where all gleeful expatriates end up, in a mill in the Dordogne?'

Not that I particularly wish to live in a mill, and not that I am gleeful. Quite the reverse. I find it ironic that I (who have so often shaken my head at the news that a fellow busker has quit because of tax problems and will in future be available only in Liechtenstein for voices-over and prolonged commentaries on the BBC), yes I (who have wagged many a finger at the young medicos about to exchange the casualty ward at Paddington Hospital for the Court House in downtown LA), should have finally decided that Britain can no longer be my home.

How could it have happened, how could they have let it happen? Of course, the Prime Minister was in Washington promising Amy a free ride on the Concorde if only she would leap into her father's lap once more, and the Monarch was bogged down in Australia watching Whitlam and Kerr trying to remember the steps of their ancient war dance. But surely Charles could have taken a hand? When is that boy going to make a start? It really is time he put down *Penthouse* and got on with it.

Had no one any inkling of disaster? Don't they say these things go in threes? *The Times*, Leyland, and then suddenly Boom Wham out of nowhere into the cancellation of the British screening of the Eurovision Song Contest.

How I agree with Lynsey de Paul who, with Mike Moran, sang

and wrote the British entry, 'Rock Bottom'. If ever a title won a contest before we even heard the tune or the lyric, this must surely be the one. 'Rock Bottom, Rock Bottom, I've gottem, the Rock Bottom, Rock Rock Bottom Bottom. On my beam's end, who needs a friend?' We couldn't have lost, and as Mike pointed out, this makes Britain look a fool and a pauper in the eyes of Europe. It isn't our tragedy, it's the country's tragedy.

I would go further: it's the country's end. Not with a bang or a song but a whimper.

Mike Moran went even further still, pointing out that the BBC had spent sixty thousand pounds just on filming the opening titles and had been involved in a year of planning. 'We are sorry for them as well as ourselves,' he said. So am I, so am I.

Sorry, too, for Angela Rippon who got the job (and I quote) 'after displaying her legs on *The Morecambe and Wise Christmas Show*'.

'The song will just vanish,' one recording executive told the *Mail*, 'they could lose thousands of pounds in record sales and appearances.'

Angela and 'Rock Bottom' sunk without trace is bad enough, but it is unthinkable that I shall be here three weeks from now when, instead of the scheduled programme, the BBC will show yet again a repeat of *Dad's Army*. No, I shall be out there somewhere in my waders trying to get the old watermill working.

For me the *Eurosong Contest* was more than a programme, it was a way of life. Three hours a year in which to rededicate myself to Universal Tolerance and National Pride. It meant as much to me as if I had been a Master of the Worshipful Guild of Fish Tasters and had been sitting in some restored mediaeval warehouse linking arms and touching bottoms and passing the loving cup, having remembered to wipe the rim with the napkin.

I would take my place at the occasional table, with the scrambled eggs still on the toast, and find a place for page seven of the *Radio Times* with the accompanying chart and picture of Katie Boyle. Is that what went wrong, I wonder? Did the gods strike when they failed to sacrifice Katie to them this year? Yet Angela surely would have proved an acceptable substitute. They are both, in the fullest sense of the word, Ladies. You had only to listen to Katie wishing us all 'Good evening and welcome' in Bulgarian to feel the first thrill of pride that here in Britain we understand Ceremony. How calm, how unruffled she appeared, how confident that a moment later she would say it all again in Dutch and delight even Queen Juliana herself. She had the extraordinary gift of making everyone seem thoroughly at home in their own country. On the whole we are not, as a nation, good with foreigners, but here was no Edward Heath causing Pompidou to flinch: here was a true Englishwoman proving herself not only a gracious hostess but a true Finnophile.

What for me gave the whole contest such exquisite pleasure was the subsequent spectacle of the Krauts and the Frogs failing to measure up to the standard she had set them.

Even when we didn't win, we palpably deserved the prize. How the others gave themselves away, time after time. The Ities, cocky and rather sweaty, gigolos to a man in ready-made dinner jackets. Only the fact that I can never remember the Italian for 'waiter' inhibited me from shouting the word to drown out the dubbed applause.

There were always the born losers such as the Micks and the Luxembourgers, countries (I suppose) too small to sustain a pop industry and too naïve to realise they must always come equal bottom with gallant little Belgium. It was pathetic, really, to see the lengths most of the foreign contestants would go to in order to disguise their musical inadequacy; some even had children lisping the unintelligible lyrics, others relied on cleavage or gimmickry such as backing groups imitating cow bells. Not that the Swiss ever won anything, nor did the entrants from behind the Iron Curtain, who always assumed a determined jollity, masking heaven knows what private problems and ultimate fate, should (as inevitably happened) failure crown their efforts with 'Hocha Hocha Bullybose Hocha'.

What a contrast with our lot; sometimes just Cliff Richard himself (and quite enough too), sometimes a group of keen young people clapping hands in unison and singing 'Bom Bom Ta Ta Bom'. Whoever wrote our songs knew how to keep them simple. Knew the sort of rhythm the Laplanders could assimilate and teach their dog teams.

It was the cliff-hanger at the end which had me standing on the sofa, waving my chart overhead.

'Can you hear me, Madrid?' Katie Boyle would ask, for the final questions were too important for her to translate. 'How do you mark?' There would be a shot of three or four nonentities with the look of suffering on their faces that comes from living abroad and teaching piano, and then the great board would flash with some perfectly unacceptable assessment. France nine points, Denmark five points, Portugal two points, United Kingdom one point. Still, every little helps. We usually managed to win in the end, and even if we didn't, it taught us not to play with foreigners. That, after all, was the whole point of the thing: a quick trip round Europe at no extra charge and the certainty that we were better off at home. Now we've removed the certainty. Anyone else for Heathrow?

The Spirit of Christmas Past

I am always delighted to see the Three Wise Men, they keep themselves so fit. I can't remember how long ago I bought them, or where, but each year I wander from room to room, holding them in my hand and looking for fresh terrain on which to stand them. In the end they always take their accustomed place above the window in the hall. There's a ledge which suits them perfectly, each walking a pace behind the other in the general direction of the golden star, with which I am not so pleased. It becomes increasingly difficult to disguise the tarnish. I am a clumsy man, not wont, or, indeed, able usually to let my fingers do the walking, but the decorations are my special province. If I was honest I would say what I look forward to most each Christmas is the brandy butter and getting my two hundredth Christmas card. I need two hundred to fix to the beams in the living-room. Without them the room is hopeless. I have tried alternative decorations and failed.

In point of fact I have tried alternative decorations almost everywhere, but each year repeat the pattern with only one or two minor alterations. The bandsmen from Tokyo can stand on the mantelpiece and the Holy Family take their places on the window ledge, or vice versa. There are some dilapidated musical instruments which pin either up the stair rail or around the grandfather clock. I am sick to death of three cardboard angels with feather skirts. Each year they come out of their box and almost at once retire back into it. It is not just that they are common — they are not, for instance, as common as the Hong Kong plastic mines, or even the Christmas Tree Fairy herself — it's just that I hate them as much as I love the owls, the beautiful white owls who perch in the holly branches, and the golden mobile, the pièce de résistance on the top landing, which only my boundless courage and total disregard of personal danger enables me to fix each Christmas Eve, balancing on the topmost of the folding steps.

I buy my new decorations each August in a shop which sells to the trade. Go in September and it's all over. In September they sell Easter bunnies. I like that very much. I admire people who plan ahead. I revere those who put things behind them. Myself, I job back. I want this Christmas to be as much like the last as possible. I hold on as a man catapulted into the water will hold on to an upturned keel, surprised at first how easily it helps him to stay afloat, feeling as yet no numbness in his finger-tips.

Talking of finger-tips, I must try not to be the first this year to pull the cracker, to put on the cap, to read the riddle, to hog the enjoyment. I have had over sixty Christmases and enjoyed them all, except possibly my first, and for all I know I may have enjoyed that one too. On my sixth they gave me the Delhi Durbar. I don't remember what I was given last year or the year before or the year before that. The only Christmas present I ever remember was the Delhi Durbar. It came complete with the King Emperor and his Queen, the elephants and the ceremonial pavilion. It came in a flat red box, the sort of box jigsaws came in, but this was no puzzle. It was what I wanted most in the whole world, it was all I wanted. It was perfection, and I have never, never forgotten the box on the drawing-room floor under the Christmas tree at six o'clock on Christmas Eve. It was not done up in idiotic wrapping paper, it was not tied with string. All I had to do was to lift off the lid and start taking the sepoys and the gurkhas, the horses and the tigers out one by one and stand them on the carpet.

So why go on, you ask, why if six was perfect try for sixty-six, why not forget the whole thing this year? Take oneself off to the splendid quiet of an Imperial Hotel at some neglected, out-of-season watering place, and hole up with an electric blanket on the bed and a 'Do not Disturb' sign on the door handle. I have thought of it. I have made a few discreet enquiries. 'Are you full at Christmas, and what are your rates?' To do it properly I suppose I would have to come down to Christmas Dinner and eat my way solemnly through to the mince pies, eyeing the solitary cracker on the table, staring out front, intensely proud, utterly alone — the sort of part Aubrey Smith (or I, for that matter) would have given our eye-teeth for. But no, I have to be home to open the cards, and before anyone else has a chance to read them, impale them with a drawing-pin up aloft. Long, short, long, short is the pattern. The picture families I do save for the mantelpiece. There are only a few of those, alas — the Yehudi Menuhins whom I hardly know, and the David Tomlinsons whom I know very well, my niece's family and sometimes the odd godchild or a celebrated photographer out on a spree. I have never had one from the Queen, but then of course she has never had one from me. I do get one from the Gaekwar of Baroda, but it is almost severely simple and although I sometimes save it for some guest to open up and read His Highness's message, they seldom seem to bother. There was a theatrical manager who used to imagine himself still an officer and gentleman and always sent pictures of regimental carnage, but these I neither pinned nor planted. They were not, I told myself, the real spirit of Christmas, and I laid them on one side to be used only in dire emergency.

For years the village in which I live used to support a company of bell-ringers, and on the appointed evening they would arrive and march into the living-room, where we had only just switched off the telly and were hoping they wouldn't notice the fumes. They put their bells on a small portable card table and kept picking them up and putting them down again with a sort of sustained patience, and if you listened very carefully and had an ear for music, it was possible to discover some sort of tune. Then came the moment for which I was waiting, when the head man would enquire whether we had a favourite carol. It was the signal that the performance was about to finish; it was the equivalent of the 'and now one final question' on the chat show. Loudly I would call for Good King Wenceslas. 'Again?' they were wont to enquire. 'Again,' I would tell them. 'I can't hear it often enough,' I would lie. Then cakes and ale and five pounds in the hat, or possibly a bit less, and God rested the Merry Gentlemen for another year. Now we have carol singers; they don't come in, but I feel just as much of a fool standing in the garden pretending I like being sung at. I would as lief have a Hungarian violinist bending over my crêpes suzette in some ghastly foreign bistro.

So what's it all about, then, you ask, and I can honestly tell you I don't know. Have they spoilt Christmas, and if so, who are they? The butchers, the bakers, the candlestickmakers? The poor we cannot forgive or the homeless we will not house or the hungry we have not fed or the prisoners we have not set free? Are they the ones who announce in the agony columns that they are not sending cards this year, but have made a donation to the Lifeboat Fund, or are they people like you and me, who always want the sort of Christmas we had last year or the year before that, or sixty years ago, who want to stand on the other side of the drawing-room door and still be able to reach up and open it when the clock strikes and find the Delhi Durbar under the tree?

RECOLLECTIONS
OF
A
RESPONSIBLE
GENTLEMAN

Prologue

The first time I put on make-up, I was about six years old. There was a very eminent cleric at Folkestone, where I spent my childhood, and he used to do what they called a mystery play. I never understood why it was called a mystery play. It wasn't my idea of a mystery play, a good old Agatha Christie play. It was something to do with religion, and, for some reason, he used to write them. Canon Elliott was a very fashionable divine. He was a great preacher, a tremendous figure at Folkestone. He ran Folkestone. Everybody rushed to obey his command, and among his commands was that the children of his parish should perform every year a mystery play, which he wrote, produced and cast, sitting at a small card-table looking rather like Tyrone Guthrie. He awarded me the role of Father Christmas:

> *Here come I, Old Father Christmas,*
> *Welcome or welcome not,*
> *I hope Old Father Christmas*
> *Will never be forgot.*

I don't say he was in the first flight of poetic dramatists, but those were the lines he gave me, and those were the lines I said. And I fell deeply in love with the leading lady. I used to walk about Folkestone hoping to see her. She must have been about nine or ten. I was a precocious child, I think. She was too old for me. I was a very unattractive child, and to be noticed was, for me, important. I suppose if you asked what had motivated my life most, it was this insane desire to be noticed. The first play I ever saw, when I was 11 or 12, was Esmé Percy doing *The Doctor's Dilemma*. And that was the moment when the penny dropped. The magic started. I said: 'My goodness, how I'd like to be someone like Esmé Percy, and come on

63

to the stage and say the lines that Shaw had given him to say, about believing in art and the mystery of Michelangelo and the wonder of beauty.' And I suddenly realised what it was all about: that you could be unattractive, and you could be disliked and unpopular, and you could still be an artist; have a very bad character and still be an artist, because that is what Shaw said. You didn't have to be a virtuous man. You didn't, above all, have to be a fit man, or a good man at running, or a good man at sums, to be an artist, to be the server of truth. This little message dropped into my idiot brain, and I thought: 'I want to be an artist.'

The standards were so different when I was young. This is a terribly snobby thing to say, but if you were a gentleman, if you spoke a bit better than some people, and particularly if you were a large man, there was always some idiot willing to pay you £4.10 a week, to fill up the company and play the butler or the doctor, or, in my case, what was called the 'responsible gentleman'. There was a fellow called Basil Loder, who used to act with Gerald du Maurier. I don't know what his exact function was. He used to play cricket or golf with Gerald, and look after the luggage on the train, I suppose. But he used to come on at some stage in the play and say: 'Hallo, I'm just going down to the tennis court,' and Gerald used to look at him and say: 'Oh, that's nice. Well, I'll see you there.' Then he walked off again. He had very pretty clothes on, always, and he looked frightfully elegant, and I thought: 'Now that's the sort of line I should like—not too long, not too difficult, and enough money to be able to afford those sort of shoes.'

I started off in films as a king—a French king, admittedly, but nevertheless a king, in *Marie Antoinette*—and stayed in that sort of income bracket. Film producers are extravagantly lazy—even lazier than middle-aged or ageing actors like myself. So, if there's a part of a duke or an earl, and it hasn't got any lines or hasn't yet got any character, they would always, up to about a few months ago, say: 'This is the part for Robert Morley or Wilfrid Hyde White. Get them in and let them write their own dialogue, because they won't bother to learn anything we write down for them. They're much too lazy.' It's not a rewarding profession. You can do any line 18 times, and you must be able to get it right once—anybody could get it.

An actor is an artist who really can't do anything, so he is the poor relation of the arts, and he plods along every night, putting on the slap, and hoping for the public to come and watch him. A sort of clown . . .

The Bluffer

'Never go on the stage laddie, without first saying to yourself – Ladies and Gentlemen, if you think you can do this better yourself, come up and try.' It was the first piece of helpful advice on acting I ever received. I'm not sure it wasn't the only one.

Bluff or confidence? Artists need both and only a narrow line divides them. I remember Balmain designing a dress for Joan Tetzel, in a play called *The Little Hut*. The dress looked as if it had come out of a bandbox instead of the sea. Nobody dared to touch it and then the master arrived. Taking a penknife, he casually slashed it into rags. Beautiful rags, mind you, the sort of rags Cinderella changes out of to go to the ball. Could anyone but Balmain have done it? Certainly no one but Balmain would have dared.

What we all crave, in life, in art, on television, in government, is the expert. Some experts are, by the nature of their calling, self-appointed. All surgeons are experts, most dentists, some criminal lawyers. The bigger the expert, the greater the bluff. The more we have to pay them, the more confidence they inspire in us. The bluff of price is the most effective bluff of all.

The first time I went to Hollywood was to play the part of the dauphin in *Marie Antoinette*. Up to then my film career had been a disaster. I had been hired twice previously and sacked on both occasions after the first day for gross incompetence. My agent knew this. MGM knew it, too. When my agent told MGM my price, they roared with laughter. 'How come?' they asked him. 'He's never earned a sausage. He's never lasted 24 hours. So how is it he's worth $500 a week?'

'He's not,' agreed my agent. 'But he doesn't want to go to America and he has a large personal fortune.' The bluff lasted until I'd signed the contract, but then I had to ask for some cash to get to the boat. Each contract has been a game of poker since then.

It is more important for an actor to learn to bluff than to learn to act. All the great figures on the world stage have one thing in common: an ability to make the public rub its eyes. Now you see it, now you don't.

How good a pianist is Liberace? If you didn't know it was Andy Williams singing, would you listen? Or Gregory Peck acting, would you watch? You might and then again you might not.

Certainly, the greater the star the less he need do to preserve his own image. The public will shine and polish it for him every day. They will tell you that a great artist learns to throw away the rule book. 'Watch the sheer economy of the man,' the public tells itself. 'He does nothing.'

But a word of caution, gentle watcher. Never, never be tempted to bluff about not wanting the job. The bluff of resignation is one which by its very nature will almost certainly be called. No matter how valuable an employee or how faithful a friend you may be, no matter how great your knowledge of where the body is buried, if you offer to resign you can bet your bottom dollar your resignation will be accepted. You are presenting your partner or your employer with a temptation he cannot resist.

I remember my stupefaction when I once told a manager who was employing me at the time that if the director stayed I must leave. 'You're both going,' he chortled. I learnt my lesson. I have never again offered my resignation on any terms. If they want to fire me, by God, they'll have to pay.

The Human Factor

'I do not understand what the feathers are for.' Mr Otto Preminger removes his eye from the view-finder and regards the property master in sorrow with a hint of anger.

'They are pens, quill pens,' he is told by that long-suffering individual. 'We need to wait until you have dressed the set.'

Waiting is the cardinal sin, whoever causes the delay is guilty of a grave dereliction of duty unless, of course, it is Otto himself. 'I do not understand,' he will tell Richard Attenborough, 'why you are not here, I have had to call you seven times.'

'Once,' Attenborough tells him, 'and I was just outside the door.'

'Outside the door is no good for me.'

I don't know what made filming *The Human Factor* such a pleasing experience, or rather I know very well. Preminger has the effect Churchill must have had on people. Beneath his stern, sometimes forbidding exterior, you glimpse genuine irresponsibility. Shall I, I asked myself in the first day's shooting, remonstrate when shouted at to keep quiet? It was, after all, Otto who was making the din. 'I am sorry,' I rehearsed my protest silently to myself. 'I am sorry, Otto, but unless everyone is kind and patient I cannot act properly.' I suspected the reply might involve my instant dismissal and kept my mouth shut for once. The scene played better than I expected.

Otto quite often tells actors to go if they're not happy. Nicol Williamson took him at his word and walked off the set pursued for once by an abject Otto. After all, his leading man was halfway through the picture. The great Gabriel Pascal sacked his star in *Major Barbara* after three weeks and reshot the entire film up to then with Rex Harrison playing the part but then Gabriel had not much sense of money. Otto on the other hand is not one to waste the pennies. He signs every cheque each Friday himself, enquiring thoughtfully about the overtime charges and, on a film such as this one, the employees number well over a hundred. His approach to actors is uncompromising, either they know the lines or they don't. Where other directors chop and change Otto sets up the camera and presses forward. Artistes who expect to cover their mistakes in close-ups are usually disappointed. He is the only director I ever worked with who tires of the scene before the actor does.

Long after the anger has gone out of his eyes he will continue staring at some luckless extra whose attention has momentarily wandered or has spoken out of turn. 'Have you never opened a door?' he will thunder at one of his cast newly arrived on the set. 'I find it extraordinary that you should come to my picture and not be able to open a door.' Here the moment of decision occurs; if the actor remonstrates, expresses his own belief that he has indeed opened doors before – the battle is lost. He will be accused of cheating, of wasting time, even of sabotage. If, on the other hand, he watches while Otto himself manipulates the knob, subsequently expressing his gratitude and pleasure at having one of life's little mysteries explained to him, he will have joined the club and quite possibly not be shouted at again for the whole morning. If and when he ever retires from directing, Mr Preminger should be preserved with a magnificent grant from the industry and required to train young actors to stand up for themselves as men, and to instruct horses intended for riot control to accustom themselves to shouting and the waving of flags.

If I have observed anything about the business of making motion pictures it is that over the years robustness has departed. Film actors grow lethargic when stroked with kid gloves, they are at their best when goaded beyond endurance and are about to lose control. Preminger keeps them perplexed and often resentful. The racehorse allowed to proceed at his own pace seldom wins the race. Before filming *The Human Factor* I had spent a month shooting another script in the gardens of the Huntingdon Library, a blissful experience with a director of immense charm and patience who listened courteously to every actor in turn and, however idiotic the suggestion, appeared to consider it seriously even though seldom adopting it, faced with a company of comedians all of whom including myself thought we were a good deal funnier than the script. His patience was inexhaustible as the strawberries and cream which he arranged to have served to us along with the cooling drinks and the quite exceptional buffet luncheons.

The only creatures who seemed dissatisfied with the proceedings were a number of exceptionally un-cooperative ostriches whom I have an uneasy feeling will almost certainly steal the picture. I don't say I acted better for Preminger but without the cream teas I certainly tried harder to do so. Actors who achieve any sort of eminence learn to soak up flattery like a sponge. In their determination to remain unspoiled and totally without conceit they grow into the dullest people imaginable. Preminger is guiltless of such corruption, he lavishes little praise, expresses the lowest level of appreciation consistent with good manners – for he remains off the set and even occasionally on camera, a profoundly courteous man. Along with his Austrian accent he has maintained a mid-European sense of style, he has a beautiful wife and two good-looking sons who came over while he was filming on a promise of tickets to Wimbledon. Another son, he informed me proudly, was born out of wedlock and is currently engaged on a book about his distinguished mother Gipsy Rose Lee. I don't know if he still goes home to the cream cakes at Deml's and the Lippizaner Horses, the Horn of the Unicorn and the Hotel Sacher. But it's nice to know he is alive and well, even if he doesn't live in Vienna any longer.

Happy as a Badger

Whenever there is an audience to watch him, the donkey in the Well House of Carisbrooke Castle leaves his dressing-room and, mounting the tread wheel, accomplishes a journey of three hundred yards in it while contriving to remain in exactly the same place. A bucket of water is thus raised approximately 161 feet from the bottom of the well and the contents inspected, after which the water is returned to the well and the donkey, acknowledging the polite applause, returns to his dressing-room until his next performance.

Perspicacious readers will have drawn the parallel but, I trust, not anticipated the question I am anxious to pose. Does the donkey enjoy himself, and if so, why? He certainly enjoys the biscuits which his visitors feed him, warm quarters and the company of other donkeys in the cast with whom he shares the work, and we are assured that the work suits the animals and one is recorded to have died at the ripe age (for a donkey) of forty-nine years. I am now sixty-six and I've enjoyed it; but it is an odd occupation though not unique, of course: there are other actors in theatres all over the world just as there are other treadmills motivated by donkeys. You can train a donkey apparently in three months: how long does it take to train an actor? Or are they better self-taught? From now on we shall be discussing only the theatre, so donkey lovers had better get off here.

Unlike most of my distinguished colleagues, and having been in the profession a bare forty-six years, I have reached no hard and fast conclusion on this or any other aspect of the trade. But I cannot help remarking that the more seriously an actor takes himself and his work, the more dedicated he appears; the more determined he is as he grows older to enlarge his scope, to accept new challenges, to break new ground, the less time he spends actually doing so. With the possible exception of Gielgud, who is ever ready to have a go, and Burton, who is ever going to be ready to do so, actors like Scofield, Guinness, Finney, Redgrave, Williamson, Stephens – all of whom are on record as finding a dedication in their vocation which has eluded me – appear at infrequent intervals and usually for limited runs. They actually enjoy learning new parts and rehearsing them – some of them even enjoy being directed by such insatiable sado-masochists as Peter Brook, who is so entirely wrapped up in the mystique of the impossible dream that he now has his actor victims running around market places in Teheran, talking gibberish to the bewildered stall holders and bored chauffeurs polishing their masters' motors in the sun and trying to listen to local football scores on their radios.

When I first left school, which I hated, and went onto the stage, which I loved, I was visited almost immediately by an ex-chum, indeed the sole chum I ever made at Wellington College. He seemed puzzled by my choice of career, and searching for a clue as to why I was immured in such uncomfortable surroundings as the meanest dressing-room of the County Theatre, Reading, opined that once the curtain had fallen we were obviously at each other like knives. It wasn't quite true, even in those days, but I think I prefer the public to think of us as belonging to what a British judge referred to this week as 'the knickers and gin crowd' than to the culture-vulture crowd. Our life can hardly be described as a very sober one. Would you like your daughter to marry an actor? Of course not. We have a higher divorce rate than in most professions – just below dentists in the league table, actually. We spend a good deal of our life out of work, sitting around waiting for our agent to call, and when he does find us a job, it is not even intended to last long. Television is a matter usually of three weeks' filming, often just days. We are always begging the public to watch when often there is really little to see. The theatre was more successful, certainly, when we resolutely declined to take Hamlet's advice to hold a mirror up to nature. Hamlet was a perfect fool. Every clown wants to play Hamlet, I wanted to myself once but I would have played him for what he is – a clown. It's too late now, thank goodness, and I have few ambitions left. One which is common to most of us, I suppose, is the wish that once, in an empty theatre, whilst we are rehearsing a new play on an empty stage, the cleaning lady at the back of the stalls will stop thumping the seats and emptying the ashtrays and generally banging around as cleaning ladies do, and, her task abandoned, sit helpless and spellbound, just watching and listening. It's only the cleaning woman I wish to hold in my spell, not the ordinary men and women who come willingly in the evenings and pay for admission. I don't mind what they do, they can kiss and cuddle and rustle chocolates and sleep peacefully, they can come as late as they please and leave as early. I have their money, I am there if they need me, but I shall be no whit affronted if they don't. I like, of course, to keep

71

some sort of control: I prefer the majority at least to stay awake and watchful, I want to make you laugh. I am, after all, very fond of you, and why shouldn't I be? You've been very good to me for close on fifty years. When I let you down, you were forgiving, and when I didn't, you seemed grateful and even congratulated me. Tradesmen are not often congratulated: a man may spend a lifetime serving the public and count on one hand the customers who have praised his butter.

Yet people come up to me on railway platforms and tell me they have enjoyed the play. True, they add that 'these days they can do with a laugh', they've been saying that, too, for fifty years. 'Why?' I sometimes enquire, 'What's so terrible about today?' They never tell me, and all those years I don't really believe I've ever really wanted to know.

It's because we actors are tradesmen and not artists that our life on the whole is such a happy one. Artists have it rough: you can paint all your life and never sell a picture; you can write music and never hear it played, or a book and never hold it in your hand; but an actor gets instant recognition though, alas, no longer instant oblivion. Before pictures, who doubted Irving? But now, with his films still orbiting in space, who believes Charlton Heston? Yet Mr. Heston is the very man who appeals for funds to buy up old pictures, other people's as well as his own, let's be fair, and preserve them. Perish the thought, and even better, perish the actor. Our performances live on in the memory of the faithful; they are safer than in a bank vault. On the staircase of my club there is a chair on which Irving is supposed to have died. He had been touring around the provinces. He was old and tired and sick. He gave his last performance to a rather meagre audience, somehow managed to get back to the hotel where he was staying, sat down in the hall and died. Should actors go on until they drop? I think so. Climbing the stairs on my way to the bar, I look at the chair and I remember what Irving once said to Ellen Terry when she asked him what he had got out of a life of endless theatrical activity. 'A few friends, dear, and a whisky and soda whenever I wanted one; what else is there to get?' Irving had no folie de grandeur about his trade. True, when after a successful first night his wife, who didn't care much for the business, asked him how much longer he proposed to go on with this nonsense, Henry stopped the hansom they were sharing and got out for ever. Well, I suppose he may have ridden in the cab again; by that time he probably wanted to leave his wife anyway. Actors' wives say worse things to them than that. Sometimes we leave them, sometimes we don't. Meeting Rex Harrison once in the Burlington Arcade – where you'd expect him to be – he was kind enough to congratulate me on a television programme I had done the night before. It was an instalment of the ever popular feature 'This Is Your Life'. For an egomaniac like myself it is well nigh the perfect programme – as long as I am the one whose life they are discussing. Rex seemed to think that on this occasion I had got away with it. 'And why not?' he continued. 'You've been so sensible; one house, one wife and, if you'll forgive me saying so, one performance.'

Actually, he is wrong about the house, but we have lived in it for thirty-five years now. It is just the right distance from London – about thirty miles – and I drive up each evening as the commuters are returning to the Thames Valley along the motorway. Their side of the road is choked with traffic, mine comparatively clear. When I come home, both sides are trouble-free, and between the motorway and my house are country lanes I share with foxes and deer and the occasional badger.

A few friends, a whisky and soda, and an opportunity to greet a badger. 'Why are you fond of badgers?' you will ask, if you've read this far, and to be honest I am not particularly fond of badgers and I would be scared stiff if I met one on foot, but it makes a good curtain to the day. We lead a funny sort of life, we nocturnals, but my goodness don't we enjoy it.

That's why, when I'm asked, I tell people I'm feeling just fine – happy as a badger.

The Play's Still the Thing

It is my gleeful task not only to encourage Americans to come to Britain but, while they are there, to watch me acting. On some nights they come on to the stage after the performance and we congratulate each other on our mutual perspicacity. They will, of course, see other shows during their visit, admire other ancient ruins, but it is a source of supreme satisfaction to me to know that I have helped construct part of this particular tourist trap and provided a portion of the bait.

Nowadays, the British wait for the tourists as the African for the rain. With both come relief and a certain amount of discomfort, but the crops and the shows are saved. Producers breathe again. Alongside the corn sprout the mink and the blue rinses. Just as the casual inadvertence of some official drafting a clause in a bill to legalise church lotteries opened hundreds of casinos all over Britain, so a grudging grant to provide meagre subsidies to a couple of theatre companies created for ourselves a great new growth industry: Theatrical Tourism. The National and the Royal Shakespeare theatres were the twin umbrellas opened on a terrace to create a *café chantant.* Now all the commercial theatre basks and shelters alongside. The tourists arrive to see Richardson and Gielgud, to visit the National and the Aldwych, and while they are waiting consume *No Sex, Please—We're British, Banana Ridge,* and *The Mousetrap.* Some of the plays in the funfair section of the exhibition wouldn't last a night on Broadway, but here they are enjoyed along with the mock-Tudor banqueting halls and Eilzabethan wenches proffering mead.

The theatre is a jungle in which the playwright, the actor, and the director struggle for supremacy. Sometimes the fight goes one way and then, for a time, another. I have lived through the reign of each in turn and now it seems to me the playwright is once more supreme. Pinter, Stoppard and Gray stalk unchallenged by Olivier and Peter Brook. Once more the audience is invited not only to look and listen but to think as they once thought with Shaw and Galsworthy. There is a rich heritage in the British theatre, but it is not, alas, the heritage of the actor, still less of the director. The playwright must in the final battle always prove the winner. His work, imperishable; his fame, enduring. I write 'alas' because although I have tried my hand at both directing and playwriting, I am in essence one of those of whom Shakespeare wrote that we were destined to strut and fret an hour upon the stage and then be heard no more.

My generation of actors was trained to entice our prey. We kept an eye open, a claw sharpened, even when we professed to slumber. However deep the tragedy or shallow the farce, we never forgot to face front. Nowadays, the relation between player and public tends to be more sophisticated. Together they share a mutual experience of pain and sorrow. Sometimes the actor seems able to dispense with his audience—to no longer need them. He may choose or chance to perfect his performance on a wet afternoon in Shrewsbury, with hardly anyone watching, and thereafter the repetition for him may stale. For me this never happens, I never perfect a performance, though obviously I am sometimes better or worse, but I have learned that without a perfect audience, my struggle to the summit is impossible. I am aware, as the curtain rises, of the texture of the house. Some nights they will appear eager and willing; on others, listless and reluctant to follow the play. Once or twice during the evening they will change course, become willing and cooperative or grow sullen and bored. Suddenly the laughter is stilled, the coughing commences. Is it our fault or theirs? I have long ceased to wonder. An audience is like the sea, ever changing, never to be taken for granted.

Like most British children, I never really came to terms with the great dramatists of the past in the classroom, or for that matter in the school plays—Jonson, Marlowe, Congreve, Goldsmith, and, of course, the great William. Possibly because of my shape, the role of Portia always eluded me. If I got anywhere at all, it was as far as Gratiano, and it came as no surprise to me, therefore, that this was to be my first role in the professional theatre, or very nearly. For a year or more I toured England and Ireland with Sir Frank Benson ('Pa' to us) in a repertoire of eight plays in which he alternated Shylock with Jacques, Peter Teazle, Old Hardcastle, Caliban, and others. Even at his advanced age, he was a very spry old gentleman, but no longer able to concentrate for very long. Unless guided to the correct entrance, he was liable to advance dressed as Malvolio to announce to a startled but never resentful audience that 'All the world's a stage.' By this time the public were as used to him as they were to the classics. They didn't much care for either, but they came occasionally, as Christians to the Easter service.

The most humiliating afternoons were those we spent performing extra matinées at girls' schools in the neighbourhood of the town in which we were playing at night. For some reason, the bus always dropped us at the gates and we had to walk up the drive in daylight and makeup, to speak the words in the gym while scores of children rustled the pages of their copies of the play in a usually vain attempt to find out where we all were. The comic, besides Benson himself, of course, was an actor called Henry Ford, the son of the famous Lotte Venne, who had inherited little of his mother's style but a good deal of her confidence. Never quite willing to learn the text, he usually made a good deal up fresh for each performance, pausing only occasionally to announce in a carefully timed aside, 'No, that's wrong, kiddies!' In a way, I suppose he was of all of us the most Shakespearean.

It is unkind perhaps to remember Benson only in his dotage, when I knew him, but it was a colourful dotage. He was the only Shylock who consistently appeared in the trial scene bereft of knife, scales, or bond, each of which he remembered at some stage of his performance, when he would walk backwards into the wings to have them placed in hands clasped behind him by the waiting stage manager. 'But why does he walk backwards?' I asked. 'Because,' I was told, 'when he is doing so, he believes he is invisible.' Most of all, 'Pa' believed in spiritualism and the ability of a Battersea medium to bring him in touch with the girl on whose behalf he had taken what was in those days the cataclysmic step of renouncing Lady Benson. Whatever the weather, whatever the distance, 'Pa' would somehow manage to journey to London at weekends to renew his faith in the life-to-come with his beloved.

For a time he purported to find something even in my Gratiano to praise. It was he who taught me to stand legs apart, the sword behind my back grasped in either hand. Alas, the scabbard was empty of all but plywood, and with my pushing out a buttock one day, it cracked and splintered and got a laugh. I was not encouraged to repeat the joke, but Benson would still sometimes send for me and try vainly to recall a piece of business perfected by Oscar Ashe, or some other ghost of his past whose performance had pleased him. I was not the stuff of which ghosts were made, and one afternoon remonstrated with him that it was long past my tea-time. 'You have seen one side of me, boy,' he told me, his old eyes flashing with anger. 'Now, by God, you shall see another.' But of course, I never did. Old men forget.

The three great Shakespearean actors of my youth were Benson, Ben Greet, and Robert Atkins. All ran companies on a shoestring. None of them ever seemed to make money, but along with a fourth, Murray Carrington, whom many held to be the most formidable and the best but who had retired on account of his legs shortly before my debut, they raked and combed and harrowed the British Isles and planted in the breasts of the children and some of the adults who watched them an abiding distaste for the works of the master.

I suppose we have done a bit better since then. They still play him in Stratford, now and again at the National, and occasionally Gielgud or Scofield or Bates plunges in and brings to town his Prospero or his Macbeth. But the plays themselves, do they really excite and inspire my fellow citizens? A few perhaps, who have found solace in them all through their lives, but the vast majority of us can tell you the plot of *Hamlet* or *Macbeth* and quote a few lines remembered from childhood about the quality of mercy and are content to leave it there. We British are not an educated people; we leave others to do the learning just as we leave others to make the rules and worry about the economy. We are proud of Shakespeare just as we are proud of the Monarch and Concorde. If other people don't want to know, we are not unduly disturbed; we don't particularly want to know ourselves. We are just glad that they belong to us—though we may wish sometimes the Concorde belonged to someone else.

Where Angels Fear to Tread

A bachelor friend of mine who persistently invests in theatrical productions attended a cocktail party the other evening, where his hostess persisted in introducing him to all and sundry as a 'professional fairy'. 'Luckily,' he told me when recounting the incident, 'that sort of thing causes very little embarrassment nowadays.' I don't know whether in his role of angel my friend makes money, but at least it gives him an interest when he goes to plays for which he has provided some of the bread. He doesn't have to follow the plot. He can be counting the house. Like the prudent angel he is, he makes a point of spreading his wings. It is nearly always fatal to put all your eggs in one basket.

About theatrical brokers I must write carefully. Most of them have employed me at one time or another, and I am always mindful they may have to do so again. Yet honesty compels me to point out that very few of them really know their business. That is not to say they won't make money for their angels on odd occasions, but it will always be the odd occasions. You won't have much chance of getting in on the ground floor unless the management concerned already suspects there is a flood in the basement. You are unlikely, therefore, to be asked to invest in a Palladium pantomime or the 'Black and White Minstrel Show'. Such rich pastures are strictly reserved. But supposing you have a few pounds to invest and would like a flutter. How should you proceed? I am assuming that you haven't a mistress whose talent you propose to diversify. In easier days there was always a place in the chorus for a pretty miss, provided her financial backing was in order, but times and choruses have changed. Another friend of mine whose belle amie is currently appearing in *Oh Calcutta* is always boasting of how pretty she looks with her clothes on.

Let us return to our moutons, and apologise for the French which keeps creeping in. Angels, I fear, are constantly associated in my mind with the belle époque. Let us consider where your money – if not safe, that would be asking too much – at least has a sporting chance of survival, and even multiplying. Should you go for the big spender who at the first hint of your interest, the first sight of your cheque book, wines and dines you at Burke's or Scotts or the Grand Véfour? 'Steady with the Château Lafitte,' you tell yourself, 'this chap will spend the ready in pre-production expenses. He will be back to demand the company's rail fare to Southsea.' At least you will have a better time in his company than you will with one of the more austere brethren who lives in a poky little attic on top of his theatre, with minimal furniture and mature lady typists. 'No room here,' you tell yourself, 'for the casting couch', and you are right. If caution reassures you, go for one of these. To my mind you might as well have your money in a building society for all the fun you are likely to get out of it. You will, of course, be sent tickets for the first night, but you will also be expected to pay for them.

No, what you need when you are starting out on your journey along the celestial way, is a little man who has the time – because until he's got your cheque in his bank account business isn't all that brisk – to show you round the stables, and introduce you to some of the colts and possibly fillies. He may even encourage you to read some scripts and get your advice on the casting, enquiring whether you would prefer Larry or Paul, and when you express surprise that either of these gentlemen is available, you will be further surprised to learn that he gave both of them their first job, and that they would do anything for him, if asked.

Eventually, if you have taken my advice and your cheque has been cleared, you may find yourself invited to a pre-production party to meet the actors who are about to rehearse your play. You will find that not only are Olivier and Scofield missing, but that you have never heard of a single member of the cast. The mood on these occasions is one of hysterical over-confidence. In the abandoned ballroom in which the first rehearsal is to take place, you are uncertain where to put down your emptied champagne glass, and are probably still clutching it as you tiptoe away, unwilling to interrupt the proceedings any longer. If this lot can get away with it, you tell yourself, it will be a miracle. But in the role of angel you should expect miracles. They are not likely to happen, of course, but you should expect them.

Depending on the size of your investment and the amount of spare time and cash you still have available, you may attend the world première of the piece when it opens in Cheltenham, and be amazed how little excitement is generated on this auspicious occasion. You will have to be constantly telling yourself that from little acorns mighty oak trees grow, if you wish to keep up your courage. Monday night is never very brisk in the provinces, and nothing alerts your would-be theatregoer in the tall grass and persuades him to leave his car in the garage and himself in the parlour more than that fatal announcement on the bills: 'Prior to immediate London production'. Granted that Cheltenham is not exactly the right venue for the piece, and it is unlikely to be properly understood by the natives, everyone agrees afterwards at a party held in the local bistro, that there were one or two good early laughs and the play held up even if the audience didn't. It needs cutting, the management insist. Cutting is the panacea invariably prescribed after a first night, even if it isn't always applied to the patient. Managements insist on cutting, just as at one time physicians insisted on bleeding. Most plays are sickly at birth, and many succumb at a surprisingly early age. Euthanasia is by no means uncommon, but no such fate awaits your little piece apparently. After Cheltenham, a week at Bognor is planned and then there is talk of Richmond, immediately prior to its arrival in the West End.

After Richmond, however, everyone suddenly decides to go to Southsea. It seems that the London theatre cannot yet be announced to the impatient West End patrons, as the play currently playing there still refuses to complete two consecutive weeks below its stop figure. But everyone confidently expects it to fold once the Motor Show is over. Southsea comes and goes, and then rather surprisingly Billingham, and by now you are in overcall, that is to say the original subscribed capital having been exhausted by unexpectedly heavy losses on the road, everyone is expected to divvy up again. You are absolutely sick of the play, and just when you are hoping you have heard the last of it, the phone rings and your manager is on the blower to tell you he has a West End theatre and all signals are 'Go, go', but there is the question of a further overcall, and will you be sure to let him know how many seats you want for the First Night, and the rush is on. He also apologises in advance for the fact that some of your party may have to be accommodated in the Circle. You tell him that your party will consist simply of your wife and yourself, and what with all the money you have spent already you couldn't possibly afford more than two seats in the Upper Circle. But on this occasion the seats are free, it seems, and when yours arrive you will find you have been accommodated with eight pairs of stalls. You have considerable difficulty getting rid of them.

On the whole, perhaps it would be better if you stayed at home that night yourself. If you do decide to attend, you will be in for a shock. First nights are not what they were. The prevailing mood can be likened to that of a first-class railway carriage whose passengers are not expecting the ticket collector to come along. Except for the critics, a faceless coterie of railway employees travelling first because it is one of the perks, no one appears to be exactly at ease. Here and there the season ticket holders add a little reassurance and there is a sprinkling of the more flamboyant characters in showbiz, some of them in evening dress – or what passes for evening dress nowadays if you have time to puzzle it out. There must surely be a man who designs clothes for such occasions, a sort of Teddy Tinling of the centre foyer.

The play is received ecstatically. You leave the theatre telling yourself that you are in the money, and the next morning the critics tear it to shreds while the management is busy tearing their notices to shreds to extract a few quotes to paste up outside the theatre. When the play comes off in a month, the final balance sheet shows a deficit of £78, but it seems you are not to be asked to fork out any further sum, and you breathe a sigh of relief and send the letter on to your accountant. You might have done worse. After all, it takes a long time to learn to play the harp.

A Church is not a Theatre – Or Is It?

The show must go on or *Don't give them back their money whatever is happening* is the first principle of theatrical management. No Play, No Pay is another from the same book. My profession has long been credited with superhuman powers of endurance and it is true that most of us act better with a high fever or a raging toothache and feel better afterwards. 'Doctor Theatre,' we tell each other, smiling bravely, as we are driven away in the ambulance.

Managers know that the public can seldom distinguish between one actor and another and certainly not between one actor and his understudy. To the Chinese and the audience we all look alike. Two things keep an actor acting on these occasions, one is he isn't going to get paid without giving a performance; the other that his understudy may just conceivably give a better performance than he does. In the second case his fears are usually groundless. In point of fact most understudies haven't a hope in Hell. I know you've seen different in the Alice Faye movies, but that was long ago, and even the suckers know different today. An understudy is paid to hold the fort, not to break out and win the war. What the other members of the cast require is someone who will enable them to score in areas where up to now they have been repulsed. With the understudy playing, everyone else expects to chalk up a few extra laughs. When the cat's away the mice insist on their inalienable right to play. They are not going to welcome another pussy!

Of course when I was an understudy myself, I took a different and more liberal view. I had ambition and genuine belief I could do better than my principal. I once put matters to the test. At Nottingham in high summer and before a modest matinee audience I lavished a week's salary on bribing the actor I covered to absent himself. In his stead I gave an intensely memorable, utterly satisfying performance, and was sacked almost as soon as the curtain fell. They simply didn't want genius in Nottingham in those days. I finished the engagement as the assistant stage manager, at a wildly reduced salary.

The show which, alas, every actor has to miss is his own memorial service. These are very popular nowadays, though not with me. I have left written instructions that under no circumstances is there to be one on my account. I don't wish to go to the grave haunted by the fear that no one would turn up.

True, the ones I go to are usually well attended, but I seldom enjoy myself. Perhaps I shouldn't expect to enjoy myself in church, I never have, and I put it all down to being forced to attend Divine Service twice a day all through my school days. I don't really feel at home in a pew. 'Forgive us our trespasses as we forgive them that trespass against us,' I used to pray in my childish treble, glimpsing through my fingers the master who was going to beat me on the morrow, and wondering what on earth he was praying about.

The same unease doesn't affect me nowadays in St. Martins in the Fields or St. George's, Hanover Square, or St. whatever it is in the middle of Soho where we actors customarily gather to pay our last respects to our departed colleagues, but I am not exactly easy here either. A church is not a theatre, but the seating is strikingly similar. At memorial services the front of the house is the responsibility of the Profession, the clergy take their place on the stage. True we are occasionally invited to read the lessons, or deliver the eulogy, but our performances tend to be muted. There is a noticeable lack of confidence at the lectern and in the pulpit.

Not surprisingly, if you are growing as deaf as I am, it is often difficult to hear.

Memorial services, too, always seem to be still in rehearsal. Only the clergy know exactly what is going to happen next; the rest of us shuffle from knees to feet and then find we should have been seated all the time. Before the curtain goes up, the late actor's friends play ushers. In the school play everyone has a part to act. Ushers speak in low murmurs, smile quietly, shuffle the mourners. No one can be trusted to walk up the aisle on their own, to find a place. While the organ plays, the ushers precede each of us in turn, carrying not a torch, but a sheaf of specially-printed programmes. There is also one on every seat and another beside each prayer book. The name of the deceased is printed boldly on page one. We can be sure the billing is as he would have wished at last, and for the first time we learn the other names he bore. A lady at the door asks our names, and we pretend not to mind. Years ago one of the newspapers used to publish the names of the ushers who were to take part, and the list would be carried by elderly and faithful theatre fans who, alas, are now all dead themselves, or at any rate past caring. 'Which are you?' they would ask, in suitably muted tones, and then put a little tick beside the name, to remind them that they had had their money's worth.

Just before the curtain rises, the ushers usher in the immediate relatives, and then relinquish their roles. The amateurs hand over to the professionals. Preceeded more often than not by a small choir consisting of half a dozen ladies in red mortar boards, the clergy take the stage. The climax of the play is, of course, the eulogy, spoken sometimes by the officiating priest, but more often by one of our lot. When this is the case, it invariably commences with the personal reminiscence. No one ever says 'I didn't know George, and I never wanted to do so.' What they say is 'I first met George when he had patently dined too well and was about to —' here a frisson runs through chancel and nave alike. Is indiscretion for once going to gain the upper hand? '— was about to help an old widow lady across the road.' Alas, the danger has passed. We all relax in disappointment. As the orator continues, we learn more and more about him, and less and less about poor George. This is not a fault of course confined to theatrical eulogies. Even Top People's obituaries when they appear in their house magazine, commence with some memory of the writer shooting tigers in Bengal, when from under the tethered goat leapt his friend the deceased.

'Neither of us,' it continues, 'were destined to be killed that day, but I think we both enjoyed our first encounter.' We don't in point of fact want to know what he enjoyed, but he can seldom resist telling us just the same.

When the eulogiser has finished, the actor climbs down from the pulpit, trying to look unassuming. There is a special sort of expression for such occasions. 'I don't want any nonsense. I have told you the truth about George as I see it. The fact that we are in church simply doesn't arise.'

When the priest is in charge, the eulogy seldom includes the personal anecdote. This is not because clergymen don't appreciate a good story, simply that this one has never met George, although he claims often to have seen him across the footlights. He is careful to stress the fact that although George never prayed, and never went to church even to read the lesson, he was in the fullest sense a Christian Gentleman, and his salvation is perfectly assured. On such occasions the church mercifully believes in a special relationship for actors where the Kingdom of Heaven is concerned. The relationship of which Nixon and Wilson once prattled so happily, adapted to showbiz, a procession of Equity card-carrying guitar players, streaming unchallenged through the Pearly Gates. Why not, pray? Who better than we can learn to play the harp?

If nowadays I find myself attending rather more memorial services than I would wish, here at any rate is an unlikely crumb of comfort.

Fame is the Spur

There are actors who shrink from recognition, playing a perpetual game of hide-and-seek. Alec Guinness, Paul Scofield, Elizabeth Taylor. No one, I told the latter, will know you in Leningrad; put a scarf over your hair and come for a walk, or come downstairs and dine with me in the hotel restaurant. The Russians stood on their chairs to get a better view. Miss Taylor ate very little.

No one has ever stood on a chair to see me. If there is any chance of my not being recognized, I stand on the chair. For everyone who can put a name to the face there are ten who can't. These are the ones who ask for autographs; mine is not the most legible signature, especially when scrawled on a newspaper in pencil. I leave them to puzzle it out. Some prefer to continue guessing, and expect me to halt until they have succeeded. 'Don't tell me,' they will urge, 'I'll be there in a moment.'

'I have to be there sooner than that,' I reply, 'the name is Morley.'

'That's right,' they tell me, 'Christopher Morley,' and we part friends.

Not all my colleagues enjoy such interruptions; they have other and more serious purposes in life than being quizzed or being told by strangers that the last time he or she met them was on a plane bound for Jersey fifteen years ago. 'I don't suppose you'll remember,' they add for further identification, 'they were plumb out of gin.' It is, of course, always impossible to recall the incident, but I for one go on my way sustained by the hope that we shall meet again fifteen years from now and one of us be sufficiently impressed to recall our second meeting.

Only on race courses do I refuse to autograph. Alastair Sim, among others, always refused to give them. He would explain, at considerable length, his objections to such a foolish request. He refused to litter the world with idiotic scraps of paper. Nowadays his signature is valuable. For some reason the Germans and the Americans are the most avid autograph collectors. They write from Bremen and Minnesota in facsimile enclosing international tokens and a half-dozen blank sheets. I never sign more than one; if, as one supposes, the sender is commercially orientated one doesn't want to flood the market.

Now and again you will be shaken by the hand by someone who knows your brother in Orpington. The fact that to the best of your knowledge you haven't a brother carries little weight on such occasions. The stranger departs, convinced you are lying and that you are estranged from your relative. You depart wondering if (as in the case of a theatrical friend) your father kept the existence of an entirely separate brood a secret. My friend was tempted to investigate further the chance remark of a bookseller, and discovered he had not one but several brothers and sisters or, more correctly, half-brothers and sisters. But in my case I have been content to let sleeping dogs lie.

Occasionally I get dead rats and even more unpleasant anonymous gifts through the post. I tell myself that it is unlikely that the former were contaminated by plague, and that I have reduced the intolerable pressure of some fellow lunatic. I refuse to accept it as a judgement on my performance. The older one grows the more pleased are one's contemporaries to see one, although not necessarily performing in the theatre. They are heartened by such encounters. There is a strong geriatric bond. Some recall how well one looks; others, an occasion many years ago when they first caught sight of one across the footlights. They strive to remember the name of the piece, or the date, or where they were at the time. It is often a slow process of gradual recall. One hesitates to prompt, even if one could. The parting is delayed but pleasurable. They go on their way remembering something entirely different. How fond they were of Aunt Maud who provided the matinée treat. One is left with the name of the leading lady on the tip of the tongue.

Americans make the best fans, perhaps because they always seem to have time on their hands. The native young pound along behind, thrust a cigarette packet into one's hand, and are off back to the shop. Worst of all are the temporarily incapacitated who demand you sign the plaster on the fractured limb. I find it well nigh impossible to scratch on plaster of Paris, yet others seem to manage.

Few ask for themselves; it is usually for a child. 'My little granddaughter will be so excited,' they urge, but surely a candy bar or a toy is a more suitable present? I can hardly bear to contemplate the disappointment. 'Guess what grandpa has for you?' The small victim searching the pocket and coming up with a squashed plastic cup bearing the signature of someone of whom she is totally ignorant. 'Don't cry, dear, and Grandpa will go out right away and bring back an iced lolly.'

New Zealanders often produce passports; there is a certain satisfaction in writing on an official document. The suspicion that in so doing I may have invalidated it doesn't seem to occur to them, as it does to me. I should, I suppose, be grateful that at least people don't seem to want to write their names on me, as they do on other ancient monuments—and I am.

Heavier citizens demand that I should follow them, to be introduced to their wives on the grounds that the latter often remark on our striking resemblance. Functioning as I do as a sort of decoy duck for British Airways, I am hailed as a friendly counsellor whose advice has been accepted, and on other occasions blamed for delays at Heathrow. Sometimes asked if I ever resent being better known for performances in television advertisements than as the definitive Hamlet of my time, no, I tell them bravely, in the world of commercials everything ends happily and that is precisely what I aim to do.

Of course, it has not been so easy for the children, and now the grandchildren, who are at times appalled by my constant *bonhomie*. My son once summed it all up. 'There are times, Papa, when you made us cringe a little, but taking it by and large we got the service.'

Critical Acclaim

I learnt my trade in the twenty years between the great wars and immediately following the last one and, whether I like it or not, am now an old dog who fails to learn new tricks. New tricks were frowned on in those days. The theatre was somewhere for the pleasure seeker to rest between dinner and an evening on the town. It was the stalls that mattered; without them life was just not possible.

The stalls put on dinner jackets and picked up their tickets at the box office. These had been reserved for them by the ticket-agency libraries like Keith Prowse and it was on the advice of the librarians that we both depended.

There were, in those days, critics of considerable reputation such as Morgan on *The Times*, St John Ervine on the *Observer*, Agate on the *Sunday Times* and even Hannen Swaffer who wrote for the *Express*. Like the monarch, their function was to advise and warn and they often succeeded in being extravagantly witty and amusing at the expense of the playwright or the cast, but the real power of life and death was vested in a mysterious and comparatively anonymous Mr Smith, who, although nominally only the buyer for Keith Prowse, also largely influenced the attitude of his colleagues who represented a number of smaller firms whose names, with the exception of Lacon and Ollier and Ashton Mitchell, I have, alas, forgotten.

It was Mr Smith who decided whether the libraries would do the deal.

If he approved, he waited on the manager the next morning and guaranteed to sell enough stalls to keep the attraction running for three, six and sometimes twelve months ahead. Although Mr Smith was not available to customers, Miss Parker, who was in charge of the ticket counter at Ashton Mitchell, became a close friend of mine and I used to drop in on her establishment in Bond Street to chat her up, as the saying goes these days.

Miss Parker's customers were the *crème de la crème*. It was she who decided how they should spend their evenings during the season, or when they were perforce up from the shires in the winter because frost suspended hunting, or unexpectedly at a loose end after Goodwood week, or simply staying at Claridges for Christmas shopping. When she booked them boxes at Ascot or centre court seats at Wimbledon, she would urge that they also took in The Hippodrome or His Majesty's later in the day. It wasn't necessary for her to describe or even name the play. All they had to be told was the venue and starting time so that they could instruct their chauffeurs.

Some names were familiar: Nares, Tempest, Du Maurier, Cooper, Buchanan, Maugham, Lonsdale, Smith and Travers. But her public usually made vagueness a point of honour. When discussing the entertainment she provided, they would seldom condescend to be explicit. 'Had a good time the other evening with that fellow who slaps his pockets at that theatre next to the Carlton,' they would tell each other in the club or at the hairdresser. Miss Parker seldom gave them a bum steer; she knew very well when, if ever, they were in the mood for Chekhov or Galsworthy. She was a magnificent saleswoman. Customers seldom rang her up or came away from her establishment without sheaves of tickets.

Where the critics were concerned, Agate and Tynan and to a lesser extent St. John Ervine and Morgan counted with my fellow actors. A good notice from Trewin or Darlington cheered but it was Agate above all who made our hearts glow and our hands reach for the paste brush to enshrine his judgement in our press-cutting books. Agate was witty at his own expense, Tynan at ours. In the war Agate was often to be met at Heppel's in the Strand or Perkins in Piccadilly; both sold patent restoratives and soap for which there always seemed an endless supply of coupons. He once thrust unexpectedly into my hand a florin bearing the head of the Prince Regent, a part I once essayed. I was immensely proud and still occasionally turn out a drawer in a hopeless and unavailing quest for it. Like the medal once given me by the Pope (though not, I hasten to add, for any outstanding act of piety, but merely that he was giving them out to callers during Holy Year) it has vanished without trace but the memory of Agate lingers imperishably for me as for all my contemporaries. A schoolmaster who placed his pupils in their order of achievement. I was not among the top of the class, but my name wasn't quite at the bottom either.

At least it was not he who wrote, 'Mr Morley was trying in both senses of the word.' I was a member of a repertory theatre in Bournemouth in those days and I have never forgiven nor forgotten.

Fifty years is a short time in the theatre.

An actor must learn to live with criticism and not only the ones in his scrapbooks. The comments of his nearest and dearest often rankle insanely over the years. Gladys Cooper never forgot her mother's observation on the first night of her earliest triumph. 'You looked, dear, a trifle peaky.' There was Mrs Irving's celebrated aside to her husband as they drove home after his resounding triumph in *The Bells*: 'How much longer, Henry, are you going on making a fool of yourself?' Irving, to his everlasting credit, stopped the cab and put his wife out of it, never to speak to the lady again. 'What did you think of it then?' I asked my mother after she had watched me portray Shylock at the Royal Academy of Dramatic Art in my student days. 'I thought your fingernails were rather dirty, dear.'

Once, heavily disguised, I bestrode the stage as Oedipus and afterwards closely questioned a favourite aunt as to her reaction. 'Your mask,' she told me, 'looked exactly as if it was made of Sorbo sponge.'

'That is because it is made of Sorbo,' I told her roughly, and never again provided her with a complimentary seat.

On the first night of the first play I ever wrote I was handed a telegram as I left the stage door informing me that a Mr Wintle was safely home again after watching only the first act of what he trusted was the worst play he would ever be compelled to witness. 'I hope,' I told myself, 'it's not always going to be like this,' and of course it wasn't. In all the years since then no one else has ever bothered to telegraph, and the danger has now passed. For one thing the cost these days is prohibitive, and for another the post office closes a great deal earlier.

Counting the House

Audiences, like salad dressings, are never the same twice running, or five hundred times running, if it comes to that. I am often accused of playing the same role too often. My defence is that I play each audience only once. Younger colleagues, and most of my colleagues are younger, hold that an audience is not there to be played with, that an actor's duty (however evocative the phrase) is to play with himself. The challenge for them lies within. Scofield, Gielgud and Olivier are high priests ministering to the faithful, while my role is that of a potboy serving my customers with gin and tonic. My patrons are a fun-loving bunch seeking a night out. They seldom leave the premises with the hushed reverence and sober mien of those who have had an Experience. They walk into Shaftesbury Avenue wondering about supper, or a bird, possibly both.

For me the supreme excitement each evening is the moment of truth. The Manager is in a dinner jacket, I in my underpants, the audience in the bars. The curtain has fallen on the first act. There is a sense of excitement, of ritual. I am invited to bid for the house. I have already decided on a figure. During the first scene I have not been idle. There are certain vantage points on the stage, certain moments in my performance when I am able to glimpse specific parts of the auditorium and note the empty seats gleaming in the dark, reflecting the lights from the stage. It is this play of light with which I have to contend. From certain positions I am inhibited from sober calculation. From others it is comparatively easy. But of course I am never stationary for very long. The closest analogy, I suppose, is with a pilot on a bombing raid. By the interval, my mission is completed. I am ready for de-briefing. I hazard an estimate, tear open the envelope, and read the figure written on a small square of notepaper. Sometimes I am spot on, on other evenings miles off target. I haven't allowed for parties at reduced prices, or hospital nurses in disguise who haven't paid at all. Purists may argue that an actor cannot give of his best whilst engaged in mental arithmetic. I can only say that I have found it a help not only to be able to do two things at once when I am actually on the stage, but to have two things to do. It was Marie Tempest who told me that she had never played a scene without at the same time being able to make out the laundry list. 'Naturally,' she added, 'I don't make out the laundry list myself these days, but I still could.'

The excitement over for one evening, I am ready for the second act. Now that I know the quantity of the house I can start to worry about its quality, which indeed may have changed drastically during the intermission. Often an audience which begins by appreciating every nuance and laughing at exactly the right moment and for exactly the right length of time, will finish the evening in sullen lethargy and hostile silence. On the other hand, a house which begins by not laughing at all, and driving the actors to despair by coughing itself silly in the early scenes, may end up as our particular pride and joy, laughing uproariously and applauding wildly. Our fault or theirs? I can never be sure. All I know is that every audience has to be watched every minute of the evening. Take your eyes off the customer, turn your back and the brute springs. I once asked a circus proprietor her opinion of lion tamers. 'Any fool can do it,' she told me. 'Only a fool does.'

One thing I learnt early in my job, miracles seldom happen. When I owned a racehorse I would watch it go down to the start, telling myself that despite the opinion of the trainer, the jockey and the travelling lad, there was nothing to stop it winning. But there was, and it didn't. It's the same when a play isn't going to win either, but as long as the race is on, there's hope. Every night when you get to the theatre you tell yourself that it might be full, but it never is, though oddly enough it is never quite empty either. There is a fixed number of determined masochists who attend performances of a failure each evening, spacing themselves with mathematical precision. There is no reason why they shouldn't all come to see you on the same evening — even then they wouldn't fill the theatre — but their singular task is to prolong the agony for yourself and the backer and nobly they achieve it. What Providence ordains that there should be just so many chartered accountants, foreign diplomats, provincial librarians, licensed victuallers, engaged couples, consenting adults and lapsed clergymen assembled each evening in the fauteuils? For us it is *you* who are the real performers, the jugglers, the acrobats, the roustabouts.

As we survey the motley crew of pickpockets who jostle each other afresh every evening in our tent, we are grateful for your infinite variety, without which it would be quite impossible for us to remain your faithful, humble and obedient servants.

The One That Got Away

*How The Other Half Loves chalked up two years and 800 perform-
ances at the Lyric Theatre, London, and during its run there grossed
over half a million pounds. It was translated into half a dozen
languages, and ran successfully in at least four of them. Why did this
particular play flourish in the theatrical jungle?*

In April, 1970 there seemed little point in going to Leicester, where
How The Other Half Loves was being given a second chance at the
local repertory theatre, the first production of the play at Scarborough some months before having satisfied neither author nor
management. The invitation had come from Peter Bridge, whom I
knew only slightly, and for whose managerial prowess I had little
enthusiasm. On the other hand, I had to find myself a play and a new
management. The firm of H. M. Tennent, with whom I had been
closely connected for much of my theatrical life, and I had come to
the parting of the ways.

The split, for which I was entirely responsible, came during the
run of *Half Way Up The Tree*, a play by Peter Ustinov, the success of
which in the West End had not been repeated in other countries
where it had been produced. I am never slow to apportion credit to
myself, and regarded the whole episode as a personal triumph for my
acumen and theatrical know-how. I had saved Ustinov from himself,
and with the very considerable help of the director John Gielgud,
had once more pulled Beaumont's* chestnuts out of the fire.

He must, I was sure, be grateful to his old friend, so that when I
needed a quick thousand pounds, I approached full of confidence
and goodwill. I had taken it upon myself to raise a few thousand
pounds to buy and equip a school for autistic children and contacted

* H. M. Tennent's managing director.

95

a number of the rich whom I considered would be fairly easy touches. There are men in our business who give, and men who don't. Lew Grade, for instance, is a natural giver. I approached him across a crowded room and sniffed his cigar for a time while he told a story. I am not a good listener to other people's anecdotes, and after a time, thinking, or perhaps just hoping, that he had reached the point, I asked him for the money. 'Of course,' he replied, 'you shall have it in the morning. Don't interrupt,' and went on with his tale. On the books of ATV Lew owes me very little. Indeed, I must have cost the company a small fortune in my unsuccessful attempts to launch a series on their network. But Lew Grade is a generous man, not given to jobbing back. I am not praising him. I don't think generous men should be praised, they are the lucky ones.

Another of my successes on this occasion was John Lennon, who whipped out his cheque book and gave me the bread on the spot. I hardly knew John Lennon. On the other hand I thought I knew Beaumont, and when he refused me I was shattered and very angry. I felt he owed me something. He felt exactly the opposite. When I told him that if he didn't give me the money I would sit in his outer office till he did, he seemed only mildly amused. When, this ploy having failed, two days later I told him that unless he gave the money I would never darken his door again, he called it blackmail, which it was. I am not a reasonable man. I have never forgiven him. I trust I never shall. When I told my wife about the incident, she looked nonplussed. 'My darling,' she told me, 'whatever made you think he'd give you the money? He's not a friend of yours', and of course he isn't. Friends are not made out of mutual obligation.

What finally decided me to go to Leicester was a race meeting at Stratford-on-Avon, where a horse of mine was entered to run. On the map Leicester seemed fairly close. There was a time when I knew every provincial city in England. I spent ten years of my life on tour, but I had forgotten Leicester. In any case it appeared to have been re-planned recently with multi-storey car parks to depress me with their cement understains and crush barriers to keep back non-existent crowds. The object of the exercise is that you should drive straight through such cities these days without stopping, or indeed noticing that they are there at all.

I was surprised to find the theatre in a bus depot, but I suppose even that makes sense in a way. A handy sort of house with raked seats and a flat stage, the convenience of a curtain was dispensed with, so that when the furniture had to be changed halfway through the first act, an entirely separate production was mounted with a ringmaster and uniformed circus hands. The audience enjoyed it hugely. I thought they quite liked the play. After the performance several patrons accosted Robin Midgley who had directed the piece, with advice on how to improve it. He struck me then, as he does now, as an eminently patient, reasonable and above all resourceful fellow. About the play I was not so certain. The most serious snag seemed to me that most of the goods were displayed in the first act, the climax of which was an immensely complicated coup de théâtre in which two players contrived to attend separate and simultaneous dinner parties.

'Is it, do you suppose,' I asked John Jonas who drives me around on these occasions and nurses me through the performances I do decide to give, 'is it, do you suppose, too clever by half?'

Mr. Jonas on this occasion seemed not to share my anxiety. 'A thoroughly good evening,' he insisted on the way home. 'I don't know why you didn't enjoy it more.'

I think it was his enthusiasm as much as anything else that decided me to go ahead. It was after all an even money chance, and this has always seemed generous odds to me. I had certain reservations, and having told Peter Bridge that I was game at least up to a point, tried for the next couple of weeks to get the play altered, but found Alan Ayckbourn, the author, fairly obdurate and inclined to prefer his own ideas to mine. I started out by demanding that the baby in the play should be replaced by an elkhound, and that I should be encouraged to participate in the celebrated dinner scene dressed in Japanese costume. Both suggestions were resisted tooth and nail, and on reflection correctly. After two years I can't pretend to have made much of Alan Ayckbourn, an eminently cautious fellow, not given to hanging round the cast, remembering the anniversaries of the play or lunching his leading ladies. About his play's quite phenomenal success he evinces little emotion, hugging himself, if he does so at all, in secret.

Having got me to agree to do the play, Peter Bridge's immediate tasks were to find the money and the theatre with which and in which to present *How The Other Half Loves.* The money presented no problem. There was an embarrassment of would-be investors. All he had to do was to circularise the list of prospective backers with which all managers provide themselves, and the eighteen thousand pounds for which he asked to mount the production was subscribed overnight. The Angels on this occasion smelt success. Both the author and myself had been previous winners over the course and almost uniquely Peter was able to produce two notices written by national critics on the strength of the Leicester production, predicting a London success for the play when it was eventually produced there. You could hardly ask for more, and no one did. Indeed one of the backers, Eddie Kulukundis, of whom we shall hear more later, tried unsuccessfully to provide all the capital required from his own pocket.

Without the Sunday notices written by Bryden and Marcus it is possible that nothing much more would ever have been heard of the play after Leicester. The local notices for the piece were not particularly encouraging, and interest in a London production had all but ceased.

The problem of obtaining a suitable West End theatre was as usual more complicated. In order to appreciate the singular good fortune which attended its arrival at the Lyric, we must inform ourselves not so much about the state of the theatre in London and the provinces, as the state of the theatres themselves.

In a business which is by nature optimistic and essentially fly-by-night, the ground landlords of theatre land have been ever since I can remember in a class by themselves for sober mien and general lack of high spirits. Grave and reverend seigneurs to a man, they are the farmers of this never-never land of ours, always complaining of the harvest, but raking in the shekels whenever and wherever possible. In the years between the wars such men were typified by the late Stuart Cruikshank, who controlled the giant Howard & Wyndham circuit in the then flourishing provincial theatre. Here was a card-index man after the heart of I B M itself. No employee however insignificant, no star however famous, no gown however dilapidated, no piece of scenery or property however unlikely ever to be used again, escaped his filing system. He once let me scan some of the cards on his desk awaiting re-deployment. 'Miss A,' I read, 'asks thirty, is worth half. Good personality and clothes sense, but poor personal wardrobe. Not a hard worker at matinees. Blonde (natural).' Then followed the dates she had fulfilled and the fees paid. The card beneath referred to a ball dress which although now alas damaged at the hem, was considered by E. J., who had supplied the information, as still suitable for second lead singer in the finale or ballroom scenes.

If there is one thing that theatre owners have in common it is a pathological horror of throwing anything away, for this would entail the purchase of a replacement. In the forty years I have been sitting around in dressing-rooms I don't believe I have ever sat in a new armchair. I have never used a lavatory which hadn't been designed half a century before, or looked into a mirror which wasn't lit by a naked bulb. I have never seen a carpet in a corridor or a picture on a wall. The higher you climb in most theatres the more sparse the furniture becomes. Understudies are not encouraged to relax. They must sit for the three hours each evening on upright chairs, no two of which ever match each other. To strip an average theatre of its furniture and fittings, most self-respecting junk men would demand a fee. Since *How The Other Half Loves* opened at the Lyric Theatre, the landlords have recovered close on a hundred thousand pounds in rent, yet the window sash in my dressing-room which has been broken since we opened, and I am not at all sure wasn't broken when I played there in *The Little Hut* ten years earlier, is still broken. Does it matter? Well, the answer is it doesn't really matter all that much to the actors. It may be good for us not to be able to relax too much backstage, and we are used to such conditions, but broken window sashes and sagging armchairs are a symptom of bad management. They do little to dispel the belief that theatre owners in this country are a bunch of frustrated property developers who spend a good deal of their time flattening their noses against the grimy window panes and gazing out enviously across the street at the car parks and supermarkets which luckier colleagues have been allowed to build.

A theatre site is rarely a profitable one, particularly if one takes into account how much more could be made by turning out the actors and installing the business men and tourists. Yet these same tourists now come to this country in large numbers partly because of the theatres and it is the height of folly that the latter should be in the hands of vast conglomerates like Associated Television, who treat them like unwanted children, allowing them each year to grow a little shabbier and more uncared for, evincing no pride in their achievement, grudging them even a coat of paint.

However, when it comes to renting them out for profit, parental interest revives somewhat. Heads we win, tails you lose is the rule, and the empty shell, for such each house virtually becomes with every fresh lease, is let to the producing manager on the harshest possible terms. The average rent demanded is in the region of a thousand pounds a week against twenty per cent of the box office takings, whichever is the larger, and the lease can be terminated by the landlords two weeks after the takings drop below an agreed sum which is known as the 'stop figure'. Over and above that the tenant is expected to pay for light, heating and staff and nowadays the landlords are chary of providing even a bulb, let alone a spotlight, so all this has to be hired afresh. The landlords, however, insist on retaining the right to sell programmes and operate the bars, an enormously profitable business. One might be forgiven for supposing that they are often more concerned with the brand of whisky on sale in the foyers than the brand of entertainment advertised on the marquee.

Not all London or provincial theatres find themselves in this sorry state. There are producing managers who maintain their establishments in reasonable repair and one house especially, acquired some years ago by Peter Saunders, has been extensively redecorated and redesigned. The Vaudeville Theatre shines forth like a good deed in this naughty world. But these theatres are not as a rule available to managers such as Bridge. Their proprietors prefer to have a finger in the pie if they have not actually baked it themselves, and do not as a rule let their theatres on a strict rental basis. Bridge was now free to proceed at his peril, the date when he would be able to conclude negotiations for a theatre some weeks off, and with no guarantee that he would get one at all, should business in the West End suddenly spurt. He could find himself as he did with his recent production of *On The Rocks*, up in the clouds circling the airport without permission to land, and if the tour proved financially disastrous, running out of gas.

Rehearsals began on my birthday at the Irish Club. I had not then, and still haven't, the faintest idea what normally goes on at the Irish Club, apart from the sale of *The Irish Times* in the hall, but I climbed the stairs to the room reserved for the first rehearsal and found Bridge had invited a few press photographers along for a drink in the hope that they would take pictures of myself cutting my birthday cake. There is surely no duller subject for portraiture, or one an editor is more easily able to reject, than an actor poised over confectionery, but the attempt has to be made.

Robin Fox turned up and I was as always reassured in his company, and managed the ritual bonhomie and drank the champagne, blissfully unaware of the impending catastrophe. A few days later I was to learn that my trusted friend and manager had terminal cancer and the shadow of his approaching death made life suddenly much colder. In the evenings after rehearsing I would drive down to the King Edward Hospital at Midhurst for a picnic in his bedroom, bearing caviare and curious mousses from Fortnum's, and drinking champagne by his bedside. It didn't really make matters better, but in times of crisis I find extravagance sometimes helps me. Late one evening I left him and walked along the corridor to where a nurse sat at a table, writing reports on her patients.

'I'm off now,' I told her unnecessarily. 'I gather the news is rather good about Mr. Fox. They haven't found anything sinister.'

She didn't answer for a moment. I had caught her, I suppose, off guard. Into her eyes came a look of disbelief, instantly checked by a professional caution.

'Oh yes,' she said, 'Mr. Fox is doing very well', and that as far as I was concerned was that. I never again had any hope at all.

It was at the first rehearsal that I met Eddie Kulukundis and learnt he was to be a partner in the enterprise which Bridge, possibly scenting battle, had christened Agincourt Productions Ltd. My first impression was that of a large, untidy and likeable Greek who was constantly ducking his head in a basin, not to cool it, but to get his hair to lie down.

His recent impact on theatreland was already proving sensational. Word had got round that there was a stranger in town and back at the old saloon they were busy polishing the glasses and getting out the old deck of cards. Here was a tenderfoot aiming to join in the poker game and there was no lack of players anxious for him to draw up a chair and sweeten the pot.

They found out almost immediately that he was a man after their own heart who never seemed quite certain of how many chips he was betting. When I asked him once how much a particular hand had cost him, he assured me he would break even.

'Come now, Eddie, what do you mean by even?' I persisted. 'You think you'll lose five thousand?'

'A bit more than that,' he told me with a smile. He is a good loser but then, of course, he's had a lot of practice these last two years.

He is the only son of a wealthy Greek shipowner.

'I suppose you would call us wealthy,' he told me. 'As a boy I lived in Wembley; it's not all that rich a neighbourhood. On the other hand my father always had chauffeurs.'

'Chauffeurs?' I queried.

'One at a time. Mother's dowry when she married — we Greeks have dowries, you know — was twenty thousand, a lot of money in those days.'

Mother was strict with him, I gathered. Until he was twenty-two he didn't go out with girls. Then, as is often the way, it all happened too quickly. He fell deeply in love and for the first time really started to go places in his father's business. He managed the English branch from the Minories. He made a small fortune, intent on marriage and settling down possibly in Wembley himself, although by this time the rest of the family had moved abroad. Eddie, as the son of the eldest brother, was more or less the boss.

'There's not,' he explained, 'much difference really between a good shipowner and a bad shipowner. In good times everyone makes money because they can't help doing so. In bad times we all lose.' He was not, however, to find the same conditions prevailing in the theatre.

Eventually his girl chucked, and Eddie surveyed his life and didn't much care for the way it looked. For one thing the cousins were growing up and began giving him advice on how to run the business, and for another he had been working so hard he hadn't really had much fun. He is not a man who relaxes easily, or one that makes friends without effort.

'I am the one,' he told me ruefully, 'who is always the host. It was the same in ship building, I pick up the check. Perhaps I go out with the wrong people — out-of-work actors, struggling playwrights. I don't seem to like the company of the sufficient, the rich, the people in society, English society. I like American society.'

'Do you,' I asked, 'know many people in American society?'

'Not really, but I think I get on better in America.'

In point of fact, last time Eddie was there he got on rather badly. He went with Bridge to produce *How The Other Half Loves* in New York.

'I intended to have only a small investment,' he explained, 'but Bridge suggested I subscribed the whole British capital, and insisted when we arrived on Broadway there would be plenty of backers eager to take most of my share and pay me a small premium for the privilege. Things didn't turn out that way and the other backers didn't show.'

In the event the production was a disaster and the money was lost. With the English profits, Eddie reckons to break about even over the entire venture, but is understandably resentful.

'I kept telling myself that in the event we didn't get the money subscribed, I had had too small a stake in the London production, and as after all this was my first real success maybe I should play up my winnings.'

If unrequited love was the main reason why Eddie decided to live it up in the theatre, he would perhaps have done better to stick to girls. After two years he has very little to show for the two hundred thousand pounds it has cost him to date.

He claims he knows more about the business. 'This time last year,' he confessed, 'I was strictly a sucker. I couldn't say no.' It started with *The Happy Apple*, a play which had a moderately good reception at an outlying theatre and Eddie went to see with one of his girl friends who thought a visit to a theatre might cheer him up. He met the director, heard of a vague plan to transfer the piece to the West

End and stepped straight on to the ice. He didn't present it himself, but put up eighty per cent of the capital required. He got his first sight of a theatre balance sheet, was fairly startled and has remained in a mild state of shock ever since. He finds it surprising, for instance, that managers with whom he presents plays should transfer so high a percentage of their office expenses to his production account. When he rents a playhouse he doesn't, or at least didn't, expect to have to pay several hundreds a week over and above the agreed sum for the illuminated signs directing patrons to the theatre. When told he can mount a production of a play already in the repertory of one of the National Theatres for four thousand, he is dazed to find his production bill has shot up to twenty thousand because the scenery has deteriorated through damp and the dresses have been claimed back and rented out afresh by the costumiers to amateur groups. The mistakes on Eddie's bill do not amount to a great deal when one considers the account as a whole, but they serve to irritate him. He is gradually being weaned from the theatre. 'If I could find a nice girl and marry her, I'd give it up tomorrow,' he told me, and I rather hope he does.

Meanwhile he flits from function to function, automatically accosted, perpetually propositioned by those who seek his patronage and his fortune. 'In point of fact,' he told me, 'it's not strictly true that I still have to pick up the checks. Quite often I get a free lunch and there's really nothing to pay at the cocktail parties. All I have to remember to do is not to take my cheque book.'

When I asked Bridge why we were rehearsing at the Irish Club, he told me proudly that coming up from Berkshire every morning I would find it easier to park. 'On the first night,' I told him, 'I am expected to make a speech excusing our state of unpreparedness on the grounds that we are all keen motorists?' I hate rehearsing in rooms as opposed to on stage. I find the space confining, the stage management sits on top of you, prompt book in hand, my mind wanders, reflecting on the decor, marvelling that people normally carouse in these surroundings, give wedding receptions and children's parties. Public rooms are haunted for me by the ghosts of failed functions.

I seldom enjoy myself at rehearsals. I am back in the classroom I so hated; the director is a beak, sometimes a decent beak, but a beak nevertheless. This is his hour, his month in fact. We normally rehearse for about that long. He is here to see we do the work as he wishes it done. Some actors suck up to the master, follow him around, take his hand on the walk, call him Sir, bring him flowers. I am not one of them. Between him and me there is always hostility of a kind often manufactured by myself. I am stimulated by conflict, like to be the one who hurls the rubber while he is intent on the blackboard. In all my theatrical career, only Guthrie willingly enslaved me. I longed to please him, accepted his rule absolutely in triumph and disaster, and no one brought the temple down more effectively on occasions than this curious Irish giant whom I met almost at the outset of my career, who directed my first two plays and later myself in. *Pygmalion.* I had stepped into the breach at the last moment, learnt Higgins in a weekend, gone on ill-prepared and triumphed at Buxton of all places, or so I thought. He came to the dressing-room afterwards. 'Very dull,' he said, 'most of it.' It seemed like praise, perhaps it was intended to be. He never bored one, was never bored himself, stopped in time, dismissed the class, sent us home for prep, a lovely man. When he died, his bailiff came to his wife. 'The great tree has fallen,' he told her. On the morning of his memorial service at St. Paul's, Covent Garden, the tree in the church-yard fell. There was no wind. A great director.

Of course I have liked some of the others, some of them I suppose have liked me, but not many. Peter Brook I found hell. I never understood what the fuss was all about. He tried everything to get me to do what he wanted, I did everything not to. We even quarrelled about who should fetch the Coca Cola. Perhaps because of him, perhaps despite him, *The Little Hut* was a great success, but I don't think either of us would ever go through it again. To enjoy oneself is the supreme duty of an actor. I cannot bear the rack of effort, if acting doesn't come easily I'd rather it didn't come at all. I cannot bear dedication when it is paraded in front of me. I like my director corked, but frothy. The late Jack Minster was the flattest director I ever knew, and the most amusing. He sat in the stalls, wrapped in an overcoat and sustained despair.

'Don't look on the floor,' he would tell us, 'there's nothing there but the play.'

'It gets a laugh,' an actor would expostulate.

'I didn't hear it,' he would reply, 'I was deafened by the ones who weren't laughing.'

Peter Ashmore directed me in *Edward, My Son,* and *Hippo Dancing* and *A Likely Tale.* I enjoyed it. Willie Hyde White summed him up. 'What a civil little chap. I find him invaluable, always ready to fetch the script when I've left it in the Rolls.' But Ashmore was cleverer than that, cleverer with me than anyone else has been. He came into money and wisely didn't press his luck after that.

Directors are alchemists, their hour is brief.

Gielgud I admired enormously, but the trouble was everyone else did the same. I was perpetually comforting the cast in the wings during rehearsals of *Halfway Up The Tree.*

'I don't think John likes what I'm doing,' they would sob.

'Has he said so?'

'No, I just sense it.'

'I like it,' I would tell them, but the tears didn't stop. After a time I began to resent it. He did rather take Ustinov's side at the beginning, but luckily Ustinov wasn't there most of the time. I like a director to take my side. I demand it.

Midgley took my side from the first. I've got so old now that I am no longer a challenge to directors, just something they wish they could move around and can't. Which is not to say I don't make concessions. I made one or two. I didn't interfere with the casting, except to insist that Tetzel played my wife. No one seemed all that keen, not even Tetzel. She had done *The Little Hut* with me, so was more or less prepared. It's strange about Tetzel. I worked with her before the war in radio in New York City when she was only a child. She was the darling of the networks because able to play opposite any leading man in the Rudy Vallee Hour. French, British, Japanese, she took them all on and I never forgot her astringent poise. When I decided to play *The Little Hut* I told Beaumont about her, adding that I hadn't seen her for twenty years and she was possibly out of the business.

'She was in my office this morning,' he told me, 'suddenly turned up out of the blue.'

'Grab her,' I insisted, and he did.

It was the same with *How The Other Half Loves.* I hadn't met her or heard of her since *The Little Hut* finished more than ten years before. On the day I agreed to sign the contract, I lunched with Robin at Wilton's. 'The girl we need,' I told him, 'is Tetzel. Where has she gone, do you suppose?' That evening I walked into a cocktail party, the first one I'd been to for seven years, and there she was by the door.

'Do you want to do a play?' I asked.

'I might.'

As is usually the case with playwrights who deliver their plays into my hands, Ayckbourn began to grow restless quite early on. He had already seen his play rehearsed twice before and had fairly set notions of what it was all about. At the back of his mind, as indeed is nearly always at the back of authors' minds, was the idea that he had written a more significant play than I gave him credit for. Moreover he insisted that all the characters except perhaps my own were fundamentally unlikeable. This didn't do for Tetzel. She was not as far as she was concerned playing a bitch and had no intention of doing so. The final confrontation was to come later at Leeds, but meanwhile there was a certain amount of muttering on both sides. I have always held that to make a steady income in our business, which should be all actors' ambition, one cannot afford to play unsympathetic parts. However much praise is lavished on you by the critics, the audience gradually comes to associate you with the unlikeable characteristics you have assumed in the cause of art. After a time they simply won't pay to go and see you. With the notable exception of Vincent Price, who cheats outrageously, few heavies grow rich. Tetzel and I were quite determined on this point. 'If they don't like us,' we told Ayckbourn, 'they won't come, and where will your little play be then?'

The other leading lady, Heather Sears, seemed much more disposed to go along with the author than we were. Heather, and subsequently Mary Miller who took over from her after a few months, both believed they were in a piece which had something to say quite apart from the laughs. They both spent considerable time with the director establishing the character. They were ready to discuss, for instance, whether the girl they were portraying read the *Guardian* before the *New Statesman,* and how many goldfish should be in the goldfish bowl, and the sort of toys they would provide for that off-stage baby. By this I don't mean they inaugurated the discussions or wasted time unduly, but they chatted around with Midgley whenever the opportunity presented itself. Midgley is a great chatter, but he is also a workmanlike director who runs a very successful theatre in Leicester and knows the curtain has to go up some time. On the whole he held the balance fairly between those who wished to find truth in the play and those who wanted to know where to stand, or more important perhaps, where the others in the cast were intending to stand.

Donald Burton played Heather's husband, and I never quite understood where he stood. He always arrived at rehearsal carrying a furled umbrella which was also a swordstick, and with a scarf tied high round his neck, reminding me of the late Queen Alexandra masking the dewlaps. He is a very good actor who also, as far as I am concerned, breaks all the rules in that he insists on altering his appearance for each role he undertakes. In my view quite fatal. They must know who you are and what you are going to do as soon as you step on the stage, in my book. Donald Burton on the other hand seems to invite them to ask which part he played. His great passion in life seems to be lighting. I don't mean what most actors mean by lighting — how many of the spots one can appropriate — I mean domestic lighting. He claimed to be able to lie in his bath and adjust the dimmers so that the perfect Mediterranean effect was achieved on the soap suds. I was always taught not to fiddle with current in the bath, but he seemed to come to no harm. Similarly, from his bed erotic effects could be created, and even the dawn simulated when it was time for the guest to leave. I hoped he'd ask me round to his pad, but he never did. I don't think he liked me very much. Perhaps he recognised a fellow egomaniac, or realised I would never be able to discuss dimmers seriously. I like the lights full up all the time, but will allow imaginative directors to keep them low until I burst into view, after which the rule, if I am allowed to make it, is light, light and still more light.

The other two members of the cast were Brian Miller and Elizabeth Ashton. Both having been in the original production at Scarborough, Alan decided that the parts could never conceivably be better played than by them, and he was right. They knew exactly what they were up to from the very beginning, refused to be swayed or disturbed by the uncertain manoeuvering of the rest of us and held firm. I cannot imagine what would have happened to the play without them. The rest of us used them as anchor buoys.

After a week rehearsals moved to the Haymarket, where Midgley could sit in the stalls and leave us to get on with it. But for some reason he seemed to prefer a chair at the side of the stage. I have never known a director who sat so long on top of a company. Otherwise I had no fault to find with him, or with the script. Normally I am a glutton for re-writing, but after my initial failure with this piece I thought it best to bide my time, say the lines the author had written and only when I found they didn't work with an audience, get him to alter them or preferably alter them myself. Directing is like cooking in the sense that all the dishes should ideally come to perfection at the same moment. Some actors boil almost immediately, while others take ages to rise.

There comes a time, too, when all of us demand an audience. 'Mummy, watch me,' we cry, and if Mummy isn't planning to visit the nursery for another week, the squabbles are liable to start. At the end of the month we were just about ready. The curtains had been drawn, the stage set. Arrayed in our costumes, we awaited the arrival of the grown-ups. They could hardly have been more appreciative in Leeds had they in fact been our relatives. We didn't pack the theatre, but business built, and we were complimented in teashops. There is nothing the English dislike more than having to talk to people they haven't met. When it happens to an actor, he knows he is on a winner.

I used to drive to Leeds, put up at the Queens and come down after the performances on Saturday and be in my own bed at four. I do not choose to linger. As one gets older, time grows more precious. Years and years ago we travelled on Sundays in special reserved coaches. Long, slow journeys without restaurant cars, but always with a pack of cards and beer, sometimes sandwiches, sometimes we rushed the buffet on the stations where we halted. A pleasant sort of day, particularly if one was sure of digs on arrival. I knew most of the towns in England then, sad, dead slums like Rochdale and Oldham and gay, comfortable, happy places like Southport and York. Blackpool was best of all, but all seaside towns were fun, Bournemouth, Brighton, Morecambe, even Southend. I was twenty-one at Blackpool and had melon flown from Manchester for my birthday party. I was always a show-off.

I opened *Edward, My Son* in Leeds at a matinee on a Tuesday. It ran for four-and-a-half hours with the hitches, but I knew we had a success. In those days the Grand was truly grand, an opera house really, with goodness knows how many floors and a lift and an enormous stage. It was a number one date, full more often than not, and when it was full there was a lot of brass. The manager wore white tie and tails and was a V.C. You put your best foot forward when you stepped on that stage. You lived in the Roundhay Park district. There were plenty of good rooms with wonderful Yorkshire teas before the performance and hot suppers afterwards. There were bits of the city which were unexpected, Marshall and Snelgrove for instance, and Austin Reeds. If like me you had a bad memory, there was always the excitement of rediscovery. Round here, you would tell yourself, somewhere round here there is a shop window in which stuffed squirrels are skating.

But Leeds has changed and like Leicester it too has barricades in preparation for some future riot perhaps, or just possibly a pageant. There is a new complex near the theatre and a new hotel and I wondered if I should have done better to have stayed there. But hotel bedrooms grow ever smaller and I preferred to be near the station. The theatre had given Bridge a guarantee, and we stayed a fortnight. Business was not sensational, but above average. The Grand breaks a good many hearts these days. There was a note for me at the stage door, left by Leonard Rossiter, who had been there the week before. 'Help!' was all it said. One morning saw a glorious row on the stage. A last attempt by the director and the author to get Tetzel to play it tough. She held firm.

'Do you mean to tell me,' asked Robin, 'that you are not going to play the part as we wish it played?'

'Yes. If you want it played that way, you must get someone else.'

'Two someone elses,' I told them, relishing the confrontation. That was the end, more or less.

After a fortnight we moved to Nottingham, where once two theatres stood side by side, like elderly maiden aunts, but one has now passed on, her grave a car park, though goodness knows what is planned as a headstone. The other remains, a dilapidated recluse. 'Do not embarrass the management with requests for complimentary passes. If your friends will not pay to see you, you can hardly expect the general public to do so.' Is the writing still on the wall? I am not sure. Nottingham is still a Moss Empire controlled remotely from the Palladium in Oxford Circus. The dressing rooms are not numbered, but labelled with great names of the past, Barrymore, Irving, Tree, or is that Wimbledon, where we went next? I can't be sure.

It is in Nottingham that I hear Bridge has been offered the Lyric. By now the production has been evaluated by head office, the reports are in. The head brass of course doesn't come itself, but somewhere in the chain of command is a warrant officer on whose judgement they rely. Years ago in the days when the libraries made deals and put down their money in advance, there was a faceless, anonymous taster to whom they appealed for a verdict. If he said buy, they bought and the success was a foregone conclusion. Once they had the seats, they pushed the show. In those days, too, everyone relied on Fred Carter. When you opened out of town he came along and if he liked what he saw, found you a theatre in London. On the try-out of *Edward, My Son* he waited till we got to Manchester.

'You can have,' he told me, 'any theatre you want in London. Which is it to be?'

'His Majesty's,' I told him, and so it was. My God, I felt proud. I didn't have the same pride with this one, but then of course I hadn't written it. I counselled Bridge to try not for the Lyric but the Apollo if he was offered a choice. He was and he didn't, and was right.

We still had three more weeks on the road, Wimbledon and Brighton, but these passed uneventfully. There was not a lot more rehearsing to be done, and no re-writes. Everything would now depend on the first night at the Lyric. The first night of a play in

London is still a formidable obstacle, the Beechers Brook of the National course. In recent years attempts have been made to modify the jump somewhat. The supreme confrontation is no longer sought by management, as used to be the case. Before the war, when the theatre catered largely for the stalls public, managers regarded their first night list as all important, and spent hours at work on the Sheet. The idea was to seat the critics in warm nests of appreciation, although taking care they should not be irritated by loud laughter and bursts of applause while they themselves were scribbling notes in the dusk. Some managers, like the late Gilbert Miller, prided themselves on knowing the social scene and which Marquis was talking to which Marchioness. Gilbert had a profound suspicion of princesses. 'If possible,' he confided in me once, 'I keep them out. They are too casual, like racehorses.' Beaumont is another who is a great expert on such occasions, leaving as little as possible to chance. He has been reported to carry a thermometer to check the exact temperature of the auditorium. But the days when first nights were great social occasions is over. In point of fact nowadays it is quite difficult to fill the house at all, and after the friends of the cast have been accommodated, the manager may be hard put to it to find a representative audience and not one composed almost exclusively of fellow managers, agents, film producers and television directors who have seen it all before and are not all that keen to see it again. This is one of the reasons why previews are encouraged. The actors get a chance of playing themselves in and the professionally interested need no longer all come on the same evening.

On the whole, *How The Other Half Loves* at the Lyric Theatre on the night of August 5th 1970 played much as it had been playing for the last six weeks and the notices, when they appeared, were with one exception uniformly encouraging. Only Harold Hobson in *The Sunday Times* was unwontedly abrasive. He reported that most of the cast gave performances which looked as if they had been recruited from the rejects of the annual pantomime in a backward village, or could he have written originally a backwoods village? We shall never know. By the time his notice appeared we were home and dried.

Miss Missouri and Miss Parker

I am descended from a long line of furniture arrangers. I lived much of my youth in furnished houses and long before the family had unpacked, my father would be in the parlour of our new quarters, impatient to begin shifting the piano. 'Just catch hold of your end, Dai,' he would urge my mother, who was called Daisy in real life — as much of it as she enjoyed with Father, at any rate. 'Just catch hold of your end and we'll try it over here.' Hours later, after every stick of furniture had been re-arranged at least three times and the dining-room table brought in from the dining-room to see if that would help, my father would consent to the rest of the family putting everything back as it was when he walked in, and depart in search of the nearest bridge club.

Similarly, when faced with the need to do yet another play I find what I most enjoy is re-siting the make-up table in my dressing-room. 'Over here,' I urge the property master, interrupted from more immediate chores. 'Over here, there's a good chap and we'll have the cheval mirror so, and the armchair in the corner.' The arrangement completed, I find the door no longer opens and the dressing-table mirror in darkness owing to a scarcity of electric points. Eventually we are back where we started, and to the altogether more mundane matter of discovering whether I know my lines, but how I've enjoyed it all . . .

'We have a rowing eight,' the director assured me, 'and we are jacking up your seat. That way the camera can see the water and the Houses of Parliament. Just come into shot as if you were taking a stroll, sit down and let us have it in twenty-eight seconds.' Behind me on the Embankment were assembled other actors, dressed as policemen, American tourists and babies. The period is early Coward, late Cochran. There is a good deal of discussion about the light, and whether Big Ben looks prettier through the mist, or would it be wise to wait for the sun to shine, supposing it ever does? Finally we go ahead, the rowing crew is positioned, the cameras turn over, and there am I, as large as life and striving to be as natural, inviting all and sundry to a one-week London Show Tour next winter, the price of the air fare to include the hotel, theatre tickets, a car for a day and a Polaroid camera. 'If I didn't live here,' I conclude, 'I'd take it myself.'

Towards evening they seemed satisfied, and I bade everyone goodbye and walked over the bridge and through the park past the grebes on the lake, and waited outside Swan and Edgars until there was a break in the traffic. It was here that I met her, a school-teacher from Missouri on the sort of package deal I had just been advertising, and actually coming to my theatre that evening. Could I, she asked me, tell her where the theatre was? I thought it prudent to conduct her in person. Who knew what other actors might be lurking around, plying for casual trade?

It was the hour when the young take over the Circus, spilling out onto the roadway, squatting on doorsteps, draining their Coca Cola tins to the last drop, camouflaging themselves like stick insects amid the prevailing squalor. What can one say to an American school-teacher about the city we have pulled down about our ears, how apologise for the filth, the litter, the stench of the hot dog stands? Years ago it was the British abroad who held their handkerchiefs to their noses and marvelled at the state of the natives, but now it is Miss Missouri's turn to walk delicately.

I took her almost to the doors of the Lyric, but not quite, for I knew there was half an hour for her to wait before they opened. How would she pass the time, I wondered. Spend it, perhaps, exploring the little alleyways at the back of the theatre, or examining the photographs outside rival establishments. She might even prepare for herself a map of this part of theatreland against the time she would perhaps venture into it again.

In the press, theatres are listed alphabetically and their locations withheld, presumably because this is the least helpful arrangement possible. If there is a boom in theatreland, it is certainly not due to any effort on the part of the bricks and mortar men. The ground landlords remain blissfully unaware of any responsibility they might owe the public. When she does gain access to the building, Miss Missouri will notice it is far from being air conditioned. She will be fortunate, should she decide to buy herself a drink, to find ice available; she will certainly not be offered iced water. No one here has heard of the sort of dispenser so common in the States, or if they have, they have recoiled in horror at the expense of installing one. There's no money in that, they have told themselves. Give them cold water and they won't touch the tepid orangeade at ten pence a cardboard carton we peddle in the interval. It's the same with the programme. If you want to know what the play is about, who's in it and where it takes place, they're not going to tell you for nothing. All you get is what you've paid for – a seat – and sometimes, on busy evenings if there's been a double booking, not even that.

I wondered where Miss Missouri had bought her ticket. At a library, no doubt. She would have had to pay a bit more for it, but it's simpler than trying to find the theatre twice in one day. There was just a chance, I supposed, that Miss Missouri had contacted Miss Parker herself.

In the days when London theatres were patronised by the indigent rich, Miss Parker held supreme sway at the most lordly of all the agencies. To her Bond Street premises flocked the fashionable and lively, in order that she might plot their social activities from Christmas to Goodwood. She snapped up the best seats at the Circus, the Horseshow, the Royal Tournament, arranged Centre Court seats for Wimbledon, boxes for Ascot, coaches for Eton and Harrow, launches for Henley, and was always cajoling, bullying, beseeching her customers to spend their evenings at the theatre. 'Of course you won't be tired, dear,' she would tell them. 'I've got a box for you at the Strand. If you don't stay for the last race, you'll be back in time for the Palace, I've managed to get you six returns. You'll want to go to the first night at the Savoy, they say it's most amusing, leave it to me.' If I or any other actor approached her during working hours, she would draw us into the act. 'Here,' she would tell startled patrons, 'is Mr. Morley himself, now you'll want to see *his* play, of course, *very* clever. I know you're only up for three days, but what are you doing Thursday? Oh, of course, I've got you tickets for the Opera. Well, you'll want to do something in the afternoon. You have a matinée, Mr. Morley, haven't you? Splendid. Hang on and I'll get on to the Box Office.' As often as not, it worked.

Her enthusiasm and expertise was boundless. I think only once did she ever speak sharply to me, and that was when I essayed a serious play about religion. 'Leave that sort of thing to Sir Alec,' she begged, 'your public doesn't expect you to handle it. I'm not even trying to sell tickets, they'd be shocked.' But times have changed for Miss Parker as they have for all of us. Her one-time clients seldom go to a theatre in London nowadays; they are too old or too deaf, they can't afford it or can't be bothered. It's difficult to get to London, it's difficult to park the motor, it's difficult to hear, and above all, there's the telly. So Miss Parker, like the rest of us, relies on Miss Missouri, and very grateful we are to her and to her courage and boundless enthusiasm which propels her along the streets at dusk, asking, and seldom being told, the exact whereabouts of the

113

Fortune or the Comedy or even Drury Lane. It's not that they don't want to tell her, it's just that most of the Greeks or Arabs of whom she enquires are strangers here themselves. It's no good asking the British, they too are only down for the day. As for the policemen, they are so besotted with their portable radios that they will only seize the opportunity to call back to London Central and chat up the Desk Sergeant, who ten to one won't be able to hear them properly. If Miss Missouri wants to know where anything is in London, she should always ask a Chinaman. It's a very old civilisation; besides, there are as yet no Chinese tourists.

Post Scripts

I read with a pang of displeasure, in the house magazine of the Windsor Repertory Company, that plans were afoot in Grimsby or some other seaport to revive *The White Sheep Of The Family*, a play by Ian Hay which I once threw into the Indian Ocean.

Emboldened by alcohol, I was explaining to a fellow passenger the criteria by which I was accustomed to judge a script and having just received a copy of this one, I removed it from the envelope and pretended to examine it for conformity by weighing it in my hand. Turning it upside down in order to ascertain the length of the speeches without troubling to read them, I promptly discarded it into the briny. A grave error; it ran and ran but without my participation in the profits.

Like most actors I get sent a certain number of scripts by the authors themselves, and what most of us look for on these occasions is cleanliness. I don't, of course, mean in the text itself, but if there are signs of wear and tear, particularly with the cover, you can be pretty sure you are not holding an instantly recognizable masterpiece in your hand.

There have been instances of plays such as *Journey's End* being submitted to a score of managements and leading men before becoming world beaters, but these are the exceptions. My own reaction is to examine the manuscript carefully for traces of Ralph Richardson's thumb-prints. Once satisfied as to the mint condition of the folio, one is still aware of how slim the chance of a strike. Good plays, like welcome guests, seldom arrive unexpectedly although my own first effort was accepted, when it arrived unbidden through the mail box, by Marie Tempest forty years ago. It wasn't, as it turned out, a very wise decision on her part, but I was never in any doubt why she had made it. She hadn't another play she wanted to do, she thought it could be improved and I had had the play beautifully typed by Ethel Christian and wisely sent her the top copy. Ethel used a special kind of typewriter ribbon of vivid blue and her name on the title page reassured. When you collected the scripts she was always encouraging. This one, she would tell you, is a smasher, my girls were simply overboard about it. We went on our way consoled by the reflection that we had given such pleasure to the staff. Like hop pickers, we told ourselves, they enjoyed their work.

Plays arriving on my desk by post are usually accompanied by a stamped and addressed envelope in which to return them. There is also a note from the author indicating the role for which he has one in mind, and sometimes the vague promise that it could be enlarged at some future date, were I to undertake it. These go straight into the accompanying envelope and after a decent interval of lying in wait on the table, go winging back to the sender. It is always a mistake to build up one's own part at the expense of others in the cast, indeed as one grows older and bolder one seeks to shed as many lines as possible. My distinguished mother-in-law seldom bothered to learn all the lines allotted to her. At the dress rehearsal any lingering hopes held by the author or the director that Gladys might have committed them to memory and be keeping them in reserve vanished. By then, too, she hadn't left a lot of time for argument.

Another great performer – adept at cutting out the sage-brush – Beatrice Lillie, was apparently so unfamiliar with the text the night before we were due to open a play of mine at Oxford that the management engaged a stand-by who (already seated in the auditorium) was to proceed on stage should a red light flash in the orchestra pit and Miss Lillie forget not only the lines but the time of the opening performance. The light flashed green, just in time for the twelfth man to catch the last train to London. Miss Lillie's performance that evening was that of a master at the bridge table; after one or two daring finesses she laid down her hand and boldly claimed the rest of the tricks without bothering to play them.

It is the aim of every actor to persuade his public that he has made the hand work no matter what cards have been dealt him by the playwright. It was Miss Tempest who taught me that it is always advisable not to encourage the latter to think he has dealt one a small slam.

At the first reading of a play she would pause in feigned

astonishment at her cue line and peer at the author in silence until the stage manager had the courage to point out that it was now her turn to speak. 'I am just wondering,' she would then remark, 'whether I really have to say this line, Mr...'

She made a point of never remembering the playwright's name.

'Why ever not?' he would ask meekly.

'It's just that I've said it so often before in all my other plays.' She would flash a smile and then surprisingly proceed to say it, although with no great conviction. Miss Tempest when reading aloud on these occasions took care to spread a trail of false emphasis and alarm and despondency in the hearts of her supporting cast. The magic came later.

Borrowing from Miss Tempest, I once nearly flummoxed the great Peter Ustinov himself by my first reading of *Half Way Up A Tree* which I felt I had left well up in the branches when the time came for luncheon at Scott's. 'You know, Mr Morley,' the manager's wife told me, 'there can be no question of any interpolations. We have script approval.'

'I only wish I had,' I told her and relapsed into moody silence. Ustinov's thoughts were elsewhere; he was planning simultaneous productions of his play in New York, Paris and Berlin. As it happened, he was the one with the interpolations; he kept thinking of additional dialogue and sending it to us air mail while he sweated it out in Boston or Newhaven.

I am not, of course, referring to the Sussex town where one takes off for Dieppe but the one in Connecticut where one hopefully embarks for Broadway. As there was always some doubt as to who was to speak the new lines, and when exactly, I used to offer them round fairly indiscriminately. There are always takers for new lines by other actors; myself, I can only learn a few at a time. In the end Peter seemed quite happy and so did I, the play contrary to my early forebodings running for a couple of years. When I left the cast, the play sailed merrily on with Jimmy Edwards, a great one for improving texts on the spur of the moment. Seizing a biscuit one evening he proceeded to munch, and noticed a hint of disapproval in the eyes of his leading lady. 'I hope,' he told her, 'you do not object to my masticating in the drawing room?' His co-star slammed down her tea cup and left the stage. 'I do not intend to sit and listen to filth,' she told the stage manager, 'Equity contract or no Equity contract.'

The other day there arrived in the post a play by an old friend whose works up to now have passed me by. In accepting it I realise it may indeed mark the end of our friendship. Dramatists, when I do act their plays, are not always satisfied by my reading of their lines. 'It's not quite what I wrote, old man,' they will urge from the stalls during rehearsals. 'It's the gist,' I tell them, 'just listen again carefully.'

THE
ROOT
OF
ALL
EVIL

Going Under...

The week my younger son passed his driving test and finally considered himself fledged, I paid a visit to my accountant and realised for the first time that I was featherless. What does an unemployed actor, in his sixties, partially deaf and weighing seventeen stone do when he discovers that he has thirty thousand pounds in the bank, and owes eighty thousand to the Inland Revenue? I shook hands all round, borrowed twenty-five pounds from my agent, and went and played roulette for an hour. It cheered me up, took me out of myself, cured my depression.

It's not the end of the road, though it is a familiar milestone. Bankruptcy figures in the index of a good many theatrical memoirs and when, as in my case, it is for a very considerable sum, it excites some of us and especially one particular colleague, almost to madness. 'How dare he!' he thunders. 'What is wrong with our tax system when it allows one man to owe fifty thousand and another to be hounded almost beyond endurance for seventeen pounds ten shillings?'

He will pose the question, but won't get an answer from me. All I know is that I have paid the Revenue roughly a quarter of a million pounds in Income and Surtax in my lifetime without ever being able to understand an Income Tax form, or to which particular year it refers. For thirty years my accountant has struggled to keep my head above water, swimming tirelessly by my side, turning me sometimes on my back and often gripping me in a vice-like frontal attack whilst striking me repeatedly on the chin lest I should panic and drown. Now, alas, his efforts unavailing, he must leave me to flounder. It is with great sadness that we part company, for although I have always been out of my depth, I have in a curious fashion enjoyed the bathe, indeed there have been moments when my feet seemed actually to touch bottom, and I believed in my ability to wade to the shore. But now I am finally and irrevocably adrift, no longer able or willing to fight the current, and only afloat because I am firmly wedged in the lifebelt of bankruptcy.

I am not sure as yet what being a bankrupt will entail. No doubt they will tell me. Do they, I wonder, give you a little individual pamphlet, or merely produce a large piece of cardboard with the instructions printed on it in bold type in the fashion of customs officials? How will it affect my wife, my children? It's idle to pretend that there won't be a slight feeling of embarrassment, even of shame. The actor always plays for sympathy, the comic exits singing a sentimental number to prove he is a good fellow at heart. No one ever suggested that he wasn't, any more than anyone suggested that a bankrupt is necessarily a crook, but from now on when I am recognised in the street, I suppose I shall not feel quite the same glow of satisfaction, or stop myself from wondering in which role I am remembered — the actor or the man who didn't pay up. They may even be wondering whether they too can manage to die owing the Revenue fifty thousand pounds.

How is it done? The first essential is to have accountants. It is not the slightest good going it on your own. Substantial tax arrears can only be achieved by a team. Provided the sum is substantial enough, and the point at issue of sufficient academic interest, there will be no lack of co-operation by the Revenue. There is nothing accountants or Income Tax Inspectors enjoy more than an appearance in front of the Commissioners. It is, after all, a day out for everyone.

There are two kinds of Commissioners, plain and fancy, or general and special, as they prefer to be known. I first appeared before the former in the late forties. I was startled to remark how many of them there were, and that they proposed, once having assembled to hear my case, not to pause for luncheon. My children were younger in those days and I had an appointment to escort one of them from Paddington Station to the dentist at one o'clock. In the end I was excused. Indeed, I think we even explained my problem to them in order that they might realise what a splendid father figure I cut, for an actor, of course.

When I returned, having dropped in for a snack at my club on my way back to the hearing, they were waiting to recall me to the witness stand.

'There is a question we should like to ask you,' said the Chairman, gazing at me intently. 'In the spring of forty-five/forty-six, did your children's nurse travel to the United States on an emigrant visa?'

I instantly realised this must be the sixty-four dollar question. I was anxious to answer truthfully. I was even more anxious to win for our side. I forget now which of the three possible answers I gave, but when shortly afterwards they returned a verdict in my favour, I invited my Counsel to congratulate me on my perspicacity. 'Things might have been very different,' I told him, 'if I hadn't answered that tricky question about the nurse's visa.' It was, he assured me, completely immaterial. 'Then why,' I asked, 'had the question been posed?' He shrugged his shoulders. 'Who knows?' he asked in his turn.

Winning the case cost quite a large sum of money, which everyone agreed was not deductible. For a long time afterwards the Revenue threatened to appeal, but when several months later they decided not to do so, everyone seemed to have lost interest. Besides, we were in that phase of my financial development which necessitated my becoming a limited company, and signing every contract twice over, in my dual capacity as actor and managing director of Robert Morley Productions Limited. I now had two sets of accountants, and a brand new office plate. All was peace and goodwill. I attended board meetings, signed minutes and cheques to the Inland Revenue as required, and if I wasn't entirely clear as to which years the sums related, I presumed everyone else was.

After about ten years the Revenue stirred again. It was, apparently, dissatisfied and wished to challenge the legitimacy of certain tax deductions which we had made. It invited me to select a year, any year, better still perhaps any two years on which a decision on principle could be made by the Special Commissioners. It took a considerable time before everyone was able to agree an opening date, but this time its performance lasted over a week, and the sixty-four dollar question was whether I considered myself justified in entertaining two of Her Majesty's judges in my dressing room at the Revenue's expense. It was not, of course, an everyday occurrence. In point of fact the judges only came once, and had a whisky and soda apiece, but it was the principle that fascinated Counsel and Commissioners alike.

There were other weighty points to decide, as, for instance, who was responsible for repairing a television set and whether a stage door-keeper wouldn't do just as good a job if he wasn't tipped by myself, acting of course on behalf of Her Majesty's Commissioners. At the end of the hearing, the Special Commissioners, of whom this time there were only three, regretted that the case had been brought by the Revenue, congratulated me as an honest man who had done his best to keep his accounts with the aid of two sets of accountants, and found in my favour on all points but one. They added they hoped the matter would now be settled as soon as possible. Once again all that was settled were my costs, which as the case had lasted a week were a good deal heavier than last time, and still non-deductible.

The Revenue announced once more that it would appeal, but that was several years ago. For me the tragedy is, I suppose, that if anyone from the Inland Revenue had ever sat down across a table with me, found out how much I could afford to pay, and asked for a cheque, I would have so happily given them one, but they never did. Instead they bullied and frightened by demanding enormous, impossible amounts, and each time they were beaten back, waited and let the arrears pile up for the final kill. When I asked my accountant if anything could get me out of the mess I am in now, he thought for a long time, and I didn't care much for his answer. 'Yes,' he said. 'Death would help.'

But for me the band still plays here in my own country. It is better to stay and face the music for as long as it lasts. I have lived beyond my means. If the Revenue has anything to do with it, I suspect I shall not be allowed to die beyond them.

. . . Or Living Creditably

I am not fond of banks. They appeal to man's lowest instincts, terror and greed. I am always nervous in a bank, dreading the moment when the cashier moves away from the counter, clutching my cheque to consult a ledger, or just possibly the police. In my youth, when I was overdrawn, I was admonished in the tone of voice usually used to those whose flies are undone. Considering banks make their enormous profits out of the inability of their customers to balance their books, I feel all debtors with overdrafts should be constantly rewarded with flowers, chocolates, or at the very least a kindly pat on the head. My father was always threatening to horsewhip his bank manager, but there's not much of that spirit left around any more.

Now that the banks have finally been persuaded to publish their annual profits the cat is out of the bag. Not that I am surprised by the fortune they make by borrowing money at one percentage and lending it out another. Small wonder they can afford all the best sites and are constantly able, like the American Ambassador, to refurbish. Who pays for the hours of television and the acres of newsprint they employ to improve their image? I do. They should divide their profits not among their shareholders, but among their customers. Those of us who regularly maintain our overdrafts should get a few hundred at Christmas, and something substantial at Easter as well. Why shouldn't we share in some of the publicity handouts? How about my picture for a start, blown up in *The Times*? 'Mr. Morley who, when he has money, keeps it in our establishment, and when he hasn't, helps himself to what's in the kitty.' Does the public really believe that if the cupboard is bare they can keep a bank manager inside as a pet? I wouldn't be surprised. The public will believe anything. Soon we shall see advertisements for special foods to keep your bank manager in prime condition.

It was, if my memory serves me, and it seldom does nowadays, the late lamented Martita Hunt who once years ago in New York was rung up by a friend, a banker of international repute, and asked to an early luncheon on the slopes of Manhattan. During the course of the meal, he quizzed her gaily as to her resources, enquiring which bank she favoured while in his city, and by the coffee had persuaded her as a personal favour to himself to withdraw her entire capital from some downtown branch and transfer it to a bank situated in the east eighties, whose manager was a personal friend, and would be so proud to have Miss Hunt as a client. On one point he was insistent, that the operation be carried out immediately, that very afternoon, and that she must withdraw her money in green-backs. 'It never does to transfer money from one bank to another except in cash,' he admonished her. 'Bankers are funny people, apt to get jealous,' whereupon he hailed a cab and sped her upon her way. Arrived at the bank, she found the process of withdrawing her savings took longer than she had expected, and it would be now too late to make the journey uptown with the loot. Cursing her friend the banker, she spent an uneasy evening guarding the treasure first in her dressing-room, then on the stage itself. When it was time for bed, she slept fitfully with the wodge under her pillow. In the morning she rose early and hurried to stash the bills away in safety, only to discover that it was a bank holiday. It was not a bank holiday in the strict sense of the word, just that some banks, and among them the one from which she had withdrawn her savings, had closed their doors forever. When she thanked the banker for his advice, he disclaimed all responsibility. He seemed to be unwilling to recall the luncheon conversation.

'To what, then,' she asked him, 'do I owe my good fortune?'

'Your timing, Madam,' he replied gallantly, 'impeccable as ever.'

When a film of my play *Edward, My Son* was being prepared, the producer insisted on a small advance party, in which I was mysteriously included, reconnoitring the terrain of merchant banking. As we processed from magnificence to magnificence I was struck by the fact that partners in a merchant bank never let each other out of sight for a moment. All business is transacted apparently not only under the same roof, but under the same ceiling, and within earshot of all.

'The one in the middle is the senior partner?' I asked the guide, as we paused to observe a pride of partners apparently slumbering after a kill.

'No, just the deafest,' he told me gravely.

I have planned for some time a treatise on the seven deadly

worries, paying particular attention to ways of increasing individual worry potentials. Money comes second in my list, immediately after health. Once a man has learnt to worry about these two, he can worry about anything. Most money worry begins at the bank, which is why we are seeing this vigorous new publicity drive to make the bank's image less alarming. All those pictures of mini-skirted girls who a few years ago were luring me to the seaside or the motor boat show now beckon me on towards the supreme folly of a deposit account. 'This is where the action is,' the message reads, 'in good old groovy Barclays or swinging Lloyds.' The scene, man, is the National Provincial. Fair enough, I suppose, if that's what attracts the customers and the bandits, but I'm not so happy when the appeal is to our children. I wouldn't want any of my children to believe that if they take care of the pennies, the pounds will take care of themselves. The pennies are for the small extravagances and the pleasures of childhood and for the nonsense of old age, for the poor of the neighbourhood, for the organ-grinder, for the fountain. Give your pennies away when you are young, or squander them if you wish. There is no happiness to compare with spending and giving, no sorrow to equal thrift.

My address, by the way, if you care to send a contribution, is Fairmans, Wargrave, Berkshire.

It is More Blessed to Receive...

The last time I saw Tokyo, from a bedroom on the seventeenth floor of what was in those days the Tokyo Hilton, I watched from the window an apparently endless procession of exquisitely-wrapped Japanese ladies bearing exquisitely-wrapped gift packages through a side entrance of the building reserved for wedding receptions. I asked what the packages contained and was told sugar. The Japanese have always been ahead of the rest of us. How sensible, how time-saving is a convention which cuts out all those hours agonising between fish slicers and fruit bowls!

What is needed by package tourists and travelling salesmen is some similar convention which decrees that the returning traveller should carry the ritual gift prescribed for such occasions and absolutely nothing else. A pair of gloves or a posy of artificial flowers never intended to be worn or sniffed and capable of being re-donated and instantly returned by the recipient. If custom ordained that such gifts should be presented at the airport they would have to be included along with passport and vaccination certificate on the outward journey, but it would be more convenient, surely, to keep them in a drawer at home and parade them ceremonially when one was home and dried.

Whether we like it or not we are leaving the world of A PRESENT FROM MARGATE tastefully engraved around miniature chamber pots. A check of the dressing-tables, mantelpieces and window ledges in my own house revealed no less than seventeen different pieces of vertu readily associated with such widely-scattered fun spots as Folkestone, Acapulco, Sandown (the Isle of Wight, not the racetrack), Catalina Island, Stratford upon Avon, the Tivoli Gardens, Copenhagen, Burton upon Trent, and Niagara Falls. One particularly crowded parking lot in the sitting-room is at present utilised by a Delft china windmill, a silver spinning-wheel, a cuckoo emerging from an ivory egg (tasteful stuff this, brought back as a gift to myself from Hong Kong), a folding mirror from Palma, cocktail swords from Toledo, a cuss box from Torquay, and the Eiffel Tower masquerading as a thermometer. Scattered around are Spanish hats, Indian jewelled elephants, camel saddles from Morocco, and a Chinese coolie costume which my daughter, who returned with it from South Africa only the other week, thought might come in handy.

These are, of course, only the tip of the iceberg, just the trophies we have acquired lately or haven't had the courage to dispose of as yet. Heaven knows how many useless and unacceptable gifts we have distributed to unoffending members of our family and circle. 'So sorry we couldn't take you with us to Madeira,' we tell Auntie on our return, 'but this is a genuine replica – in miniature, of course – of the kind of sleigh they use to come down the hill just outside Funchal.' From the moment she holds it in her hand she is uncertain what to do with it next. How grateful both of us would be if a stop could be put to the nonsense, the last two or three days of the holiday not spoilt by the shopping. Forsaking the beach and bistro and cutting out the after-lunch brandy, we drag ourselves around in the heat pricing handbags, shawls and leather flagons of undrinkable wine. There is no country left in the world which does not specialise in leather work, glass work, copper work. The whole world glints with saucepans.

Worse still, there has been a recent migration of indigenous rubbish. Thus, Eskimo carving is on sale throughout Canada and pre-Colombian bric-à-brac parades itself shamelessly on Bond Street and Madison Avenue. No one rash enough to purchase a Bolivian church bell in situ can be certain it wasn't cast in Stockport. A good deal more is made in Japan than meets the eye in Osaka.

I have never subscribed to the myth that it is the thought that counts. With me it's the gift every time and in choosing what to bring back on such occasions I favour the consumable – scent, wine, joss sticks, salami, shark fins – as opposed to the durable – beads, ships in bottles, papier-mâché, pill boxes, animals stuffed in their own fur, and cheap – and, for that matter, expensive – cuff-links. If I *have* to go into the durable market I select sponges, laundry baskets, pool sweepers, coins in plastic cubes and executive desk toys. I know I can buy such things at home but somehow I never seem to spot them except in Abercrombie and Fitch. I once returned with a genuine Japanese pachinko machine as a present for the grandchildren. A great success. I still have it. You simply cannot buy them in this country and now ten years afterwards people ask me where I got it. Boy, that's prestige!

Normally I avoid shopping in transit lounges, but in a Bahrein boutique I recently purchased, for reasons still not clear to me, an instant computer capable, or so I imagined at the time, of multiplying thirteen to infinity. I set about my task with one ear cocked to the public address system – I wasn't proposing to be there all night– and almost at once the magical screen packed up. The nines predominated and tended to endure. I hastened back to the counter and with a smile which clearly said 'You picked the wrong guy, chum', held out the machine and the receipt. The salesman gave in without a word, ripped a new computer out of its cardboard box and handed it over. It just shows, I told myself, the state of the computer market. There could easily be an epidemic of poisoning among pocket calculators involving the whole Middle East. No wonder oil is costing so much.

My worst fears were confirmed when, after a few manoeuvres, this one also stuck, and at the same moment the flight was called. Back in my safety strap I sulked.

'You should not,' I told my hostess, 'allow innocent passengers with travellers' cheques loose in transit lounges. I have been conned.' I held up my purchase and she took it from me and deftly set it to work.

'You don't,' she told me, 'know how to use it. As soon as I've taken round *The Gulf Times* I'll come back and teach you.'

It's still working fine. I never use it, but it's still working. Pocket calculators are, come to think of it, the ideal gift for returning travellers, they have built-in play value. They amuse and stimulate far longer than jade buffaloes, book markers, miniature bottles of schnapps, and old motor car horns. They are more useful and only a shade less decorative than Burmese temple bells, carved ivory or Arab gongs. They are not, of course, preferable to the jug I came across recently in a top cupboard. A real find, I fancy. This exquisite piece of old china bears a picture of a small boat passing under the cast iron bridge over the river Weare which was begun by R. Burdon, Esq. on September 26th 1793 and opened on August 9th 1796. The jug apparently commemorates the return not only of the vessel, but of Henry and Jane Davidson of Monkseaton, who sailed in her in 1848. Someone thought fit to inscribe it as follows:

> Thou noble bark of brightest fame
> That bears proud England's honest name
> Right welcome home once more.
> Welcome, thou gallant little sail,
> In England's name I bid thee hail
> And welcome to our shore.

Repetitious, possibly? Valuable — ah, who can tell? I might just be persuaded to part with it. Perhaps some honest dealer reading these lines will tell himself, and possibly me, that I have in my possession and in pristine condition the Monkseaton jug, the only other known copy of which is in the Getty collection, and invite me to state my price. Which is why I have ended this chapter as I have done.

Home Cheap Home

I am not a man for the small economies. Better to splurge, as is my
custom. If I am not making money most days, I am at least, thank
God, able to save it. Only this morning I am already richer by some
hundreds of dollars simply by not accepting Prince Alexis
Obolensky's invitation (what a party thrower that man is) to the
Thirteenth Annual International Grandmasters' Tournament at
Manzanillo, Mexico. For one thing, I would have presumably to
learn backgammon and then, having paid for the lessons, enroll for
the contest as a non-member ($185) and get myself to Mexico (say
$2000), and put up for the weekend sharing a bedroom at Las Hadas
(a princess resort in Manzanillo) —say another $2000. By my reckon-
ing, and in all fairness I cannot honestly deduct the prize money
which I just possibly mightn't win, there would be little change
from a five thousand dollar outlay. Well, five thousand dollars is not
a bad sum to make before breakfast. At any rate, it's a start.

Of course, life will be duller for me over the period of the jolli-
fications, which included a more than ordinarily busy Sunday starting
at two-thirty with 'Fourth Round of the Grandmasters' followed at
3 pm by the 'Continuation of the International Obolensky Cup' and
immediately after tea the 'Start of the Consolation Tournament in
All Flights', carrying on right up to the 'Beach Fiesta and Dinner'
and then, at 8.30, the 'Third Round of the Grandmasters'. Goodness,
I would have been tired by then. I might not even have had the
energy to enroll in the special 'One Day Getaway Tournament for
All' next day.

Well, there it is, a quiet Sunday at home and five thousand dollars
put aside for a rainy day. If the reader detects a certain smugness in
my attitude, if he is inclined to think my sacrifice isn't all that great,
I would like to remind him of the discipline involved in the daily

donning of the hair shirt. I am a pleasure-loving chap, and before deciding not to proceed to Mexico, I spent a few moments determinedly anticipating the pleasure I had forgone. I am not, I hope, the man to give up peanut butter for Lent simply because he never liked the stuff anyway. No, every sacrifice I make must be a conscious effort of will—first to conjure up pleasure and then to eschew it. I would like, which of us wouldn't, to get myself once more to the airport, to stand in line, to check in, to be invigilated, searched, lined up and counted, processed along the ramp into the bus jammed tight with passengers but missing, as usual, a driver, up the last flight of stairs to the cabin, spend a few frantic moments impeding fellow travellers while trying the hand luggage for size, first beneath the seat, then on the rack above, and when the stewardess approaches with the welcoming smile of a traffic warden, return it to my lap, begin to search for the leaking biro to fill up the Immigration form, and climb around my fellow passengers seeking my overcoat and extracting my passport to ascertain where it was issued and which of us will expire first.

I like it, I tell you . . . and it's true! Besides, I am eagerly looking forward to the Immigration formalities awaiting me on the other side. The cliff-hanger of the search in the official's black book to see whether or not I am an undesirable alien likely to commit crimes or overthrow the government of the land; the rummaging Customs official; the heavy physical exercise involved in the sport of lugging the luggage.

Last time I went to Acapulco I drove in a taxi across the border at Brownsville and restrained my companion from showing our travel papers to the policeman on the bridge. 'A mere formality,' I told him, as we sped happily across and into the desert, having by that time exchanged the taxi for a Drive Yourself. So it was to prove, until sixty miles further on when, still ahead of the game, we were stopped in a police trap and very nearly shot. 'Back to the border,' they urged, 'and get your exit permit.' 'What we need, surely,' I pointed out, 'is an entry permit.' 'True,' said the guard, 'but first you must get yourself an exit, and that may prove difficult as there is no evidence as to when you entered our country. Later, when your exit papers are in order, cross the bridge, turn the car round and come in again.' Actually turning the car round proved the most difficult part of the whole operation—it being a Mexican car, we weren't really supposed to drive it over the bridge in the first place.

We live and learn, I hope. Mexico is not for me this year, or, come to think of it, Switzerland either. If there is one piece of information calculated to bring the colour back into the cheeks of my accountant it is that I am not going to take my annual winter sports holiday. In point of fact, I haven't taken it for quite some time. It is for me the supreme sacrifice of the whole financial year.

As autumn edges into winter and the first snowflake shimmers down and dissolves on the grass, I realise that the temptation of Saint Morley has begun. Geneva, I tell myself, what must it be looking like now? That fun-crazed city with the single spout. Of course I know they've turned off the water by now, but the Swiss gnomes will be there. Those deadly dwarfs hurrying to and fro from their banks, sacks of the precious stuff slung over their shoulders; and the strangers in their midst, collars turned up, hats pulled down, repeating to themselves over and over again the magic number of their account, lest one day they forget their identity and can no longer enter the cave and count the treasure.

But it is not this city of wealth by stealth where I would choose to linger once the snow is falling, but one of those ravishing little villages up the slopes hidden in the mist, with the rutted streets black with frozen oil, and the ice providing free sliding for the unwary. Oh, the fun of watching, as I once did, my entire family fall down one after another while they peered into a cake shop, and then joining them in the gutter.

That was, in fact, the only time I took a ski-ing holiday, not that any of my lot actually got any nearer the slopes than a sort of sports pavilion at the top of the chair lift. My lot were younger then and easily discouraged from attempting feats of physical prowess, in competition with so many clean healthy teenagers striving to perfect their balance, earn the ritual medals, and show off their speeds, and elbow them out of the queue. Like Scott at the South Pole, we realised that others had been there before us, and packed up our dog sledges and came home. On our first and last night at Château d'Oêx we tried the après-ski bar in the basement of the hotel, but it was full of people demanding that I signed their plaster casts, which is something I have never learned to do successfully. 'Rosemary,' one mother told me proudly, 'broke her arm on the first day, poor child, but we must be glad it's only a green fracture.' Rosemary seemed as pleased as Punch. It is a status symbol, of course.

But, as I told my accountant, I simply can't afford a status symbol this year. I reckon a fortnight at the Palace Hotel, St Moritz, with a small dinner party for the Shah and Prince Rainier, and a couple of sleigh rides, would set me back about five thousand. It's already entered in my savings account, along with the £17,000 I didn't spend on my world cruise this January (private suite with verandah on A Deck, naturally. Where else?). It is no use economising when one is economising.

Insecuricor

Nothing makes me feel less secure than Securicor itself. Sometimes on the motorways we pull up next to these grey, grim armoured vehicles in which the banks reportedly move bullion from branch to branch; one inspects the po-faced gentlemen behind the wire netting and they inspect us, with their trained expression of hostile, wary contempt, and I marvel that they should be allowed not only on the roads, but in the country, and fall to wondering how, given half a chance, I would burst in and, seizing their clubs, remove their helmets and after a few sharp blows, leave them, not for the first time, trussed and bound in the back of their own vans while I speed away, the booty in my boot.

Half the world, and I have no doubt the other half as well, but I have not yet been to it, is spoiled for me by the private armies of the security organizations which infest the beaches of Africa and the linen shops of Fifth Avenue. I don't want to be guarded as I lie toasting under an umbrella on a Mombassa beach, clad only in my bathing dress. What could I possibly be wearing that anybody else could want? Yet up and down and round me are steel-helmeted and gaitered (against snakes? Are there snakes on the sand, and if so, why wasn't I told?) Securicor patrols. Each time he passes, he tucks his baton under his arm, halts briefly and raises his hand in some crazy, quasi-military salute. Why? What is the purpose of this foolery? Are we expecting a tribe of cannibals? Are the Masai on the march? Or some sneak thief, bent double, flitting from coral rock to coral rock, collecting cameras, sunglasses, half-opened bottles of Ambre Solaire? Outside, inside the jewellers' shops, the banks, the hotel lobbies, circle the vultures, reminding visitor and citizen alike that nothing is secure until they have secured it. What nonsense, what rubbish this great protection racket has become. How foolish of Government and citizens alike to allow it, and how fatally divisive the device, foreverlastingly reminding the haves that the have nots are ready to snatch, challenging the criminals, encouraging the tear-aways. 'Here it is,' they tell them, 'come and get it if you can.'

A policeman should, and often does, reassure. He is there to see fair play, to tell us the time, to point in the direction of the Post Office, to take our side against the criminal. But the private cop has no such allegiance to the public and is suspicious of any enquiry. He is there to protect the booty, no matter how it was obtained. He is there to see that the rich grow richer and the poor keep their distance, and if they don't know what their distance is, he is ready to give them a shove back behind the ropes.

It started with the Corps of Commissionaires. If your daughter was being married, you hired one to keep an eye on the presents and help park the cars. Later some of the more expensive shops hired them to ameliorate the feelings of their overcharged customers. In America between the wars they elaborated the notion. They armed private cops with guns and let them patrol motion picture lots to keep the actors from escaping. I don't think they ever shot one; in those days we were too valuable.

In New York recently I was horrified by the hysteria. As dusk fell, the hotel lobbies filled up not with the café society fun lovers of yesterday, or the out-of-towners intent on an evening of hell raising, but with security guards. Main entrances were closed, swing doors secured, entrance effected through side passages and up emergency staircases.

Even the New York taxi cabs have been refashioned into armoured cars; steel bulwarks protect the drivers from such desperate characters as myself. Payment is made through a slit in the armoured glass. What rubbish, what nonsense, what poltroonery! A friend, driving from the airport recently at two o'clock in the morning, found the driver had not only secured himself but his passenger, locking the doors of the cab by remote control before switching off the taxi meter. This is kidnap, my friend told himself, and was astonished to arrive safely at his destination. His relief was almost as great as the fare demanded and gratefully paid.

No wonder the New York theatres are empty, the restaurants deserted, the night clubs closed. Let us beware lest London follows this pattern of defeat. We are not all extras in a new horror film. There is no King Kong loose in our cities, we do not have to rush hither and thither in senseless panic to heighten the dramatic effect and satisfy the director. We are the many perfectly able to protect ourselves against the few; if we need more policemen we can afford to hire them ourselves. What we cannot afford is big business trying to persuade us that they can take over law and order if we are prepared to pay extra for the service. If we don't stop the rot now, the next body of men to demand protection at their hands will be the Police Force.

I warn the Home Secretary that when the first security guard shows up on Bognor beach, I shall emigrate.

Any Reasonable Price Considered

With the possible exception of the Monarch waving a languid and perfectly-gloved hand at them from an open carriage, nothing gives visitors to our shores more pleasure than the phenomenon of the 'floating pound'. Fiscal purists may affirm that the pound is not so much waving as drowning, but I prefer the simile of a prolonged float, always bearing in mind that the pound is attached to the end of a fishing line and liable, when seized in the jaws of currency speculators, to be dragged ever deeper and deeper for fairly prolonged periods.

American visitors particularly have always spent a large part of their holidays abroad finding out where they can change their travellers' cheques advantageously. Where the Englishman opens a conversation with some penetrating observation on the weather, Americans are accustomed to compare notes with fellow Americans not so much on the beauty of Hampton Court or the majesty of St Paul's, but on how they are faring on the exchange mart. 'There is a little kiosk almost directly behind Madame Tussaud's where the fellow will take your dollars, provided no one is looking, and give you sixty-three cents,' they tell each other.

Indeed, it is to be doubted whether Americans would see as much of our cities and countryside as they do if they were not perpetually engaged on extended forays to outlying money-changers. Nowadays, of course, there is not only the right place but, even more important, the right time. To have changed your money last Tuesday, before the pound went down another two and a half cents next day, can effectively dampen the spirits of the most optimistic Blue Rinse.

The British abroad are frankly appalled by the treatment afforded their currency in the *bureaux de change*. They are overwhelmed with self-pity and frustration. How dare foreigners behave in this manner? We remember the time when, having changed a few pounds, we simply hadn't the pockets in which to put the francs and lire. We were constantly fishing ten thousand lira notes out of our wallets to reward subservient waiters. 'He seemed so pathetically grateful, poor fellow,' we used to tell our companions, 'and of course in our money it's only seven and six', for in those days we did not speak of thirty-seven and a half pence lest people should have thought we were mad.

In those days too, once we had got our hands on the folding money, we were just as keen on exchanging it for useless and unacceptable gifts as are today's visitors to our own shores. We adopted an easy but superior familiarity with all and sundry. 'Come now,' we implied, if occasionally left unspoken (for our manners were always apparent), 'you need the money, old chap. We're halving the price of these shoes just to give you a sale. We don't need them, we have better shoes at home.' We spoke slowly and loudly so that there would be no mistake. We smiled and shrugged our shoulders and even waved our hands a little as though to the manner born. In the end we got the shoes for twice what they were worth, or half what the shop-keeper was asking originally. We had enjoyed ourselves and were delighted to find that the shopkeeper still smiled and bowed as he wrapped up the footwear, having apparently enjoyed himself too.

The French love bargaining, we told ourselves. Not any more. Nowadays we do not hesitate to pay the price on the *guichet*, before the pound takes another lurch.

Now that the foreigners swarm playfully all over us, ransacking our chain stores for woollies and goodies on day trips from the Channel ports, we have swallowed our pride and forgotten our indignation at having once been called a nation of shopkeepers. And how good have we become at striking a bargain? There are still stiff-necked Britons who stick to the price demanded. Magistrates, traffic wardens, members of the professional classes, newspaper vendors and one or two of the better hotels, such as the Connaught or Claridges. The rest of us, including the Commissioners of Inland Revenue, can mostly be tempted with the ready. On the rare occasions when I have been able to settle my debts to the Revenue, it has always been the prospect of immediate cash which enables them to drop the odd nought out of their wildly optimistic earlier demands.

We British, unlike our American cousins (in these difficult times we like to claim kinship with all and sundry, knowing that to boast an Egyptian mummy in the house makes it easier to open a charge

140

account at Harrods, are keen on the ready. The one thing that really upsets an American store is the prospect of the customer paying cash. If you are not in a position to flourish a credit card the assistant feels it wiser to summon the house detective than to accept your patently forged currency. But for visitors to Britain who announce their intention of paying cash, our arms as well as our palms are wide open. There is nothing we like more than cash and carry, as long as you pay the cash and are prepared to do the carrying. Delivery is one of the things we don't do any more, or rather we do do it but you will have left the country long before the goods arrive, as, in all fairness, we point out to you.

Never be afraid to try and strike a bargain, however august or unlikely the surroundings. There is always a first time for the custodian of the Royal Mews, or an up-and-coming funeral director, to shade his price, but remember, the best bargains here, as everywhere, are to be obtained in the Arcadian fields. Where may they be, you may ask? Why, among clusters of olde antique shops where you can obtain the useless trivia which make life more bearable— the Toby jug from which you will be wise not to drink, the Dresden shepherdess not quite intact, the musical box which does not play. All the things which you picked up for a song and from which you will never more be parted, because they remind you of how happy and foolish you were when you bought them and the going was good.

My younger son gave me this Christmas an enormous, exquisitely-constructed model of a sailing ship.

'Thank you,' I told him. 'I shall sail it on the swimming pool at high summer.'

'On no account,' he demurred. 'The man particularly warned against putting it in the water.'

'Then it shall stand beside the pool,' I assured him, 'but meanwhile? There is no room for it in my study.'

When my son prepared the surprise on Christmas morning he moved out the radiator to display his gift. Since then I have gone back to the radiator and laid up the yacht in the garage. I look at it every time I take the car out and avoid striking it a glancing blow. My eyes fill with tears, for he is far away in Australia, but my heart warms to a chip off the old block. When I asked him how he had known such a gift was exactly what I craved, he replied, 'I didn't, Pa, it was just luck. You see, it was a bargain.'

Where There's a Will

It is extraordinary how seldom I ever make wills. I take a vicarious pleasure in the stories of dustmen who have taken pains to bury old ladies' gin bottles in their back gardens and are rewarded by being left their fortunes. 'She would come into the shop sometimes, and we would have a bit of a chat, but I never dreamt she was worth all that, and that she would leave it to me,' says the delighted village postmistress when the eccentric dog-breeder down the road suddenly snuffs it. Of one thing I am sure: it's no good being too close if you want to inherit. Everyone longs to spring a surprise at the last, even if they can't be there to watch the fun.

I have a particular aversion to the poetic flummery which leaves everyone the sky at morning or birdsong at night or the corn ripening in the meadow, and then gets down to the nitty-gritty and discloses there's no estate worth mentioning. On the other hand, I am fond of the quirky testator who plans to leave his millions to as yet unconceived heirs, on condition his daughter's husband has nothing whatever to do with the fur trade and has never ridden a horse.

I like the idea, too, of beneficiaries having to change their name, or better still, add a hyphen and go double-barrelled if they want to inherit. 'In future Mr. Tom Jones wishes to be known as Mr. Tom Bardslay-Jones' – *wishes*, indeed! Why not say straight out it's either that or goodbye to fifteen thousand?

Literature about wills always delights me. There's that unlikely play by Barrie in which the couple keep changing their intentions and end up with no one to leave the money to anyway. Then there is the whodunnit in which the family gathers at midnight at Aunt Tabitha's, whose testamentary intentions are not disclosed until the last victim is found in the rock garden, bludgeoned to death with a flower pot. In fact, as in fiction, Aunt Tabitha outlives them all. In these days of death duties and possible wealth tax, a will no longer matters as much as it did to the next generation. Keep in touch, certainly, but don't hang around should be the guide in these more realistic times. Both my grandfathers tied their money up in quite complicated wills, and my father, who was usually in need of the ready, was forever thinking up ingenious ways of getting his hands on some of it. I remember his ecstasy on being once informed by a new solicitor he had engaged to assist in the task, that there had never been an entail yet through which the fellow could not drive a coach and horses, given a little perseverance. Father delighted in the phrase; he had been a notable coachman himself in his day, but I don't think the solicitor delivered the goods because he was dismissed after a time, and Grandfather's money went where he had intended, more or less.

I had an uncle whom I used to vex a good deal by taking taxis when he thought I should travel by bus, or better still, walk to visit him on his deathbed. He was not a mean man, but spending money made him unhappy, and to watch others spend it saddened him immeasurably. He left a small fortune, of which the government took their share, and I thought how much more fun he would have had spending the stuff, but of course he wouldn't have. There are the savers and the spenders, and woe betide us when the balance is faulty. Uncle left me ten thousand and I spent it quite easily in no time at all: he wouldn't have expected anything else. People live on a plateau of money from which they seldom stray; a man hard up for fifty at twenty will be hard up for fifty all his life, allowing of course for inflation. On the other hand there are people like myself who are hard up for a bit more than that. If you remove a man artificially, say by leaving him a million, from one plateau to another, he may not survive, although I have a friend who spent his youth in comparative penury, always hoping to buy a car, then his father died and left an undertaking business to a brother, who died in his turn, intestate. 'Ask me,' my friend demanded next time we met, 'how many cars I have now.' I obeyed and he told me he had twenty-seven Daimlers to follow the hearse and a Jaguar for himself to pass it on the road.

I am at the age when obituary columns make news. I look in *The Times* and find the name of an acquaintance I thought was still around and now obviously isn't, and ask myself whether perhaps he has left me something. There's no earthly reason why he should; the chances must be a thousand to one against, but I like the long shots. I browse in the bath, hopes as high as the water going out the waste pipe. There's always a chance, just as there is the chance that I may be remembered by a loyal matinée fan or even a distant relative in Australia. Whatever happened to all those wealthy Australians who used to return loaded and cut up for millions? Did they only exist in Act III of the plays we used to go to? I had another uncle in Australia, and one by marriage in Canada. Of course they've been dead for years, but posts are very slow nowadays and so, come to think of it, are executors, unless of course you choose your bank manager. Why not go along right now to see him about the disposal of your earthly goods, and it might be a nice idea to leave me a little for the suggestion.

FLIGHTS
OF
FANCY

Death of a Snailsman

The death of the man reputed to be the most successful snail trainer in the world highlights once again the danger of competitive sport. There is, thank goodness, no shortage of men and women still prepared to face fearful odds. And the late Mr Hudson was certainly no ordinary snail trainer, as visitors to his extensive snail stud and training establishment just outside East Grinstead will bear witness.

I have never forgotten the first time he invited me to 'Slimetrails', the lovely country house which adjoined his paddocks. Trophies, photographs and shells covered the walls of every room in the house while in his own office I even spied several privileged ex-champions crawling on the ceiling. Indeed, one actually fell into my coffee cup as he passed it across the desk.

'With or without?' he remarked cheerfully while he extracted the creature expertly with finger and thumb and transferred him to his blotter. 'He will probably dry out this time,' he assured me. 'Snails have a natural sense of self preservation but I am afraid Perce Agincourt III is getting a bit old for that sort of caper. Perce won the Cheltenham Grand Prix way back in '74; I made a packet that day,' he confided. 'Came in at eight to one backed down from fourteens.'

He stirred his own coffee and gently propelled Perce a few inches. After a shock like that, he informed me, they must be kept moving.

'Tell me,' he asked, 'what do you want to know?'

'Everything,' I told him. 'How did it all start?'

'Well, I suppose I was ten when I first decided to become a snail racing trainer. Father wasn't too keen at first. He was a window-cleaner himself and kept pigeons so it's in the blood I suppose, but it was my mother who really encouraged me not to follow Dad with the old chamois and the step-ladder. Mind you, it's a good business, even today, mostly cash, but I never fancied heights particularly after Dad had his fall and had to go around on crutches. Mother thought I would be safer on the ground and so it proved – mind you, this game is not without risks, it's the travelling really.

'Snails have got something we humans haven't. They never try to go too fast or too far. That's what makes the sport so fascinating although, mind you, I once had a fellow who could do 50 yards in 16 minutes flat. But I could never win a race with him – wonderful on the home gallops but when he saw another snail near him he refused to budge, even in the mating season. I often thought he must be a bit bent but when I entered him in cobbler races it was the same story.'

'Cobblers?' I queried.

'Cobblers are the same as colts before they've been cut, of course. Mind you, you only cut a snail if he plays up. Never had to cut old Perce here and look at him now. Fit as a flea though not so active as he used to be. Still, he looks as if he's recovered. I'll just put him back on the ceiling, and then I expect you'd like to look around.'

'What does he eat up there?' I asked.

'Nothing, he comes down for his tea,' he told me. 'Bran and lettuce, that's what they all get. Snails will eat anything except garlic, you know. Natural I suppose – they get a sort of foreboding about garlic. Cruel stuff, I always think.'

'Do you ever eat them?' I asked.

'Do horse trainers eat horses?' he replied. 'Well, they do in France you might say, but not in this country, thank heavens.' Outside he introduced me to one of his assistants. 'This is Fred, he looks after the walls and the gallops. You have to keep both in tip-top condition, that's the secret or one of them. The others are training and especially breeding.'

He took me to see the snail nurseries, delicate little crustaceans following their parents around the small, well-kept lawns in front of the breeding pens. Each enclosure, I noted, had its own individual plunge pool.

'They don't do better than this in Vegas,' my host assured me. 'It's important they should learn to swim as soon as possible, best thing for their muscles. At six months the training begins in earnest.'

He took me over to where half a dozen pretty girls in breeches and boots were each concentrating on drawing a plastic lettuce leaf gently across the sward pursued by one of their charges.

'Keep it straight, lass. Hold it there, let him get a sniff, right, off you go, reckon that one's had enough, rub him down and put him back in his stall.'

For each girl he had an encouraging word of advice but his eyes, I noticed, never left the shells and their occupants.

'Sometimes,' he confided, 'we do have to go in for a bit of lemon on their tails – seems to sting them up. Start them off. Mind you, none of that on the tracks, they have to do without the lettuce and the lemon, except in Miami for some reason. The authorities there allow it.

'The real trouble,' he confided later back in his den, over a whisky and soda into which he occasionally dipped his fingers and moistened Perce Agincourt III's antlers, now waiting for his tea, 'the real trouble is keeping the owners happy. Mind you, it costs a bit to keep a snail in training and then, as I mentioned before, there's the travelling expenses. If they're keen they like to come and see for themselves. Luckily the prize money is getting bigger all the time. Then there's sponsorship. The garden fertilizer firms are beginning to come in. You must excuse me now, I have my race entries to make. The European telephones are the very devil but you can say one thing about the sport. It's clean, we don't have any bloody jockeys in this game, thank God, not yet anyway!'

One for the Pot

'How would you feel, Head Master, if I were to tell you that we have a cannibal in our midst?'

The Provost took another walnut from the silver dish on the table and cracked it in his teeth. It was an accomplishment of which he was particularly proud. Very few men of his age had the strength of jaw, or, indeed, the teeth. The Head Master, as was often his wont, appeared not to have heard the question, but Small knew better than to repeat it. Dinner, he reflected, had been a particularly vile meal even for the Head Master's table. There were very few cooks left in the world who could do what had been done that evening to white fish, and he could see no point whatever in the rabbit pie. Where on earth did the cook get the rabbits these days?

'I should want to know,' said the Head Master, 'whether the cannibal was on the staff or among the children?' It was an affectation of his to refer to the loutish adolescents in his charge as children, thereby excusing—at least to himself—some of the more bizarre habits of which they were capable.

'He is a member of your staff,' Small told him.

'Then I am relieved,' said the Head Master. 'Cannibalism among the children might involve us in difficulties—that is, if it were on any scale. One wouldn't expect the craze to last long but while it did . . .' The Head Master shivered delicately. He was not nick-named 'The Unicorn' for nothing, thought the Provost . . . He wondered what would happen if the Head ever put his head down and charged.

'More port?' The Head Master propelled the decanter towards him and remarked that the Queen might come to the Wall Game but he wouldn't know definitely until the first of the month. 'I hope she does, and brings some of the children.' The Head Master had never abandoned hope that one of the little Princes would revert to the pattern.

'Did you want me to tell you about the cannibal?' asked the Provost.

'My dear fellow,' the Head Master replied, 'you must do as you think best.'

'I was in New Guinea just after the war settling the tribes,' Small reminded him. 'I saw a certain amount of cannibalism, learnt to detect the signs. As you know, it was the custom of those who practised eating their neighbours to file their teeth.'

'First?' The Head Master seemed genuinely startled.

'How do you mean, first, Head Master?'

'Before they got down to the munching . . . Whose teeth are we talking about, Small? . . . Let's be explicit, shall we . . . the victim's teeth?'

'Not the victim's teeth, Head Master. They didn't eat each other's teeth.'

'That's what I thought, Small—I just wanted to clear up the point. What you are saying is that one of my staff has filed teeth?'

'No, I didn't say that.'

'Very well. I was just trying to think. . . . Bertram has had all his teeth out. Is there a clue there, I wonder?'

'It isn't Bertram.'

'Now let me think . . .' The Head Master was obviously delighted by the game. 'Filed teeth? Whom do we know with filed teeth?'

'No one,' Small told him. 'They don't file them any more—too risky.'

The Head Master seemed disappointed. 'So we can't tell who is the culprit? It wouldn't be any good asking him to own up? Imposing sanctions until he does?'

'In this case we know who the culprit is. When I was in New Guinea,' Small went on, 'the practice of teeth filing was discontinued as being too much of a give-away. Another method was adopted whereby the man-eaters could recognise each other.' He opened his third and fourth fingers and pointed to the fold between them. 'There,' he said, 'a small black spot just there.'

'Good heavens,' said the Head Master, his attention caught for the moment. 'You? My dear fellow, I had no idea.'

'Not me,' Small told him, 'Potters.'

'Fancy,' said the Head Master, and then, again, 'fancy.'

For the six hundred and tenth time that morning Mr Potters hit the blind cord and realised simultaneously that he had lost the thread. He looked round his division room to see if anyone had noticed. On the blackboard a half-finished and enormously complicated equation caught his attention. 'Burgess,' he said abruptly, 'clean the blackboard.' He watched Burgess hungriiy: a small plump child newly arrived from his parents' crumbling ancestral home somewhere on the Welsh border. Country-fed, thought Potters. It made such a difference; and he sighed. 'None of you appears to have been paying the slightest attention to what I have been saying. I shall dismiss the division.'

He watched the last of them shuffle out and closed his eyes. By his calculation he could reach Suva in exactly forty-three days from now. After that, of course, there would be a week's trek into the jungle, but that was a period of exquisite excitement. The problem was how to sweat out the next six weeks: it was always worse in June; the waiting was sheer torture. Each year it seemed to get worse; each year the temptation to cut and run became greater. He knew it would be no good getting there early. Arrangements had to be made months in advance. You couldn't just rush into the forest and grab a human steak; there was a good deal more to it than that. There was the ritual dance which lasted all night and which quite frankly bored him these days; then the ceremonial slaughter which he had once been allowed to witness, and even to assist at. In any case, it wouldn't be the slightest use arriving without the money; and the Bursar never paid out the cheques until the last Wednesday of the half.

The question of expense bothered Mr Potters . . . each year he paid a bit more. That was only to be expected; the air fare had gone up as well, and the price of the hotel bedroom, and even the water melon; but the amount asked by the tobacconist became more and more outrageous. Mr Potters always thought of him as the tobacconist; in point of fact if he sold anything at all in his shop he suspected it was soap. It was always too dark to see what exactly went on . . . Mr Potters always did exactly as he was told; he never went near the shop before sundown and always entered through the back door. The shopkeeper stayed in the shadows while he counted the money, then introduced him to the courier who explained how he was to leave the town and at which bus stop to alight the following afternoon. After that it was just hard slog; three night marches through the jungle—to work up an appetite, he always told himself.

By day they rested on the beaches eating exiguously, drinking from coconuts. It wasn't so much of a holiday; more of a pilgrimage. That was what he was, Mr Potters told himself—a pilgrim.

Towards the end of the half Potters was surprised to be asked to dine at the Lodge with the Provost. The other guest was the Head Master. Over dinner the Head Master discussed Chaucer ... a subject on which he was famed both for his erudition and an unique ability to bore his listeners profoundly.

Potters sought profound refuge in the wine. Pouring himself a fourth glass of port, he sensed danger.

'Where are you going for your vacation, Potters?'

'Fiji. I always go to Fiji; I have friends there.'

'Do you know Chief Matabomba at all?'

'No, sir. I've heard of him, of course. He is the Paramount Chief of the Balatse, isn't he?'

'I shouldn't be surprised,' said the Head Master. 'He was Captain of Skates here, you know.'

Potters didn't know; it was news to him that Chief Matabomba was an Old Etonian.

'I'll write to him if you like,' said the Head Master, '... ask him to keep an eye on you.'

'Most kind,' said Potters, and assured himself that the old fool was not likely to do anything of the kind.

He was wrong, of course.

Next half started without Potters; Chief Matabomba saw to that.

The Head Master thanked him personally when they met outside the tea tent in the grounds of Buckingham Palace next spring. 'It doesn't do to have cannibals on the staff,' he told him. 'It would be awful if the papers got wind of it.'

'It doesn't really do to have cannibals in Fiji,' Matabomba assured him, 'but it happens occasionally.'

'I wonder,' said the Head Master, taking a gargantuan bite out of his Swiss roll, 'where on earth poor Potters acquired the taste—personally I prefer a quiet evening at Scott's or Prunier's.'

Hugo, or Back to the Crawling Board

Slumped in our chairs, Hugo and I were spending the afternoon on the lawn. Time was when we would both have napped, but my grandson has passed the age for sleeping in the afternoon, whereas for me the habit becomes more and more compelling. But now, alas, a sense of duty prevented me from nodding off. Hugo seemed in no immediate danger, as he presently climbed from his chair and started to crawl around, searching for daisies, a diet of which he never seems to tire. He reminded me, as I watched him savouring their subtle flavour, of some dedicated oyster fancier.

'Now that you have been with us nearly a year,' I said, 'have you formed any general impression of our predicament?' I did not expect an answer. I spoke merely to distract his attention from the feast. There is a theory, propounded no doubt by Dr. Spock, that too many are bad for the appetite. I was surprised, therefore, when, having considered my question, he answered it, at the same time carefully expelling the beard of a flower.

'It's curious you should ask me that. I was pondering the matter in the early hours of the morning, while awaiting my orange juice. How late you all sleep, to be sure. Are you referring to your personal predicament as an ageing comedian, or to the state of the human race as a whole?'

'Both,' I told him.

'You must understand,' said my grandson, 'that before one was born nearly a year ago, one was briefed in general terms as to what to expect, and indeed what would be expected of one. There are available to those about to be born all the latest baby books, and droll reading most of us find it, I can tell you. Not that one doesn't occasionally get ideas from them, but besides them one has lectures on the crisis days. A new-born babe, you understand, dreads two things — precipitation and confrontation. He has a morbid fear of

154

being dropped, and a reluctance to accept his parents at first sight. A lot of babies imagine that the doctor who delivers them is a parent, and are often bitterly disappointed when introduced to their actual fathers, and indeed refuse to accept them for some time, and on occasions permanently. On the other hand, they nearly always seem to settle for the mother. They are a pretty adaptable lot on the whole. What was it Tennyson wrote? 'Ours not to reason why'? In any case, we are all sworn to silence for at least a year, and then there's a general agreement not to say anything significant for some time afterwards. As soon as we start to talk we go back to square one. We have to learn to grope around with the rest of you in the dark.'

'Before the light goes out, is there any help you could give, any advice you care to offer?'

'About yourself? A good deal. For instance, I never understand why you *read* the papers.'

'What would you do?'

'Tear them up. Haven't you noticed, I always tear up newspapers? That's the only possible satisfaction to be got out of them. It's not as if you were interested in what's going on around you.'

'What do you mean? I'm passionately interested.'

'In the theatrical gossip, perhaps, but famine in India, earthquakes in Persia, fighting in Nigeria — despite them you still eat a hearty breakfast, slumber on the lawn. Nothing shakes you. Tell me, when was the last time you ate a daisy?'

'I don't happen to like daisies, but I suppose I munched a few of them when I was your age.'

'They taste quite different,' Hugo assured me. 'They've entirely changed the flavour of daisies. And the grass, don't you notice the grass is a different colour? And the trees, how tall they are nowadays. When did you last chew a lump of coal, or pull the pile from a carpet, or bite on a door? When did you last sprinkle milk, or choke on a rusk, or dip your fingers in custard? You see, you're really not alive at all. You don't do any of the exciting things. You just sit there, oblivious of your surroundings, missing all the fun. Why don't you crawl over there to the path, and try sucking a pebble?'

I felt rather foolish, but the pebble was cool, and not at all unpleasant.

'There's a clever boy, then,' said Hugo, joining me on the gravel. 'Be careful you don't swallow it.'

'You were going to give me some advice,' I reminded him.

'I have just done so. The trouble with you, Grandfather Robert, is a basic lack of perception. You have discarded your own senses in favour of instant touch, instant smell, instant taste. You glance, you never gaze, hear but you never listen. What you need is a refresher course in babyhood. Back to the crawling board.'

Suddenly I saw it — a vast building, perhaps in Bond Street next door to Elizabeth Arden, where men of my age would be lifted out of their executive Bentleys and carried screaming across the threshold, to be plonked down on a giant-sized nursery rug, and encouraged to crawl one step at a time up an enormous staircase to the giant playroom, where great blocks of plywood, decorated with lead-free paint, were waiting to be piled on top of one another, and where teddy bears as large as themselves were ready to be bitten and sucked, and have their button eyes gouged out. At mealtimes, too, what pleasures would lie in store for the customers. To taste tapioca and jelly again, to be fed, from the giant economy size tins, sieved bacon and egg with added cereal breakfast, grated mutton, carrot and custard lunch, and genuine hip syrup rusks for tea. A crash course of babyhood to attract all the more go-ahead tycoons. A fortune was in my lap, and all I had to do was grasp it. 'Hugo,' I cried, opening my eyes, 'how can I ever thank you?' But Hugo had disappeared. Panic seized me. I scanned the lawn, then started up and began a guilty search. How could I have been so lacking in grandparental sense of duty? 'Hugo! Hugo!' I cried. 'Where are you?', and came upon him suddenly under a gooseberry bush. 'You haven't eaten one? They're not ripe.'

Hugo didn't answer. I sensed he was back to square one. In his eyes there was a look of pity. 'Where did you expect to find me?' he seemed to be asking.

2076: The Future Lies Ahead

This is, I understand, the last issue of *Punch*; it is amazing really that it has lasted so long and that I should still be writing for it as did my great-grandfather, grandfather and father, thus continuing a family tradition that when rough games were forbidden at home we should sit down quietly and write a piece for *Punch*. Sad to think that rough games are over as well, but we are all too old for them now. Indeed, since that memorable day in 2020 (was there really, as is now thought, some significance in the double score?) when procreation—at any rate for man—ceased all over the earth, almost everything else has also ceased, so I accepted with . . . (I almost wrote enthusiasm, but that, too, is a thing of the past) the Editor's suggestion I should revisit America which has bravely decided to celebrate its Tricentennial this month by returning the country as far as possible to its natural state.

I did not, of course, venture into the Mid-West: recent visitors to Chicago have insisted it has changed out of all recognition since the reintroduction of the buffalo herds into the down-town district. Apparently these great creatures, although rapidly becoming urbanised to an extent which has quite frankly amazed anthropologists, are still in a somewhat confused state and have a tendency to stampede on occasions, trampling unwary pedestrians and, as yet, completely disregarding the traffic lights.

I flew to New York on one of the old Concordes and was amazed to think that great-grandfather travelled in the prototype of this venerable craft in which in those days they actually served food to help the passengers while away the hours.

I heard in a news flash that the decision has finally been taken to close down Wales completely, and about time too. I found New York basking in hot sunshine; an effort is being made to reintroduce cooked food, and surprisingly, ice cream. Instead of the daily ration of pills, people are being encouraged to devote certain hours of the day to sitting down to meals again in the company of what is left of their families; it's even recommended that they lay an extra place or two in memory of the recently departed. There is a streak of maudlin sentimentality about Americans of which I have always rather disapproved.

New York is peaceful but still heavily patrolled; indeed, every other citizen is an officer of one kind or another. It is odd to think of the violence which erupted here in the 'thirties when the young who apparently felt cheated of their birthright sacked Manhattan, a district which has never been rebuilt. Life today centres round the Battery where, indeed, for their ancestors, it all began. I could never understand why the generation after mine felt so bitterly the deprivation of not being able to breed. It is all so much quieter now without youth, and we are all so much nicer to each other than we were when I was a boy. I was taken to the new United Nations headquarters and shown the vast laboratory complex where earlier mankind concentrated its energies on trying (unavailingly, thank heavens) to get the race started once more. There are still dedicated scientists toiling away in the labyrinth, but most of us are now, I believe, satisfied with things as they are. Life was after all getting absurdly complicated; it may sound selfish, but enough is enough, for me at any rate, and it is no good pretending that a great deal of the pleasure I have experienced in my life has not been due to the approaching extinction of my own species.

On leaving I was subjected to the mandatory FT (Fertility Test) to which every visitor has to submit, but it was not an unpleasant experience, although as I remarked to the (I almost wrote young) lady in charge, it was, I feared, a forlorn hope. There is always a chance, she rejoined, and added: 'Have a nice child.' Truly the Americans will try anything!

Now that only three of the original forty-nine states are still designated residential areas, I flew on to California, deciding to take in Florida on the way home; but, alas for plans, the closing of Florida (with the exception of a small area around Disneyland) while I was in Los Angeles, caught me unawares.

California is still functioning normally, at least as normally as it ever did, but there are basic problems of water supply and, looming on the horizon, an increasing shortage of electricity. There are some people still willing to work but it is becoming difficult to persuade anyone to hang around the power station at Boulder Dam, for instance. For a time Las Vegas was reopened to gamblers and the odds substantially tilted in favour of the players as a bait. But, alas, to no avail. Most Americans, like ourselves, have little use for money ... what has really caught their fancy is the campaign launched by the Government to ensure that every citizen has a place in the earth when the time comes. Enormous posters bearing the slogan 'Get Yourself Buried' have appeared on billboards that once advertised British Airways and Coca-Cola.

The idea is for everyone to dig their own grave right away and find a friend to swear to fill it in when the time comes. It is ironic that the whole venture is sponsored by the Wild Life Trust which once used to try and preserve tigers. No need to do so these days; Ceylon and for some reason Windsor Park are literally teeming with them, or so they tell me.

I was surprised to find several film studios still at full stretch: apparently artists and directors alike donate their services and bribe the technicians to carry on. Plans are afoot not only to show the films on television (which unlike our own BBC still survives here) but afterwards preserve the negatives in specially protected vaults in case human life should one day be re-established. I find this insistence on the part of the American people that someone some-where is still watching them rather touching. There is an immense interest being shown still in religious belief, and the churches are sponsoring an inter-denominational campaign to find the man most likely to survive to hand over the kingdom of earth to whomever the Almighty decides to send. This is what judgement day will really be like, they tell us, and, working on a sort of points award scheme, vital statistics of selected human beings are being fed into a giant computer and the longevity champion will then be selected and specially trained for what is envisaged as the final ceremony. The notion that he may well be a Britisher or even some crazed Eskimo does not seem to have occurred to them.

Bathing in the sea is no longer possible round Malibu as the water is crowded with marine life, and although most of the fish are harm-less, there is more than the occasional shark and whale to make swimming dangerous. There has been a considerable exodus to the desert, where neither wild life nor vegetation engender a feeling of envy, and many seem determined to sunbathe until the last possible moment.

The rats are a problem, especially in Burbank where the Mayor has appealed to the citizens and urged them to make peace with their friendly neighbourhood rodent, the idea being that the creatures now have the living space they have always craved and are unlikely to harm anyone. This is not the lesson we learnt in Bognor, alas. Still, one wishes the Yanks luck, as always.

I was not sorry to touch down safely at Torbay and pick up the threads again. It has been an exceptionally balmy summer. Mother Nature seems determined to remind us what a pleasant earth we are leaving. Like a hall porter, all smiles as he stows the luggage in the boot.

P.S. Since writing this I have had the most extraordinary communication from official sources about my test. I am to fly to New York this evening by rocket.

Pipe Dream

'You mean to tell me,' said my neighbour, 'you have been living on top of an oil field all these years and mistook it for a vegetable garden?'

'That's right,' I told him, 'still, better late than never. They're coming with the equipment on Friday. A week, give or take, and I shall be in production.'

He asked whether it might be noisy.

'A sort of rhythmical tapping,' I told him, 'and of course a faint smell, but the gantry, I think that's what they call it, is pastel blue to match the shutters. I can give you a booklet if you like, they're the people who used to do the swimming pool, but now they've switched. Most people already have pools if they are ever going to have them. Oil is the new status symbol. They put it rather cleverly on the cover: "Rig yourself out".'

He took the literature and went back to mowing his lawn, but I could tell he was no longer concentrating. My firm, they pay for introductions.

One of the leading estate agents prints small symbols under the photographs of the houses he has for sale nowadays, designating the amenities. A horse means stabling, a dog kennelling, a diver indicates a swimming pool, there's a radiator for central heating, and now, lo and behold, a small derrick for you know what. We are keeping it pretty quiet in Berkshire, we don't want a lot of the big boys moving in, and among the crowd I go to cocktail parties with, a second derrick is considered a bit much. Three oil wells on the property and you buy your own gin and go back to dusting the mantelpiece.

Most of us sell the stuff direct and just keep back enough for the Rolls and the radiators and a little for special needs, and to give to friends. Berkshire Spirit is that much richer and visitors driving down for Sunday lunch really appreciate a special fill-up.

Our neighbourhood oil prospector was a pleasant man, dressed in the traditional costume of worn denims and tin helmet; he might have stepped straight out of the celebrated TV series. He parked his van in the drive.

'If you will just show me where the boundaries are I can get down to it,' he explained, producing a survey map.

'Get down to what?' I asked. He looked round nervously, waited for a load of hay to pass the gate and uttered the magic word. 'Oil. You're loaded with it here – didn't you know?'

'I had no idea,' I told him.

'You're right in the middle of the biggest oil field between Marlow and Sonning,' he went on, 'there's no point in taking a soil sample really, just a formality; still, it's all part of the service. Help us site the rig; I suppose you don't want it on the croquet lawn? Under the swimming pool, too, would be a bit awkward, come to think of it. We'd be better in the kitchen garden, I suppose; anyway, there's where I'll make a start, and Bob's your uncle.'

I hadn't heard anyone say 'Bob's your uncle' for a long time, but, come to that, I'd never seen anyone prospecting for oil among the raspberries.

'I'll be a fair time,' he told me, and asked if I was planning to go out to work. I explained that I worked at home and would be available.

'You won't have to do much more of that once we've got rigged up,' he assured me. 'You can just sit in the shade and watch the old jigger go up and down and every time it comes up means another bob or two in the old pocket.' He fetched a spade and a bundle of drain rods from the back of the lorry and marched off in the direction of the Brussels sprouts.

I don't quite know what I expected at this point; I am not even sure I believed the fellow, but it was impossible not to admire his optimism. In any case it was justified. About an hour later he interrupted a short piece I was working on for a well-known travel magazine to bring me his report.

'First the good news,' he told me, 'you're stashed. I don't think I'd be far wrong if I called if half a million barrels, give or take a couple of thousand. Now for the bad news . . . the rhubarb will have to go. For a time I thought we might save it but the pipe will have to come bang down the middle.'

'Forget the rhubarb,' I told him. 'We never eat it anyway.'

'I like a bit of rhubarb myself, there may be a crown or two we could save, we'll have to see,' he went on. 'But the important thing just now is to order the equipment and find a day to install. Would next Friday suit? I shall be in the district, so if it's convenient for you it'll suit us both.'

I told him Friday would do admirably and asked how long the operation would take. Apparently they'd improved the technique out of all recognition. He reckoned, with luck, and given a fair crack of the drill, the whole thing would be accomplished in about five hours; in six we should be fully operational with the oil flowing, in the first instance into a static water tank which he was letting me have second-hand and siting by the garage. Later he proposed to connect the tank by pipes to an outlet point further down the drive.

'Much the same arrangement I see you already have with fuel for the central heating system, only this time in reverse. The tankers will arrive about twice a week to start with and instead of you paying them they'll pay you and give you a receipt.'

I suggested that I might be the one to have to give the receipt but he demurred. Better not have anything in writing. 'With this Government you never know, they'll try and get a piece of it, you can count on that. They screwed those North Sea boys, and they'll crucify you if they get the chance.

'It's your land, it's your oil; I reckon you're doing them a service, making a patriotic gesture. In war-time we had to grow our own greens, now we have to grow our own oil. The only trouble, as I see it, is if we get too successful over here, we'll have another Uganda on our hands. Only this time it won't just be one wife they'll want to bring in, it'll be the whole bloody harem!

'I reckon,' he went on, 'it was a poor day for those old sheikhs when the Americans thought of Skylab. It was a poor day for America too, come to think of it. Didn't do Texas much good.'

'You mean,' I asked him, 'the Berkshire Oil Fields were spotted from Gemini?'

'Where else? That's what they were looking for. That's what they found. Anyway, you don't have to pay for that little caper, all you have to pay for is the rig and installation, and that you can do on the never-never if you wish. A cheque for a hundred pounds and your signature is all I'm asking at present, and whether you'd like the rig any particular colour. Any particular colour that's on the card, that is.'

I chose blue and wrote out the cheque to cash. I spent the rest of the day trying to find out the asking price for crude oil and how many gallons are in a barrel. That sort of information is hard to come by, unless you are in the oil game. Finally I rang Paul Getty. I met him at a party, nearly met him that is. Just as I was going to walk over to his table and say, 'Hullo, Mr. Getty, I'm Robert Morley,' he got up and left.

I wasn't more fortunate this time; apparently he doesn't care to speak on the phone, or else it's a trade secret. I made up my mind I'd have to wait until Friday.

I suppose you're thinking I was a bit of a mug; that when Friday came my neighbourhood prospector didn't turn up, and there isn't an oil rig at the bottom of my garden! I'm sorry to disappoint you. At two o'clock in the morning, if I open the window and listen, I hear, not as Kipling wrote 'the feet of the wind going to call the sun', but the tap, tap, tap, tap of the well. Twice a week a plain lorry calls to collect and hands over the cash and I now know the price of crude oil; and how many gallons to the barrel. But it's a secret. In this part of the Home Counties we don't have to discuss money, we just count it.

Folie de Grandeur

I am a Minister, but not of the Church. I sit in an enormous office at an enormous desk and am enormously occupied. It is enormously difficult to see me. Appointments have to be made months ahead.

I have got much thinner and am now beautifully dressed. I have two private secretaries, one young, the other not so young. They are both dedicated to serving me. Simpkins would give his life for me. Matthews will do just that, but doesn't know it yet.

The pictures are my own – two Rembrandts and a Manet. Only I would dare hang them on the same wall. When I go I shall take them with me, but that will not be for a long time. Meanwhile there is work to be done.

I never speak on the 'phone. My decisions are always final. They are written in a hand I would not have recognised as mine when I came here first. My visitors know my time is precious: they seldom stay more than a few moments. I listen (something I have learnt to do) and occasionally interject a sentence or two. I stand to signal that the audience is at an end, and my guests leave, refurbished utterly from head to toe, their faces glow, they walk backwards. Backwards? Am I the Pope? Royalty? The Aga Khan? Not the Pope certainly, nor the Aga Khan. There can't be all that pressure in Sardinia, even though he's married. Am I getting married? Am I married already?

There is a private apartment somewhere, but my family life is a closed book. I am not certain whether I'm married or not. If I have children they're 'Spanish type'. They are exactly the right number, the right sex and the right age. We are to be seen dining en famille at the Ritz, flexing in beach cabanas, playing touch football. We refused a fortune to be photographed advertising brandy en plein air. Are there ten, fifteen, seven of us? It depends on what we are doing. Sometimes we play chess, and then of course we are two. The one behind, bringing the coffee, is the footman.

Preparing a few personal notes about myself, at the request of some learned foundation or other, I described myself as an adequate man. *The adequate man* perhaps would have been more honest. I have never met another. I am always hoping to. Every time the doors open at the end of the room, and I rise to meet another stranger, I search his face for a sign that he too is adequate, and will be ready to share my burden. How heavy this burden is, I can never exactly find out. I am tired, naturally, but by now resigned to fatigue. When I smile it is as if the sun shines. When I furrow my brow in displeasure, people have remarked that it actually gets darker.

I have one of those watches that can be worn on the high diving-board, not that I dive often these days, there simply isn't the time.

Simpkins has just come in with some papers for me to sign. I have just decided to make it mandatory for motorists to drive a minimum of eight miles on every occasion they exercise their cars. Neither they nor their passengers must alight from the vehicle until an hour or more has elapsed from the moment of entry. I have solved traffic congestion, but Simpkins was not pleased. He lives in Highgate and prides himself on doing the journey in fifteen minutes. From now on he will have to drive to the Alexandra Palace, wait thirty minutes in his motor, and walk back. If he parks his car correctly, the journey here in the mornings will present no problems as long as he leaves forty minutes earlier. The curious thing is that I am practically certain I am not the Minister of Transport, but Simpkins seemed to find nothing unusual in my demand. Possibly I am Minister without Portfolio, charged with special tasks.

I have decided to return Gibraltar to Spain forthwith. I can see no point in retaining it any longer, and it's not as if I ever intended to go there. Of course this is not my only reason. I plan later this year to summon King Juan Carlos, the Generalissimo's successor, to London. I am almost certain that is where I still am. I am going to demand that he accepts my offer to run tourism in Britain. When he has had time to grade our hotels and hang up those price lists in the closets, we can make ready for influxes of Spanish day trippers at Lords. It will be the salvation of cricket.

Simpkins has just come in to ask how he will know when he has been in his car for an hour, as he has broken his watch. After next month, cars will be fitted with time locks. There is no problem but the problem itself, I tell him. (One for the book, I fancy.)

My plan for the compulsory retirement of all workers at forty seems to be working well. Speeding up the rat race makes it a spectator's sport. After sixty, spectators are free to get back into harness. They can apply to be taken on as traffic wardens, night watchmen, domestic or civil servants.

166

Promotion in all walks of life is rapid. If a boy hasn't got it made at seventeen, there's not much hope for him. The average age of bank managers in this country is now nineteen; doctors can qualify three years earlier.

On my seventieth birthday I shall definitely give up the editorship of *Punch*. It is extraordinary how I have been able to combine it with my other activities all these years. In some ways it is the least arduous of my tasks. One merely sets the subject of the essay and leaves the rest to the hacks. I shall probably appoint a schoolmaster to succeed me.

Simpkins and Matthews are back. It seems it is time for my tea. I wonder why they persist in wearing white.

MORLEY
AT
LARGE

The Scuttlebut

At a party the other evening I was taken to task by my host. 'The story you have just told,' he chided, 'I found excruciatingly dull and almost certainly inaccurate. It's not as if you had attended the funeral, or even been asked to do so. You don't, I imagine, know Princess Margaret.'

'I don't have to know Princess Margaret,' I retorted, stung by his sudden venom, 'I was merely recounting a remark made to Her Highness. I am sorry, I thought it would amuse you.'

'It doesn't. I cannot abide gossip.'

To say that I was shocked by his attitude is an understatement. As far as I am concerned, to tell me he doesn't like gossip is like someone telling me he doesn't like Queen's Pudding. I simply cannot understand it, nor do I approve.

In my dictionary, gossip is defined as idle talk or rumour about the private affairs of others. It lists 'scuttlebut' as an alternative. I learnt to scuttlebut in early childhood, and have been at it ever since. One of my uncles wore stays. If you hugged him in a certain place, you could feel the whalebone. He must have thought me an affectionate child, but having spread the rumour, I was forever trying to verify the fact. At school, at least the ones I went to, there was a tremendous amount of scuttlebut about sex, some of it fairly inaccurate, but none the worse for that. In an effort to dispel surmise, the headmaster used to entertain chaps who were leaving for public schools to a final briefing. Not a good scuttlebut himself, he contented himself at the session I attended with chalking up on the blackboard the imperishable phrase, 'Smut is rot'. I never had any intention of heeding his parting admonition to refrain from discussing the matter further. I have always wanted to know who is going to bed with whom. I suppose I feel that in some ways it enables me to see more clearly the shifting patterns of life. It doesn't, but no matter.

I like, too, knowing how much money people left, what exactly they died of. I have a friend whose morbidity on this count exceeds my own almost to the point of madness. He spends most mornings with *The Times* obituary column in one hand and the telephone in the other, trying to contact distant relatives or casual acquaintances of the listed deceased, to verify what finally carried them away from us.

'Surely,' he will say, 'you knew Mrs. Perkins?'

'No,' I tell him.

'But I am almost certain I met her at dinner at your house once. Mrs. Perkins. She lived in Oswestry, you must remember her.'

'No,' I tell him, 'why?'

'She's dead. I have an idea she had a weight problem. It could have been heart, I suppose. What do you think?'

'I have no idea,' I tell him, but before the end of the morning he is usually back on the blower. 'It was angina,' he informs me reproachfully. He believes I don't take sufficient interest in other people, but of course I do. I am passionately interested in other people. I can't wait to find out what everyone is up to. If I think it's worth repeating and it's not actionable, be sure, gentle reader, that you will be the first to hear.

The House of Windsor

At the time when arrangements were being finalised for the launching of the great Jubilee celebrations, American network executives were summoned to the Palace for informal discussions on procedure.

They explained to the courteous officials that, ideally, they would like Her Majesty to make an appearance on the networks and perhaps give a short interview to one of their anchor men.

The officials of the Royal Household were tremendously impressed by the number of Americans who would be watching, preferably round about breakfast time, but politely pointed out that it had been decided that Her Majesty would not be appearing on television chat shows this year or, for that matter, any other.

Would it be possible then, enquired the disappointed media men, for some other member of the family to help us out? The Prince of Wales or Prince Philip, who, after all, like Princess Anne, were occasionally to be seen on the box fronting a programme about playing-fields or shire horses or launching an appeal for distressed tigers? Not this year, they were told .There is such a thing as over-exposure, you know.

However, one evening Her Majesty did appear on our own TV screens to talk briefly about the Crown Jewels, or, more specifically. the jewels in a couple of her crowns, one of which she even wore obligingly on her head. She spoke for perhaps five minutes, and the effect on my trade was devastating. Most West End theatres were down that night a couple of thousand pounds and the one I was playing in was no exception. By tactically delaying the curtain rise on the pretext I had snapped a bootlace, I was able to catch most of Her Majesty's performance, and it would have been difficult to fault it.

Standing very erect, she articulated slowly and carefully into the lens as a previous generation was taught to speak into the telephone. Because it was understood that the invention had been by no means perfected, it was considered in those days quite fatal to gabble. In point of fact, the Queen seldom gabbles, but those observing her manner on the box must sometimes ask themselves whether she is not at times enjoying a gigantic leg pull. No one who is in her confidence doubts that she has a sense of humour, and when, in the course of her explanation of how and why exactly so much loot came into the possession of the family, she was obliged to mention the dreaded words 'Oliver Cromwell', she conveyed by a subtle raising of the eyebrow that anyone who could be so foolish as to deal harshly with a monarch might be relied on afterwards to dispose of the booty on strangely disadvantageous terms.

Cromwell, apparently, sold quite a large ruby for four pounds, and there was a perceptible royal wince. Money matters to royalty, one imagines it has to, and we all shared her glow of contentment, that with the coming of Charles II, those who had rushed in to buy, prudently returned the gems, not knowing, of course, that they had been stolen in the first place.

Splendid, too, was her tale of the Cullinan diamond which caused the Dutch diamond cutter to faint as he split the stone. 'My Grandmother,' Her Majesty told us, 'always referred to the two sizeable chunks hived off from the centre block as the "chips".'

There was no reference in the Court Circular the next morning as to where Her Majesty was on the night of the transmission, so presumably she was at home, like most of her citizens, watching herself. Home for the Queen is Windsor Castle, where, like her Great-Great Grandmother, she is presumably happiest, although, unlike Queen Victoria, she commutes to London on a good many days in the week to her office in Buckingham Palace. Among the most extraordinary traditions of the Royal House of Windsor are the migrations undertaken when the seasons change. What impels the inevitable visits to Sandringham, Holyrood and Balmoral? It cannot, surely, be the outward manifestation of a restless and unhappy monarch. Quite apart from the fact that Her Majesty must do an unconscionable amount of travelling each year on official business, what inducement is there in constantly pulling up sticks, packing up the gold plate and moving her family and their considerable staff of ladies- and gentlemen-in-waiting and second scullery maids from pillar to post and back to pillar? Nor are the visits arranged on sudden impulse. There is a time designated annually for the flight of the swallow and the royal visit to the Highland Games.

Ours not to reason why, but we in Berkshire like to think the Queen enjoys life most in what is sometimes referred to as the green or stockbroker belt and officially designated by Whitehall as the Home Counties. Driving along the M4 in the summer, one sees across the spires of Eton College the floodlit castle of Windsor with standard fluttering at the mast, and hopes the family are at home for once and enjoying a good wassail.

The most colourful of the royal wassails takes place after the annual Garter ceremony during Ascot Week, when the Queen and her party attend the races and, weather permitting, drive along the course in open carriages while the spectators raise their hats and a cheer and the bands play the national anthem. But for me it is when the Queen and her family have passed us and hats are back firmly on our heads, that interest quickens, as in the fifth, sixth or even seventh carriage come Her Majesty's 'castle guests', invited for the four days not only to dance attendance but to be given one free ride each in a state carriage.

It may, for many of them, be their first and last taste of the royal roundabout. 'One day, my darling, if you're a good girl,' Nanny once told them, 'you too will ride in a coach behind the Queen', and ride they do, these oddly assorted young men and women, dreaming of last night's banquet in the Waterloo Chamber or the game of dumb crambo arranged for tonight after their visit to the Windsor theatre. Here they are in what they hope are suitable clothes, girls holding on to their hats, the young men with grandfather's topper firmly crammed on their head, sporting ancestral or hired morning coats and wondering if the royal trainer really knows what he is talking about and whether there is a hope in hell of his landing the Wokingham Stakes for his patron. I don't know why I find it so moving, I suppose because I have always been a sucker for the carousel.

A. L. Rowse, the eminent if rather quarrelsome historian, has written a splendid account of *Windsor Castle in the History of the Nation* where English Kings and Queens have, on the whole, enjoyed themselves hugely for more than eight hundred years. And, like the good tourist I hope I am, I sometimes spend an afternoon with a friend pottering around the precincts, avoiding the crowds and the conducted tour and losing the occasional grandchild in the process.

I am not much of a one for history and not at all one for guides.

I loathe jokes about dungeons and being shown where they roasted the oxen and being told that meat was cheaper in those days. I am not the shape for which armour was originally fashioned, and although sometimes in the course of my own professional duties I have been forced to don fustian and double for Oliver Cromwell or the Duke of Manchester, I have seldom felt comfortable in the costume or certain in which century I have temporarily landed up.

I am aware that I am profoundly ignorant of history, and have never felt it necessary to apologise for the fact to anyone, still less to myself. There is always someone who can tell you who succeeded William II, if you have to know, just as there is always someone, I hope, to tell me how on earth to get to Peru, a journey I am contemplating.

What I find it impossible to do is suddenly to evince interest between three and five-thirty in Chinese ceramics or a stamp collection or even, as in Windsor Castle, the celebrated Doll's House, which I am probably quite wrong in thinking was presented to Queen Mary on her jubilee; but I am able, thanks to an entirely fortuitous conversation with my American daughter-in-law, to pass on to my readers one supremely unimportant piece of information about the latter. The school where my grandchild is being educated clothes its captives in an extremely expensive and, to me, rather unattractive blazer. When hard-pressed parents suggest to the Mother Superior that it might be possible to substitute a less expensive garment, the Principal raises her eyes to Heaven and points out that a minute replica of the school colours is presently worn by Royal Dollies. If it is ever decided to re-dress the puppet, consideration will be given to a cheaper cloth, but not before.

The trouble, of course, with dolls that are not played with is that they remain, like the Crown Jewels, in pristine condition.

Inflation, alas, gallops ahead.

Out of the Mouth of Babes...

Late December, early January is the time when most people can get a New Year if they want one. Most people don't. They grumble a good deal about their present model, they pretend to be delighted with the prospect of the new one, but in the end they decide to make do with what they've got already. 'Why bother to change?' they ask. 'There's sure to be teething troubles. Then again, supposing we did get a New Year, would we be able to drive it?'

I asked my year-old grandson whether he thought I ought to get a Happy New Year.

'It depends, I suppose,' he told me, 'what sort of New Year you want – a good resolution New Year?'

'I'm absolutely sick of those,' I told him. 'Besides, they don't work.'

'A year of endeavour, perhaps?'

'That's a bit vague. What sort of endeavour?'

'This could be the year when you took over, came to power, ran the country.'

'Yes,' I told him, 'that would be quite nice.'

'It would mean a lot of work.'

'But I don't mind work as long as it's interesting work. That's why I'm so grateful I don't have an assembly line job.'

'I expect they're grateful too,' he observed. He seemed to be having difficulty balancing his bricks. I tried to give him a hand, but for some reason he bit it.

'If you ran the country, what would you do?' he asked.

'Certainly get rid of the slums.'

'How?'

'It's perfectly easy to get rid of things. I'd just knock them down, like you do.'

'And meanwhile, where would people live?'

'They could live in huts. If there were an earthquake, they would have to live in huts.'

'How about their coming to live here?'

'What, all of them?'

'Some.'

'It wouldn't do, wouldn't do AT ALL!'

'There's no reason to shout. You're the one that's deaf,' Hugo reminded me rudely.

'Let's forget the slums for a moment,' I went on. 'There's the question of unemployment. That's something I could deal with. I should adopt the Japanese system. In Japan when a firm takes on an employee it assumes an obligation. It looks after him and his family for the rest of their natural.' Hugo flinched: he is opposed to slang. 'In Japan,' I continued, 'they believe in jobs for the boys.'

'So do our lot,' said Hugo.

'But this is entirely different. There, all the school leavers are automatically absorbed. It's a point of honour for employers to take them on, even if at the moment they don't need additional staff. They never sack anyone. Once an employee, always an employee, unless you are criminally dishonest, and even then they will try and save your face for you, if not your job. In Japan losing face is very tragic, which is why no one calls anyone a bloody fool.'

'The British,' sighed Hugo, 'like sacking each other and calling each other a bloody fool.'

'Yes, and look at the economy. Bad labour relations, that's the trouble.'

'If you had your way, would you sack the present government?' asked Hugo.

'Yes.'

'Why?'

'Because they're a lot of bloody fools.'

Hugo seemed to have arranged the bricks to his satisfaction. 'What would you do about the trade gap and sterling as a reserve currency?'

'Absolutely nothing – it's only book-keeping. I've never kept accounts. It's a mistake to put down what one spends, or to add up what comes in. Just be grateful for the stuff when it's around. I had an uncle, well, you had a great-great uncle, come to that, who used to put down every penny. On his deathbed he asked me whether I'd taken a taxi or come by bus to get to it. I thought it the saddest thing anyone ever asked. How could it matter, then or ever? He was the kindest of men, too, in some ways.'

'Leave you any money?' Hugo asked me.

'He did, as a matter of fact.'

'I wish you would keep accounts,' said Hugo, 'It might be a help to all of us. But go on with what you were going to do if you ran the whole caboodle.'

'It's quite simple,' I told him. 'I would get the country on its feet, get the economy moving.'

'Everyone,' said Hugo, 'always wants to get someone else up on their feet. It might help if you got up on your feet a bit more yourself, instead of slumping in your chair all day, watching the television.' He rose, I thought a trifle unsteadily, and tottered in my direction. Then he sat down abruptly.

'Hard luck, old fellow.'

'What do you mean, hard luck?'

'You didn't quite make it.'

'I had a partial success. In her present mood, Great Britain might argue that I also had a partial failure, but I prefer to ignore that aspect. I travelled three steps; tomorrow or the day after I shall walk right across the room. Then in a few weeks across the garden, then in turn across the street, and the town, and the country, and the whole wide world. Why? Because instead of commiserating with myself for what I haven't achieved, I continue to congratulate myself on what I have. That's the difference, and try to remember it in future.'

'I'd like to congratulate you,' I said.

'Why me especially?' asked Hugo. 'If you want to congratulate anyone, congratulate the entire human race, and especially the human race between the ages of one and five. That's the testing time.

'Why do you wrinkle your nose up like that?' I asked.

'Because I smell success.'

'I wish I could,' I told him.

'You have to sniff for it. It's there more often than you might suspect. It's one hell of a sweet smell.'

I was surprised at Hugo's vehemence. He hardly ever swears. One of his attendant slaves came to collect him and carry him off to his bath. At the door he turned and waved gravely.

'A Happy New Year,' he said, 'and mind you sniff for it.'

In Praise of Mr Robinson

It is not true that clothes mean nothing to me. When I was ten I sat sucking a straw on a stone wall and a child rode past in corduroy breeches and I was aware of sex for the first time, and for years afterwards haunted agricultural shows, bored to sobs, unless I could discover small girls in riding breeches, posting up and down on their ponies. Later I discovered in a shop in Monmouth a weekly magazine with a correspondence column of highly suspect letters, dealing with the dressing of little girls in breeches and hunted avidly for back numbers of the same paper, which did not continue to publish for long. There was a limited demand for such specialised fetishism. Nowadays, perhaps because my perversion seems slightly disreputable, I dislike the sight of little girls mounted on horseback, wearing those hard black hats and carrying whips. 'There's a streak of cruelty in that child,' I tell myself.

As for my own clothes, I have never taken kindly to them, although I am not of the stuff of which nudists are made. My own flesh burns rather than grills. I am seldom cooked to a turn. When I lie in the sun I take care to be fully clothed. I have a very old pocket watch which dreads the sand and for that reason I seldom venture onto the sea shore unless it is stony, and then only when fully shod and my watch well wrapped up in a handkerchief. People who lie for hours face down on the sand dunes should be removed by mechanical scoops.

My watch is the sole inanimate object to which I am attached. I care nothing for my pen, my cuff-links, my Pissarros. I once had a cigarette case of which I was moderately fond, but now I no longer smoke. Above all, I am not fond of my clothes. It gives me no pleasure to meet them every morning. I am bored by my underclothes, irritated by the constant failure of the elastic in my underdrawers, dread the days when I have to walk round constantly hitching my waistline. I seem unable to foretell elastic fatigue. I am not attached to my handkerchiefs. When Cilla Black was a child she once waited for me outside the stage door, and begged a memento. I handed over my handkerchief and am still haunted whenever I meet her by the fear that it may not have been laundered at the time.

Only my ties occasionally give satisfaction, even a fleeting pleasure, but my favourites are always the first to become disfigured by gravy stains. I have learnt never to give my heart to a tie.

My shirts have to be custom tailored. I am too thick in the neck, too broad in the chest, for the fashionable rubbish on the ready-to-wear counter, where I sometimes glimpse a colour or a pattern which would favour me. 'Those are nice,' I tell them. Instantly, crushingly, comes the rebuke. 'Not your size.'

The real discrimination in the world is not between colour, but shape. I am segregated in New York, forced to shop at the outsize store next door to the Tall Girl Boutique. In the old days inns were obliged to provide food and lodging for the traveller, no matter how inconvenient or unprofitable such an exercise proved for mine host. Nowadays stores should be compelled to carry lines to accommodate the full figure. How insufferable are the advertisements for men's wear in the illustrated glossies, the bland assumption that the skinnies get the fat. How I loathe the arrogance of the well-groomed skeleton, stooping condescendingly to open the door of the sports car to decant the flashy bird. I even resent the horse in the background. I do not live in the world of cavalry twill. No dog nuzzles my legs if I can help it. Damn and blast all spindly-chested, unbuttocked men.

Years ago the discreet tailor enquired 'Which side do you dress?' I remember I was so taken aback I had to grope before I could answer. These days, men dress to the front. Before I die, we shall see the return of the codpiece and men will carry swords, if they're not doing so already.

What happened, I wonder, to all those elaborate trouser presses with the thumbscrews? At school, the prefects made the fags, as we were laughingly called, operate the contraptions. The expert among us could produce three or four different creases in the same pant leg, but were seldom thanked, except with a beating.

That habit of pulling the trouser slightly upwards with the thumb and forefinger as one sat, seems to have gone out of fashion, thank goodness. It always struck me as the height of economy. Not that I am extravagant where clothes are concerned. I buy my suits sparingly from a tailor to whom I was originally directed by Gabriel Pascal, who had engaged me to play Undershaft, the millionaire armament king in *Major Barbara,* and insisted that only Mr. Robinson, his personal cutter, could give him a run for his money.

Gabriel Pascal was a splendid, larger than life figure of a gypsy. His career was a superb confidence trick, although the confidence evaporated surprisingly on the studio floor, where he was perpetually bereft of his cool, and made me, at any rate, so nervous that I had to insist that once he had shouted 'Action!' he would leave the set — a procedure I have never been successful in adopting with any of my subsequent directors, though I once worked for one who kept a large packing case on the premises, into which he could creep and hide whenever I started to act. For the film, Pascal ordered and paid for a dozen suits, of which I wore at least three, and a black overcoat with a velvet collar which I still have thirty years later, but, alas, can no longer get into. A pity, as in the picture I only carried it over my arm. Rex Harrison, who played Cousins, was also directed to the same establishment, and wore his clothes with a good deal more panache. Later, when cast as a convict, he wisely insisted on Mr. Robinson cutting his prison garb. I once taxed the maestro with preferring to make clothes for Rex rather than myself, but surprisingly he was unenthusiastic about the pair of us. I could never understand what upset him about Harrison's figure, but I think I have presented him with a perpetual challenge. I suppose he has come to regard me with all the tolerance of a doctor for a chronic patient whom he manages to keep alive and reasonably active in the face of a crippling disease.

Mr. Robinson himself is now over eighty, but still stands all day in his establishment, ripping and pinning, and always careful to run every pin through his hair before inserting it into the cloth.

'Why do you do it?' I asked.

'I have forgotten,' he replied. I am reminded of the spot of carmine greasepaint I deposit in the inner corner of my eye when making up for a play. Some actors put carmine, too, on the ear lobes, but not I. There was a theory long ago and before Mrs. Patrick Campbell's devastating comparison of her leading man to a rocking horse, that one should also apply carmine to the nostrils.

Mr. Robinson, like myself, can be forgiven for forgetting. He started cutting, or at any rate devilling for a tailor before the turn of the century. He has a relish for the days when dukes drove up to his establishment in their dog carts, complete with tiger. 'You do know about tigers?' he said to me once. They weren't animals, but boys who sat on the back seat with folded arms and were as much a part of the scene as the dalmatians who followed behind. When dukes arrived for their fittings, they would leap from the driving seat and race for the entrance, trying to reach it before the tiger had time to leap from the back and, flinging himself at the horse's head, strike the trusty steed on the back of the knee (or is it a fetlock?) so that he should stand properly. 'It was important how he stood,' Mr. Robinson assured me. Dukes apparently were intensely jealous of each other. They still are, as a matter of fact. In those days if they saw a carriage drawn by a better horse than their own, they couldn't wait to steal their rival's coachman. 'But surely,' I queried, 'it was the horse they coveted?' No. According to Mr. Robinson, the secret was always the coachman. I am reminded that Louis B. Mayer once wrote down for me in the order of importance, as he saw them, naturally, the qualities of a star. The ability to act came comparatively low on the list. Turn-out was all important.

'Here you are at eighty-two, still standing on your feet all day, while I am still a boy twenty years younger and get tired just sitting around. How do you do it?'

'You've named them,' said Mr. Robinson. 'You must have good feet, and know how to look after them.'

We were lunching at Buck's, a club started by my father-in-law, the late Herbert Buckmaster, to which I have belonged for many years, without making much impact. Mr. Robinson made an immediate impact. The members clustered at the centre table to listen. A good many of them, of course, are customers, who seldom catch him in a mood of relaxation. After luncheon I escorted my guest back to his premises around the corner, passing on the way a male boutique of alarming modernity and expense. I hoped that Mr. Robinson wouldn't notice the window, which displayed clerical collars in surprising colours and hair shirts complete with chains. 'I often go in there,' said Mr. Robinson, 'and give them my advice. They are young chaps, you know, just starting in the trade.'

There is a clue to my cutter. He is very loyal to his trade, although he does not subscribe to *The Tailor & Cutter* and refuses to exhibit at their annual exhibition. He has never won an Oscar. I once gave the Oscars, or at least their equivalents, away to the tailors, and if you think the Hollywood version is strange, you have no idea what sort of statues tailors cherish. Silver labradors, silver pheasants, miniature huntsmen pursuing miniature foxes across silver fences, silver chalices, silver beer mugs, silver stags grazing on nuggets of the stuff. 'Have you no gold?' I asked them. The ceremony was a lengthy one. There was an enormous list of prizewinners. All around the room were tailors' dummies, displaying the coat of the year, the waistcoat of the month. I made an impassioned speech, berating my hosts for their lack of adventure. I told them that their work on the whole was as dusty and fusty as their premises, and they were delighted. I told them they should petition the Queen to allow her subjects to dress informally for Ascot. I told them how unattractive I thought my countrymen looked in hired morning coats, and they clapped.

My speech gained great prominence in the trade papers, and three days later the Palace announced that men could wear lounge suits to watch the Ascot Gold Cup. But of course they didn't. I was the only one to avail myself of the privilege. Strolling around the lawns in my flannels and panama, I was annoyed by the number of people who peered at my name on the label which the Duke of Norfolk's lackeys pin to my chest on these occasions. Usually the start of recognition, the half-smile of delight suffices to put me in good humour, but on this occasion I was incensed by the fleet of elderly admirals, who kept reading my name as if for the first time, and looking at my clothes as if they had never seen a chalk pin-stripe before in their lives. *The Tailor & Cutter* offered me a suit, but Mr. Robinson refused to make it.

'I heard about you,' he told me, 'making a fool of yourself. Very bad for me.'

'How on earth,' I asked him, 'could it have been bad for you? I should have thought if your customers wore their own clothes to Ascot it would have put money in your pocket.'

'My customers,' he replied loftily, 'do wear their own clothes. It's only the actors who hire them. You don't understand the trade,' he went on. 'Why, there was a man came in here the other day who has a suit for every day of the month. Of course, he dresses for dinner every night, and naturally he has seven dinner jackets. But he was bored. "I look the same every night, Robinson!" he complained. He lives alone since his wife died. Won't come up to London, thinks it's dangerous. He could be right. He comes to Guildford. He lives just outside.'

'Mr. Getty?' I hazarded.

'Certainly not. I wouldn't dream of telling you the gentleman's name. Anyway, I solved his problem. I suggested cummerbunds, seven cummerbunds. He's as pleased as Punch, and different.'

Mr. Robinson demands a high standard of conduct in his fitting rooms. He has a particular horror of wives who accompany their menfolk to offer advice. When one of them confessed to a feeling of disappointment that her man still bulged in all the wrong places, and incautiously enquired if Mr. Robinson couldn't do something about it, he is said to have replied, 'Willingly, Madam, were I only a surgeon.' A duchess who complained that the waistcoat wrinkled when the duke sat down was invited to inspect his shirt, and forced to agree that that wrinkled as well, whereupon Mr. Robinson opened the garment. 'You will observe, Madam, that when he is seated, his grace's stomach is also prone to wrinkle.'

'What happens,' I asked Mr. Robinson, 'between the day I choose, or rather you choose the cloth, and the first fitting?' 'You wait,' he told me. On the other hand, if you are really in a fix or, in my case, a film, he will make you a suit in twenty-four hours without a fitting. He knows the rich like to be kept waiting, long to be rejected. My father-in-law was the same about his club. He would refuse people a table occasionally, even when there was room. 'They mustn't always have what they want,' he would remark.

In Mr. Robinson's and my father-in-law's world, people are children. 'I'll be with you in a minute,' Mr. Robinson says, and means 'sit down and wait quietly and don't make a fuss, that's a good boy'. We sit and wait and Mr. Robinson comes in with the jacket and waistcoat and puts them on a chair and goes away, and we are now in our underpants in a little cubicle, feeling as if we were going to have a medical examination, when the trouser cutter comes in. In all his long life, Mr. Robinson has never cut a pair of trousers, and wouldn't know where to start. The trouser cutter is quite unlike Mr. Robinson. He is not a star, and he is deferential. He has his jacket on, while Mr. Robinson is always in shirt sleeves. But perhaps the most marked difference is that the trouser cutter's trousers always fit perfectly at the first session. They are always quite perfect, and he is never surprised that it should be so. He leaves them on for Mr. Robinson to see, and we sit down again, waiting for the boss.

When he comes he surveys the trousers, but says nothing. He puts on the waistcoat, pins it roughly over the stomach, and enquires after my health. He removes the tape from around his neck, and measures my chest. 'Put on a bit, have I?' But Mr. Robinson in diagnosis doesn't answer the idle questions of his patients. It is just, but only just possible, that the fault is his. He puts on the jacket. It is not, of course, in a finished state. There are facings of canvas, a lack of buttons. The tape is produced once more, and this time worn by me briefly as a belt. Mr. Robinson pats the front. 'Very nice,' he says to no one in particular. 'Very nice.' The only parts that fit are the shoulders and the sleeves. Mr. Robinson pulls out a penknife, makes some deft incisions, gives a few swift tugs, and I am suddenly in my shirt again. Mr. Robinson calls out loudly for Albert. His name is echoed through the shop, as if we were in the corridors of justice, and Albert was a missing witness.

When he appears from the attic, or possibly the cellar, he is straight out of Galsworthy. His clothes are calculated to suggest immense deprivation. He is collarless. He gives me a humble smile of duty, touches his forelock and is instantly engaged by Mr. Robinson. 'I want you, Albert, to look at this revers. It wants taking up into the flèche. The shoulder will have to be lengthened.' The coat is now in pieces. The sleeves on the floor. All Albert's work — if it is his work, and I sometimes suspect that Albert is kept there as a whipping-boy and has no hand in the task — all Albert's work and Mr. Robinson's work is now destroyed, and you might think the pair of them would be down-hearted. But not a bit. They know that, unlike Humpty Dumpty, it will all soon be together again, only to be taken apart once more on my next visit.

Perfection will be achieved on the third and final occasion. Indeed, has already been achieved. The very appearance of a penknife at the third fitting is unthinkable. The coat fits, can be seen to fit and Albert is once again summoned, this time to be congratulated. 'I want you, Albert,' says Mr. Robinson, 'to see this for yourself. Very nice. Very nice indeed. And Mr. Morley, if he will forgive me saying so, is not an easy man to fit.' After I have thanked Albert comes the moment when Mr. Robinson ceremoniously adjusts the cheval mirror in order that I may admire the back. 'Just look at that back,' he urges. But I am not fond of the back. It is the moment of truth when I see how bald I am. Because my hair still grows in front and is there for me to brush every morning, I am always chagrined to observe in Mr. Robinson's cheval mirror that on top it doesn't grow at all.

Some years ago, visiting a mental hospital, I was introduced to a little old lady who was convinced that she was Queen Victoria, a monarch whom she closely resembled. Her condition was character-ised by the medical staff as extremely disturbed, but she was calm-ness itself while receiving me in audience. I noticed that when she graciously dismissed me, Her Majesty spoke a few words in Welsh to the doctor who acted as her Chamberlain.

'What did Her Majesty say to you?' I asked him when we had withdrawn. He hesitated fractionally before replying.

'She wondered who the bald bugger was.'

'Bald bugger?' I repeated. 'Are you quite sure she said bald bugger? Surely from her height it must have been difficult to detect?'

I often wonder if those we think mad are not psychic into the bargain.

One thing about Mr. Robinson's suits is that they last forever. It is his habit to inscribe the date of each masterpiece on the label which he causes to be affixed to the right hand, inside pocket. It is always the same pocket, because that's how the police like it. Instant identification in the face of the untoward is a fringe benefit enjoyed by his customers. I am not a believer in the tradesman's right to stamp his name on the goods which he supplies. I don't really care for the name of my hatter on my hatband, nor am I remotely interested in the provenance, if that's the word, and I'm pretty sure it is, of my toothbrush. But I do not resent Mr. Robinson's intrusion. I am not a frugal or well-balanced man financially. I often puzzle over why Mr. Burton can afford so much, and I so little. But I like sometimes to remind myself that though in the debt of the Inland Revenue to an extent which neither of us exactly relishes, I am on the whole a sober citizen, and in such moments open my jacket and find reassurance by squinting downwards at Mr. Robinson's meticulous handwriting, to discover that the coat I am wearing was first buttoned by me in 1951, and what's more that I am still managing to button it.

The one outfit I have never purchased from my tailor, or worn, save in the pursuance of my trade, has been a tailcoat and the accompanying white tie and waistcoat. When still a comparatively young man, and appearing as Oscar Wilde in a play of that name on Broadway, I was asked to a supper party after the performance by the late Mrs. Cornelius Vanderbilt, who in those days still lived it up in her mansion on Fifth Avenue. I had already been to tea with her on several occasions among the roses, each in their separate silver vase, and the photographs of reigning monarchs and others who unlike Mrs. Vanderbilt had thrown up the sponge. But this was the first occasion on which I had been invited to a soirée. The dress, she indicated on the invitation, was to be formal.

'What would that entail?' I enquired of the social secretary.

'It means a white tie and tails.'

'I haven't got either, so I shall come in a dinner jacket and a black tie if that's all right.' I never dreamt for a moment that it wouldn't be. I was, after all, the toast of Broadway that season. Every taxi driver knew that my grosses were only topped by Raymond Massey impersonating Abraham Lincoln. Queer waiters used to thank me for what I was doing for them as they ushered me to the ringside seat at the Cotton Club. Walter Winchell had awarded me 'five orchids' and although his quote slightly interfered with my prominence on the playbill, this was heady wine.

On the morning of the party the social secretary rang back. It seemed that Mrs. Vanderbilt had been considering my problem, and thought it best if I were to come some other evening. I went to bed supperless, scarred for life, and vowing never to own a tailcoat. On the whole, my decision has been a wise one. It has caused me little inconvenience and has saved me a great deal of boredom. I have never wanted to conduct an orchestra, or play a cello. Moreover, I am reliably informed that men in white ties make even worse speeches than men in black ones.

The last time I was in Paris, emboldened by after luncheon brandy, I left the Ritz hotel and wandered 'lonely as a cloud' down the Rue Cambon and entered, in a moment of *folie de grandeur,* the Katharine Hepburn shop, or, as it is still known in Paris, Chanel's, and asked to see the collection. It was not the normal hour for viewing, or I believe the right time of the year, but I was told that if I cared to arrange myself they would do what they could. Presently, several lovelies appeared, wearing the little coats and skirts, the beaded cocktail dresses, the woollen evening gowns which are so instantly recognizable as Madame's handiwork, even by incognoscenti such as I. Halfway through the show, the brandy began to wear off, and I to be alarmed. How to get out, without buying anything? In that moment of panic, an idea for a story occurred to me — a hideous hunchback, or perhaps just a fat actor, enters the premises of a leading couturier and demands a fashion show. A frightened vendeuse accedes to his brutal request, whereupon he selects a dress on each of the models in turn, writes out a cheque and presents the delighted birds with their own feathers, gets into his carriage and drives silently away into the afternoon. On this occasion I simply got up and left before the bride put in an appearance. Maybe they hadn't planned to give me a bride anyway.

When it comes to collections, women still have all the fun. How pleased I would be if I found on one of my visits to Mr. Robinson, his sober premises transformed. The bolts of Harris tweed, the books of little square patterns banished, the pictures of drag hunts (no Freudian connotations here) and the portrait of the Japanese Emperor taken down. The leather armchairs replaced with rows and rows of the traditional small gilt chairs on which were seated merchant bankers, film producers, Venezuelan Ambassadors, Mr. Paul Getty, the Prince of Wales, even perhaps Mr. Hefner himself, watching 'the clothes of tomorrow worn by the men of today'. Down the staircase they would march, each one dressed to kill, in the bedroom, on the moors, perhaps on the battlefield itself, dressed to love, in the motor car or beside the swimming pool, dressed to dine at some glittering banquet, or merely to lounge elegantly, the tray on the lap, watching television. Dressed, in the final tableau of all, on this occasion only, on the arm of his bride, or perhaps, wiser to stick to his best man. We can't have women littering up the place. They will see the clothes later, and by the time we get round to such displays who knows, they may even be ready to pay for them.

For someone who doesn't enjoy dressing up, I have had my share in the fitting-rooms of the theatrical costumiers over the last forty years. I have stood patiently confronting the cheval mirror while a procession of wardrobe mistresses have tugged and sweated, have cut and pinned silks and satins, genuine ermine and synthetic chain mail to my resisting person. I have been laced into corsets and padded out with rubber foam. Even, on one occasion, fitted with angel wings. Always the perpetual struggle has gone on between the designer who tried to make me look different, and the actor determined to look much the same. In the end, of course, it is I who have triumphed and despite their efforts, all the great historical characters I have enacted, from Alexandre Dumas to Oscar Wilde, from W. S. Gilbert to Louis XVI, and from the Emperor of China to Prinny, have ended up looking extraordinarily like Robert Morley.

Only on one occasion has the disguise triumphed. In one of my very early professional engagements I was cast as Oedipus and prevailed upon to speak Greek tragedy through a sorbo-sponge mask. Understandably, my beautiful voice was muffled. An aunt who witnessed the débâcle summed it up forever as far as I was concerned.

'I didn't enjoy it much,' she told me. 'Do you know your mask looked as if it was made of sorbo-sponge?'

Tailor's Dummy

I was once hailed as one of the ten best-dressed men in the world. Like a fool I have lost the clipping which conveyed the joyful news and all I can state positively is that I came equal fifth with another national hero called George Best, that a tailor himself was top of the list and Lord Snowdon just scraped in as number ten. Mine is a remarkable achievement, as I have never before even entered the lists, and I cannot think why I haven't preserved the press cutting to add to my collection.

There wandered into my dressing room the other day the innocent grandson of a famous criminal lawyer with some notion of interesting me in a television series based on his granddad's more sensational *causes célèbres*.

'Do you know,' he told me, 'Grandfather actually kept a scrap book into which he stuck newspaper clippings about himself. He must have been a rather conceited sort of chap.'

'Very,' I told him gravely, and thought of my own bookcases bulging with the laudatory mentions earned by myself all those years ago in the *Wirral Advertiser,* and now preserved for ever in stout scrapbooks. I know few actors who do not follow my custom, but Q.C.s are made, it would seem, of more modest stuff.

I don't feel at all modest about being one of the ten best-dressed men. I am proud of having crashed the weight barrier, to have struck a blow for the properly-made man. I am heartily sick of those skinny ginks who figure in the advertisements, climbing in and out of shooting brakes with girls and dogs.

Years ago, when I went to the cinema and watched the Pathe Gazette cockerell, we were treated to seasonal fashion shows and after the wickedly seductive slinkies in cloche hats and silver fox, there came a glimpse of a stout matron who was, I believe, called Dorothy. Dorothy fashioned the more mature models for the more mature woman, never the bride or even the bridesmaid. She was that most revered of guests, the matron of honour, and I was always impatient to greet her from the one and three pennies. Dorothy always came up smiling, and I caught myself smiling back. It doesn't matter, she seemed to be saying, if one is no longer young, if one was never pretty. It doesn't matter if one is on the big side, indeed it helps.

On the big side, that's me, and I am proud to take my bow a little late in the proceedings, smiling bravely as I essay the catwalk and listen to the commentary. 'Here comes Robert in double-breasted blue flannel with just the faintest suggestion of a pin-stripe. Notice the outsize lapels, the slanted breast pocket with just the right amount of clean handkerchief displayed, the trousers cut generously to accentuate the *embonpoint* of the seat and the turn-ups kept wide to enable them to be pulled over the shoes. The coat is worn un-buttoned to give additional ease and avoid any appearance of strain. Thank you, Robert.' Thank you, Dorothy, if it comes to that. I wonder whether she still lives. Mr. Robinson, alas, is dead. All the years he cut my clothes he resisted the suggestion that I should include his name on the list of credits in the programme. Actors rather like to get an additional mention in the small print, along with Lux and Schweppes and the Post Office telephone. 'Mr. Morley is dressed by . . .' but alas, it was never to be.

'I'd much rather not,' he would tell me whenever I brought up the subject.

'Are you ashamed of me?' I once asked him.

'Not ashamed,' he replied, 'but then of course I'm not exactly proud either. It's not so much how you wear my clothes as the way you treat them. When you go to bed at night, why don't you hang them up?'

'I sometimes put them over a chair.'

'But mostly on the floor?'

'Mostly. Don't you think clothes like to be free occasionally, like pit ponies?' I asked him. 'It can't be good for them to spend their life on hangers. If you throw them around, they relax. That's my theory, anyway.'

'It's not mine,' Mr. Robinson told me.

Mr. Robinson took on all comers. I played Gilbert in a film of Gilbert and Sullivan. Osbert Lancaster, by no means an unintimidat-ing figure, was the designer and attended one of the fittings. Mr. Robinson surveyed his sketches with distaste and refused point blank to cut a slit for a watchchain in a tweed suit. When Lancaster eventually withdrew, Mr. Robinson bundled up the designs and gave them to me.

'If we're going to get on,' he remarked, 'we'd better get rid of these.' Then, unable to leave well alone, he shuffled through them resentfully once more. 'What I am wondering,' he observed, 'is whether this gentleman ever *saw* a morning coat.'

'Mr. Lancaster,' I told him, 'has always moved in the best circles.' But Mr. Robinson remained unconvinced.

I would have liked to have seen my old friend's face when I told him I had finally made the team, but it's too late now. There are some men in whose debt I shall always be proud to have been, and one of them is Mr. Robinson.

Why Can't the North be More Like Me?

When I was a touring actor there were some dates which struck terror in my feeble heart — Rochdale, Oldham and Darlington. I don't know whether Darlington's changed much. It didn't seem to have done the other morning, when I glimpsed it from the railway track, but my heart certainly hasn't. Every man has his particular Hell, and for years I have been preserving mine. 'How would you like,' I tell myself, 'to be stuck forever in a faceless street in the north of England, with only good neighbours for company?' I should hate it. The northerners' hearts may beat warmer than southern ones, but the real difference between us is that northerners put up with things which we southerners wouldn't. They put up with ugliness and gloom, their buildings have a positive tradition of grime and neglect. Any shed is good enough to house a railway engine. It doesn't matter that it's made of tin and rusty, and half falling down. Eyesores are acceptable north of Welwyn Garden City.

It's not only what the northerners put up that worries me, it's what they leave lying around. They are so untidy. They go out of their way to make the worst of themselves. I know I am sticking my neck out, but sometimes even elderly tortoises such as I have to stick their necks out, have to plod up the A1 and see what's happening the other side of the fence.

On just such a journey to Durham last winter, I chose the day when the snow fell. I was as surprised as everyone else to gaze out and see beautiful Berkshire covered with the stuff. I started off up the M4 in the general direction of Durham, and after an hour's crawl, reached the airport. I hadn't intended to fly, but I couldn't see much chance of getting there any other way. At Heathrow no one seemed to know what had hit them. 'It's snow,' I told the girls at the enquiry desk. 'Someone will have to sweep it off the runways.' 'No good doing that while it's still snowing,' they told me. 'In any case, there's an industrial dispute.' They cancelled the flight to Newcastle as soon as I bought my ticket, but everyone agreed there was a good chance later, if the aeroplane which was still waiting at Newcastle could be persuaded to take off from there. They rang Newcastle, but nobody seemed to want to commit themselves. 'Better to be safe than sorry,' I told myself, and if the worst came to the worst I mightn't have to go north at all. I should simply telephone Durham University, where I was due to speak, and point out it wasn't my fault. Meanwhile I sat tight. Every now and then the Director General of Civil Aviation, Heathrow, addressed us personally through the loudspeaker. He kept apologising for the weather and for the strike.

About lunchtime we were urged to proceed through Gate No. 1 and after waiting the customary ten minutes for the bus, were stowed inside the plane, fastened our seatbelts and listened to a short speech, by the pilot this time, in which he expressed the customary good wishes and gratitude for our patronage, and announced a delay of an hour before we were airborne. For some reason this produced an absolute storm of protest from the passengers. Why, they demanded, had they been strapped in, and what about dinner? The business babies among us banged their mugs on their plastic trays and screamed for Nanny. Nanny came, and handed out biscuits, and after a certain amount of tantrums, gin and tonics. She gave us clearly to understand that she was not pleased with her charges, and it was not the policy in the nursery to serve drinks on the ground.

When we got to Newcastle at a quarter to three, I fell straight into the cleverly arranged booby-trap. The restaurant, although still full of diners, had closed ten minutes earlier. I was directed to the cafeteria, where I ate two poached eggs and a chocolate biscuit, reading the social diary in a glossy to keep up my spirits and try to pretend I hadn't arrived after all.

The hotel in Durham had a plaque boasting that it had been there when Oliver Cromwell arrived, a fact which interested me a good deal less than the immediate awareness that it was not centrally heated. However, to be fair – and we southerners do try to be fair to the north – there was a very jolly chambermaid, who made me welcome, turned on a small electric fire in the bedroom and enquired whether I would like a hot water bottle. I thanked her for the offer, and was assured that she would put the bottle in the bed last thing before she went off duty. 'When will that be?' I asked, and she indicated round about five-thirty. At six, when I left the hotel, clergymen were streaming out of the dining-room and off to bed, no doubt before their bottles cooled. On the river, men were rowing, snow settling momentarily on their oars.

I was delighted, when I arrived at the Union, to find that the noble lord who had earlier promised to refute me in debate, had chickened out because of the weather. 'I found no difficulty in getting here,' I lied, and subsequently dazzled the students with a display of verbal fireworks – or did I? To be quite honest, I was a bit disappointed by both of us. I am used to being disappointed by myself, but the students were so tremendously un-trendy. One of the girls even brought her knitting. The speeches were mild and unexceptional. Files, sit-ins, demonstrations, student unrest, were not topics about which they wished to comment, or indeed to listen. Six out of six whom I quizzed later, over cider and sandwiches, were determined to vote conservative at the next election.

'I simply don't understand you,' I told them. 'It's so different where I come from.'

'Where do you come from?' they asked.

'The south.'

'That's where we come from too.' Few Durham students, I learnt, are Geordies.

In the morning I found they had rebuilt Durham Railway Station, or were planning to do so. That's the impression one gets from the north, there's always a plan – a plan to rebuild the hotel, widen the main street, knock down the old terrace house. There's a plan to clean up the Town Hall, a plan to build a theatre, modernise the hospital. 'Patience,' the north counsels. 'Rome wasn't built in a day.' Alas, it's not Rome we're considering, but Darlington. Perhaps I'm short of patience. I expected to be able to buy a newspaper on Durham Station. I expected a seat in the waiting-room. I even expected the railway carriage to be heated, and so it was – once we got to Hitchin.

Surgical Spirit

It was one of my 'bilious days'. As a child I used to have them at regular intervals. 'Come here,' Doctor Farr ordered. I rose from the sofa where I habitually spent bilious days, and tottered to the dining-room table still covered with a white cloth. Doctor Farr used it to demonstrate his problem and mine. He drew a small circle in pencil. 'This, boy,' he announced, 'is the size of your tummy, and this,' now he drew a much larger circle, 'is what you persist in trying to cram into it.' I am still incensed when I recall his diagnosis. Even allowing for the fact that medicine, like myself, was in its infancy at that time, he should have realised that such a brutal statement was likely to offend such an artistic, delicate child as myself. It would have served him right if from then on I had patronised the pharmacist, not the doctor.

Fortunately for the medical profession I still prefer to wait in the consulting-room, rather than the chemist's. I don't, of course, relish the dingy grandeur of Harley Street. I am depressed by large central tables and dog-eared copies of *Punch*. Sitting round with other patient patients, I think how much nicer it would be if we were actually invited to a meal in the room in which we now all sit equidistant from the polished mahogany and on our reproduction Hepplewhite seats.

What happens, we wonder, at closing time? Are the magazines tidied away, the gilt horses taken from over the fireplace, to serve as a centrepiece for the richly-laden table? Do the doctors' families feast here together, and if so are they attired in Victorian dress to match the furniture and the drapes, or is it all pretence, and does each doctor, cash-box under arm, creep stealthily down the stairs from his consulting-room, to sit round the table with his colleagues, sharing out the booty? Is there, in the manner of casinos, a *chef de partie*, supervising the counting of the petty cash when the table closes? The truth is, I suppose, that everyone gets out fast and that few doctors care to linger in their own waiting-rooms, where anxiety clings like cigar smoke to the pelmets.

There is a lot to be said for the country surgery which I patronise. For one thing it is always full of babies attending for their jabs, and for another both partners employ a phrase in consultation of which I am particularly fond, and which I always find immensely reassuring. Whether it is pink-eye, incipient tonsillitis, an ingrowing toenail or high blood pressure from which I believe myself to be suffering, they allay my anxiety with the simple statement that there is a lot of it about. I find it so comforting to realise that most of the inhabitants of my village, and all the babies, are currently fighting the same dread symptoms.

Actors who accept film engagements have, like racehorses when they come under the hammer, to submit to a medical examination. There is nothing I dread more. The questionnaire which precedes the examination is fiendish, the weighing and measuring an affront to human dignity. The very idea of having my blood pressure taken sends it sky high, and when the ceremony actually takes place, I am aware only of my pounding heart and the startled expression on the face of the apparatus. By the time the ritual beaker is presented, I am a prey to the final anxiety. Ah, the relief of filling the goblet to the brim!

On the operating table, on the other hand, I am comparatively calm, telling myself that with modern techniques and apparatus there are few places where a man is safer. Should anything stop on the work bench, it is a comparatively easy matter to start it up again. The spanners and blow-torch are to hand, to say nothing of the increasing spares which hospitals carry these days. My own operational experiences have been on the whole enjoyable. To have subjected oneself to the knife is still regarded by family and friends as something of an achievement. Once the operation is over, there is a definite scent of courage mixing pleasantly with that of the surgical spirit. Beside being able to boast of one's own sangfroid, one can and one does pay tribute to the chap who actually did the job. Surgeons, like schoolmasters and portrait painters, are on a shilling to nothing before they start. However atrocious their manners, however inept their execution, they cannot be judged by us ordinary mortals. We are prone to praise our surgeon extravagantly without the slightest knowledge of the form. If he stays too long at our bedside, it is we who are to blame should the conversation flag. If his manner is brisk, even brusque, and his visit fleeting, we remind ourselves of how busy he is saving other lives besides our own.

Once, believing myself to be recovering from major surgery, I pressed my surgeon to drop by one evening for a chat. I hinted that there was so much about his own life that fascinated and enthralled me. I pointed out that, having afforded him the opportunity of exploring my guts, the least he could do would be to let me have similar facilities with regard to his libido. For some reason he took me at my word, at four o'clock one morning. I opened my eyes to find him sitting by my bedside, and realised I was dying. In vain he protested there was nothing amiss, that he had been on his way home from an emergency call and had dropped by on the chance I was awake. 'Alive, you mean,' I told him, and demanded to know the exact nature of the complications which I was convinced had now arisen. Was it my breathing, my heart, my brain which was about to pack up? When he finally took his leave, we had not mentioned his libido. My own, however, has never fully recovered.

Down with Preservationists!

There are few people I find myself more often in profound disagreement with than John Betjeman. He is forever discovering the beauty in the eye of the beholder, extolling the tile-work of a public lavatory in Bootle. I dread Bootle. Most of all I dread being caught short in Bootle. One of Betjeman's recent campaigns concerned the preservation of the Criterion Theatre, another underground building famous for its ceramics. Personally, like the Brighton Belle, I should not mourn its passing. A most uncomfortable train, a most uncomfortable theatre – that is if you hate stairs, as I do. Ave atque vale! Ave atque vale, Betjeman, too!

I know such sentiments may shock the reader. John Betjeman is a good thing. Property developers are a bad thing. It's as simple as that. Property developers seldom write poems. They are not often photographed in floppy hats on Euston Station. When their photographs do appear in the papers, they do not reassure; hard-bitten men, signally lacking in charisma, whereas Betjeman is soft, cuddly, the sort of chap you could warm your feet on. He goes to church, if not to pray, at least to explain to the rest of us how important it is to recognise a Norman tower.

Did we create Betjeman, or did he create us, the silent majority who approve of the olde order, who already have our houses in the green, green belt, who chortle over the plight of those who wish to join us? A caravan site, a housing estate, a council cottage, these are bad things. A forge, an oast house, a castle, a cathedral, these are good things. We are nice people, not quite as nice as Betjeman perhaps, but nice enough. We simply cannot understand why people should want to spoil the field next door by coming to live there. We acknowledge the need for new houses; indeed, if we are fortunate enough to have land on which building restrictions can be lifted, or seem as if they might be lifted one day, we are not averse to selling it for a packet, explaining to our friends that we simply had to see little Edward through Harrow.

But on the whole we resist by all the means at our disposal anyone else coming within a mile of us – to live, that is. 'You are lucky,' my friends tell me, 'what's the secret?' 'Double Green Belt,' I tell them, preening. 'It's as simple as that.' At the bottom of the road, a mile away, the Belt stops abruptly, the houses jostle one another. The proud owners have the worst of both worlds as they sit in their little gardens, gazing at their neighbour's garage. They do it for the children, of course.

Most children hate the country. When I was young, nothing bored me more than walking in the country; walking in towns was a different matter altogether. Happily I trudged the streets, peering into strangers' faces, each one a new delight, a new surprise. I gazed into a shop window as if into Aladdin's Cave, and when at weekends I was banished to Kent, surely the dullest of all counties, I fretted with boredom, glowered at the chickens with displeasure, hated the cows. What madness pervades Betjeman, that he can be content to stare at the steeple and browse among thatched cottages in some stagnant backwater of England? What excites me is not land, but living. I would that every man was allowed to live where he liked and how he liked, and if I had it in my power I would grant Betjeman the gift of living when he likes, and banish him to the Victorian era which he professes to admire. For the rest of us, I would decree that a man may build as he chooses, and where he chooses, a shack, a bungalow, a castle, a cathedral if he has the money, and is so inclined. I would give him squatters' rights in all the broad acres. He could even come and build in my wood, if he chose. I do not believe that human beings spoil the land by living on it, quite the reverse. If a man wants to live on his own, let him. If he wants to live in a cluster, let him. If he wants to live like a pig, let him. But most men do not want to live like pigs. They are as house-proud as badgers, forever striving to improve their set. Like badgers too, their time is brief, there is no proof it comes again.

There is nothing more boring than the elegant formality of ordered living, nothing more heartening than the chaos of people and children, even dogs. Let us give back to the English the belief that their home is their castle, and that they are entitled to build it where and as they please. It may not always look like a castle; it will never please Betjeman. Buildings, like men, crumble to dust, and when the last of us have slipped away and the children have stopped playing, and no one is untidy any more, and the silence is total, then and only then let us give the country back to the woodpigeons and the butterflies and to old, old, old, old Mr. Betjeman himself.

Travelling in Style

Thank goodness I am not a snob about travel. I go first class whenever possible, even when on rare occasions I am actually paying for
myself, because I prefer it. It is not that one meets a better class of
person in the first class (one does, but that is beside the point), but
that quite often, if one is lucky, one doesn't meet anyone at all. The
first class is full of men and women struggling to stay there, they do
not engage in idle chat or stare out of the window; they are far too
busy filling up personal time sheets, assessing, as far as they are able,
the success or failure of their recent meeting with His Excellency, the
Faquir of Swat. For most of the time, especially when flying, their
heads are in the clouds. When the canapés come round, and the
champagne, they reach out instinctively, their eyes still focused on
the company report on their laps, assessing the correct location of
the last Angel on Horseback. Then, too, they have the grace to get
off where no one else wants to, leaving me in mid-Gulf as sole
occupant of the upstairs bar, while I continue my journey to Beirut.

I can never understand why my fellow travellers should boast of
the petty economy of travelling tourist. Apart from the humiliation
of having to step on and off the plane at the wrong end and wearing
those tell-tale green boarding cards in their breast pocket, there is
the knowledge that, except possibly for the ritual distribution of
orange juice, one's drinks have to be paid for on the spot. The tourist
passenger, too, has the absurd notion that once the flight is completed
and he is back on the ground, we all, in some mysterious way,
become equal once more, yet very often the tourist person doesn't
even arrive at the same time as we first class chaps—by which I don't
mean, of course, that the tail falls off in flight (nothing so drastic is
needed to separate the classes, thank goodness, and I for one should
never approve of such Draconian methods); no, the tourist passenger

very often misses the first bus and joins the queues a respectable distance behind us.

A first class citizen is still a first class citizen when he collects his luggage. I don't say it comes off the plane any too soon (it ought to but it doesn't), but those matching suitcases, even the occasional fitted dressing case with the dust cover, do something to brighten up their drab plastic companions and are not snatched off before they reach us by some idiot who mistakes them for his own imitation leather hold-all. It is not that I dislike tourist passengers (if it wasn't for the occasional glimpses of them, we others might forget how fortunate our lot is), but I can't help feeling an odd surge of pity when I see a fellow creature forced to economise so blatantly. However confident, even defiant their bearing, however boldly they sport their casual clothing, I know that each and every one is acutely conscious of his or her predicament and embarrassed to meet my gaze. It is only with an effort that I can resist raising my celebrated eyebrows as I pose the silent question: 'You ... of all people ... tourist?' I remember on one awful occasion I spied David Frost clutching a badge of verdant shame. 'Has it really come to this?' I asked myself. How to avoid a confrontation which must only prove embarrassing to us both? I loitered behind the check point until I judged David would be at least in the transit lounge. Imagine my relief when I discovered that there was no first class accommodation whatever on the plane. Thank God, I told myself, and was able to speak to him later as if nothing had happened.

Normally I avoid the one-class flight as one avoids the one-class liner. Indeed, these days, because of the increase of this form of seafaring, I seldom put to sea at all. Even having engaged a state-room before the war, crossing the Atlantic was not all easy sailing. Once aboard one had to be quick to interview the head waiter and reserve a table in the verandah grill in case one was not expected to sit with the captain; sometimes even if one was.

My bearing aboard was that of a laird returning on August Twelfth to his moor to commence the ritual grouse slaughter. An easy familiarity on my side exactly matched with the affectionate deference of the head ghillie or steward. 'Here we are again, Crosby, and I know you're going to look after me,' meant exactly that. On board ship, to attend boat drill the first morning was as important as occupying my family pew in the manse back home, but to place a suitcase outside the cabin door as instructed on the evening before the ship docked was only slightly more of a *faux pas* than wearing a dinner jacket on the first night out.

As always when travelling, one must know the ropes, and if one does not personally know the cabin staff it is better to pretend one does. A cheery 'Good evening, Bridges,' on boarding the plane does much to reassure the head steward, even if his name happens to be Alfred, and ensures an invitation to visit the flight deck later. I always graciously accept and make a point at least once during the flight of paying a visit to the crew's quarters, where I feel my interest in their welfare and turn-out is appreciated. I insist on informality on these brief inspections, urging the captain to remain seated and at the controls. Usually I ask him about his background—where he comes from and whither he is bound (quite often his own destination differs from my own). I try and find something on which to compliment the second officer, praising perhaps his smart appearance or his understanding of the controls.

A word to the navigator—usually a joke about his map-reading—then I leave them to get on with it. Protracted conversation is not easy in such comparatively confined quarters, and I feel flying these days is a complicated operation demanding their undivided attention at all times. For this reason I am never entirely happy when the captain leaves his bridge, as sometimes happens, and strolls among the first class passengers—even, I regret to say, the tourist portion—seeking information on whether everyone is or is not enjoying the flight. One doesn't expect an engine driver suddenly to appear in the restaurant car, so why should we tolerate the pilot in the cocktail lounge? In the air as well as on the track there are such things as signals, surely, to be disregarded at our peril?

I have a friend whose attitude to travel differs completely from my own, and who frequently is forced to pay his own fare. On such occasions he never buys his ticket across a counter but invariably becomes a life member of The Hornsey and District Piano Tuners' Club, or some similar organisation. Having served an apprenticeship for several months during which, as far as I know, he never volunteers to tune a single instrument, he is then entitled to deduct a substantial portion of his fare and travel by charter, as the saying goes. I asked him once whether he did not find the proximity of so many piano tuners wearisome on the flight, as he is even less musically inclined than I, but he told me, much to my surprise, that as far as he was aware none of his fellow chartists were employed in the trade but, like him, availed themselves of the perks.

Personally, if ever I am forced to economise over travel and join a group, before buying the ticket I shall choose an organisation more suited to my needs and station. The Land Owners' Association or Stately Homeowners Inc., or better still, inaugurate my own group. Would all those who wish to join it kindly send me their cheque for one hundred pounds and some hint concerning their lineage?

Away From It All

I have a friend who spends a fair amount of his life on junkets. He is a travel correspondent – the cinnamon on the holiday custard. I thought it might be worth asking him where he spends his own holiday. 'Reading,' he told me. Quite a large town, in Berkshire, but I had never heard of anyone going there for a spree. He chooses it for that very reason. He does not want to be too comfortable and in Reading, apparently, there are any number of small, private hotels which are really mean – mean with the butter, mean with the bathwater, mean with just about everything. The bedrooms still have linoleum on the floor and a light which switches out by the door. No soap, either. It is such little things which count with him.

It is always fatal to ask an expert. Me, I go for the swinging holiday. I have always yearned for the sort of Mediterranean clubland where they wear bead necklaces and shorten them every time they need a drink or a partner – missionary stuff in reverse. I used to like the idea of dug-out canoes and small desert islands with tree-climbing crabs – until I made a film in Tahiti. I've tried boating in the Aegean, submerging in the Bosporus. I have dunked myself cautiously in the Pacific, paddled in the Indian Ocean. And then come happily home to Folkestone where it all started. I can still remember digging down furiously to reach Australia which some fool nurse had explained was underfoot.

In those days I wore striped cotton bathing costumes and shining white sailor suits with a genuine whistle on Sundays, when we didn't go down on the beach until after church parade. I wore the same sort of linen hat that I wear now, because I have a dream that one day some elderly crone in a Bath chair will pass me, a large and portly figure sandcastling for the grandchildren, and observe to her companion that I am the same dear little chap who used to dig there when she was a girl and I haven't changed a bit.

For most holiday wear, however, I shop nowadays at special boutiques which cater for the fuller figure and have names like 'Big and Beautiful' or 'Giant Strides' or 'High and Mighty'. I see people looking at me out of the corner of their eye when I'm in a bathing suit and saying to themselves, 'So that's what happens if you let yourself go.'

Myself, I cannot understand the craze for the body beautiful and the deep tan. *I* look out of the corner of *my* eye and notice the hiatuses – the last little bit of the canvas which stays obstinately white and spoils the picture. It's not that I'm jealous, but I can't help wondering how long it has all taken. And I resent the unhooked brassière, the face in the sand, the essential inanimation of steak on a charcoal broiler. I find this basting such a bore: so much cold cream squeezed out of tubes and spread endlessly over the torso and then the awful problem of the back and sides. Where to stop? Occasionally I employ a Flit spray-gun and little bubbles of oil burst and trickle down my chest.

On a beach, I am happier to be off and into the sea. The fat float easily. And I have found that each time I come out I am obliged to start again with the suntan treatments. I lose heart, and finish up in my bathing wrap. With burnt insteps. This is not to say that I do not enjoy holidays, I thoroughly enjoy shopping for sandals and buying the funny-tummy preparations. I appreciate the feel of the air-tickets in my wallet. Indeed, I count the days to freedom as I lie around at home with my eyes shut, telling myself that in a week's time I will be doing just that on the Lido. And sure enough, when I get to the Lido, I am happy to be Away From It All.

Though not entirely, of course. My feelings are perhaps best summed up by another friend, a bookmaker, whom I once asked why he chose Venice every year. 'I like it,' said the fellow. 'I don't say it's perfect: for one thing, you can't get the greyhound track results unless you ring up home – but nowhere has everything, has it?' How true.

The Super Seven

When I have to die, I should like to do so in the foyer of the best hotel in the world. For one thing I feel most confident in hotel foyers, and for another, disposing of my corpse would be a final test for the Hall Porter. I have always been a snob about hotels — about people too, I suppose, but that need not concern us. For me the best hotel in whatever place I happen to be, is a must. Ensconced in any other establishment, I tend to sulk. Once, on the steamer to Capri, I was examining the luggage tags of one of the most beautiful girls I have ever seen, when I discovered to my dismay that she was bound for a different hotel from the one I had selected. I decided there and then to adjust my itinerary, to stay where she stayed. Yet it was not the child's beauty that prompted my action, but the obvious wealth of her companion. He was, I decided, an Indian princeling, and as such, could be relied upon. When we landed, I followed hard on their heels, up the mountain to Annacapri and through the revolving doors of their Shangri-La, only to be dismissed by an obdurate reception clerk. Forced to return to the hotel of my original choice, I spent my holiday in jealous despair.

Each new hotel has for me the excitement of an untried mistress. I am impatient with the preliminaries, eager to register, and afterwards to rid myself of the attentions of the bell-hop who has preceded me with my key along the corridor, and unlocked my room. I watch him demonstrating the central heating, the public address system, the television remote controls, and long for the moment when he will withdraw and leave me in possession. I know from experience it will be a considerable time before my luggage arrives, and meanwhile my room and I will be getting to know one another. As soon as the bell-hop collects his fee and withdraws, I hurry into the bathroom to inspect the plumbing, to admire the tumblers wrapped in cellophane and the lavatory pan decorated as if for a marriage. Is there a bidet?

How large are the soap tablets? How many towels? Flannels? Gift samples? I test the heat of the towel rail, the noise of the toilet flush, make sure I understand how the taps function. These grow more complicated with every year. I am particularly fond of the built-in thermometer, although I can never remember the exact temperature at which I prefer to bathe.

I hurry back into the bedroom itself to inspect the thickness of the drapes, the pile of the carpet. I adjust the lights, toy with the television, take in the view. This is the moment of truth, and I must ask myself whether this is really the best bedroom I can expect — for the price. Am I on the right side, at the right height? Do I want to look out over the swimming pool, or the garage? Now is the time for action, if I decide to change. I must pick up the phone, demand to be connected to the desk clerk, get into the poker game, and be prepared if necessary to have him call my bluff.

My decision as to whether to accept the original accommodation proffered, or to try and improve on my hand, depends largely on the ambiance I have already encountered at the reception desk. I can usually tell whether I am being given the bum's rush. One day I will accept a small back room over the dustbins, on another even a penthouse suite is inadequate. Having decided to stay put, I start to explore the closets, paying particular attention to the way the doors are hung and the drawers slide. I assess the writing paper, read the breakfast menu, and the other brochures provided. I can never have too much of any of these. I like to know that I can write letters on all kinds of differently-shaped paper, and that there is a wide choice of breakfast cereals, bars and restaurants. I am always ready to sample Frosted Grape Nuts, to plan an evening in their Sapphire Room or the House of Genji, to have a cocktail in the Eagle's Nest or the Imperial Viking, a nightcap in Nero's Nook. On the whole I avoid coffee shops and grill rooms, believing that if a man takes the trouble to find a name, however bizarre, he may equally have taken the trouble to find a chef.

When eventually my luggage arrives, I am already unpacked. The actual disposing of my belongings becomes something of an anticlimax. I am conscious of the inadequacy of my wardrobe, beset with a longing for a hundred handkerchiefs, a thousand ties, a multitude of socks to fill every drawer, an infinity of suits to exhaust the coathangers.

I have always believed in myself as a world jurist where hotels are concerned. I still hope that even now in the afternoon, the early afternoon, of my life, I may be invited to become one. How pleasant it would be to travel the world in the company of a few others like myself, sampling the delights and extravagances provided by great hoteliers, and to award the annual ROBERTS. There would have to be several, naturally. For the hotel which had the best cellar, the hotel with the best plumbing, the one with the best hall porter. The best hotel built in the last year. The hotel with the most beautiful setting, or simply the most beautiful hotel. If actresses are entitled to Oscars, why not hotels? The latter are more exciting, more unpredictable, and with notable exceptions, better behaved. Moreover hotels, except those in the very top class have, like film stars, to show off. I am never intimidated by ostentation; being in the business myself, I understand it.

Once, staying in a hotel in Fez, where the uniforms of the staff were the most magnificent I have ever encountered, I approached a lackey even more gorgeously attired than the bell-boys, whom I imagined to be the hall porter, with some trivial request about procuring a fleet of camels for the afternoon.

'I think you are making a mistake,' remarked my accosted, 'I have the honour to be the personal aide de camp to His Majesty the King of Libya.' I shook him warmly by the hand, but did not apologise.

In selecting what are in my opinion the seven great hotels of the world I am tempted to include this beautiful Moroccan Caravanserai, but things I am told have changed in Morocco since I was there; besides, a simultaneous visit of myself and the King of Libya may have ensured an unnatural and temporary standard of excellence. An even more potent reason for not including it in my list is that I have entirely forgotten its name.

I am not in favour of the Award Committee, when it is formed, arriving anywhere incognito. Let us see the *best* you can do — not the worst, should be our admonition. Personally I am careful, when arriving at any hotel where I suspect I may — initially at least — be unrecognised, to employ a gamesmanship ploy of which I and not Stephen Potter am the inventor. 'I think,' I remark casually, leaning across the reception desk and addressing the clerk, 'you may be expecting me. My secretary has made the reservation: ROBERT MORLEY.' I speak the last two words slowly and loudly. The impression I wish to give is that I am far too modest to believe that the name will mean anything to him; and if as sometimes happens the idiot hasn't in fact heard of me he will begin to check his list.

'Nothing here,' he will not unnaturally remark when he has done so.

I take care to appear thunderstruck. 'Are you quite certain? My secretary has been with me a number of years and this is the first time anything like this has happened.'

After this I play it by ear; if, as sometimes, there is plenty of accommodation available I like to believe that I will be offered something a little better than would have been the case if I had not established that I had a secretary.

When my darling mother-in-law Gladys Cooper was alive, we were once in Las Vegas together; I employed my gambit and had the clerk on the ropes and about to produce the accommodation. Suddenly Gladys spoke. 'You know perfectly well, Robert, you haven't reserved anything. You are only confusing the poor young man, and in any case I don't want to stay here. I am sure we shall be much happier in that nice motel next door.'

That would have been the end of that, except that the motel was full and we were obliged to crawl back ten minutes later.

'Another time perhaps you'll leave it to me,' I told her, surveying the inadequate accommodation with which I had eventually been provided.

'Another time,' replied Gladys, 'I will have *my* secretary handle the reservations. We stand a better chance with her; at least she exists!'

The reason why I am so well qualified to serve on the ROBERT Committee is that I have a nose for good restaurants. Put me down anywhere in a strange city and like a truffle hound straining at the leash, I will lead my party to the most delectable morsels. Where hotels are concerned, my perception is equally uncanny. Half a dozen steps across the threshold and I can tell whether a hotel is fully adjusted. If not, then I prefer to put my polo sticks back in the boot of the Rolls Royce and drive on. However imposing the façade, splendid the foyer, extravagant the furnishing, gorgeously costumed the bell-boys, luxurious the beds, unless a hotel is 'adjusted' neither you nor I are going to be happy there. In a restaurant one can return the boeuf Stroganoff to the chef with a courteous request that he should try again, and if he is prepared to do so, continue to toy with the caviare. The meal can still be salvaged. But there is nothing to be done with a hotel that is ill-adjusted, except pack and leave. It won't be difficult for you to do so early on your first morning, because the chambermaid will already have made an entrance, or at least knocked loudly on the door demanding to know if you rang. She does this to ensure that you will not oversleep and fail to give her a chance to do your room when it suits her to do so.

In all ill-adjusted hotel you will not be able to enjoy breakfast in bed. If you persevere with the telephone you will eventually be able to contact room service; but having done so you will be well advised to allow for the inevitable time lag and order luncheon. Last time I stayed at an hotel in New York I was amazed to find the breakfast trolley being trundled to my bedside a bare twenty minutes after I had put down the phone. 'This can't possibly be my breakfast,' I told the waiter. 'I ordered it under an hour ago.' The waiter shrugged his shoulders sympathetically and started to wheel the individually-gathered, sun-drenched blueberries with pasteurised double cream and thin (as you like them) hot cakes out of the door and back along the corridor. After a struggle I regained possession. 'Finders Keepers,' I told him.

The best room service in the world is enjoyed by guests of the Westminster Hotel, Paris Plage. Here one can reach out and press the bell push (suitably decorated with a picture of a waiter) and within two minutes the breakfast tray is resting lightly on one's stomach. The Westminster is, as I have noted, a supreme example of efficiency in this respect, but all over Europe, unlike the U.S.A., there are hotels which expect their guests to order breakfast around nine o'clock and are prepared to serve it within five minutes or so of their having done so. The secret is to have a kitchen on each floor; it is a secret which, except in rare instances, the Americans have not yet discovered; and for this reason, among others, it is not possible in my list of great hotels to include a single one in the United States. The absence of a bell push on the bedside table indicates that a hotel, despite its other pretensions, is understaffed.

For my money, and I admit a good deal of it is required whenever I am a guest there, the greatest hotel in the world is the Ritz in Paris. It is really two hotels, one situated in the Place Vendôme and the other in the Rue Cambon. I have never quite understood the geography of this beautiful building. To walk from the Place Vendôme to the Rue Cambon takes me at least five minutes and I have to cross several streets in order to do so, and yet if I make the same journey through the Ritz itself, along the elegant arcade with its show cases glittering with diamonds and broderie anglaise, I am there in half the time. A simple explanation may occur to the reader; one way one goes round, the other direct; but what happened to the streets? They certainly don't run through the Ritz itself, indeed in the centre of the hotel there are only a number of mysterious secret gardens, gravel-pathed and silent. I haven't the least idea how many bedrooms there are in the Ritz, only that in proportion to its size there are very few. It is the extravagance of the building which attracts me; I do not care for hotels which conserve space. I do not approve of batteries for hens or humans.

I am essentially a Rue Cambon man myself, although I often enter the hotel from the Place Vendôme, and admire the vast foyer, peopled at tea-time by archduchesses, elaborately bewigged and ex-monarchs waiting with well-bred boredom for their cucumber sandwiches. In the evening a small string orchestra plays in the restaurant, and an indescribable and reassuring melancholy hangs in the air. The diners have for the most part eaten all the caviare they are ever likely to actively enjoy on this earth, but the spoon still travels to the mouth loaded with the little black grains, and returns stained with carmine to the plate.

In the Espadron, which is the restaurant on my side of the hotel, the pace is altogether brisker. Caviare is eaten, but on toast. There is no vast entrance hall, and a comparatively narrow passage leads from the Rue Cambon up a short flight of steps to the reception desk; immediately opposite the hall porter's. Further on, where the passage ends and the glass doors of the Espadron open invitingly, is a small foyer usually cluttered with tables overflowing from the restaurant, and with French windows opening on to one of the gardens, where on summer evenings it is also possible to dine.

There is no better food, no more perfect setting for a meal in Paris except perhaps the Grand Vefour in the Palais Royal, with its ancient window engraved with an advertisement for Cherry Cobblers and its justly famous sommelier who refuses all invitations to try his hand at making one. You cannot, for that matter, get cherry cobblers in the Ritz, but you can get practically anything else and see practically everyone except le Président himself.

But it is with its bedrooms that the Ritz really scores. The timeless elegance of the furnishings, the gilt and the glitter, the huge wardrobes, the small sofas, the brass bedsteads – and the golden clocks, which I can never look at without a twinge of conscience; for once, long ago, I stopped all the clocks in the Ritz by yanking out a wire from one over my daughter's bed when she complained the tick was too loud and kept her awake. 'I'll soon stop that,' I told her, and I did. The trouble was that next morning no one would believe I was the culprit. In vain I telephoned the hall porter to confess my guilt.

'Impossible, Monsieur, you are not to blame,' he assured me. 'We are searching for the fault; it is the same in all the rooms; be patient.'

'At least,' I begged him, 'send someone up to my suite to investigate.'

'Useless, cher Monsieur,' he protested, 'the fault is with the electricity supply. Our engineers are in conference with the Minister.'

In the end I climbed on a chair and poked the wire back into its socket. At once my clock, like all the others in the Ritz that morning, started again. But, for me, the Ritz is the best hotel in the world not because of its electric clocks, or even despite them, but simply because it is the most comfortable to stay in. A guest in the Ritz is a guest of the Ritz, and no member of the staff ever forgets this simple fact for a single moment.

If you walk out of the Ritz into the Place Vendôme and turn left into the Rue de Rivoli you will come in a moment to a tea shop. Last summer, seated inside, I found an old friend and joined her for an éclair. It is sad how éclairs have almost entirely vanished from the tea table; in my youth they were obligatory, like conversation and visiting cards. In any case, my friend, a lady of enormous wealth, was lamenting the passing of the tea-cake.

'It is something I miss,' she remarked, 'like Baden Baden.'

'But surely,' I urged, 'Baden Baden remains.'

'Not for me,' she replied, 'and even if you were right, I don't suppose I should care for it nowadays. I used to go there when I was a little girl and what I remember most about Baden Baden were the Grand Dukes and their enormous trunks. The porters at Baden Baden railway station were the strongest porters in the world; they had to be. Nowadays,' my friend continued, 'one seldom sees a trunk as large as those, and when one does one has to be on one's guard. Last year I saw one at the Ritz, of all places. It was late at night and they were wheeling it along the passage. I happened to open my bedroom door and there it was. Behind walked the owner. I am certain he wasn't a Grand Duke. He looked,' she stabbed the air thoughtfully with her fork, 'as if he might have been a travelling salesman. One couldn't be sure, naturally. As you know, Robert dear, I am not a snob, moreover I am a very simple woman. I do not like cluttering up my life. I have entirely ceased to buy diamonds. I am no longer interested in property. I have a suite of rooms at the Ritz, another in the Hotel de Paris at Monte Carlo and a small house in London. With these, unlike most women I know, I am content, but if I am right about that traveller — and I hope very much I am not right — why then, I may have to consider reopening my apartment in Versailles, at any rate during the summer months; the danger, I imagine, would hardly arise in the winter; in any case at that time of the year I prefer Monte Carlo.'

'So do I,' I told her, and indeed I do. Summer and winter, come to that. I am drawn to Monte Carlo like a pilgrim to Mecca, or an art lover to Florence, because Monte Carlo still represents for me the centre of gambling in the world. In the centre of a whirlwind, although I have never proved this theory personally, there is said to be a vacuum. I *can* prove, however, that at the heart of Monte Carlo, in the great entrance hall of the Hotel de Paris, nothing stirs. You might argue that the real heart of Monte Carlo must be the casino, but the hotel is linked with it by a tunnel, so that it all really counts as one building. Here in the entrance hall, arranged possibly by some fabulous interior decorator, sit sometimes on sofas, sometimes on upright chairs, the Ladies and Gentlemen in Waiting. In enormous hats and wearing great quantities of jewellery and eye shadow, or blue-blazered and occasionally toupéed, they sit in the hotel as to the manner born. Elegant, resourceful, infinitely patient, they neither fidget nor fuss. Their purpose is to reassure the ordinary traveller that he too has arrived. Every now and then one of them will rise and make his or her way to the elevator, or out on to the terrace. It is not for us to enquire where they are going. They are going off duty, and that must suffice us.

The Hotel de Paris has more to offer even than its clientèle. It moves with the times and now has a superb roof restaurant and an indoor swimming pool. It also has the prettiest breakfast china in Europe and the unique advantage that people never stay here on business, or because they want to look at churches or trudge round picture galleries. They come some of them to gamble, all of them to put their feet up and to enjoy themselves. There are not nearly enough places where one can simply put one's feet up in Europe, but just on the edge of it, just before you cross the Bosphorous and find yourself in Asia, there stands at a small Turkish village called Yesilkov, twenty miles from Istanbul, on the sea of Marmora, my third great hotel, The Cinar.

There is something very attractive about the Sea of Marmora. I would not care to stay on the Bosphorous, which is surprisingly narrow, so that the Russian tankers finding their way up the channel occasionally lodge fast in some unfortunate Turk's front parlour. No such danger presents itself to guests of The Cinar, which passed all the tests to which I subjected it, and one that had not occurred to me — an earthquake. I am not fond of earthquakes, and this one caught me, as is their custom, unawares and about to step into a bath. I draped myself in a towel and hurried into the passage. A few doors opened and one or two guests made for the elevators, and others returned to their rooms as the tremors subsided. I hesitated, uncertain which course to pursue, and then happened to glance out of a window.

What I saw decided me to hurry down the staircase and rush pell mell into the garden, where I joined the dozen or so chefs whom I had spied from the corridor. Instinctively I felt these were the men to follow. They seemed content to stand around for a time chatting, and so was I. We were presently joined by an American professor who was, I had learned previously, in Turkey to arrange a program for a computer. It appeared that the American Government had given the Turkish Government a computer, for which naturally the latter were unable to find a use and to help them in their dilemma the Americans had now added a professor, whose task was to find a job worthy of the computer's prowess.

'I am thinking,' he told me, 'of putting it to work analysing the drinking water from various provinces. I don't know about the local authorities, but I am pretty sure the computer will get quite a shock.'

On the occasion of the earthquake I was delighted to see him. 'Has the danger passed?' I enquired. 'Is it safe for me to return and have my bath?' He consulted his watch and advised us all to wait another four minutes. We should either have another almost immediately, he insisted, or we shouldn't. I waited patiently while he continued to observe the minute hand. Eventually he looked up. 'Bath time,' he said reassuringly, and I and the chefs returned to our tasks.

While still in this part of the world, a word perhaps about the Hilton Hotel in Athens. Although not one for my list, it stands head and shoulders above all the other Hilton hotels at which I have stayed, including the London Hilton — which stands head and shoulders above Buckingham Palace. It would be foolish to belittle Mr. Hilton, or to deny that in many cities, such as Athens, he has imposed new standards of comfort and cleanliness not only on the natives but also on some of his guests. He reassures the American traveller — although not, oddly enough, the British. But then does *anything* reassure us? For myself it is the Hilton elevators which alarm. A slow mover, I am frequently attacked by the doors.

At the inaugural party to launch the London Hilton, I was retained to introduce the cabaret, which was performed between the courses and intended to emphasise the international flavour of the feast. Japanese jugglers following the birds' nest soup, a French singer the *poulet,* and so on. The waiter assigned to our table took a look round the affluent and distinguished guests, who included Mr. Paul Getty and Mr. Hilton himself. 'This looks,' he told us, 'as if it might turn out a funny evening. Ladies, will you please put your handbags in the centre of the table where we can all keep our eyes on them.' The American waiter is, of course, an expert on cutting the proceedings down to size. How often he demolishes the elegant, sophisticated atmosphere so carefully built up by host and proprietor by that honest shout of 'Who gets the consommé?' But his English cousin is seldom far behind. The best waiters, like the best lovers, are Latins. What the Englishman, the American, and for that matter the Australian, lack in technique both in bedroom and banqueting hall, they attempt unsuccessfully to cover up with bonhomie. Alas, there is more to laying a table or a lady than high spirits.

Outside of London, the traveller who stays in a British owned and operated hotel must not expect to be pampered. He will find meals are served when it suits the Hotel Catering Act to do so. Bedrooms are kept at a temperature which will encourage the client to spend money on gas or electric fires to stop shivering. Bathrooms are scarce, bleak and remote. What I find most depressing about British hotels is the display of literature in their public rooms. A British hotelier would rather shoot himself than buy a paper or a book for his guests to read. Such magazines as one finds in the smoking-room of The Crown, The Feathers or The George must not only be at least a year old and bereft of cover, but must also have been issued free, and deal with such subjects as canoeing or topiary. Anything, indeed, unlikely to excite or stimulate even the passing interest of an itinerant biscuit salesman.

The more modern the hotel in Britain the smaller the bedroom, the longer the corridor. The emphasis is on discipline. You are not, for instance, expected to upset your morning coffee. Having done so in Manchester one morning lately, I phoned for assistance. I was prepared for the staff to remove the sheets, but not the mattress. There was nothing for it but to get up — never a wise thing to do in Manchester until one is actually required at the theatre. I was stepping into the bath when the phone rang. Big Brother had been informed. 'We understand,' a voice told me, 'that you have soiled your bed. There will be an additional charge on your bill.' How different from the hotel in New Orleans, where after a stay of a fortnight there wasn't a bill at all. 'We like actors,' they told me, and charged only for telephone calls. Were it not that any hotel quite so recklessly conducted must have long since gone out of business, I would proudly include it in my list.

On the whole the British find little pleasure in staying in their own hotels, possibly because there is very little pleasure in doing so, with the exception of the top ten or so in London itself, and of course Claridges. No praise can ever be too high for this superb annexe to Buckingham Palace. It is the refuge of monarchs and presidents, protecting them while they reign and caring for them long after they have abdicated or been deposed. Uneasy lies the head which wears a crown, except on a Claridge's pillow slip. The management also entertain film producers, landed gentry, ambassadors, débutantes, actors intoxicated by their press cuttings and sober citizens. Immensely comfortable, superbly intimate, faultlessly maintained, more of a club than a hotel, and more of a home than either. The shining exception which proves the rule that the British don't understand the hotel business. Most surprising of all, there are few foreigners on its staff.

Oddly enough there was a British waiter on the staff of my fifth great hotel, the Imperial, Vienna, when I stayed there shortly after it had reopened. Vienna is a city of make-believe. Where else would you find the horn of a unicorn on display next to a golden rose? It is a city where horses prance under the chandeliers in the riding school and where the Russians, taking a hint from their hosts, stabled their own cavalry in the ballroom of the Imperial Hotel and roasted an ox on its marble staircase. But when they left, their hosts, no whit abashed by such vandalism, managed to get everything back in place along with the gilt mirrors and the chandeliers, and opened for business within a year.

Very comfortable it was when I was there making a film with Yul Brynner and Deborah Kerr, and first fell in love with Anne Jackson. Yul's part in the picture demanded he should be constantly chewing on a wine glass, but the rest of us sat around happily in the hotel dining room, munching Rhine salmon and wild strawberries, and occasionally venturing forth to the location, accompanied by a vast quantity of cardboard on which cotton wool had been affixed and which had to be scattered over the countryside to represent the snows of yesteryear in which we had optimistically commenced the shooting, and which had long since melted away.

Presently I was joined by my wife and children who in those days were fascinated by the enormous gas balloons sold in the Prater just beside the Great Wheel immortalised in *The Third Man*. These they would bear home in triumph and then, forgetful as ever, release, whereupon the balloons would sail upwards and bump along the ceiling. As long as the children stayed with me it seemed as if in our sitting-room there was always a porter perched on a stepladder.

'You really mustn't bother him again,' I would tell my son.

'But he likes it, Pa, he really does,' would be the reply. Not of course the only reason for including the Imperial, but certainly one of them.

A hotel is only as good as its staff, and my sixth among the giants, although it possesses an exceptional one, will persist in the supreme folly of dressing it up as if for a children's fancy dress party. Let not the traveller be dismayed, therefore, when on arrival, the door of his car is opened by a gentleman sweltering in the guise of a Beefeater, or when his luggage is unloaded by another dressed as if for the paddy fields. He is not in the Tower of London or Vietnam, he is not even in Disneyland, he has merely arrived at the Century Plaza in Beverly Hills, California. There are various theories about the costumes. The hotel is built on part of what used to be the Twentieth Century Lot and some think the film company threw in the wardrobe along with the land. Others see a sinister attempt to lull the nation into a false sense of security so that when the threatened Chinese invasion finally takes place, the American citizens will be caught unawares. 'Don't worry,' they will be telling each other, 'they are merely bell-hops from the Century Plaza.'

Once you have winced over the threshold, however, you will be very comfortable indeed in this hotel. It has the most efficient elevators, the best room service and the most comfortable beds of any hotel in America. It is beautifully quiet and, except for the dressing up already noted, quietly beautiful.

Not as beautiful, of course, as my last great hotel, the Gritti Palace of Venice, but then the latter has the manifestly unfair advantage of the Grand Canal. No other hotel in the world can compete with such a setting, and one can pay no higher tribute to the Gritti than to note that it deserves to be exactly where it is. It has the incomparable advantage of not having been built as a hotel. It was originally intended to be, and indeed still is, a Palace. The corridors meander, the bathrooms are never quite where you expect, the furniture not dreamt up by an interior decorator, but collected piece by piece over the years, until at last the room is complete and fit for a guest. Last time I stayed, I sent a bedside lamp crashing onto the marble floor. 'If I can afford to pay for it, I will,' I told the desk. They dismissed the suggestion with a chuckle. Venice is a long way from Manchester.

There are other hotels I have stayed in and been comfortable and content: the Mandarin in Hong Kong, the Tokyo Hilton, the Pierre Marqueez in Acapulco, the Black Buck in Wiesbaden, and, surprisingly, the Europa in Leningrad, but the seven I have written of are the tops. They have a reputation for perfection which over the years they have cherished and striven successfully to maintain. Most of us go through life haunted by a few anonymous, pleasurable scents. A flower sniffed in childhood, a special kind of wood fire, hops drying, a horse being shod, furniture polish, vanilla, honeysuckle, straight bourbon. Now and again, perhaps in a strange house, or walking in the country, or passing along some city street, there comes borne over the air towards us a remembered fragrance, which delights. Thus, when I first cross the lobby of a new hotel I will pause for a moment with my nostrils hopefully flared. What is the scent for which I am patiently sniffing the air? It is the smell of confidence which comes from perfection.

The Trouble with Holidays

There was a fellow who lived in our village during the recent hostilities who kept his family on exceptionally short commons, even for wartime. Such economy was not achieved without a good deal of ingenuity on his part and his behaviour on the night the fish and chip van called did not go without notice among fellow parishioners. It was his custom to purchase a portion of newspaper-wrapped goodies and devour them up a side alley, after which he would return to his loved ones with the information that the quality of the cod was such that he advised a supper of bread and cheese for all concerned. Eventually someone thought of a flashlight torch and spotted him one evening in full gorge, whereupon the game was up for ever and his family were happily back to the rock salmon.

I instance this story because in my time I have, as a family man, been guilty of similar heinous conduct. Indeed, only this year we planned a summer holiday on the Riviera and I dispatched myself come Easter on a scouting mission, staying at the Negresco, in Nice, and spending a small fortune on self-indulgence. I returned after a week to report that the Reserve at Beaulieu was not what it was and the new casino at Monte Carlo was run Vegas-style with double zeros and was not to be recommended. 'France,' I informed my wife, 'is out of the question this time, prices have gone through the roof.' 'The children and I weren't actually planning on haut luxe,' she told me, 'and in any case we don't play roulette. However, no doubt we shall be happy as usual at Weston-super-Mare.'

The main problem of a holiday is how to unwind gracefully while doing absolutely nothing at all but waiting for the sun to shine, the sea to warm up and some bird to alight on the terrace who is anxious for a crumb left over from the breakfast toast (don't get me wrong, we are on holiday en famille at this time of the year). In order to unwind most of us have to be wound up already, so let us suppose you are an up-and-coming or, just conceivably, an up-and-just-leaving business executive with a worrying bank statement, some hungry children and a wife who is still wondering whether she remembered to stop the papers, and you are installed in a holiday concrete block on the Costa Something or Other and it's raining. How then to spend your first few hours, or, if the rain persists, your first few weeks, cut off from home and the television and wondering whether you should complain about the loo in the children's bathroom?

The first thing to realise is that the bar is open although it is not yet ten o'clock, and you are ready for the first gin and what passes for tonic in these parts, and that the children's Coca-Cola is at least constant. There is no need to worry about the wife, who already has the old portable iron working and is busy taking the creases out of the summer dress and singeing the counterpane (there will be time to settle for that later). Off to the bar, then, and at least congratulate yourself that the sunburn problem which was such a menace last year is not likely to bother any of you this time. The curious thing about abroad is that the weather and the natives are never constant. The barman is no longer the laughing Andalusian Peasant he appeared last night, but this morning insists that the weather is not going to get any better for several days because of some mysterious freak wind native to this part of the coast. You are well into your second gin and the children into their third game of ping-pong, at which neither of them is the slightest use and which in consequence both find extremely boring. Suddenly the sun is shining, the clouds have disappeared, and there is not a moment to lose if one is to bag the chaise longue and position it correctly on the sunny side of the water chute.

This, you tell yourself, is what you are here for, sun and splash, a moment of shut-eye. Your wife when she joins you is surprised you didn't reserve her a chair and wonders where on earth the children have got to. You tell her you thought they had gone to their bedroom to collect their bathing things and wonder that they didn't tell her on their way. By now you are alerted sufficiently to go and look for them, and discover them not kidnapped as you had begun to fear but pricing local pottery in the shopping arcade. You persuade them to join you at the pool, and the holiday is off to a good start.

Twenty-four—possibly forty-eight hours—later you have had your fill of the prison-yard, you have got to know a few of the other inmates, your nose has started to re-peel, and you begin to think of possible escape and that a visit to San Pedro del Fidelio might be just the thing for the children. San Pedro seems the right distance on the map, although, of course, you didn't allow for the time it took trailing heavy vehicles up steep mountain curves into the cloud belt of the lesser Sierras. The village, when you arrive, is tightly shuttered, along with the Church; everyone else has apparently had lunch and is now asleep. We really are off the beaten track, you tell the family triumphantly, this is the real Spain that few tourists see. 'And yet,' says your wife, 'San Pedro del Fidelio contains the Black Madonna—you'd have thought someone besides us would be having a look. Unless we are in the wrong village.' Your wife is seldom fooled; you extract the car from the local pound and try again.

Three-quarters of an hour later you find not only the Black Madonna but also somewhere for an early tea and a place to buy souvenirs of the occasion. Later you join a long queue of fellow pilgrims and peer briefly at a heavily-robed madonna behind bullet-proof glass, and the children light candles and seem perfectly content as usual to watch money going up in smoke. On the way home you try to tell them something of the history of the monastery founded by Carlos II on the spot where a young peasant girl divined a spring of healing water a thousand years ago, but having spent their child-hood up to now in blissful ignorance of Spanish folklore, they are not prepared for an instant course of guidebook lore and nor, come to think of it, are you.

The ability of the casual tourist suddenly to steep himself in the history of, say, the Spanish Inquisition or early Mycenian ruins, is vastly overrated. A great deal of holiday boredom can be avoided by previously consulting the family on what they really want to see, and the answer will be found to be almost invariably a new supermarket or the actual swimming pool where once upon a time and very long ago Goldfinger tried to down Bond, or at least have him eaten alive by crocodiles. Though such historic sights are, alas, few and far between, it is still possible to awaken family interest by discreet invention. Having myself made two or three films in Italy and at least two in Spain, I am always ready to show the grandchildren the spot where Gina Lollobrigida waded ashore at Amalfi, or where Alec Guinness's beard blew off outside Pamplona, or, if we are too far away, maybe Sitges. My family are not exclusively cinema-orientated, but here again the new generation, as their parents did, like to concentrate not so much on the ancient stonework of Padua as on a cinema poster displayed on the walls advertising a film whose title, in a foreign tongue, is susceptible—after some puzzling over—of being identified and often, if time permits, visited.

Because I have learnt to be tolerant of my own holiday behaviour, because I never know quite what is expected of one when one emerges from the bright sunlight into the contrived gloom of a Gothic cathedral, because I cannot make out the grimy pictures and find myself idly counting the candles and grading them for size, because I have no desire to climb to the belfry or explore the relics in the sacristy, I can understand that once the family have pushed open the small door, held back the curtain and taken a hurried look around, they will want to be off again hunting for ice cream and, in my case, for *The Times* of last Friday week. I am sorry we are not, on the whole, a cultural group, sorry, but not unduly disturbed perhaps. Appreciation of Byzantine Art will come later or never awaken.

A final word of advice: if you can't relax at home, don't try to do so on holiday. If you have acquired the worry syndrome, indulge it. There will be plenty to worry about in the next fortnight—health, exchange rates, smuggling on the return journey, flight cancellations, jelly-fish, rabies, the constant dread of losing your passport from your pocket or your cache of reserve currency from the unlocked wardrobe. On holiday, hope for the best, prepare for the worst, and above all expect the one big family row which is absolutely certain to occur, and be eternally grateful for the fact that no holiday can last for ever.

Hell is . . .

Hell is a play by Brecht, Hamlet acted by Nicol Williamson, a word from Lord Soper. Hell is a medical examination for an insurance policy, a shop like Harrods. Hell was always macaroni cheese, and lately the Earls Court Road. Hell is a story I've told too often and a letter from my accountant before I've opened it. Hell is a letter from my accountant after I've opened it. Hell is knowing how much I have in the bank. Hell is the bathroom scales and the unexplained blemish on the end of my nose. Hell was my name on a games list at school, and a lout who terrorised me when I rode my tricycle.

I know my Hell can't be the right one. Good heavens, there are people who are prepared to pay to see Nicol Williamson, sane, ordinary, well-informed folk who probably shop at Harrods on the way to the theatre. It is patently absurd to worry about health or money. I don't really worry about my weight. I certainly don't want to know about it, any more than I want to know about Hell.

I shall feel a perfect fool if I open my eyes after I've died, and find things exactly as predicted by the devout, by the Seventh Day Adventists, Jehovah Witnesses, or Aimée Semple Macpherson, who once explained the whole thing to me seated on a motorcycle and dressed as God's Cop, or so she claimed. Could she have been right? Could they all have been right? Is there a final reckoning, and if so, how shall I fare?

'But we told you,' they will insist, 'we kept on telling you. Why on earth didn't you believe us? It was perfectly obvious, surely? You weren't just there to enjoy yourself. You were supposed to be preparing for the life eternal.'

'But what happens?' I shall ask piteously. 'What happens now?'

'What do you expect will happen? You flunked, you're for it, old man.'

But who will be there with me? None of my aunts, that's for sure.

They all believed in the life eternal, and they were right. I always contradicted them, and I was wrong. Not all of them, of course, would have expected me to go to Hell. Some of them might even have been mildly surprised, especially my aunt Evelyn, my champion aunt, who bought three vacuum cleaners from me my first morning in the trade. She surely must be in Heaven by now, that is of course always supposing there is a heaven, which I don't. It's not that I cannot visualise myself in a state of permanent preservation, even in a position of perpetual worship. I am confident that I am the sort of person God would like to have around, but on my journey through life, if indeed it is possible to travel in the recumbent position I have so frequently and for such long periods adopted, I have met so few who seem qualified to accompany me to Paradise. There simply aren't sufficient of the right people to fill the place and if the Almighty doesn't want Heaven to look like Lord's Cricket Ground on the final day of The Test, He will be well advised to cancel the match. Most people are so much more boring than I am. Very few of them have the quality of being able to amuse the Almighty, indeed I can count on the fingers of one hand (I have four) the men and women I have met whom God and I would welcome as they stepped through the pearly gates — Bernard Shaw, Sybil Thorndike, Wilfrid Hyde White and although I am not absolutely certain about him, Marty Feldman. A personal choice, you may argue, and one that does not include members of my own family, but then naturally we shall enter in a body. Nevertheless, even at this rate the place can hardly be said to be filling up, and though I imagine there may have been a few early arrivals, such as Michaelangelo, Shakespeare and just conceivably Moses, it is unlikely, in my opinion at any rate, that the party would ever really get off the floor.

At school Divinity was my best subject. It usually is with backward pupils. But I have never had much subsequent joy from the Bible. I don't really care for the style, but I have always been very fond of the Parable of the Vineyard. It has always seemed eminently fair to me that workers who arrive late on the scene should not be penalised. I arrived very late on my scene. Indeed I was thirty before my weekly wage reached double figures, and I was usually the last one to be hired in the casting office. I am not a man who has read widely, preferring to keep my mind relatively uncluttered with the ideas of others, so that any of my own thoughts may have room to manoeuvre. Unless you have a first-class mind it is a great mistake to afford it a first-class education. It is daunting to discover that everything has already been said and thought. My ideas may not shatter, but I am always pleasurably surprised to have conceived them, and cannot help being struck with their originality and brilliance. Better and especially classically educated men are, on the other hand, often bored when I expound them. 'Plato said that,' they tell me. 'Did he, indeed?' I take care never to read Plato, but it would be an overstatement to maintain that I have taken care not to read the Bible. The idea has simply never occurred to me, and therefore I do not know whether there is in the Good Book a reliable description of Hell, or for that matter Heaven, though I seem to remember both subjects were touched on in Revelations, but it is too late now for me to bother.

If I believe anything about a God, it is that He is a God anxious for me not to worry my head about life after death, or for that matter death after life. I never expect to meet Him, and I cannot go along with those who believe in a sort of instant judgement. It would take far too long to decide most people's cases (not mine, perhaps, but most people's) for considered judgement to be practicable, let alone just. I don't know why I should expect judgement to be just, but I suppose that comes of being British. Italians, for instance, may find it easier to believe, but I am not Italian, and I would certainly be the last to wish Heaven to be filled with them. They are a gifted race, and in the kitchen at any rate, superior to ourselves, but cooking in Heaven is not seriously envisaged by the faithful, although I suppose it's more than possible it might take place in Hell, in which case it would surely be the sort of cooking I watched on television the other evening, where the butter was shaped like a rose, and dusted with edible gold dust. Is Fanny Craddock really the Devil in disguise? 'Why on earth should she be?' you ask, and alas, I cannot answer, except to postulate that anyone could be the Devil, or anyone could go to Heaven or to Hell for that matter, and I should not be a penny the wiser. All I can affirm is that Hell for me is butter shaped like a rose and dusted with edible gold dust.

I Could Have Danced All Night

'This dance,' Mr. Durrell assured me, 'is native to the village. It is performed nowhere else on the Island.'

'I don't wonder,' I replied.

'I hope,' my companion went on, 'you are not thinking of buying a house; there are far too many of us here already.'

I reassured him. If anything would decide me not to settle permanently in Corfu it would be the spectacle of three elderly crones, arms linked and ankles swollen in unison, stirring the dust. Not a good mover myself, I am jealous of the leaping crowd. Not that these ladies leaped, they shuffled. Shuffling is the fashion abroad. Sitting in the sunshine in Capri last summer, the whole square erupted with conga madness. One moment the British were chewing their olives and the next they had snaked off down the water's edge and hopefully, as far as I was concerned, into it, crazed and dishonest lemmings, leaving their campari bills unsettled. Ten minutes later an aged and solitary Member of Parliament returned in the manner in which he had departed, two steps forward and one back, but now with no girlish bosom on which to rest his elbow.

'Not dancing, Morley?' the fellow enquired, helping himself to my frozen daquiri. 'In Capri everyone dances.'

'I don't,' I told him.

I believe the Monarch shares my inhibition. I catch her sometimes on my television screen, sitting curiously upright and tensed in the green canvas chair under the palm tree, surveying her own, or nowadays, alas, more often other people's subjects, prancing around the totem pole. Do we, I wonder, feel the same about ballet when we are obliged to watch it? Is she, too, miles ahead, as I am, of the programmed scenario, optimistically but mistakenly believing we are past the wedding rites and approaching the final pirouette, only to discover that what we took for the marriage ceremony was merely the rape of the temple dancers and that there is at least another bad twenty minutes to go?

Why am I always so impatient for the dance to end? Is it because as a child I was taken by my father to so many musical comedies when all I longed for was to see a play? I sat hunched with boredom, watching the orchestra pit for the moment when the occupants would submerge and I could be sure of at least a few moments of plot or comic relief. How quickly the magic moments flew by until the dreaded musicians began groping their way back again, the conductor resumed his seat and tapped with his baton, and some fool spoilt *The Maid of the Mountains* for me by bursting into song and prance.

Or is it simply because I was never able to dance myself? In adolescence I tried to learn. I took ballroom dancing lessons from a Miss Peeler in the very best part of Pimlico; at least I took one from her and the rest from her assistants. The day Miss Peeler personally intervened is one I shall always remember. At first I mistook her interest in me for admiration; she rarely taught the beginners herself. She must, I thought, have discerned some hidden talent in me and was anxious to exploit it. There was a slight hesitancy on the part of my regular teacher when she announced that Miss Peeler herself desired to hold me in her arms and we were to go to the main ballroom, where we found the headmistress all in black with a rather more superior gramophone than the other studios boasted, and eager to commence. We took a few steps around the floor and stopped abruptly. Miss Peeler spoke, and I realised her role on this occasion was not that of a talent scout, but of a trouble-shooter.

'I didn't believe it,' she told me, 'and I wanted to see for myself, but, Mr. Morley, I wish you to know that for you I am breaking a lifelong rule and returning your fee in full. I have only done it once before in thirty years. You will never learn to dance.'

It was a snap judgement which has not been reversed. True, I later comported (if that is the word, and I fancy it is), comported myself in a musical comedy at Drury Lane believing, wrongly as it turned out, that anything Rex Harrison could do, I could do better, but my reason for accepting the engagement was not so much to prove Miss Peeler wrong after all those years as to enjoy myself at someone else's expense (considerable, as it turned out). At last, I told myself as I signed the contract, I shall see a bit of life as it should be lived backstage. I can only report that dancers are not the romantic crowd they are made out to be. Backache, not heartache was the sole topic of conversation in the wings, unless we happened to be joined by the singers, in which case we discussed tonsilitis.

But to return to the global scene and to the dancing girls and boys who were once the prerogative of emperors, but are now to be found supplementing the table d'hôte of resort hotels from Kenya to Katmandu. 'The Commodore proudly presents its troop of genuine native dancers,' announces the bandleader, and out from the service entrance trip the proud creatures themselves, arrayed in traditional plastic to re-enact with remarkable detachment the ritual stomp preceding a long-since discontinued, and indeed in their case never actually sampled, cannibal feast. Not a missionary to be seen, but alas, a certain number of pots, my own included. At least Her Majesty is not expected to participate when, their performance concluded, they invite us to rise from our chairs and join them in a simplified version of the Hula Hula or Beri Beri. This is when I put on my bravest face and indicate as best I can in local miming slang that I have a wooden leg. I shake my head and smile until the danger has passed and some other idiot is hopping in my stead, blissfully aware that it is all included in the cover charge. He may even be hoping to strike up some form of rapprochement with his coy partner, little realising that long before midnight has struck she will be off once more through the service hatch in a puff of steam to climb into the minibus at the staff entrance and on to her next engagement.

How perfectly Lewis Carroll anticipated the advent of the dancing tourist:

'Will you walk a little faster?' said a whiting to a snail,
'There's a porpoise close behind us, and he's treading on my tail.
'See how eagerly the lobsters and the turtles all advance,
'They are waiting on the shingle. Will you come and join the dance?
'Will you, won't you, will you, won't you, will you join the dance?
'Will you, won't you, will you, won't you, will you join the dance?
'You can really have no notion how delightful it will be,
When they take us up and throw us with the lobsters out to sea.'

I wish I had had the wit to quote him to Lawrence Durrell as we sat in the taverna, waiting for our stuffed vine leaves, while the staff, arms linked with the visitors in suspect bonhomie, imitated a drooping line of aged Tiller girls, and to hell with the service.

Promises, Promises

Now that we have learned not to wash our cars, and suede has taught us not to clean shoes, we may achieve the third freedom—not to keep promises. Indeed, some of us have learnt this already, or like me, have avoided making them since childhood. Nowadays I say, 'We'll see about it', or, 'We'll do what we can—we never promise.'

Like most children I endured the tyranny of the promise, was indoctrinated into the sacred oath and abjured not to break it on pain of forfeiting my honour. Brought up on a diet of Sabatini, Hornung, Sapper, and even that cad Yates, I believed a gentleman keeps his word and a promise is sacrosanct. I kept my honour brightly polished, like my shoes. When I gave a promise I kept it. What was worse, I expected others to do the same. 'But you promised,' I would tell my parents. 'You promised I could stay up to see the New Year', or 'You would take me to Wembley' (for the Exhibition, I must remind readers, not the football—I was never a common child). 'You promised to increase my pocket money.'

I forget now whether they had actually done so or whether I had simply imagined it—not that it mattered. What mattered was the row, the whole dramatic exercise, the charges and counter-charges. The screams of temper—the kicks on the shins. The breaking of a sacred oath which ensured that I would never believe another word they said.

How different life is today when, with the possible exception of the currency, nothing has been more devalued than the promise. Like sterling, the promise has now to be perpetually and vainly supported. No one simply promises any more—they promise faithfully. The sweep will call, the garden seat be delivered, the boiler serviced. We clap our hands and wait. At least, we used to clap our hands—now we just wait.

There was a Spanish word which we mispronounced to indicate the state of the world abroad. It meant 'tomorrow', or so we thought. 'Mañana,' we used to confide pityingly to each other, 'that's the trouble with this country. It's always tomorrow with them.' Goodness, how the world's changed now. When the Arabs want something in Britain today, they get it. The rest of us have to wait till long after tomorrow.

Does it all matter? I am inclined to think, not as much as all that. For one thing it prolongs anticipation, a great deal of it pleasurable. One day, we tell ourselves happily, we shall have the new telephone, or the new cooking stove, or the man will come to fix the roof, and we picture our happiness when the bell rings and the smell of gas evaporates and we can dispense with the slop pail in the middle of the drawing-room.

In point of fact it never happens quite like that. Our tight little island is now geared for continuing disaster. We are more likely to have to move out of the house. The roof proved a bigger job than they thought, or the kitchen just blew up, and now the telephone is ringing once more there's no one to answer it.

Perhaps it is easier for me to be philosophical about these matters because my world has been the theatre and not, for instance, the Church, where promises are still, I presume, hard currency. Congratulating a colleague in his dressing-room only the other day on his bearing and resilience and on his having emerged unscathed from a gruelling matinée performance of a not very good play to a not very good audience—with the notable exception of myself—I sought and found the right word for the playwright who had engaged our dutiful attention for the last three hours.

'Promising,' I told him, 'a most promising first play. You would be well advised to get an option on her next.'

He won't, of course. Full of promise, in our trade, means it hasn't quite come off but is likely to do so quite soon. Lest the author of this play should happen to read these lines and identify the occasion, I hasten to add that in my opinion, and it's not worth much, she will do a good deal better next time. In which case, besides enabling me to make, I trust, a graceful exit on this occasion, I shall have once again demonstrated my perspicacity.

But, alas, on most theatrical occasions when the air is promise-crammed, it is difficult to detect the sweet smell of success at the box office. The present generation of grandchildren appear to accept with equanimity the devaluing of the promise. They no longer scream and shout and flood the world with tears and accusations when they find that after all they are not being taken to the circus. Nor, I think, do they experience an undue feeling of shame when they manifestly fail in their own solemn undertakings not to turn on the television until they've finished their homework. I suppose, strictly speaking, one shouldn't let people down, but now that it's more or less accepted practice from cradle to grave, I do find it makes them easier to live with. More important, it makes it easier to live with myself.

Shaving, I can concentrate on essentials. The stubble, for instance. It is impossible, however, not to regret the passing of the breach of promise case. What happy reading these always provided. How we used to marvel at the folly of the blushing plaintiff. Could she really have believed the fellow, we asked ourselves, and with what admiration (we fellows at any rate) regarded the defendant. What panache, what cheek! Remember, these were the days before deferred payments and hire purchase. Occasionally the ladies collected for supplying the goods on credit, though not often if the judge could help it, but we enjoyed the blow by blow account of their attempts to do so.

We may not believe in promises any more, but as a nation we insist on our right to pretend to do so. Politicians promise us the earth and we reach out our greedy little hands to grasp it. We cannot forget that President Kennedy once promised the moon and when we got there it was quite dead—and so was he. Do we really want it all to come true? Do we want all the promises fulfilled? If they were, what would become of us? Nothing left to hope for, nothing to get annoyed about, nothing to pardon, nothing to understand. The best of all possible worlds in which everyone kept his word because there was nothing else to do with it, would be a dull place indeed.

Better, surely, to survive as we do, waiting for the window cleaner, chivvying the Gas Board, bouncing the post-dated cheque. It's when things seem most unpromising that I have learnt to expect the best. With the signals set fair, I know I'm in for trouble. All fate ever promises is surprise. If, for any reason, and against my extra-sensory expectations, I fulfil a promise from time to time, I feel everyone should share my astonishment—especially commissioning editors.

The Case Against Conservation

Whatever happened to the pink-footed geese, the ones Peter Scott used to chase after on that tiny Arctic pony of his? I never knew where my sympathies were supposed to lie, all three seemed to be having such a terrible time. In the end someone wrote to *The Times* and said the geese didn't really care for it, and in the process the young ones got separated from their parents and died of fright. I kept waiting for Scott to write back to defend the birds' right to wear one of his patent foot tags, but as far as I know he never did. Nowadays you see his tag mostly on knitwear.

I hope Mr. Scott won't think this is a personal attack on him on behalf of the geese. I couldn't care less if I never saw a pink-footed goose again, indeed I am not even sure I have ever seen one. True, there are geese living on the river bank at Henley, and I like watching them at dusk, circling the supermarket, very pretty and squawky and in a way threatening, but I doubt they're pink-footed, just muddied.

On the other hand I am always seeing Peter Scott on the box – the Kenneth Clark of the Marshes. I even once took tea with him at the Wildfowl Trust, but there didn't seem many wildfowl about, or trust either, come to that. The birds crouched against the imprisoning wire netting. Some of them, indeed, seemed to be missing a few wing feathers. They seemed extravagantly listless.

I suppose it's all part of 'Civilisation'. The children come to see the black-tailed godwit, just as they flood in to see Tutankhamun's death mask. Once they have glimpsed it, they don't have to bother again. Off to the salt mines with them, they had their chance.

How awful, claim the conservationists, if the child never saw a dead Egyptian or an okapi or even a butterfly. We must set to work and make sure they do. The first thing to do is raise the ready. No conservationist ever admits to needing money to conserve himself, but of course there are things he simply must have – helicopters and poisoned darts, landrovers and rhinoceros nets, recording equipment and cameras and miles and miles of film stock. The cinema industry started to decline when it was discovered that all the world needed to satisfy the demand of its customers was roughly one hundred and fifty feature films a year. Up to then they had been making an average of five thousand. Similarly, if no one ever again photographed a lion, there would still be sufficient shots of lions to last the human race for another six hundred thousand years. (The statistics in this chapter are entirely my own invention.) There is, luckily, absolutely no chance of the human race lasting that long. In our case, as in every other case, the conservationists are fighting Mother Nature, and no one ever gets the better of her for long, but it doesn't stop them trying.

Once they have kitted themselves and their friends out and booked the air freight space, they are off on their lugubrious task of counting the puff adders or upturning the giant tortoises, and back before you can say David Attenborough to record the commentary and book prime time on BBC 2. They know that the rest of us have little if any chance of ever making the trip ourselves. We shall never feel the sun on our backs or smell the frangipani leis or drink guava juice. We shall not bathe on warm beaches or eat fresh coconuts, fly over the volcano or shoot the rapids. We shall live out our proscribed lives in the shadow of South Kensington Underground Station. 'Don't worry,' Peter Scott tells us, 'just put up the money and we will bring you back the colour transparencies. Hold them up to the light bulb and you will swear you, too, are standing in the Gobi Desert.'

What right have these people to represent us on these junkets? Who appointed them our ambassadors of pleasure? Is it on our instructions that they bundle up a drugged rhinoceros and move him thousands of miles up country or down country? 'He'll be happier now,' they tell us, 'and wasn't it exciting when he nearly impaled old Fred on his horn? Did you know that rhinoceros horn is widely regarded by the Chinese as an aphrodisiac? That's why we have to keep moving this one around.' 'We do know,' we shout back to the unheeding box. 'You've told us a thousand times, and now we have news for you. Rhinoceros horn is an aphrodisiac. That's why the Chinese don't need conservationists.'

If Peter Scott never drew another flying duck, if he opened all the cages and set the geese free, and if he never conducted another package tour to wrap up the penguins or stopped telling me that if something isn't done soon there will be no more white leopards around, I should be so grateful I'd even buy one of his sweaters, supposing I could find one to fit me.

But what, you ask, is the poor fellow to do in future? Well, here's one suggestion. Collect some money, buy a shooting truck and some poisoned darts – the ones that put the rhinoceros to sleep, but not so strong this time – and creep up one night to Notting Hill Gate and capture a little family of human beings living in the dried-up waterbed in Ladbroke Grove, put them on board and set them free in clean new quarters in Windsor Great Park. The game warden is his old friend and patron, H.R.H., so that should be all right.

Death to the Flannelled Fools

I have a friend, W. Rushton, an actor like myself, a creature of the dusk who earns his living lampooning Prime Ministers on the Box. I came upon him the other afternoon in a meadow, dressed all in white, a forlorn uneasy moth of a fellow unaccustomed to the daylight and in boots which seemed to be causing him discomfort. He was, he affirmed, playing cricket for money: the fact that he wasn't going to get the money himself didn't seem to disturb him as it surely would have done on a more normal occasion.

Living as I do in Berkshire, I am used to oak trees displaying posters advertising charity cricket matches – indeed am grateful for the warning not to approach too closely on such occasions – but Rushton, not for the first time, had caught me unawares. I withdrew hastily. I would rather watch a man at his toilet than on a cricket field, but such is the madness of the players that in time they come to believe that the spectacle they make of themselves dressed in white wielding a willow (to use their own revolting phraseology – and why not?) is something their betters should pay to see.

'Car Park two shillings,' the posters proclaim. 'All proceeds to H.R.H. Duke of Edinburgh', and blow me if the public don't drive their cars through the gate over the cart tracks, park in the cow dung, wind down the windows, turn up the radio and tell each other that they are getting a bit of fresh air.

It is not, of course, everybody who rolls up on these occasions, mostly people who still have drawing-rooms and take the *Telegraph* and *Punch* and who, like myself, were brought up in the shadow of The Awful Game.

I have never got over the shock of seeing my first cricket ball. I simply couldn't believe that there was anything so dangerous loose in what up to then had seemed a safe sort of world. A terrible master at a terrible prep school introduced us. 'This is the bat, Morley,' he said, 'and this is the ball', and flung it at me. A small red leather bomb, which for some reason failed to explode. I have lived in terror of the thing ever since. In vain I pleaded to be allowed to continue playing with a soft ball. 'I might even

236

learn to like the game,' I told them, 'if I played with a soft ball.' Of course I lied. I had already played with a soft ball and hated it. My governesses were always urging me to join up with other children standing in front of groynes or spread out over the pebbles while Father bowled. (Never *my* Father, thank God.)

Blind in one eye, I discovered early on that I was never to stay long by the breakwater. While others made a meal of their innings, my own were brief to the point of incomprehension. A moment of top dogmanship holding the bat, a quick swing and back to Long Stop for the rest of time. Later at my Public School I used even to hasten the process by taking guard and then, before the ball could reach me, knocking down my wicket. A protest which enraged the jolly cricketing house captain, who beat me nightly in the bathroom.

Right-minded boys were supposed to like cricket.

The masters used to read out the scores of the country cricket matches after prayers. They believed in a God who liked cricket and prep schools named after His saints.

Not being of the faithful I particularly dread the Test Match season, always fearful that switching on the radio or television I shall be exposed to a cricket commentary by Mr. Arlott.

I cannot explain why I dread being told that Sun Yet San has now bowled more overs in his sweater from the gasworks end than any other fool in first-class cricket, but I do. Readers may think me mad if they wish. I am, but I am also brave. The other day, taking some of my old phobias out and examining them, I decided to go back to cricket for the day and to see what really goes on at Lords during a Test match. When I arrived nothing whatever was going on. It had been raining and although the sun now shone, the wicket was covered over with what appeared to be collapsed sight screens, and a number of mackintosh sheets of various sizes and colours were laid out to dry on the turf. Someone had obviously been shopping at the army surplus supply stores and was now keen to display the trophies. No one seemed keen to play cricket. While I watched, two men in blue took the field with the measured tread of police officers approaching an incident which they trust will have sorted itself out before they get there. 'Umpires inspecting the pitch,' one of the custodians informed me. They go in for custodians at Lords. Sports which were once the privilege of the few and are still run by the gentlemen of England, Polo, Cricket, Racing, concentrate as far as conditions still permit on the 'enclosure within the enclosure'. At Lords there are stands marked Members Only and others bearing the legend Friends of Members.

Always one to dramatise my situation, I asked how I could make a friend. 'It's no use today,' the custodian informed me, 'friend or no friend, it's another fifty pence.'

By now the Umpires had reached the centre of the ground, cautiously lifted one end of the tarpaulin and sniffed. I wondered what they were looking for, could it be wet grass? Inscrutably they returned to the Pavilion. I bet Mr. Betjeman likes the Pavilion, I bet he likes cricket. 'The Players,' announced the public address system, 'will take lunch . . . another inspection will be made at two-thirty.'

'But I've paid,' I told the custodian.

'You should read the small print.' No one having asked me to lunch, I lingered by his side while he reminisced about the time when as a boy they paid him sixpence for eight overs. 'Who paid sixpence?' I asked. 'Why, the players, of course . . . we were glad of the money in those days. Cricket is dying,' he went on, 'it's been dying ever since I can remember.' I went over and read the menu outside the restaurant. Everything was cold. I was cold. I took a taxi and went to an Indian restaurant up the road. If I wasn't going to watch them playing cricket at least I could watch them cooking my lunch.

When I got back they were ringing bells, just like they used to at St. Christopher's. An Indian stood outside the Tavern shouting at one of the players coming out to field. 'Encouraging him?' I asked. 'He is my kid brother, he insulted my mother, now he can never go back to India. I shall cut him in small pieces.' He insisted on buying me a gin and tonic. 'Keep the bottle to throw later,' he advised. He was a very cheerful fellow.

I sat down beside a man who knew all about it. He had spent a lifetime playing and watching the game, a helpless hopeless addict. Perhaps he was happy, perhaps they were all happy, even the little man in a turban who bowled and kept rearranging the fieldsmen and seemed more grown up than all the others. The Father figure on the sands, he bowled all through the long afternoon, slowly, cunningly, patiently, and the children got out one after another, trying to prolong their time at the wicket, not really scoring, just staying there so they shouldn't have to field in their turn. Nothing had changed. Halfway through the afternoon I found myself almost enjoying myself. It was the bars, I suppose. Lords is full of bars and barmaids. I always like barmaids. 'We come down from Lincoln every morning,' one of them told me. 'We enjoy the change.' If they could why couldn't I? The very last ball of the very last over bowled Edrich. He had stopped trying to score half an hour earlier. He wanted to bat another day. I was glad he went.

I watched them all go home, the old men and the boys, the mothers and the custodians, the waitresses from Lincoln, the decent quiet people of England – and, oh my God, you should have seen the filth they left behind.

À
LA
CARTE

A Movable Feast

'There is no need to make it a picnic,' was one of the most frequent admonishments of my childhood.

My mother was wont to utter it whenever one spoon or plate was asked to do the work of two, or when the jam jar was not put back on its saucer: yet the picnic itself was in those days far from an informal affair especially when celebrated on a railway journey. The sandwiches all neatly packaged in white grease-proof had the legend of their contents clearly written in pencil. Ham and tomato, chicken and tongue paste, sardine and watercress.

One thermos contained lemonade, the other tea already milked and sugared. There was a special tin for the ginger nuts. We preferred a carriage to ourselves but if this was not possible there was still a lack of furtiveness about the feast. How sad it has always seemed to me to watch a guilt-ridden soul feeding himself from a paper bag, dipping his hand deep into the folds and fishing out some tiny morsel of sustenance to convey to his mouth with surreptitious gesture as if he hoped he would be thought to be merely coughing. There are still men today of such hideous refinement that, popping an acid drop between their gums, they give the impression that they are prisoners on remand poisoning themselves with strychnine rather than face their accusers.

Not so my family: we held up our egg sandwiches for all the world to admire and if there was any plum cake left over we would offer it around to fellow travellers. In those days the railways put up picnic baskets of their own which were ordered in advance and handed through the window at certain specified stations en route. The passenger was asked to state his preference for wing or thigh, and the bird came with ham rolls, cheese, fruit and a half bottle of wine. Passengers were on their honour to hand back the basket, or at least leave it in the carriage; any breach of trust on their part was unthinkable. Picnic baskets were usually single and in that sense not really a picnic so much as a ration. The package lunch is seldom convivial; I always sigh for those individually-packed British Directors assembled in the Albert Hall when they come to undo their little cardboard boxes and inspect the contents. Each one exactly similar to another, nothing to share, very little to swap. No cheating allowed. I remember my own field days at Wellington College when each man was supposed to fill the knapsack of the soldier in front of him with the regulation pork pie and chocolate bar. The trick, of course, was to pretend to do so – at any rate with the chocolate, the pork pies were usually filthy.

I have always enjoyed food on the move. 'Is there a restaurant car?' has been my constant enquiry and nowadays, alas, how often am I disappointed. But where it is forthcoming I can still relish the excitement with which the food on British Rail is served. Whoever is responsible for the training of our restaurant car attendants imparts his own particular flavour to the service, if not to the food. There is always an element of Mack Sennett, of the early films in the manner of the attendant – a hint of Chaplin in the walk. Then there's the speed with which plates of soup are placed before the customers: not a drop splashes over, but then there is never more than a drop to start with. The way in which the empty plates are hurled onto the table, the lightning portioning out of the slices of mutton, fair do's for all with potatoes and sprouts. Speed is the essence. One is perpetually reminded that we are all, passengers and staff alike, catching a train. In almost no time at all the meal is over, the bills distributed, the money collected, the tables cleared and we have been persuaded to return to our carriages and leave the attendants in peace. Woe betide the passenger who tries to linger – or, worse still, returns for another drink. How enjoyable a journey which didn't end when the platform arrived but lingered on in the refreshment car, a band of happy voyagers carousing till the dawn and joined perhaps by others about to start their journey, or even with no travel plans whatsoever.

Our local station has over the years been cut down to size; where there were once two tracks only a single one remains. All hints of the booking hall have been effaced – even the waiting room is usually locked. .

On this deserted but tranquil scene there happened the other evening a band of youths and their girls intent on recreating that pastoral scene so seldom witnessed these days save in the Hovis advertisements on television. They took the station to be abandoned, like themselves, laid a cloth on the platform, produced cakes and ale and sat there among the midges, strumming their guitars, when suddenly the five twenty-nine commuter train from Paddington arrived with the exhausted daily breaders carrying brief-cases and umbrellas and searching their pockets for car keys. There was a confrontation, terror assailed the bowler-hat brigade; they scented squatters, they remonstrated, they urged retreat. 'You won't like it here,' they told the gipsies, 'this station is used every morning by people like us trying to make a living. If you've opted out please opt out somewhere else.' But the girls and boys laughed at them. 'We are here for good,' they assured all and sundry, but in the morning they had gone.

In Switzerland, even still sometimes in France, the station restaurant is the best in town; how curious that British Rail have never understood that a station can be the focal point of a community; that every time they give up Liverpool Street to the developers or Sandhurst Halt to no one in particular they are destroying themselves. How pleasant in the evening to take a train out of the smoke, to journey down the line to some Elysian field, to find a picnic spread outside the waiting room and lobsters and champagne in the booking hall. How pleasant and how unlikely. Heigho.

As for just taking the pony cart, the *foie gras en croûte*, the cold grouse, the lobster patties, the quails in aspic, the champagne and the sherry trifle, and driving out across the heather – those days are over for most of us. The last vestige of gracious living has been banished to racecourse car parks, where one can still have one's Rolls and eat them. We indulge our national proclivity to get there and spread out now that the Empire is over and the races begin later.

The picnickers that delight me most are the lay-by layabouts, that cherished little family parked at the side of the road with a field or a heap of gravel at their back, facing the endless ribbon of cars which, unlike them, are getting on with the task in hand. Why, oh why, I ask myself, have they stopped where they have? A call of nature? A child who wants to be sick? A dog who wants to run? But not, surely, simply a meal demanding to be eaten off plastic plates? Sometimes there is a kettle boiling, sometimes an aluminium chair unfolded, always there are tomatoes. The tomato is the patron fruit of picnickers. It gives the seal of approval to the cold collation. The sort of people who pull up in lay-bys to feast are the same people who drive their cars right up to the edge of the esplanade and don't get out. For them the sea is best observed through a windscreen, the ozone let in through a half-opened window. They will not explore the sand any more than they do the turf. They have long since forgotten, if once they knew, the terror of seagulls.

When the children were younger, we used sometimes to go for river picnics, tying up the hired launch to a tree stump and squatting among the reeds, anxious always lest the boat should drift away or the engines fail to restart. But it was adventure of a sort, and for one like myself who is

245

frightened of almost all wild creatures, particularly chewing cows and running dogs, a time to muse on just how far one was prepared to go if one's loved ones were threatened by the horse grazing in the distance who m ght turn out to be a stallion.

The best of all picnics was once organised for me on the Island of Marmora by the champion Turkish lady sculler of her generation (how I love to drop names). We hired a caique and after a bit of bother beached on a deserted stretch of sand and swam and ate bread and butter and wild honey and figs and grapes picked in the fig groves and vineyards of an unknown farmer who, when we had finished, suddenly appeared, not to scold or demand payment, but to offer wine and a home-made liqueur. Well, Marmora was fun while it lasted, and I suppose it is just possible that I shall be picnicking again before long – on a train to Newcastle with no restaurant car but with those little labels stuck on the windows reserving our coach for 'Ghost On Tiptoe Company', and what shall we take with us – chicken sandwiches on brown bread, cucumber sandwiches heavily sugared, a pork pie, a bar of chocolate and a bottle of wine, and just possibly a corkscrew? More or less what I stuffed in my haversack fifty years ago on field days in the dreaded Officers' Training Corps.

In Praise of the
Great British Breakfast

Like dresses that do up at the back, the English breakfast was invented as a status symbol; just as there were people to dress you, there were others to rise at dawn to lay the table, scramble the eggs, shred the kedgeree, devil the kidneys and light the lamps under the chafing-dishes. A generation or two ago there were slaves and slavies, domestic and outside staffs, where today there is only cellophane.

It would be idle to regret the passing of bath chaps, and by that I do not mean male sauna attendants, but a peculiar cut of bacon which, on the rare occasions I sampled it, tasted like brawn—another departed side dish, along with the porter and lamb chops.

Breakfast scenes today are strictly for period television serials. The actor in the plus-fours, his hostess still apparently in the ball-gown of the night before, other ladies in hats. The chafing-dishes, the fresh toast, and almost before the meal has started we are away to the butts or the stables, or down to the kitchen.

The English breakfast was a time to get a grip on oneself for a change, for these—if memoirs are to be believed—were licentious times indeed. A time for the knowing glance at one's companion of the night before, but also at *The Times*, warmed and ironed ready for inspection. Whereas today men's thoughts are concentrated on the pound, in those days it was Consols and lust.

Consols have vanished along with the porridge, and what remains? Precious little. 'What do you like for breakfast?' enquires the hostess of her visitor. 'Just some coffee, if it's not too much trouble, but I can easily come down,' replies the perfect guest. Come down to what? A deserted dining-room not even bearing the traces of last night's meal. ('We'll eat in the drawing-room, there's a rather interesting programme on BBC2 my husband thought you'd like.')

The hostess rinsing the milk bottle, her husband all ready with bowler and umbrella, sipping scalding instant coffee, munching a cold sausage lightly smeared with last night's bread sauce. What happened to grace and favour? What happened to Time? Has no one ever thought of a calendar on which certain days every year are unrecorded, simply don't count as time at all, allowing the world to catch up with itself? Days on which no one grows older, no one has to go to work—Recovery Days. If Time is really money, what a way to increase national wealth.

There is a fellow in Neal Street by Drury Lane who runs an excellent restaurant and claims that all his cooking was learnt at the breakfast table of some noble relative on whom he was dumped at the start of the recent hostilities and who all through the war demanded and received proper sustenance on which to commence the day. Certainly his fish cakes, finnan haddock and chicken hash have just that touch of aristocratic know-how which distinguishes English nursery cooking from all other kinds. Whenever you penetrate the enclosure within the enclosure in my country, sit down with the Prime Minister or the Governor of the Bank, invade a Bishop's palace or the private dining-room of one of our great counting houses, you will find the food served for luncheon is not only nursery food, but nursery breakfast food, with the possible exception of the Grand Marnier employed to inflame the bananas.

Oysters, Gammon and Spinach, Pease Pudding, Steak and Kidney Pie, Rissoles of Duck, Golden Syrup Roll, Welsh Rarebit, even the humble Rice Pudding, all have a place in the dining-rooms of power. You may find it hard to credit that British children once took such fare in their stride every morning, and the answer must be not every British child, of course, but the ones who survived. In those days an Englishman started the day as he meant to go on, and before you could say 'Robinson's Golden Shred' we had gobbled up half the world.

Still searching for some answer to our economic plight today, our leaders clutch hopefully at the treacle spoon. 'What we must do,' they tell each other, 'is to pour golden syrup over everything and then our troubles will simply disappear.'

Alas for their hopes, the treacle tin is simply not on the table. They will be fortunate to find individually wrapped packages of the synthetic maple stuff and the battle of finger nails before them. The barrier of class in Britain is gradually being superseded by the barrier of cellophane. Citizens are divided between those who can deal with the stuff and those who can't. For myself I despair easily.

Confronted with what now passes for an English breakfast away from home, I brace myself for an encounter in which inevitably I shall be worsted.

My first disappointment is with the butter pats—too few, too small; even if as nowadays it is sometimes wrapped in foil, which is comparatively easy to remove, it has, I find, a lingering metallic taste on my buds. Butter is something I like to get my knife into. Of course, if the butter is in one of those plastic cups which are supposed to be paratively easy to remove, it has, I find, a lingering metallic taste on by stabbing the surface repeatedly, all control abandoned, and the butter emerges in droplets suffused with shreds of transparent paper.

The terrible little pots of jam and marmalade are the same, only worse. By now I am enfeebled, besides I have taken two preliminary bites out of the colding toast and finished the butter ration. I know I am greedier than most, less effectual than a few, so why not allow me to order a king-size breakfast and pay extra to slice the butter and spoon the marmalade and generally make a beast of myself?

As for the cooked food, that too is nearly always a disappointment. Sausage, bacon and egg is usually just that; with *two* eggs, *two* sausages, *two* rashers of bacon one would get a chance to satisfy one's hunger and then start to enjoy the taste. Kippers, when ordered, usually do arrive in pairs, but, alas, it is rare to find two of the same standard of excellence. I once started a fairly successful correspondence in *The Times* on the comparative excellence of any one pair of kippers—successful to me at any rate, because the Kipper Board sent me a whole box full of them.

It is sad but true to find the best English breakfast these days in America. Not, of course, ordered upstairs in the hotel bedroom, but partaken of in the friendly neighbourhood drugstore with the complimentary extra cups of coffee, the chilled orange juice and, of course, that most superb of all breakfast dishes, the corned beef hash.

To get out of the habit of eating a full breakfast is to get out of the habit of leading a full life. The fall of my country started when we sold the first of our antique silver chafing-dishes to go abroad. When we have the oil once more to keep the lamps alight under them, we shall be able to afford to buy them back.

Eating Up

'Eat up, Master Robert,' nurse would urge, 'show me a nice clean plate. If you can't manage that last piece it means you don't want pudding.' It meant nothing of the kind. I always·looked forward to pudding, still do. Eating habits formed at the nursery table are irreversible. An overweight child grew into an overweight adult. It's true that there was a school of nursery thought which encouraged me occasionally to leave something for manners, but this referred to the last piece of bread and butter before it had been actually transferred to my plate. Once that happened it was my duty to gobble it up. Even mustard was not lightly set aside. Mrs. Colman was apparently gowned on the proceeds of mustard waste. My mother enjoyed repeating a story about a maid reproved for not washing the dishes properly. 'The mustard, Ma'am, was there before I came.' My enjoyment of food was constantly being interrupted by bilious attacks which necessitated my lying fully dressed on the sofa, eyes closed, a water biscuit within reach, alongside a small basin.

I was not a child who shone on the sports field. There are no pictures of me cross-legged, squatting at the feet of the Cricket Captain, supporting the shield which I had assisted the team to win, but there is·a fading sepia print of myself at the age of eight, presiding at a feast at Geronimo's, looking in my Eton collar and with my hair carefully quiffed, like a young Al Capone. Geronimo's of Folkestone was a restaurant of renown, famed for meringues, a dish of which I have always been a connoisseur. Meringues Chantilly, and not of course the vulgar Meringues Glacés. At schools I complained bitterly of the fare, at the age of nine protesting to the Headmaster of the establishment at which I was spending a term — I seldom stayed longer at any school — about his serving me up fried bread and jam and maintaining it was a pudding. The argument ended, as arguments are wont with schoolmasters, in blows, but not before it had produced my first aphorism. 'There is a time,' I told the entire school, 'when catering ceases to be catering and becomes rationing.'

I repeated the remark not so long ago at Ayres Rock, finding myself hungry in the great open wasteland of Central Australia after the table d'hôte lunch. Dinner that same evening, and after my protest, was more plentiful, but I remain unconvinced that food in the Outback is not cooked and served up by chefs specially imported from English boarding schools. Travellers in Australia should at all costs avoid the counter lunch offered in public houses, but in most towns and certainly in all cities there are delicious meals to be found for the trouble of looking for them. In Lorne on the Victorian coast and not far from the celebrated Geelong Grammer School, there is a marine café which serves the best crayfish I have ever eaten. In Freemantle there is the Oysterbed Restaurant, in Adelaide The Barn, in Melbourne Fanny's and in Sydney Mon Coeur, all superb; even their specialities can be safely recommended, although I am always somewhat chary of such taste sensations, and make it a rule to eschew dishes which the chef must have been asked to prepare time and time again.

Nowhere does the national character assert itself more stridently than at the dining table. The French, who conceived the idea of cooking for gain and opened the first restaurant in the Palais Royal once it had been vacated by the aristocrats, have now lost heart. They have had it too good, too many tourists have professed themselves satisfied with the tarte de la maison, the lack of fresh vegetables and the endless monotony of the sauce Béchamel now go unchallenged. Only the bread is what it was. Here in England we meet our children fresh out of school, but at noon the French parent has a rendezvous at the baker's.

In Spain service continues late into the night; the rich eat too much, the poor not enough. In Germany everybody eats too much. Italians eat extravagantly, Greeks cautiously, Americans at speed. They seldom linger longer than is necessary. In elegantly contrived Beverly Hills bistros, baroque Chicago Pump Rooms, Fifth Avenue Regency parlours or exotic San Francisco fish tanks, nothing ever stops the hired help destroying the ambiance with 'Who gets the check?'

But what of the British? Where do we stand, or rather, sit? Well, at least we have learnt that no visitor in his senses would ever eat the sort of food we dish out to ourselves. They will never, unless they are very unlucky indeed, have to eat in our railway stations, in our prisons, in our hospitals, in our schools or on our racecourses. We know better than to advertise English cooking. Our restaurants and hotels are staffed by foreigners. In London, and indeed throughout the whole of the British Isles, you will find the French cook better than they do in France, Turkish chefs exert themselves more in London than in Istanbul, and the best Chinese food in the world is prepared in Cheltenham.

When you have had enough of our towers and palaces, our cathedrals and castle ruins, you will find the bistro in the keep, the take-away curry shop in the pantiles and the wine bar (Spanish type) triumphant where once stood ye boring olde English Tea Shoppe.

The Business of Lunch

Nothing convinces me more of the determination of this country to show our headmaster that we are worthy of his trust and confidence than the way our senior prefects and sixth-formers are prepared to work through the lunch hour.

Anyone fortunate enough to get a table in one of our fashionable restaurants soon after noon must be aware of the quickening tempo in the heart of our great city as one o'clock and decision-time approaches. Is it to be the Vichyssoise, the cold lobster, the duck and orange and the trifle or the oysters, the sole, the steak and kidney and the Gorgonzola? When this has been settled, and settled it must be, speedily, there remains the question of the wine to follow the gin and tonic or the vin blanc cassis.

The ideal number of the working party is probably five. Any more, and the conversation is apt to split; any fewer, and there is a danger of a decision being taken. For various reasons, luncheon conclusions are undesirable. Ideally, matters should be discussed, territories explored, approaches reconnoitred, information exchanged, and whoever picks up the check congratulated on his initiative on assembling the guests.

After some luncheons he may receive a more formal letter of thanks: *Dear Bill, I was so glad to meet R.W. and S.P. under such pleasant and helpful circumstances and will certainly consider the suggestion you made and perhaps we might meet again in the not too distant future to discuss it more fully? How about luncheon on me this time, one day next week?*

After many years of participating in these kind of forays I have learnt that any decision I have made over the coffee cup and the biscuit is almost always the wrong one. I rise from the table, collect my hat, thank my host, and come to my senses a few yards along the pavement. 'Morley,' I tell myself, 'you've been a bloody fool. You should never have agreed to walk alongside the horse, steadying Lady Godiva, especially for charity.'

In my early days, managers wouldn't have dreamt of asking me to luncheon. I waited in their office till they returned from theirs and was then handed a few leaves of manuscript chopped in half (such was the tradition) and told the part carried four pounds. Take it or leave it.

Of course I took it. I never read the play in prospect, just the lines I was to speak and three words of cue. The advantage of this system is obvious. Actors did not indulge in long conversations about the merits of the piece and went home convinced that the part of the Player King was at least as long as Hamlet's.

Later I graduated to the ritual luncheon when the plan for my employment would be delicately broached about halfway through the meal. If it was to be a film, the one thing you could be quite sure would never be produced at this stage was the script. This was because films took, and for all I know still do take, an unconscionably long time to set up. The producer, having launched himself and the project, needs to eat and drink as do the rest of us. In this period of pre-production, every double gin served to Tony Quinn, every plate of oysters offered to Miss Taylor, has to be accounted for and, naturally, shared with the producer. He could never afford to eat alone.

I learnt early on never to speak out of turn in any case. My agent, who had to eat too, usually accompanied me, and as the party was usually made up of the director presumptive, the writer apparent and an aide to the producer, sometimes a useful hint could be obtained of the latter's would-be lifestyle and what sort of meals one might expect on location.

I remember (and what is the point of writing if not to do so?) an exceptionally happy luncheon, or what I imagined was to prove to be so, with Billy Wilder, some years ago. I had already had a preliminary meeting in his office and, for once, had done my homework so that I had memorised the titles of his biggest bonanzas. The names came trippingly off the tongue, Mr Wilder dealt with the compliments, and my agent with the terms. We were all set and I was given the script to take home, or rather, as I was staying with her, to my distinguished mother-in-law's home in Pacific Palisades. That evening, after reading the part I was to play, I began to have doubts. I didn't take kindly to Opera Bouffe and consulted my hostess.

'Robert,' said Miss Cooper firmly, 'as far as I know you have never made a picture with a proper director or, if you have, you have ignored his direction. Here is a chance for you to redeem your career. I beg you to stop criticising the script because you weren't asked to write it and if Mr Wilder has really offered you the part, just pray he won't change his mind.'

He didn't; at least not straightaway. My agent rang and arranged a confirmatory luncheon. 'It's all set, Bob,' he assured me, 'just go along and discuss costumes etc and find out his ideas on how the part should be played. I don't even have to come, he's so mad keen to get you.'

I waited a week, during which Mr Wilder nursed a cold, and then on the eve of the celebration Gladys read the script which I had left meanwhile on the hall table. 'You are not,' she abjured, 'surely going to accept a role in a film like that?'

'I need the money,' I told her, 'and I prefer to remember your earlier advice.'

All might still have gone well if halfway through the meal Mr Wilder hadn't asked me what I thought of the script. 'Look,' I told him, 'you are a great producer. Mr Diamond,' I indicated his writer, who hardly ever spoke, 'is a great scenarist. Who am I, a hack actor, to give an opinion? I have accepted the part, I shall do all I can to play it. With your help I must surely succeed.'

I gave ingratiating and confident smiles all round but still they pressed.

'Well,' I told them, 'if you are really keen to know what I think, although it is not of the slightest importance, I think the script is,' and here I paused, searching for the *mot juste*, 'metricious.'

'Metricious?' asked Mr Wilder. 'I've never heard the word. What's that mean?'

Mr Wilder, of course, is a foreigner—at least, he was not born to the native tongue. Nevertheless, I was surprised he had not heard the word. I turned deferentially to his writer. 'Perhaps you had better ask Mr Diamond,' I suggested.

'There's no such word,' said Mr Diamond.

I really got quite annoyed. 'Just because neither of you has heard the word,' I assured them, 'that doesn't mean it doesn't exist . . .'

'But what does it mean?' they asked.

'Second class,' I told them.

That did it. 'I could do,' said Wilder, 'with a little more enthusiasm.'

'That's something you can't buy,' I told him. It was magnificent but, alas, it was not the contract.

'You will be glad to hear that I am not doing *Irma La Douce*,' I told Gladys that evening. 'I simply couldn't work with a producer who doesn't include the word metricious in his vocabulary.'

'You might have tried him with meretricious,' said Miss Cooper, 'but I don't suppose it would have made any difference.'

On the whole, of course, I have happier memories of pre-production lunches. There is a depressing tendency in these stringent times for managers to invite one to share a cheese sandwich and Coca-Cola in their office. Nothing, in my opinion, gets a play off to a worse start. In my Caesar Salad Days each theatrical manager had his own corner table to which you were bidden. Cochran at the Empress, Shepherd at the Savoy Grill, Sherek at the Caprice, Beaumont at Scott's. Here plans were unfolded, casting discussed, flattery exchanged, the manager picked up the bill and, if all went well, you picked up the contract some days later when your agent had hammered out the terms.

What our hosts implied but never stated was that if one accepted the engagement, today's occasion with the caviare and the Château-briand would on the morrow become commonplace. When, at the end of a long and arduous career, they asked Henry Irving what he had got to show for so much effort, he replied, 'A few friends and a whisky and soda whenever I need one.'

Expense accounts had not then been invented, but today a few good luncheons and the friendship of Sir Tom, Sir Dick and Sir Harry may still be the reason why the chairman soldiers on.

Confessions of a Pudding Man

I am a pudding man. Nothing depresses me more than a meal which doesn't finish with one. 'Just coffee for me, thanks,' is not a phrase in my book. However boring the occasion, I perk up when they wheel in the sweet trolley. I inspect it as I would a guard of honour, I insist the jellies should be standing to attention, the rhubarb, although I never touch it, pale pink, the chocolate sauce dark and mysterious. I cannot contemplate a spoilt trifle. 'What was in that?' I ask, as I wave away the half-filled dish and wait for the replacement. Sometimes there are several trolleys going the rounds. It is as well to inspect them all. They are seldom identical. The first lesson I taught my children was never to show your hand when being served from a trolley. Never ask for a little of that and a little of that, please. If you have decided on profiteroles and syllabub, encourage the waiter to pile your plate with the former, and only when he has put back the spoon, suddenly, and on the spur of the fork, as it were, demand the syllabub.

Because I am a great artist myself, I know the disappointment of rejection. I know what it is like to 'bang on the slap' and find the house empty. I know what it must be like for a chef to send out a Crème Honoré and have it returned untouched. When no one bought his paintings, Gauguin, or was it Van Gogh, cut off his own ear. A kitchen is full of knives. I must put no similar temptation in the way of a pastrycook.

I look forward to the petit fours, often nibbling the spun sugar in the swan's beak, or breaking off a piece of the basket and chewing the wicker work. I am not fond of marzipan. It is not a medium in which a chef does his finest work. The best sweet trolleys are always to be found in Italian restaurants, the most meagre in Indian ones. The two finest puddings I have ever tasted are the circular mille feuilles obtainable at the Château de Madrid and an Orange Boodle

Fool my daughter occasionally makes at the weekends when we have company.

I am a lifelong enemy of tapioca, but every now and then am seduced by a prune. I am still fond of a good meringue, but never hope to taste again quite the perfection of my grandmother's. I was smaller in those days, but a meringue should always be judged, like a vegetable marrow, by its size.

Of my schooldays I remember with pleasure only the tuck shop on the days I could afford a tenpenny mess (one banana, two scoops ice-cream and extra cream). I don't say I was happy then, but I was a little less miserable. While others dreamt of success on the playing fields, my private fantasy was a box of milk flake bars to myself.

For a time after I left school I was hooked on Walnut Whips, but ever afterwards have been a milk chocolate addict. I share my craving with one of my cats. Together we prowl the house, searching for the cache where my wife has hidden the bars she buys for the children. When we discover the hoard, we demolish it. Naturally, my share is larger than Tom's, but once we have awoken our taste buds, nothing can stop us. I have even known Tom to eat the silver paper. I have left many things unfinished in my life, but never a bar of chocolate. I haven't a wisdom-tooth in my head, but thank the Lord I still have a sweet one.

Afternoon Tea Now Being Served

How perfectly Oscar Wilde understood the importance of afternoon tea. There is a line in one of his plays about the dearth of cucumbers for the sandwiches which wrings the heartstrings. 'No cucumbers, Lane?' 'Not even for ready money, sir.' I have always been devoted to afternoon tea, an afternoon without it seems purposeless, and yet quite often these days I have to go without. Not at home, of course, there is always tea at home, but without guests – and especially grandchildren – the fare tends to sparseness, and more often than not the butter has not been left out of the refrigerator. Why cannot anyone design a reasonable compartment for the butter where it doesn't freeze to death? I sometimes look at the advertisements for soft margarine and wonder whether it's worth a try. Tea, then, for what it's worth, at home is flapjacks or crumpets, shortcake and gingerbread, swiss roll and chocolate biscuits and one or two cakes which need eating up. On Sundays and feast days when we sit round the dining-room table with the family it's altogether a more elaborate affair, with ginger snaps filled with cream and playmate biscuits and cucumber and pâté sandwiches and scones and jam, and the cakes of course are fresh, like the brown bread.

Ah well, having declared my interest in tea, as they say these days, or are supposed to say, let's venture further afield and contemplate how seriously this beautiful meal is taken by the catering trade as a whole. High praise to start with to the Savoy, where I once gave a tea party to about twenty guests and was allotted a private sitting-room, two waiters and a maître d'hotel who processed around with tea and cream and milk on silver trays and offered poached eggs in muffins and five sorts of sandwiches and *millefeuilles* and chocolate cake. Just about right, and of course a butler at the tea table makes all the difference. In Kent when I was young there were Sunday teas under a cedar tree and cake stands carried in procession across the lawn and silver trays, and large cups for the gentlemen and small for the ladies. They were not my teacups or my footmen, but for the rest of the week selling vacuum cleaners from doorstep to doorstep I would hug the memory of gracious living and Dundee cake.

Since the War, things have never been quite the same. Two who never survived the holocaust were Fuller's Walnut Cake and Sainsbury's Breakfast Sausage. I count myself fortunate that in my formative years, and indeed for some time afterwards, I ate my share of both. But tea shops are not what they were, particularly down South, though there is one opposite Kew Gardens which specialises in Maids-of-Honour, and Fortnum's still does its duty nobly. Indeed, their restaurant off Jermyn Street with its soda fountain is open unexpectedly late in the evenings in case you've missed out earlier, and there is deep consolation to be found in one of their elegant rarebits washed down with a chocolate milk shake.

Do my readers remember, as I do, Gunter's in Berkeley Square and Stewart's in Piccadilly, and the Trocadero in Shaftesbury Avenue? One is tempted to ask what on earth people do in the afternoon these days. Of course, there is always the Ritz.

In an endeavour to find out what happened to the trade I looked up tea shops in the Yellow Pages, to find the sole listing of such establishments is now confined to Capone, A., 38 Churton Street, S.W.1. I rang up to enquire about reserving a table, but something in my voice alerted the member of the staff who answered.

'You won't like it much here,' he told me, 'this is a tea-room for working men and we don't reserve.'

A similar enquiry to Gunter's, now in Bryanston Street, provided a more puzzling response. Tea was apparently available as long as I knew Mr. Vincent, who was out at the moment. I said I looked forward to meeting him and would it be all right if I brought a friend? The voice raised no objection and asked for the name and initial and when I'd given it, the time.

'I thought about four,' I said.

'And you're a friend of Mr. Vincent's?' Again the fatal enquiry.

'Not yet, but I hope to be a great friend after tea.'

'If you're not a friend already, I don't think you'd better come. Who are you, exactly?'

'A member of the public,' I replied with unaccustomed humility.

'We've given up entertaining them,' the voice rebuked, and hung up.

I tried Bentinck's, who used to serve tea in Bond Street and Wigmore Street, but now apparently only do so in Sloane Street, and never after five thirty. Marshall's tea is cleared away by five, as is the custom in most department stores. I feel slightly embarrassed taking tea where I am not proposing to shop or spend the night. It was not always thus. Hotels especially used to promote tea time, and Selfridge's Hotel still has a pianist. But what happened to the Gypsy Bands, what happened to the thés dansants, what happened to the trios and the quartets of gallant lady musicians who played amid the palms up and down the country from three-thirty till six, spreading a little happiness and extravagance with their repertoire of light music? 'Two teas with buttered toast, and will you ask them to play something from *Lilac Time*?' How proud, how happy I used to be when my request was granted; how appreciatively I would smile at the leader and clap all concerned. Dare I ask for the Cobbler's Song from *Chu Chin Chow* as an encore? I dared.

You will have to go a very long way indeed to recapture such pleasure, but intending travellers to Canada might care to know that in the Château Frontenac in Quebec they still strike up in the Palm Court as soon as lunch is over, and that the gentlemen of the ensemble wear wigs – not false hair pieces, you understand but genuine period wigs – tied with bows. Come to think of it, I enjoyed it more than Niagara.

The Chance of a Meal

The plight of the food critic on a crash-diet course is similar to that of a judge of a beauty contest devoid of a tape measure. How to compare the wilted lettuce, the raw cucumber, the aggressive tomato? The salads in Guy's Hospital are dreadful and in the whole world there seems no such thing as an orange with a thin skin. For the social occasions at which I felt strong enough to appear I made elaborate arrangements for a thin soup and 'hutch' sustenance to be placed in front of me. I was surprised therefore to notice how small the appetite or how great the customary restraint of others. At the *Punch* table, separated only by the distance of Harry Secombe from Princess Anne, I observed Her Highness, having refused the biscuit, crumbling the minute portions of Cheddar cheese before devouring them like a fairy-tale mouse. Opposite, her Lady-in Waiting delicately peeled a single grape with an expression sometimes observed on the Monarch's countenance whilst watching Zulu dancers.

People on the whole do eat less than me. I, who am incapable of refusing a pudding without a relentless explanation, find others merely shaking the head as though they have never even touched a profiterole and don't intend to.

I was enchanted by the tale published in a London evening paper about high officials of the IMF over here to promote a loan to Britain who were, like all good money-lenders, ready for a modest splurge on a Saturday night and couldn't get a table at two of our local fish-and-chip shops because they had omitted to reserve. Symptomatic, surely, of the state of the country, the editorial implied. We cannot afford to go on eating in this country, yet we persist.

Myself, nothing heartens me more than the sight of restaurants already replete at six-thirty or seven . . . They are eating early, I tell myself, and then coming on to see me. So they are, sometimes. Between the matinée and evening show on a Saturday some of my company stay in the dressing-room, some go round the corner to a club. I am, I think, the only one who regularly fortifies himself with a cut off the joint and two veg and hot treacle roll. 'How can you,' my fellow actors enquire, 'act after a meal like that?' 'It makes me feel good,' I tell them, 'except for a touch of wind, and when I feel good I act better.' To be honest, I don't think it would make any difference to me even if it was true.

I love food and for some reason I am particularly fond of it on Saturdays. So is my friend who invariably accompanies me and shares my passion for suet, and ritual. We sit always at the same table, greeted by the same maître, waited on by the same waiter. We order the same food after a lengthy perusal of the menu. Occasionally the thought crosses my mind, I will vary the diet, try the steak and kidney or the silverside, but I never do. I drink the house claret, my friend the cider. At precisely twenty-to-eight I glance at my watch, call for the bill, scurry back behind the scenes, slap on the slap and feel good. What pleasure life affords to a man of habit. How admirable, how satisfying. Once in a blue moon my friend has business which takes him elsewhere and I am lost. I moon about the streets or walk to a casino or just stay in my dressing-room slumbering over the television. 'I don't feel good,' I tell my fellow buskers when we meet later on the green. 'Give us our cues, get on with it,' they beg.

I have often thought there should be a *Punch Food Guide*—not like all the others, of course. It would be a guide which specified the mood one was in and matched it with suitable ambience and cooking. Where to take your aunt, your lover, your common-law wife. Where to go when you are angry, worried, bored, to celebrate passion spent. 'But you are the one who is supposed to know the answers,' you may say. 'Tell us, for instance, where to take our dog. Where are there special menus for pets?'

When ambience and the interior decorator first arrived on the scene and waiters first wore tight trousers and red aprons, and witchballs hung from fishermens' nets, a mild revolution occurred and patrons patronised the Bistro. Now the trend is Brasserie and American Disaster Areas. Soon perhaps we shall be back in the Speakeasy, but meanwhile, where is the most sinister restaurant? The smallest? Are there restaurants for singles, for children, for hat fetishists? Where would I choose to entertain Prince Charles, Patti

Hearst, Mrs Thatcher? I wish I knew. 'Tell me,' asked an American tourist the other day, 'where do the actors eat?' 'Here,' I told him, 'in the Wimpy Bar.' But he was not exactly satisfied. 'This isn't Sardi's,' he rejoined. 'Where do you sit around after a first night awaiting the notices?' The queries are endless.

If the *Punch Food Guide* appears there must be a chapter, surely, on the great trenchermen of today and yesterday. And another on how to listen to triumph and disaster and continue to spoon up the Poire Hélène. Such was indeed my dilemma when lunching a few days ago with the United Nations at Quaglinos, seated beside the immensely likable and courageous Mrs Williams who was in London to promote the Peace March. Mrs Williams's account of the perils and dangers of life in Belfast had my spoon poised motionless over the ice cream for some minutes, and only when she compared the menace of the Provos with that of the multinational television crews who are seldom out of her kitchen these days, did I feel emboldened to help myself once again to the chocolate sauce. I realised that Mrs Williams's tongue was in her cheek but in the brief respite afforded me, I managed to get the poire into mine . . .

All my life—at least as much of it as I remember—I have played my own version of Russian Roulette, not with a revolver loaded in one chamber, but on the pavements of London Town. 'If,' I tell myself, 'I do not overtake the lady with the ‘dachshund before she reaches the next lamppost but one, I shall be dead in a week.' I command myself to meet the unknown poet in the Gannex exactly opposite the To Let sign fifty yards along the road. Were I not to do so, I must instantly assume his personality and he mine. Above all, I am by nature an omen-taker born out of my time. In less happy days I should have surely have spent long hours in the queue before the Temple of Diana at Ephesus, if indeed that was where it was sited.

On my way to casinos I decided to back number eleven the whole afternoon, provided the man mending the gas leak is entirely invisible once I have reached the No. 9 bus stop where the manhole he is contemplating is situated.

In pursuit of my destiny I have become an amazing judge of pace, not, alas, on the race track, or indeed behind the wheel of a car, but I can gauge the exact speed needed to overtake, encounter, or even stop dead beside a moving object, without sudden acceleration or undue loitering. Smoothness of pace is demanded—any fool can break into a jog trot at the last moment. Besides being able to defy and often get the better of the malign powers always attempting to destroy me, I am rather good at securing the only taxi on the rank, as happened the other morning at Paddington Station. Coming up on the blind side of a mother and child, two collies and a variety of luggage, I was in the taxi and away before the dogs, at any rate, had grasped what was happening. I think the taxi driver was grateful, too; at any rate we became friends from the start.

'I want,' I told him, 'No. 45, Cheapside.' I thought I had better pretend to be a property entrepreneur or an underwriter to excuse my ungallant conduct. I sought to give the impression that sheep-dogs have more time on their hands than I.

'You will be wanting that French restaurant, Mr Morley?' he said.

Well, fame is fame, I might as well accept it. 'That's right,' I told him, 'you know it?'

'Often drive city gents there. I believe it's quite the place for stock-brokers to nosh up their clients before the shearing.'

'It's a wicked world,' I replied.

'We've all got to live,' he told me. Being the same age as myself he lived on his pension and about fifteen pounds a week he made as a part-time cab driver. His wife's pension brought his weekly income up to around thirty pounds. He owned his house, paid rates of four pounds a week, and managed quite nicely.

'I don't think,' I remarked, 'I have spoken to a single Englishman for the last twenty years who has told me that.'

He and his wife had a great many Continental relatives who came to stay and whom they visited in their turn, mostly in Belgium, he told me, then he took the occasional weekend package holiday out of season by the seaside and went fishing. On the last occasion the automatic tea-maker had failed to function, so he had overslept, but then he had forgotten to plug it in. He seemed to have few worries and throughout the whole journey failed to criticise a fellow driver. I felt I had been in the company of some sort of saint.

I was ready for the sinners at Le Poulbot, if not for the bill, which came to thirty-two pounds, just about what my taxi driver and his wife lived on for a week. Thank goodness no one expects a moral from a food critic . . .

Once in New York, impatient at the lack of service, I walked out in the interval between ordering the food and having it served me. At the door I was inveigled back by the fellow who stood behind the

small bar. 'Mr Morley,' he called in dulcet tones. 'Do me a favour?'
I approached all smiles, autograph pencil at the ready. 'Don't come
back,' he begged. I don't know why I've never forgotten an incident
which caught me unawares forty years ago.

TRAVELLING
HOPEFULLY

It is Better to Travel Hopefully. . .

Somewhere in the pocket of one of my suits is an advertisement for the Pakistani Airline. I have an idea their address is in Regent Street, and I have walked up and down past Hamley's and Mappin & Webb, searching for it lately. Why on earth don't I find the page or look it up in the telephone book? The answer is I don't really want to set out immediately for Katmandu. It is in the nature of a project. One of my many projects, like my visit to China, my stay in Bolivia, temporarily shelved after reading about the place in a Sunday supplement, or my insistence on seeing Naples again before I die, but meanwhile, and just for the moment, I am still hanging around Shaftesbury Avenue, lying low, waiting for the break. This is the time of the year when I cross the road to look in the windows of travel agents, but it's not a holiday I am seeking. I am not attracted by the gay poster or the cheap inclusive rate, with the individual shower and balcony. I yearn for sterner pleasures. In the Earls Court Road there are notice boards offering the most exhausting experiences. 'Small mixed party proceeding overland to the Upper Amazon have vacancy for spare driver. Bivouac-style accommodation, own sleeping bag essential.' I dream of joining a student group intent on studying primitive life in the lower Sudan, but fear rejection.

No, when I do set off I shall travel alone, as usual. It's not speed I'm after, but avoiding embarrassment. The truth is I don't really like other people to watch me en route. I am a slut where sightseeing is concerned. I have no particular love of churches. I dislike the castles and palaces once they have been gutted of treasure. I don't care for history unless it's quirky. On a hill outside Lebanon I searched for and found the grave of Lady Hester Stanhope, and later chided our ambassador in Beirut that it was neglected. I had been attracted to the tomb by a sentence in a guide book. 'Finally abandoned by the Sheiks, she took to the hills and the study of sorcery.' She who had once ruled England, or at least had advised her uncle on how it should be run, ended up in the wilderness, brewing up bats' wings. It's not how they start, but how they finish that interests me.

I hate shattered sculpture, ruined forts. I love camel markets and bazaars. I like noise and filth and stench. I detest the smell of incense burning in empty cathedrals or full ones either, for that matter. I get no kick from a twelfth-century reredos. I am not the stuff of which Kenneth Clark is made.

Arriving in a new place, I am invariably disappointed. This is not how I pictured Samarkand, I tell myself. The truth is, of course, I never pictured it at all. As soon as I arrive, I want to be off. I find the harbour or the bus station, and read the destination boards. If the lettering is indecipherable, so much the better. I hop on the coach and pretend I know where I'm going, pay the conductor the same amount as the man who sits beside me, alight where he alights, and wonder what the hell I'm going to do in a hillside slum for three hours before the bus returns. But I find something, even if it's only to sit in the café in the square, and if possible in the sun. I watch nothing whatever happening, and am content. On the way back I grab the seat next to the window and am disappointed that the route is familiar.

In Belgrade there never seemed more than one way out of the town. I chose the bigger bus, always hoping to get further. One evening I found myself back at Munich. Another time I reached Kotor after a hell of a journey and rang up to see if they had missed me on the film I was making. They had. 'Come back,' they urged, 'all is forgiven.' It had taken me three days to arrive, but the guide-book insisted Belgrade could be reached from Kotor in four hours by a new crack express operating on the recently-built line linking the capital with the Mediterranean.

'Get me a first class ticket,' I urged the porter.

'On what?' he asked.

'The train, the express, the Trans-Yugoslavian Queen.'

'There is no such thing,' he told me.

I showed him the guide-book. 'Very well,' I said, 'book me by the slow train.'

But he seemed unimpressed. 'There is no line,' he replied. In the end I commandeered the light aeroplane which transported the mail. I used up a lot of stamps, but of course no one got their letters for a week.

In Istanbul, boats are always leaving the quay. The game is played by rushing up the gangway at the last moment, and then starting to worry in case one is bound for Australia and not just another island in the Sea of Marmora. Why all this rushing around, Morley? Why can't you keep still, stay put? Heaven knows, you're old enough. To me it's awful to have lived sixty-odd years on an earth which I haven't seen properly. Geographically, I don't suppose there are any more surprises. I have taken in sea coasts with palms and sea coasts with mountains and sea coasts with houses. I have driven across deserts and through country lanes, along American highways and Turkish mule tracks. I have pottered in Hong Kong and Huddersfield. They are different, of course, but not all that different. The cities and the plains of the world are the same basically, but it's the people living in them who vary. The maids bathing fully dressed in the Bosphorus; Japanese ladies exchanging gift-wrapped sugar at the Tokyo Hilton; the trussed live crabs with bass in Macao; Sinatra in Vegas. In Istanbul I found a bear trained as a masseur. How I longed to bring him home with me and set him up in business on some shady Soho landing. I would have pinned a card to the bell push; 'Bear Massage', and waited for the terrified customers to remonstrate over the spelling. I always like to have the last laugh. I must really go through my suits again, and find that address.

Mr Morley, I Presume

Of all the madness I experienced as a child, nothing reached a higher quotient of insanity than the geography lessons. I was instructed to draw the course of the Euphrates River and to mark and name the principal tributaries. Who was I at the age of eight to decide the relative eminence of rivers? I still do not know where the Euphrates rises and falls. I sometimes wonder whether, indeed, the Euphrates is still rising and falling, so seldom do I hear it mentioned. And even today, as I travel the globe, I am still trying to hide the fact that I have only the haziest idea of how the world fits together and why, for example, when flying out of Britain, I must pause at Frankfurt en route to Kenya. I had decided on Kenya for a holiday, because if one is to bask in the sun, it's smart to get as close to the equator as possible. Mombasa is not only near the equator, it is thoroughly spoiled. I am not one for the unspoiled terrain, the empty beach, the thornbush, the flyblown kiosk with the lukewarm beverage. Give me the marble terrace, the steps leading down into the water. I can ignore the high-rise apartment at my back. I am looking the other way.

When I leave the water, I like elegant patio furnishings and a cool drink – not out of the coconut but from the refrigerator. I like the loving care of the barman, not the childlike friendliness of the noble savage. I am not interested in ecology. I refuse to worry about the fate of the spotted hartebeest. If it's had its day, that's all right with me. I shall manage without the creature. On the other hand, when it's hot, I prefer not to manage without ice and air conditioning. Why should I?

It was exceedingly hot in Mombasa. I had only to put my nose outside and the skin peeled. Fellow visitors coated their features with cream and wore plastic shields. My world was full of the chicken-mayonnaise crowd and I was content to lie in the shade behind some rocks and watch a honeymooning French couple play chess every afternoon under a coconut tree.

In the bar one evening I met a man who had a house in Lamu, a town farther up the East African coast toward Italian Somaliland; and the next morning I was flying there. I decided against making the journey by road and dugout canoe through the mango swamps, as I didn't fancy having to stand upright in the latter, watched by rapacious crocodiles. When we landed, the pilot warned us against taking photographs of the ground staff, who were convicts. They seemed remarkably young to be serving prison sentences. But farther along the path to the jetty and the motorboat that was to take us across the lagoon to the town itself, we came upon a more mature group breaking stones.

In Lamu, I was welcomed by the curator of the museum, who introduced me to his parrot. The parrot came from London and hadn't learned to fly, on account of a defective wing. Each afternoon at four local time, which is petshop closing time in Britain, the parrot insisted on being put to bed in a dark room with the door locked. Until that happened, he screamed.

The rest of the town came from *Alice in Wonderland*. Once upon a time, Lamu was the richest port on the coast, with plumbing far in advance of anything Europe had experienced up to then – including the bidet. Wealthy residents even drove gold rods into the walls of the houses by way of ostentation. Little remains of the elegant extravagance that demanded four slaves to a canopy as the local sherifs paraded the main street. The sherifs still parade, holding their own umbrellas; the sons of the prophets are everlastingly marrying the daughters of the faithful, and everlastingly divorcing them the next morning. A night with a sherif for her virgin daughter, and mother goes to heaven, or so they tell her.

A great deal remains in Lamu, including even the British. There are many cannons on the waterfront and a plethora of bones in the sands beneath. Lamu played a home match around 1800 against the neighbouring island of Pate and won 1700 to 6 – a famous massacre, as when the tide went out suddenly, the away team couldn't get off the reef. Usually when Lamu lost, she lost to the cannibal tribes, the Portuguese, the Ethiopians and, of course, the British.

One afternoon I lunched on my hotel terrace and noticed the beach being patrolled by soldiers. The oldest of all the English residents had taken to exposing himself by the water's edge and the newly-appointed district commissioner was determined for some reason to catch him in the act. 'Will they shoot him?' I asked anxiously. 'They won't even catch him,' I was told. 'His wife is keeping him indoors.'

Later, I signed the visitors' book immediately below the Aga Khan, who had just left. There is one family in Lamu that subscribes to his faith

273

and he had taken pains to meet them, but not while he was alone. If you are a follower of the Aga's and catch him alone, he must accede to your request. The family was anxious to buy the local mosque at a knockdown price, knock it down and build a hotel. The Aga Khan was courteous, circumspect and perpetually accompanied on his walks along the waterfront.

On the way back from Lamu I stopped in Malindi, Kenya, to lunch with the British and take tea with the Krauts. Nationalism is encouraged by the package tour. The Germans are winning hands down; there are at least four jumbo flights each week from Frankfurt. Of the Americans, there is little sign along the coast. They simply haven't the time to lie around in the sun; besides, that sort of life comes easier and cheaper at home. If they come to this part of Africa at all, it is to Mombasa or Nyali Beach, and then only for two or three nights, to rest up between safaris. Americans are in the game game, and how well they play it. The men try to look and dress like Stewart Granger; the women favour Dorothy Lamour — the head turbaned, the figure sheathed in fiery African colors. They are armed with cameras, not rifles; zoom lenses, not cartridges.

There is not really a great deal to buy in Africa, but Americans have a stab at shopping. Occasionally, they are stabbed themselves. One party, in particular, was nearly speared to death by the Masai because they laughed too loudly and bent themselves double, pretending to have been wounded by the dancers' spears. The tribesmen, suddenly bored by audience participation, decided to play it for real. None of the visitors was killed, but the guilty tribe was punished by being deprived of the dance concession for a spell.

Some tourists also ask for trouble by stepping out of jeeps to feed an elephant the remains of a picnic lunch or by climbing down from a tree hut to proffer a leopard a drink. Punishment when it comes is condign; an elephant takes its time trampling a man to death. When it's finished, all that's left is a thin, red mush.

Of course, not all trouble is invited. There can be no harm, surely, in tea on the lawn and no blame attached to anyone, except the lioness herself, if she chooses to hunt and catch a baboon among the chocolate biscuits and buttered scones. 'Two of my guests finished up in trees and quite an old lady up to her neck in the pond,' Mr. Pascoe told me. Mr. Pascoe is manager of the appropriately named Hunter's Lodge, which stands just to the side of the Nairobi — Mombasa highway. 'We have a good many lions here,' he went on proudly. 'I usually take guests for an evening ramble and we nearly always see something, even if it's only a snake.'

Water-holes are a great feature of the game lodges. Floodlit and with a thoughtfully-provided artificial salt lick, they provide an opportunity for the game to have a look at the guests in their natural habitat. All day the latter have been bouncing around in jeeps, making it difficult for the elephant and particularly the leopard to count them accurately. But here, bunched at the bar, they can be inspected by the wart hogs and hyenas at leisure.

Sitting next to me at the bar was a Kenya policeman's wife, who had lived in Africa all her life and who knew a good deal about the Mau Mau. 'We had a cook in those days,' she told me, 'who was one in a thousand, the kindest, most obliging, most dedicated cook in all of Africa, famous for his spaghetti soufflé. With this talented man in the kitchen, I couldn't go wrong as a hostess and he might have stayed forever, had not my husband come home one evening and told me that our splendid chef was the senior Mau Mau oath administrator for miles around. It was a terrible oath, you know,' she continued, 'the worst sort of black magic and quite unmentionably obscene. Arrangements were made that he be arrested in his own village because he was such a charming old man. That night the fellow cooked his last soufflé, or so we thought, and the next day we drove him back to his home, where a dozen soldiers were waiting. He got into the truck and bumped off to prison and, as we thought again, his death. Then about three months later, my husband and I went to dinner at the home of the police commissioner. The meal began with spaghetti soufflé.'

I asked her about problems confronting white Kenyans these days and she thought cattle rustling was as serious as any. The whole farming economy is undermined by the necessity of enclosing the stock every evening. It means cows can't be left out to pasture but have to be driven into pounds. Their grazing is interrupted and the milk yield and growth rate are far lower than they should be. When cattle are stolen, the farmer must do everything possible to recover his beasts, otherwise he will lose more of them next time. The thieves have to be tracked, sometimes for weeks, and all other work on the farm comes to a standstill; and when the cattle are found they have to be driven home and they lose more weight in the process.

My companion was one of the few white Kenyans I met who didn't seem affronted by the way things were going. The others always prefaced their opinions by confiding how long they had lived in Kenya. They felt a peculiar sense of injustice at the nationalism they were now encountering. Whatever their attitude had been before independence, they no longer clapped their hands and shouted for Charley. When they spoke to their African servants, they almost whispered their requests, couching them in

275

the reasonable terms in which one might address a difficult seven-year-old. 'Don't scream,' they seemed to be pleading, 'and don't stamp your foot, but just run along like a good boy and see if you can find Mummy a little more ice. Won't that be fun, now?'

How much fun the Africans have these days is difficult to assess. The women lead lives of incredible austerity; each day they must walk miles in search of firewood and to fetch water from the communal tap. They also must do the housework and till the fields and mind the herds and contrive at the same time to dress elegantly and to carry their youngest on their back.

For men, life is easier. Unless, that is, they elect to work in the hotels, where they must watch the guests waste the bath water and leave the food untouched on their plates. What do they think of the luxury in which we wallow, compared with the deprivation and undernourishment of their own folk? I asked the proprietor of Leisure Lodge, arguably the most comfortable and certainly the most beautiful hotel in Kenya. He told me that the African wasn't undernourished, that most Europeans were far from clean and only with the greatest reluctance would he be willing to entertain one in his home. This was particularly true of hippies, whose physical presence nauseated him.

According to the proprietor, his staff had no need to work; they were all possessed of small-holdings that brought them adequate incomes. They worked in order to pay for more wives. The acquisition of wives was a complicated and lengthy game. 'It is played,' he explained, 'rather like Monopoly.'

'But if you were an African awakened in the night by your child crying for a drink of water, how would you feel if you knew the nearest tap was five miles away?' I asked. 'Would you go yourself? Would you send your wife?'

'I would wake my wife,' he told me, 'and she would give the child a coconut or a glass of goat's milk. Very few Africans drink water.'

I wasn't sure whether I believed him or not. I recalled the experience of one settler who had taken his head cattleman, a Masai tribesman, to the Royal Show in London last summer. After two days he was asked what had struck him most forcibly. 'Those taps,' he said, 'all those taps.'

There is a man called Donovan Maule, an actor like myself, who went to Nairobi after the last war and decided to stay and found a stock company. Curiously enough, he made a fortune, retired and built himself and his wife a bungalow on a creek near Mombasa. The theatre is now run by his daughter. They still play Rattigan and Coward and Priestley and

Maugham, but the heart and the profit have gone out of the business. 'A lot of our patrons have had to pack up and go home. They don't like it, you know; England isn't what it was, any more than this place. What they dread most is having to retire to somewhere like Canterbury.' He poured me another gin and slapped his wrist. 'We don't get mosquitoes here, you known.'

'Nor in Canterbury,' I told him, but he seemed unconvinced.

In what was once called the White Highlands, beyond the Aberdare mountain range, the British still farm the land, but no longer with the confidence they used to display when the Mau Mau was around and each settler had a gun at the ready. They have put their guns away but still greet the stranger on their stoop with caution. They know that his briefcase hides no fearsome machete, but more probably just a letter from the President himself, inquiring in the politest possible manner whether perhaps the present owner might care to sell his property. After that, of course, it's only a matter of time before Canterbury, or a bungalow near Mombasa, becomes a reality.

The mission pilot was on his honeymoon and lived in Abyssinia. He was the only man I saw in Africa actually eat a coconut and he did it with expert ease, even producing a bowl for the milk. He had been married only three days, which was perhaps why, in true African fashion, he neglected to offer his wife any until he had almost finished it. There was plenty of coconut meat for both of them, and as he munched, he explained why he found it necessary to spend an hour on his knees each week, specifically asking the Almighty to put an end to the permissive society in West London.

'Are you praying for a holocaust?' I asked him.

'If necessary.'

'Tell me,' I urged, 'about Addis Ababa. Is it true the penalty for stealing is to cut off a hand?'

'Sometimes.'

'My goodness,' I told him, 'I wouldn't like to see that sort of thing in Britain. Think of the number of one-armed shoppers you'd meet. I think I prefer the permissive society.'

On my last night in Africa, I hired a launch in order to inspect the carmine bee-eaters. Extraordinary birds, which look like psychedelic starlings, who choose to roost each evening in one particular clump of mango trees three or four miles upstream from the creek on which stands the Mnarani Country Club. The club is an elegant establishment, much patronized by big-game fishermen and, especially, the present Lady

Delamere. The murder case in which her husband, Delves Broughton, was tried and acquitted of the killing of 'Boy' Errol in the Fifties still provokes raised eyebrows and lowered voices wherever two or three Kenyans are gathered together with a stranger who will listen to the tale.

Upstream, we dawdled by the riverbank. I was convinced the boatman was uncertain which mango clump harboured the birds. But no, it was too early and they hadn't yet arrived. Meanwhile, he showed me huge pelicans perched in banyan trees and egrets fishing from the bank and sea eagles circling above and, rounding a bend of the river, a village built on the mud flats with children calling us to come closer and be inspected for cigarettes. My boatman ignored them and, turning the boat suddenly, brought us back downstream. He's lost, I told myself, we'll not find them now, it will be too dark to see. Then suddenly the carmine bee-eaters came swooping and soaring, settling for a moment and then flying away, and returning, and all the time the beat of their wings and the sound of their voices filled the air with excitement.

This is Africa, I told myself. This is what I came to see, and wondered if it was true that these were the only carmine bee-eaters in the world and this the only mango swamp they patronized. But when it was quiet again and darkness fell and we journeyed back downstream to the country club, I found myself considering for the hundredth time the riddle of Delves Broughton.

The rip-roaring days are over for the British. Now they walk abroad as delicately as the Japanese. In Kenya, they are remembered, but without gratitude. They set an example of incorruptibility in the administration that has not been followed. They planted sisal and grew groundnuts and became croppers. They left Kenya no richer than they found it, but look, an African will tell you, look what they got out of it for themselves.

The Great
South American Adventure: 1
Up the Amazon

Each year around the winter solstice there appears in my morning paper the picture of assorted passengers dressed overall making their way heavily laden up the gangways of some great liner tied up at Southampton. Underneath, the familiar caption, 'Travellers on world cruise forced to carry their own baggage, owing to dock strike.'

Nothing makes me more envious—not, of course, that they are permitted to carry their own suitcases, a facility nowadays increasingly extended to us all, but that they are up and away before the rest of us have had our morning bath, to spend a delirious three months or so encircling the globe. This could be me, I used to tell myself, if only I'd played my cards right, and this year I dealt myself in.

I am not pretending ours was a world cruise, and in point of fact our luggage did get carried on board at Callao just up the road from Lima whither my wife and I had flown to await the arrival of the good ship *Viking Sea* and sail around the Horn, or more prudently perhaps, through the Straits of Magellan. We didn't get off to a very good start, as fog more or less closed down Heathrow and even the Monarch Lounge where I normally shelter before a flight was already overcrowded. I work here, I told others less fortunate, and shouldered my way to the gin and tonic fountain mercifully still working (and about the only thing that was for the next twelve hours). But we got off at last and even managed the connection at Miami, which was more than a prominent British banker contrived en route for Bolivia, where he was to lend more money than I thought we had available just at present.

The number of British bankers travelling alone and in pairs that

I was to encounter in the right places along the route was quite phenomenal. One of them confided to me that they borrowed the money in Dallas before lending it to any available junta which then in its turn did the right thing by the old country by ordering another hundred gross of machine guns for internal security purposes.

A word here, perhaps, about my own attitude as contrasted, say, to that of Bernard Levin. While he never goes abroad except to Salzburg but continues to animadvert lustily on books he hasn't read, TV programmes he has never seen, and countries he has no intention of visiting even in the unlikely event of their being willing to admit him, I for my part peruse and potter wherever I am permitted to do so. I do not approve of police states and torture and firing squads, nor, for some far more inexplicable reason, of Bernard himself.

On, then, to the jungle, which is where we landed up after only three days in Lima. We found the city rather cheerless on our first visit. It has been palpably poorly sited, sheltering on a ledge straight down from the Andes. Here, like some unfortunate mountaineers trapped and bivouacked, the residents await rescue and realise—as we did—that the sun simply isn't going to shine on them. Peruvians have the saddest faces imaginable. I was reminded of Salt Lake City and Brigham Young's fatal mistake in not going on a little further. Not that there are many Mormons in Peru but then, of course, one never knows for certain who exactly still lives in the vast jungle which steams and sweats all around them. There are wonderful stories of this Rider Haggard-Stewart Granger world where helicopters disappear into swampland and aeroplanes laden with gold take off, never apparently to land again, at least in Peru.

There is much talk of a tribe of fair-skinned and red-haired warriors entrusted with the guarding of the Treasures of the Incas from marauding explorers. In Callao there still lives the sole survivor of one disastrous encounter who, feigning death, was able eventually to escape and managed *en passant* and in headlong flight to cut off with a machete a golden thumb from a huge idol. 'I shouldn't have thought,' I told my informant, 'you could cut gold with a machete.' 'This was soft gold,' he told me.

'But didn't our friend go back?' I asked. Apparently not; once is enough.

I must say once in the jungle was enough for me. After two days in Lima, and still hoping for warmer weather, we decided to fly to

Iquitos and thence travel up or quite possibly down the Amazon to a sort of leisure lodge which had better remain nameless. Whatever Iquitos was once in the days when rubber was booming, it certainly isn't any longer: a few rusted wrought-iron balconies of great elegance cling to crumbling colonial mansions, most of them designed by Eiffel who seems to have had a hand in most of the architecture of Peru and whose speciality—besides towers, naturally —were appalling little cast-iron churches.

The Iquitos Municipal Council, years ahead of their time and no longer relying on dustmen or employees in the public sector, have created (or encouraged the citizens to create) an enormous rubbish dump in the centre of the town and turned all waste disposal over to a flock of voluntary vultures. We ate a poor lunch and ambled downstream in an open launch on which someone had constructed a rickety and utterly ineffective shelter of coconut matting to keep out, or possibly in, the rain.

Almost at once the rain sheeted down and the boat halted in midstream to avoid the enormous logs which float aimlessly and in considerable quantities down to the ocean thousands of miles away. When it rains everything stops on the river to get thoroughly wet, but the storm eventually moved away and round about tea-time we arrived, not without first having had to transfer to a sodden dug-out canoe, at our rest camp. If you have ever wondered—or indeed experienced—what it must have been like in a Japanese prison camp on a damp Sunday afternoon, you will know something of the conditions prevailing down river.

The proprietor was American and made a short speech of welcome before offering a glass of rum punch and a warning not to stray off on our own. The sleeping cubicles, lit by kerosene lamps, were open to the jungle, windowless and shutterless, and duckboards led to jungle loos and washing huts. 'Not,' I told the proprietor, 'quite what I expected.' 'It is exactly what you should have expected,' he told me brusquely, 'a chance to live for a couple of nights as the Indians do.' 'But not at these prices surely?' I asked. I got little change and was violently ill all night, my spirits not improved by innumerable walks along the duckboards and a horror that a snake might be ensconced in the lavatory bowl and I would die of snake bites on the bottom, miles from civilisation, leaving my poor wife to cope with my corpse. But in the mornnig, although it was still raining, I felt well enough to crawl back on to the launch and head upstream for Iquitos.

We said farewell to our fellow guests, to whom, indeed, I had hardly said hello before the rigours of the night. They consisted of a couple of amateur lepidopterists who seemed surprised we were leaving so abruptly. They were themselves spending an enjoyable week apparently, finding the jungle no problem as long as one remembered to keep moving. Otherwise, they explained, one was liable to be bitten by snakes or spiders or eaten alive by ants. The other guest was a keen French photographer armed with cameras and a quantity of bead necklaces which he was hoping to exchange with neighbouring tribes for shrunken heads.

For myself, on my way back to Iquitos and the friendly vultures, I could see no traces of tribes on the river bank. Only a few isolated huts and a general air of damp depression underlined the fact that to avoid the intolerable boredom of the rain forest the Peruvian is willing to live anywhere, even in a shanty town outside the capital. We got back to Lima just in time for the festival of Our Lord of Miracles and to find everyone wearing purple cloaks and, in the streets, to watch the procession of their most venerated image, a picture of the crucifixion painted by a black Christian slave on the wall of a monastery which, unlike the artist and most of the inhabitants, survived the earthquake of 1665. The bishop, mitred and walking delicately under a canopy, followed thirty of his stout churchwardens bearing the heavy golden frame while priests, conducting a massive walk-about, snatched children from the faithful and held them aloft to kiss the painting before returning them hopefully to the right parents. The bands played and the flowers piled up and we partook of very special nougat baked for the occasion while having our pockets most skilfully picked of all loose change but none of our credit cards.

By now the sun was shining and we spent two happy days exploring the museums, admiring the elegance of the early Spanish settlers with their golden bedsteads and the examples of pre-Columbian art with their golden penises. We found an extravagantly beautiful hotel and drank Pisco sours and dawdled till the ship was due to sail. We sat high up in the Windjammer Bar, still clutching our Piscos, and watched the pelicans and the not-so-secret police on the quay fade into the haze, and hoped that one day the money will flow in to start the oil flowing out, the copper surfacing, the gold rushing to bring prosperity to this melancholy land where a patient people wait to catch a glimpse of their ruler (through a fence of British sub-machine guns) , held at bay by steel-helmeted members of his bodyguard.

The Great
South American Adventure: 2
Once Aboard the Lugger

I was a much-walked child; from an early age nurses, governesses and even sometimes my parents had me out on the roads practising putting what was called one's best foot forward. For what marathon I was intended originally I never discovered, suffice it that the process cured me effectively of ever wanting to go for walks when not obliged to do so. To my protests and enquiries as to where on earth we were bound for on a freezing March morning or sweltering summer afternoon, the reply was inevitable. All the way there and back again to see how far it is.

Thus, on board the *Viking Sea* off the many coasts of South America, I had nothing but pity for those unfortunate fellow passengers who, although by this time too well advanced in age, were still in thrall to ghostly governesses and perambulated the promenade deck beneath the window of our cabin. Heads down, mufflers up, or on a warm morning in nylon track suits, they would complete their self-imposed quota of twenty-eight times around and chalk up just so many nautical miles to keep them in the Race Around. For among the many trophies to be competed for, along with the deck quoits, the table tennis, the shuffle board, the whist, the Monopoly and clay pigeon shooting, the walk-around individual free style long distance championship was possibly the most prized.

For a long time after we had come aboard their undisputed leader was a spry octogenarian whose actual age was considerably exaggerated by early morning drinkers in the après-walk bars along with the distance he had already covered. Not much was known about him, save that he started walking when the boat was still tied up in San Francisco and had been at it more or less ever since.

Sadly the lone eagle, as he became known, bruised his wings against the funnel one windy morning off Valparaiso and for the rest of the voyage perched disconsolately on a deck chair. For myself, it was quite enough excitement to be on board such a splendid ship and to know that in the very next and exactly similar cabin to ours nested a genuine Getty.

It is no good pretending I don't like the rich. I love them. I know it's common and vulgar to be impressed by wealth and titles, but I am common and vulgar and the fact that nearly everyone on the boat was a great deal wealthier and some even older than I, pleased me inordinately.

Nor was I overawed by the hints contained in the booklet entitled 'What Every Viking (sic) Should Know About The Royal *Viking Sea*'. I wasn't likely, for instance, to appear in the dining-room in anything but informal dress for breakfast or lunch and needed no reminder that shorts, swimsuits and hair curlers were inappropriate at all times.

Even if I hadn't already known that 'for gentlemen unwilling to pack a tuxedo, today's fashion scene covers a variety of comfortable and colourful evening models', I was soon to discover for myself that sports coats studded with sequins show up well after sundown, and to wish I owned just such a garment. Clothes should announce the intention of those who dress in them. A man sparkling like Liberace is patently out to enjoy himself and will probably do so, just as surely as a lady clad in a well-cut trouser suit is not expecting, still less inviting, rape.

In actual fact, most of the five hundred passengers on board were not passion-orientated, although one of the ship's officers admitted that on the last leg of the cruise, sailing back into home waters, there is a slight increase in the alcohol consumption among those who dreamt of tall dark strangers and are about to find them at long last in the person of custom officers. But most of us have banished such fantasy a while back and for the most part are surprisingly still attached to our lifelong partners with whom we walk cautiously but still hand in hand from the Windjammer Bar to the Hedevig Amalia Room or the Emerald Club to attend yet another cocktail party hosted by some surprisingly sober couple from the Palos Verde Estate, Newport Beach, or Boca Baton, Fla. The passenger list discreetly identifies each of us with our home town but not, of course, the exact address, and a horrible suspicion crosses one's mind that not everyone lives where he or she pretends. Corona del Mar, San

Juan Bautista, Pebble Beach, Chula Vista, Baxter Springs. Is there no one from Brooklyn or Flatbush? Suddenly reassured, one comes across Mrs Jane Hulsen from Brisbane and even a couple from London, England.

Modesty was my watchword, even witnessing in the theatre a collection of some of the worst films I have ever made including *The Blue Bird*, assembled by an over-confident cruise director as a Mini-Restrospective Morley Festival. When I remonstrated with him as to the wisdom of including a picture in which Cathleen Nesbitt, dressed as a Mother Superior, strangled me with the cord of her habit, he riposted that although possibly enough was enough, this was for him a collector's piece, and he confidently expected that all the passengers would be opting for an early bedtime as he planned to screen it the evening before docking in Buenos Aires.

Indeed, after such special treats, I modelled every thought and gesture on the Queen Mother herself. However tired my ankles, I stood erect to receive compliments and gently correct the impression that I had also been extremely good in *Mutiny on the Bounty*. I shared the limelight with a charming CBS front man who lectured directly after breakfast each morning on 'What Really Happened To Amelia Earhart' and how he once found a missing American fighter plane at the bottom of a lake, too late, alas, to do anything much about the occupants. He had tried to do something about Amelia on a series of expeditions he and CBS had made to the Solomon Isles, once even boxing up what was thought to be her skeleton and conveying it back to the States, only to find the bones didn't belong to Amelia and politely returning them once more to their earlier resting place. There was always a good attendance at that hour of the morning when passengers liked to vacate their cabins, in order to have them made up by the stewardesses, and had a happy hour to fill in between breakfast and bouillon. Once aboard, the passengers were happy to repeat the exact pattern of any day that had proved agreeable, rather in the manner of the *Mad Woman of Chaillot* who read the same paper each morning. Indeed, we all did that, only we read it in the evening, picking it up from the cabin floor where it invariably lay immediately after dinner.

True, sometimes the captions were slightly altered and even rearranged, but such headlines as 'Soviet Slick Threatens Sweden', 'Commerce Index Not Optimistic' and 'Carter Says Wait Till Next Year' were not only what we came to expect but invariably found. The page we turned to most eagerly was headed 'Daily Program', starting at six-thirty with Early Risers' Coffee Club and carrying on through Spanish Class with Rev Rudler, Keep Fit with Clive and Jane, Complimentary Dance Class with The Revells, Walk-a-Thon, Meet Barry, right through the day to Grandmothers' Tea with Master Barry, Music for Discerning Listeners, Ann Offers After-Dinner Liqueurs and ending with Late Night Buffet and Sounds for Night People. The entertainment staff (Rabbi: J. Schwarz) doubled and trebled throughout the day in the manner of circus performers, now in spangled tights and the next instant dressed and behaving like Yugoslav tumblers urging the passengers to keep their eyes down for bingo or up for clay pigeon shooting, to bend and touch their toes, or reach for the last trump in the dummy's hand. They never seemed to tire or weary the customers, in whose breast there existed for them an almost romantic attachment as they 'sang along with Jack' or urged Barry to wrap up an unwanted éclair for their stewardess.

As the kidnapped are reported to become increasingly attached to their captors, so cruise passengers become almost morbidly attached to those who organise their activities aboard. On the *Viking Sea* many of the entertainment staff were already well known to the voyagers from previous cruises. Although the line is comparatively new, most had made half a dozen trips already aboard this one or her sister ships *Viking Star* or *Viking Sky*, and as seasoned churchgoers they had taken part in previous services and were ready with the responses.

They were able to explain to new communicants the difference between formal, informal and casual dress when it was urged upon them in the ship's programme, how long to pause before and after shaking hands with the captain at his inaugural reception, and the compulsory attendance and due solemnity with which shepherds and sheep alike celebrated the first boat drill. They knew when the library opened and the swimming pool closed, the exact minimum temperature at which luncheon would be available on the sports deck, and in rough weather (which happily we never encountered) they were familiar with the ropes and where they would be slung, to assist us to keep our feet.

It was surprising, really, that not more of us slipped up even in calm waters, considering how many already relied on aids to balance or a spouse's arm to propel them. The maintenance of equilibrium under the most trying conditions is the overriding preoccupation of the wealthy, and on board ship it is often easier to maintain than on dry land. There are no relatives or charitable causes to importune, no fears of robbers breaking in or revolution breaking out. No one has ever been mugged on the Mediterranean Deck. When they venture on shore, they do so in large parties. There are buses at the ship's side to convey them where they wish to go, to bring them safely back; all they have to remember is not to leave their cameras on the rack and to drink bottled water. Besides, there is no necessity to go ashore in the first place. Many preferred peaceful days tied up to the dockside, observing the cormorants and the pelicans. Best of all are the long hours spent at sea with their fellow Flying Dutchmen, when slumber and silence are broken only very occasionally and no one ever quite hears exactly how many fathoms lie below the keel. Do you find it difficult, I asked a retired banker, to understand the captain when he speaks over the intercom? I expect I should if I listened, he told me contentedly.

Peace is what they seek, although not at any price. For all of them, no matter how little it still matters, are motivated from time to time by the latent profit motive which once urged them onwards to capture and store their treasure. Now they are able to indulge, however fleetingly, their love of a bargain in the gift shops and duty-free stores of the world, and here they shop, triumphantly saving a few cents on a bottle of perfume purchased in Lima instead of Valparaiso and produced but never broached as an example of thrift and caution. It was Mr Getty himself who explained to me how much could be saved on shore excursions by not travelling with the team but making up a small party willing to share in the expense of a taxi. You see twice as much for half the price, he told me, and knowing Mr Getty he was probably right.

Everyone is out to gun the rich; it is churlish surely to confiscate the water pistols they still carry for their own protection.

The Great
South American Adventure: 3
How Green Was My Valparaiso

'A little bit of heaven fell from the sky one day; when the angels found it they sprinkled it with Shamrock and called it Ireland,' my aunt used to sing, and no doubt elderly maiden Chilean ladies were, and possibly still are, wont to voice much the same sentiment about Vin del Mar, a little town on the outskirts of Valparaiso boasting a Bournemouthian tranquillity in the midst of the rugged realities of present-day Chile. Our guide assured us that practically the whole of South America was apt to flock there during the summer months, the Argentinians finding it so much less crowded than their own Buenos Aires and Brazilians preferring it to Rio during the carnival. It was certainly not crowded in October; indeed, there were few people even playing the slot machines in the casino and none at all in the Salles Privées which were closed along with most of the restaurants, but the guide assured me the town came to life in December and even the floral clock would be going again by then, and I would like to have believed him for he was a patient fellow and dealt with considerable tact with the endless problems of explaining to my fellow tourists (on a later excursion) why there were quite so many police barriers on the main road from Valparaiso to Santiago.

'The government are anxious to bring home to the motorists the trouble that can be caused by worn tyres and faulty brakes, consequently these are now examined from time to time and of course the oil pressure checked.'

But why is it necessary for them to search the boot and apparently be asked at the same time for the passengers' papers?

'There are, alas,' he explained, 'a number of stolen cars on the roads, but I hope you will notice that under our new and benevolent rulers there is an entire absence of graffiti and the streets are cleaner.' Then, added as an afterthought apparently, 'The views I am giving you are not necessarily my own but those of the Tourist Board.'

I am not a man to be daunted by lack of experience in depth; give me, say, twenty-four hours, a brief shopping expedition and a couple of drinks in the local, and I am ready to publish my findings. I found Chile on the surface an altogether jollier land than Peru. There were plenty of shoppers in the street, a good deal to buy in the shops and, in Valparaiso at least, an enormous number of buses, clean, comfortable and not unduly crowded. Yet only the rich and middle classes seem to be comfortably housed, and the rest of the population is often not housed at all but shacked in conditions of extreme squalor. By six in the evening work was by no means finished on the land, and along the highway from Valparaiso to Santiago we passed palatial farmhouses and, at a respectful distance, the circles of one-room sheds in which the help is normally housed. In the capital there are avenues of beautiful houses and here, as elsewhere in South America, the more money you have the further you live from the centre of any city and the higher the wall of steel mesh which fences you in. The Moneda Palace is still closed for repairs, but the windows through which the rockets exploded are nowadays securely shuttered and the name of Allende does not exactly hang in the air. One day the Chilean poor will undoubtedly try again to secure a fair share and a free say in their own land, and this time they may have the private soldiers if not the generals on their side, and remember to close the windows once the firing starts.

Meanwhile, from the Restaurant of the Pyramids, you get the most beautiful view of the snow-capped mountains standing out above the smog and the heat haze and marvel at the good nature of the American tourists who, at four in the afternoon and still without lunch, exhausted from a marathon bus trip, join cheerfully in the Chilean National Dance, waving the white handkerchiefs loaned by the management, and wait without rancour for all the appalling food at long last to be served to them.

Five hundred miles farther along the featureless coast of Chile, we take another of the shore excursions but this time all goes well. Puerto Monti, in the shadow of the not quiescent volcano of Osorno, was originally settled by the Germans a hundred years or so ago in their eternal search for Leben space, and some of the houses and the churches they built are still there along with their descendants. It is a very different Chile from Valparaiso, with solid-looking cottages and well-kept gardens, and fields with grazing cattle and sheep, and the beautiful lakes, the water of one of which is emerald in colour and mirrors the wooded mountains and occasional pastureland in its green stillness. What happened to the German dream is not clear, for although early settlers sent home glowing reports of the opportunity the new lands afforded those who were willing to work it, they never arrived in sufficient numbers to do so, possibly dissuaded by the truth that it is not the tranquil Eden it appears.

There is a history of savage earthquakes, the latest only a few years ago when, besides the eruption of the volcano ruining thousands of acres of arable land, enormous avalanches descended on the villages and decimated the population. In a nearby resort, fifty terrified guests woken by the earthquake fled their hotel and were buried for ever under the snow. This is to be expected in our country, our guide told us with surprising equanimity, remarking that he himself had been away in Punto Arenas at the time. One remembered London during the buzz bombs. How remote Wimbledon seemed from Putney in those days, and how unfortunate.

All the way through the Straits of Magellan the sun shone from a cloudless sky and wonderful mountain peaks covered in snow played hide and seek with the passengers, who searched the water for seals and penguins and the banks for glaciers. The land, never far away, and sometimes creeping in almost alongside, and sudden low rocks protruding just above the water, remind us of the necessity for two pilots on the bridge at all times, an obligation imposed by Chile on all ships which sail in these waters.

It took Magellan thirty-eight horrific days to find his way through the maze of canals and past the hundreds of small islands normally wreathed in fog, but we were fortunate and three centuries later. Punto Arenas, the southernmost point, is a small robust settlement of neatly arranged squares, with houses and people built to withstand the almost perpetual blizzards which swirl around them. In the supermarkets prices are still going up, and Chile seems caught up in a hopeless spiral of inflation with her neighbour Peru. In Punto there is no sense of the police or the military and the alarming tales of torture and repression receded as, strolling into the local municipal theatre, we watched the children rehearsing their end-of-term dance display and listened to the kindergarten recite a poem in praise of education. How effective a propaganda weapon is universal education in action. Look at our children, urge the dictators of the

290

world, and hold your peace. In Punto Arenas they danced the folk dances of South America, the handkerchiefs waving, the feet strutting, the eyes shining—and what beautiful eyes these are and what beautiful children, perhaps this generation will after all grow up to inherit the rich earth. I, who had been prepared to glare at every policeman and follow the advice of the guide book about exercising restraint with officials and never growing impatient with or arguing with authority, telling myself that I was scarcely condoning the regime by so brief a stop along the way, found myself lulled into the belief that after two steps forward one step back still means some sort of progress.

Or does it? Would I have felt more sanguine if the children had been dancing and singing not the forgotten legends of the past but brisk stirring marching songs along the road to the future? More sanguine perhaps, more entertained certainly not!

Back on the *Viking Sea* that evening we have a sudden desire to find out what is happening at home, and picking up the telephone are connected within a few moments with Waltham St Lawrence, Berkshire, at a rough guess some ten thousand miles away. Asking how it is done, I am told it is just a matter of linking up with one of the satellites forever circling the Post Offices of the Universe. The moon men have earned my gratitude. My son sounded naturally as if he was in the next room, and wondered what on earth we were calling about. 'How is Pa?' he asked his mother, scenting trouble, and I am reminded of those happy days before the war at the New York World Fair where free calls were on offer by the Bell Telephone Company provided the caller didn't mind talking in public. All he had to do was to speak his mother's number in Idaho, and immediately the lights lit up on a giant map along the route taken by the wires, and the soft voice of the telephonist alerted Mother that her son was calling from the fairground and we listened on headphones while he tried to reassure her. 'No, Mother, there's not been an accident. Mother, if there was something wrong I'd tell you. It's a free call and we don't need a thing. Please try and believe me.' But Mother was seldom convinced by the time she was cut off, which was why there was always a queue for the headphones.

It wasn't all that of a free call to Berkshire, but well worth it. Travellers do well not to forget to send the postcards, reminding themselves they are having a wonderful time.

France and the French

During the First World War, the punishment for homosexuality in the French army was execution. However, if you were an officer you were allowed a final charge against the enemy, on the understanding that you got yourself shot. In one rather exceptional case the accused, who was the heir to enormous wealth and a proud title, was granted special leave from the battlefields until he had managed to consummate his marriage and procreate an heir. Eight months after he was killed in action, a child was born - a girl. That's the French for you — they take every trick but the last.

But for an Englishman there is always the fear that the French will win in the end. Every now and then one of my friends will put it to the test and retire with his ill-gotten gains to perch on one of those green-brown hills at the back of Cannes. But I am always struck by the sense of suspended animation which envelops him when he has acquired the sun blinds and the swimming pool. Once he has collected the sunshine and the gin, and of course the English papers, he is constantly obsessed with the price of butter.

My attitude to France was, I suppose, inherited from my father, who always felt perfectly at home there because he never attempted to talk or make friends with the natives. He admitted that there were certain things they did better than we did — sex and gambling, for instance — neither of which is true today. When I was sixteen and had left my last school, he decided that I should go into the Diplomatic Corps. He used to play bridge at his club with the Greek Ambassador, and usually won his money. 'They are a very decent class of fellow,' he told me. 'You'll enjoy being an Ambassador. Come on,' and having prized some money from his trustees, spirited me across the Channel to Tours, where he had been told the best French was spoken. Twenty-four hours in Tours shook him. He found himself encircled by the French. Hitherto he had always had his back to the sea, and a good hall porter at his elbow. In Tours there wasn't even a good hotel.

'You don't care for this, surely?' he asked me. 'You wouldn't be happy here? There's nothing to do.'

'Learn French?' I asked him.

'Yes, but not here.' He was already fingering the money entrusted to him for my further education. We left for Monte Carlo that afternoon. 'This will be better for you,' my father assured me. 'You get all nationalities here. In the Diplomatic Service you'll find you have to mix.' My parent was anxious not to leave me alone with the wrong ambiance. Ambiance was one of his four French words. His other three were Le Bon Dieu.

'I believe,' he would reiterate, 'in Le Bon Dieu, which is why I find the Church of England service so frustrating.'

'You never go,' my mother told him.

'That is why,' he told her. 'Le Bon Dieu is everywhere except in an English church.' There was no arguing with Father, while the money lasted, at any rate. In Monte Carlo it didn't last very long, about ten days, and we were posting breathlessly home before the cheques bounced. In France it was an offence for cheques to bounce, and Father dreaded not arrest, but banishment from the casinos.

I myself was arrested in France when I was eight years old. I had swung a fishing line off the jetty and caught the hook in my thumb. I was led away by a gendarme, with blood streaming from my hand. As he marched me through the streets I sobbed, not with pain, but with terror. True, he took me to a doctor, and not the police station, but why didn't the fool tell me what he was doing? An English Bobby would have given me a toffee and told me I was a brave little chap. The French are a logical people, which is one reason the English dislike them so intensely. The other is that they own France, a country which we have always judged to be much too good for them. France has for centuries blocked our way to Europe. Before the invention of the aeroplane, we had to step over them to get anywhere. I was particularly conscious of this geographical fact as a child, because I lived at Folkestone, where the Channel is at its narrowest, and the packet sailed daily for Boulogne. When the gales blew, my nurse used to take me down to the Harbour to watch the homecoming passengers staggering down the gangplank, and crawling across the cobblestones to the Pavilion Hotel for a steadyer. 'Serve them right,' she would tell me. 'That's what you get for going abroad, Master Robert.' Intolerance was one of the subjects she taught me in the nursery, and I was a willing pupil.

For me intolerance is still the adrenalin in the vein of society. Without it we should perish, with it we get into trouble. The intolerance of white to black, Gentile to Jew, rich to poor, and vice versa makes for battle, murder and sudden death. It also keeps everyone who stays alive fighting fit for a short time. In the intolerance league, the British are still top — an unaccustomed position for this old country these days. Over the years we have hung labels round the necks of foreigners. Americans are brash, Spaniards lazy, Germans gross, Turks treacherous, Russians dangerous and the Italians pathetic. We suffer them to live in their own lands only because they have to be there to be ready to fetch and carry for us when we have our holidays.

It is this concept of the British as the absentee landlords of the world that has served us so splendidly in the past, but it is one that the French have never accepted. They persist in believing that France belongs to them. The argument has been going on for some centuries. At various times in our history we have had to resort to fisticuffs, and one day no doubt we shall have to do so again. But it would be foolish not to recognise that the present is a period of stalemate, and there is little we can do just at the moment but pay up and look pleasant. We don't like paying bills any more than the French do, but at least we struggle to do so. When De Gaulle died, his epitaph was spoken by the landlord of my local inn. 'I'm sorry the old chap's gone, but he never paid the bill for Dunkirk, did he?'

Another fact I learned in my nursery was that the Frogs were a violent lot. In those days every revue, and most musical comedies, contained an Apache Number, in which a French Cad in sidewhiskers and a tight fitting black suit assaulted a girl in slow tempo around the stage. The girl wore, as we believed all Frenchwomen did, a slit skirt, and had her hair pulled a good deal before being finally knocked down, rolled over and abandoned. She would lie unconscious on the floor until resuscitated by her partner for the curtain call.

Years later I had my earlier impression of the French confirmed, while staying in the Rue de Rivoli. The Rue de Rivoli, as most readers probably know already, is an absurdly long colonnaded street, running from the Place de la Concorde to the Louvre, and a good way beyond. For a time when I was making a picture in Paris, I lived at the Hotel Brighton, and had a bedroom overlooking the Tuileries Gardens. In the evening, after a day's shooting, I would repair to the bar and sit watching the television before dinner. If it was raining, and it usually seemed to be, I would then walk under cover to a restaurant in the Place Vendôme.

One evening, as I stepped into the Arcade, I saw at a distance of two hundred yards, a man carrying a body emerge from a lighted doorway and crossing the pavement, attack the colonnade with his victim's head. Half a dozen times he swung his human battering ram, and then casually abandoning it, let what was left of it fall into the gutter, and returned to the bistro. I suppose I could have arrived on the scene quicker, but when I did, the horror and fright I felt had been replaced by righteous indignation. With scarcely a glance at the crumpled corpse, I tore into the café and into the half a dozen silent, sulky Frenchmen who sat there. A torrent of pidgin French, stage argot and half-remembered phrases from the Folies Bergères poured from my lips.

'Bêtes sauvages! Canaille! Méchants hommes! Quelle bêtise, quelle exposition formidable! Que va dire Le General? Appellez les gendarmes!' I looked round for the man who had committed the crime, but could not identify him, yet they had all been there. They had watched, they had done nothing, and now a man lay dead in the gutter, and still no one moved.

'Ambulance!' I shouted, 'Appellez un ambulance, vite, vite! Very well, if you won't do it, I shall.' I seized the telephone, and realised I hadn't the slightest idea how to proceed. I pushed the receiver into the hands of the one I took to be the proprietor. 'Appellez,' I ordered. 'Appellez, vite! Pas de nonsense! Attendez!'

I really had them mesmerised. I think in that brief instant I realised why it is Englishmen are so good in a crisis. Slow to anger, perhaps, but when we are aroused our fury is really magnificent. 'Venez!' I reiterated, 'venez, vite!' and for the first time employing physical force, drove my finger deep into the patron's chest. There was a hint of menace now in the way in which he replaced the receiver on its stand. His eyes were fixed on something at the back of me. I spun round, ready for a surprise attack, to find the corpse had now got to his feet and was dusting himself off. Then he started to laugh. I can never forgive him that laugh. I like to think he was concussed, but I can never be sure. All I know is I had to pay for the telephone call before I could leave the bistro.

But at least on that occasion I didn't have a Frenchman on my side. The French are never on anyone's side for very long. When they capitulated in 1941, the general feeling in my country was that at last we could get on and win the war. 'Now we know where we are,' we told each other. I was making another picture at the time, and the mood in the studio when we heard that Paris had fallen was one of quiet optimism. Only the director was silent and apprehensive.

'Come,' I said to him at luncheon, 'surely the rushes can't have been all that terrible. No worse than yesterday's, at least.'

'It's not the rushes for once,' he told me. 'It's Paris. You wouldn't understand what Paris means to me. It's the last place left in Europe where one can purchase genuine chamois leather gloves, buttoning to the armpits.'

I imagine if chamois leather gloves are being stitched these days, the British have the monopoly. It is curious how the pole of sexual permissiveness has shifted. Now it is the French who are the Puritans and we the libertines. A friend of mine, who recently had a few hours to kill in Nice, decided to spend them in a brothel. Being a writer, the word bordello came eventually to his lips and his need manifested itself to the hall porter of the hotel in which he was lodged. He was directed to an appartment on the Front, and in the parlour explained to the proprietress that what he enjoyed most was a sound whipping. A moment later and he was back on the Promenade des Anglais, Madame's rebuke still ringing in his ears: 'Pardon, Monsieur, c'est une maison serieuse.'

'Of course,' he told me when he recounted the incident, 'I may not have made myself understood.'

It's always a mistake trying to speak French to the Frogs. As Noel Coward once remarked when he was sustaining a role at the Comédie Française, 'They simply don't understand their own langue.' How true. 'Place de la Concorde,' you say to the taxi driver, and he sits uncomprehending while you repeat your instructions a dozen times before he consents to shrug his shoulders and get going. Once he has secured you as his passenger, he will take his time before deciding on the destination. 'Place de la Concorde,' he will suddenly announce, braking abruptly, and turning the cab round come scuttling back from the Bois de Boulogne, where he has been enjoying a skelter at your expense. In England a taxi driver doesn't make the foreigner pronounce Waterloo twenty-seven times before conveying him to the railway station. He doesn't have to. He knows he's going to miss the boat train anyway, because of the traffic jam.

The French and Ourselves these days both keep boarding-houses. Our windows face each other, but whereas there is usually a sign hanging up in our front parlour advertising vacancies, the French always seem to be Complet. When an American rings the bell over the road, the door is opened immediately. There is little fuss, hardly any formality, no questions asked. He just signs the book and pays up. Naturally, we on this side expect him to pay up, but before doing so there are a whole lot of questions to be answered. Is he respectable? How long will he be staying? Whom are we to notify if he dies? What is his purpose in coming? Was his mother an Armenian? We don't mind if she was, but we like to know.

Every year, little pieces of the white cliffs of Dover crumble away and fall into the Channel, which you might think would have the effect of increasing the distance between our coast lines, yet today the French stand nearer to us than ever, and with the Hovercraft service, a projected Channel Tunnel and the Common Market, we seem to be in danger of actually touching. It will not be an easy embrace, if I have my way.

The other day, deciding to find out for myself how real is the danger of a final clinch, I bought a ticket on a Hovercraft, a vehicle of which I have always been slightly ashamed, believing it to be another British invention which failed to jell, and imagining the South Coast of my beautiful land littered with these rusting giants, and set sail for Boulogne. True, when I came upon it in Dover, it was stranded, apparently helpless on the sand, but a spirit of optimism prevailed among its attendants. Concrete ramps had been constructed leading to the doors of the monster and soon passengers were being invited to climb on board. I found the loading procedure unnerving. Care has to be taken lest the thing should tip sideways, and when I stepped on to the port side, two other passengers were hastily urged forward on the starboard deck. Hovercrafts apparently cannot decide whether they are boats or planes. Lifebelts are circular, but on the other hand there are air hostesses, young ladies with bossy manners in identical uniforms, barking instructions and soliciting orders for duty-free demon alcohol and Customs-exempt cancer sticks. For those of us who have never worked on the roads, Hovercraft travel is perhaps the nearest they will get to operating a pneumatic compressor. Once aloft, they are not, of course, grasping it by the handle, but actually bouncing up and down in the saddle. Sucking up a gin and tonic through a straw — conveying a glass to my lips nearly knocked my teeth out — I learnt that the fellow in the next jump seat was paying his first visit to France. He was planning to return that evening, reckoning he would be able to see all he wanted to of 'abroad' in six hours, provided he wasn't poisoned by the grub.

My own plans called for a rather longer visit. I didn't propose to return for twenty-four hours, just in time to scuttle through my stage door on Monday night in time to receive the customers. Visiting France while one is acting in the London theatre always adds excitement to the trip. I have never yet been posted as a defaulter, but there's always a first time. The nearest I ever came to it was when

David Tomlinson flew me to Le Touquet, and on the way home his engine started to cough. On that occasion I wasn't worried so much about missing a single performance, but the rest of the run.

Boulogne served in the war as a bomb dump for returning allied missions who had failed to locate their intended target further inland. It has been rebuilt with both eyes on the car ferry. I was reminded of a Christmas toy for eight-year-olds. The nursery floor is covered with sections of motorway, some of it not yet assembled. Stepping out, except along the promenade, is unattractive and dangerous.

The French cannot bear to look out through a restaurant window without being able to read the price of the crustacea and coq au vin they are consuming, in reverse. They insist on being constantly reminded of the cost of living expressed in rump steak and chips. The only thing that makes us British suspicious lest the French have more of the stuff than we have, is they never think of anything else. A nation always ready to put its hand in anyone's pocket except its own. I chose a bistro where I could glimpse the sea between the lines of graffiti, and after lunch joined the proprietor and his friends for a discussion on the Common Market. Everyone agreed that it was in our interest to join. Meanwhile it was in their interest to pop over on the Hovercraft and shop in Dover.

After luncheon I took a taxi and drove over to Le Touquet. In the Casino, in the vast hotels, on the deserted plage, nothing stirred. For most of the year Le Touquet is a ghost town, only coming to life for a few short weeks in the high summer. Out of season its mood is set by the shells of the great hotels standing derelict in the forest, like the ruins of Ankhor Vat. Legend has it that Le Touquet died just as the war was ending, the result of a drunken escapade by four American airmen who wanted a little action. If you want action these days, Le Touquet is the last place in which to find it. Perhaps the French never intended to rebuild it. Perhaps they didn't want to be reminded of the English milords who patronised the place between the wars, accepting that in any case they wouldn't come back even if they could afford to. Those stuffed shirts who cried 'Garçon!' and 'Banco!', and competed on the golf links and polo grounds for perpetual challenge cups given by English clubs and British regiments, and presented personally to the victors by the Prince of Wales or Gladys Cooper. In those days we actors used to queue up at the barrier at Victoria Station on Sunday mornings to catch the boat train with our share of the week's booty, anxious to join our betters on the green turf or across the green baize. We were bound for a continent to which we British have never really belonged, but which in those days we really believed belonged to us.

It was dark when I returned to Boulogne. The ferry had stopped running, the waterfront was deserted. I had dinner in the empty hotel dining-room, and went to bed. In the morning when I got into the bath there was no soap. When I stepped out of it, there was no towel. I rang the bell, and no one came. Eventually, to stop myself shivering I dried myself on a sheet, calculating how much the French must have saved themselves over the years by not providing their customers with soap or bath towels.

Nowadays they don't even come when the customer calls. They surely can't imagine that it's our turn to answer the bell?

O My America!
My New-Found-Land: 1
Crossing the Pond

It must be forty years ago that I caught my first boat train to New York. The boat trains were specials supposed at any rate to run non-stop to Southampton Docks, although even in those days they usually stopped unaccountably just outside Brookwood Crematorium. The passengers dressed to catch them, wore orchid corsages, the extra fur coat carried over the arm, the latest novels under it. Luggage for the first class was matched and heavily labelled, the larger trunks occasionally snubbed by a sticker emphasising they were not wanted on voyage. Voyage was the word, not journey or trip. To cross the Atlantic was not only eventful, it was to follow in the trough of adventure. Great ships founder; the Titanic and the Lusitania were not forgotten; even the smaller and less significant liners carried musicians to strike up Nearer My God To Thee, should the occasion arise.

I went on the German-owned Bremen, a curious choice for Louis B. Mayer who was paying my fare, but there was an urgency about the proceedings. I was to make a film test in Los Angeles. The Bremen picked up her Southampton passengers by tender; in those days there was a mad rush to get going. It was unfashionable to be more than five days at sea, but the Bremen took six. Otherwise there was little else of which to complain, the cabins were comfortable, the food lavish and myself highly over-excited. Just to stand by the rails sharing the night with the gulls gave me a sense of urgency – so much effort to get me to the studio on time. Crossing years later on the Queen Mary, I encouraged a fellow traveller to hurl his empty champagne glass into the sea, then went to the barman and told him to be sure when the ship docked to bill my friend. My friend was tremendously impressed; he recalled it had been midnight and pitch dark with no one else about when the incident occurred, and yet in some uncanny way Cunard had realised they were a glass short. They ran a tight ship, he affirmed ever after.

Holiday camps started on board ships. We didn't have knobbly knees, but opportunity knocked at the ship's concert, and we had shuffle board and ping pong and deck quoits and bridge and horse racing and funny hats, church services and boat drill. No one shirked the last; there was a sense of responsibility aboard. This may look all right, it seemed to warn, but beware, big ships turn turtle. To don your lifejacket, to find your boat station and stand beside it, awaiting the roll call, to answer your name and wait for the ship's sirens to sound the All Clear before marching off was a chance to rehearse one's own performance in the event of the real thing happening. I was meticulous in allowing women and children to precede me, if not into the boat, for the cover remained on it, alas,at least back to the elevator. We had an elevator in the Bremen. Later, on the S.S. United States, there were no less than three elevators and bell-hops who answered the bells in the cabins and then passed on the request to the stewards. At the time this seemed the height of gracious living. It took a good deal longer to get a drink, but there was plenty of style aboard ship. Plenty of time too for romance, the clinging embrace at midnight, lovers proving to each other that seasickness was not in their make-up, that they could enjoy a force five gale together. Alas, such things were not for me. Squeamish, I always felt the slightest swell, and only with the coming of pills, invented so they said in the war to make invasion possible for G.I.s, did a feeling of drowsiness supplant the fear of throwing up over the railings.

One voyage I lay, dry of mouth but tolerably comfortable, on my bed while the ship rolled and pitched, and then suddenly I had my sea legs under me and walked up flights of stairs to reach the open sea and sky. The ship lay motionless, or what passed for motionless, in the heavy swell; the engines had stopped. Some secret rendezvous, I wondered, or had we already come further than I imagined? Was New York just around the corner, if indeed there had been the hint of a corner and not just a vast expanse of colourless sea? The ship, they told me, had buckled a plate in the storm and precautionary examination was under way. Almost at once we started again. There seemed at the time little else that we could do. I spent the rest of the voyage worrying half-heartedly about the seriousness or otherwise of buckled plates. There was always something to worry about on board ship; sudden fog, seamen's strikes, what to wear at the fancy dress ball, whether to try and improve one's cabin. One of the first and abiding anxieties was the seating arrangements in the dining room how to ensure a jolly crowd or, as years went by, no crowd at all, and by tipping the chief steward and paying the supplement, to have one's permanent table in the verandah grill.

Once, crossing with Graham Greene and Carol Reed, we spent five days giving the children, including my own, a whale of a time, turning the Queen Mary into one vast adventure playground. There were treasure hunts and games of Sardines, and Hunt the Captain, and Flood the Cabins, and the children arrived exhausted and the rest of us thoroughly pleased with ourselves. The Customs officials came on board and because for some reason my lot were on immigrant visas, discovered that I as head of the family had defective vision, which, in the opinion of some official in London, might affect my ability to earn a livelihood. 'But you're some sort of actor, aren't you?' his opposite number enquired, just off Staten Island. 'That's right,' I told him. He tore up the document. 'Why, in your profession I reckon you're blind half the time anyway.' America was different then. Five days and not five hours different. Will they ever come back, those great ocean greyhounds, the Normandy, the Ile de France, the Aquitania? Not them, of course, but perhaps their whelps. Perhaps as the oil gets scarcer the day of the liner will return, the dinner jacket once more laid out on the bed, the bath run, the ship's news slid under the door, along with the passenger list.

Something tells me that in the plane crash I shall not have the time or courage to behave myself, but at sea with the ship slowly sinking in the fog, with the band playing, I see myself standing on the bridge, my hand raised to wish God Speed to the survivors as the boats pull away. It is true there is still one place vacant, it is also true that I am large of girth and heart. I will not add to the difficulties of the lifeboat crew, besides I am a splendid swimmer. Che sera, sera. What an actor is always seeking is an exit.

O My America!
My New-Found-Land: 2
Out of this World

Flying out of Miami where the temperature registered a neat eighty degrees Fahrenheit, I fell to reading the National Airlines parish magazine.

What held my attention in the magazine was a glowing account by a fellow travel-hack of a visit to Key West where, apparently, you can not only see the clapboard house (if that is the apposite nomenclature) where Tennessee Williams lives, but visit the bars, too numerous to list, where Papa Hemingway got drunk. I fell to wondering what on earth Hemingway would have made of Disney World where I had spent the last five days, shepherded by the grandchildren, and only chickening out once on the helter-skelter ride in the space age. Perhaps this would have been the one attraction Papa would have enjoyed. At least no one travelling on it with him would ever be allowed to doubt his courage. I remember once asking Mary Hemingway what she found so special about her late husband and she told me it was his insistence that all his wives should learn to shoot straight. The last thing most husbands would wish in my neck of the woods.

Disney World is surely everyone's neck of the woods. Forty-six square miles of Florida's remote and hitherto inhospitable terrain encircle the magic city he has created. It is the characteristic of magic that no one knows how it is done, and if you ask any of the twelve thousand assistant conjurors how the tricks are performed, all they will tell you is that, in vast underground caverns, computers know when an automaton falters or someone is rude to a customer, in which case a light flickers and an alarm sounds. The genius of Disney is that he created a mirror which shows the world not what it looks like but how it ought to look. In all his kingdom there is not only never a cross word, there is never even a rude protest. Nothing is defaced, nothing is spoilt.

A few years ago my family did what they could to repair and maintain a small shelter on the river bank in Henley as a memorial to the late Gladys Cooper who lived there. 'We must,' the Town Clerk told me when passing the plans, 'make provision for vandalism.' Sure enough, after a few weeks the small tablet recording her name had been ripped from the wall and stolen. Nothing like that happens in Disney World; in some miraculous way we are all on our best behaviour. The only security guards I saw manifested themselves at dusk to ask me to move from a seat in the square while they released the doves who swirl and dart across the Plaza each evening as the flag is lowered. The birds seemed the only things that were in a hurry to get home to supper; each evening we found it more and more difficult to tear ourselves away from the bands and the parades and a last Adventure.

In the five days we achieved all we set out to do, but it was a near thing and on the final one we had sometimes to divide our forces so that the Mad Hatter's tea party was not left unattended while the world of Mr Toad was explored. Nearly all the great children's classics are honoured, certainly all the ones Walt read, and while the birds talk and the bears sing and the elephants squirt, while the pirates fight and the submarine captain nearly but not quite loses his cool and his ship to a monster of the deep, there is always time before we disembark from jungle launch or flying carpet for a last reminder to wait until we are tied up or nailed down before, with caution and keeping our arms out of trouble, we disembark. Caution is the key word. We heed the parrot's warning, Captain Hook's final admonition, even the ghostly voice of Vincent Price, to take it easy and keep out of trouble. There is a fortune, surely, waiting for some prudent maker of safety tapes attuned to the various domestic situations and factory emergencies which befall day by day. 'Good morning, children, get out of bed and take it easy till you find your slippers, the bathroom is now yours, proceed in an orderly manner and do not slip on a wet surface. When you are ready, come downstairs, one step at a time and holding on to the banisters. Handle the butter with care, knives can be sharp too.'

I must admit after a time the care syndrome started to eat deep into my subconscious. I resisted all efforts to dislodge me from The World and visit neighbouring attractions which abound, although (thanks to the Disney prudence and foresight) at a discreet, and if you travel by taxi, an expensive, distance. Though that was not the reason I gave the grandchildren. 'It's just that I feel safe here,' I told them. 'Let's stick to the monorail, shall we?'

The monorail runs slap through the Hotel; every time we rode we were greeted by a different host bidding us welcome, urging us to enjoy the ride, warning us not to try and open the doors ourselves. Would it work elsewhere, on the London Tubes for instance? Perhaps I alone of all of you rather think it might.

Was Disney World what Orwell was dreading? Should every country build a Disney World? Alas, there was only one Walt and I think they've thrown away the mould, and though he didn't live to see it completed, it was his dream and it came true. The most perfectly planned exercise in human extravagance, and, as is always the way with extravagance, it pays off. I like to think of him seated at his desk poring over the plans, asking how many restaurants were needed, how many lavatories, how many engineers and roustabouts, and then telling them to double the number they first thought of and, by God, they did.

It's wise before returning to harsh reality to fly as I did to Vegas, where the sucker gets anything but an even break, where the sell is hard and the taxi drivers uninhibited as they drive twice round the citadel to put the money on the clock. But if like me you ignore the strip for the down-town area and try the Golden Slipper rather than the Dunes, you will still rub shoulders at breakfast with the last American optimists, who, after a night of stud poker, have just enough reserves left to order two eggs easy and a dish of cornflakes before they fall asleep and rest weary heads on the short order counter.

God bless America and particularly San Francisco, where I ended up having the best haircut I remember since my village barber used to do it at his kitchen sink. Of course, the San Francisco barber came from Brighton. (Why did I write 'of course'?) The airports of America no longer warn againts pickpockets, enormous signs bid us beware of flower children, but I saw ne'er a one. A hundred years ago we British travelled abroad with a pistol. I don't think we've become any more sanguine now that we are armed with our credit cards.

O My America!
My New-Found-Land: 3
Las Vegas

Fifty years ago, give and take a few, after an appalling luncheon of cold ham and stodge, my housemaster at Wellington College summoned me to his study and sent me packing. 'You're not looking well, boy. You need a holiday,' he told me, and a few hours later I stood beside my tuck-box on an empty platform, praying that the train would arrive before I woke up. It was the best holiday I ever had, and in some ways it was to last forever. At least, I never went back to school.

I am a great believer in the idea that lightning can, and often does, strike twice in the same place, but alas, no one has ever again sped me on my way in such a totally unexpected fashion. One day, perhaps, I shall walk through the stage door of a theatre in which I am performing to find the proprietor waiting for me with an airline ticket. It doesn't have to be the proprietor, the stage door-keeper will do just as well. I would take my dismissal from anyone and start my holiday as a holiday should be started, on the spur of the moment. A holiday which is planned in advance isn't really a holiday at all, just another engagement. All those elaborate arrangements finalised in January for a brief fortnight at Frinton in August with one's loved ones, are self-defeating. By all means take the children for a paddle, but remember that for most of us it is part of our working year, and very often the part where we work hardest.

The ideal holiday should start as my first — and I begin to think only real — holiday started, just before the exams, or halfway through a conversation with one's bank manager, or getting the tea ready for the kids. That is the moment to put down the phone or the tray and get out fast. A holiday should be a walk-out, a wildcat strike. Leave the pieces, you can pick them up later. Get away. But where? Norway? I suppose there are people who enjoy those roofless grottoes and the midnight sun which never seems to get up high

306

enough to warm them, but for me there is a limit to the simple life, and that limit is often exceeded around the Arctic Circle. The scenery is magnificent and when I was making a picture there, I was never allowed to forget it. There was always someone at my elbow reminding me how much they were enjoying the vista, and expecting me to do the same. Beauty is in the eye of the beholder, but what makes the beholder themselves so unattractive? Nature lovers out on a hike dress worse than coursing enthusiasts at Altcar.

But back to the stage door and the airline ticket. Where would I fly to? Now, this minute, tomorrow or the day after? The answer is always the same — Las Vegas. The man who doesn't gamble has not been born. Life is contrived in such a way that to gamble is as necessary for survival as to breathe. People who profess to despise the more overt forms of gambling, like roulette and marriage, might find Vegas was not the place for them. It is, however, *the* place for me. When I first went there in the thirties it consisted of a couple of saloons at a crossroads leading to the silver mines, and for the first time I watched silver dollars being thrown around by men who kept their safety helmets on at the bar. It was a hideous little town. It was also attractive. Today it is still the ugliest, most attractive resort in the world.

On a fine Labour Day, and it is nearly always fine in Vegas, you can see a quarter of a million tourists on the Strip, or at least in the hotels that are built along it. Uniformly hideous, improbably named, and almost indistinguishable from each other, they are spaced at a nicely-judged distance so that to travel between them except by taxi-cab is uncomfortable in the heat and the occasional sandstorm. There is nothing to choose between the Stardust and the Thunderbird, the Dunes and Caesar's Palace. They are all extremely comfortable, expertly staffed around the clock, scrupulously clean and air-conditioned. Each has a pool compulsorily vacated by the guests at seven o'clock, a restaurant in which one can hear Frank Sinatra or Dean Martin or our own Tom Jones, and a casino which never closes and in which the crap tables, the pontoon dealers and the roulette wheels are all assembled in a mathematical ratio. There are just so many of each, spaced just so far apart and presumably patronised by just so many customers at any hour of the day or night. Somewhere there is an architect who works out the arrangements, and since all the casinos are identically arranged, must be the sole arbiter on such niceties.

As in all deserts, great importance is attached to drink, and most men and some women carry a glass in their hand when moving around the hotel or walking to their cars. They are not encouraged to take them with them into the swimming pools, but often do so. Carrying a glass in his hand reminds an American that he is on holiday and to be with Americans on holiday is why I go to Vegas. For I, too, like to be reminded of the hell on earth in which most of us survive. And we do survive, often despite excruciating difficulties, in acute despair and unbelievable squalor. We survive the wars and the peace. We survive childhood and middle age and we very nearly survive death. We survive love and hate, inflicting appalling cruelties on ourselves and each other. We are gloomy, sullen, silent and lachrymose, and in Vegas we are often gay, noisy and drunk. We are as brave as lions. We shiver in our shoes, but we also occasionally dance in them. We are raucous and boorish and we are alive because we don't know what else to be, and I like to be reminded of all this. I don't want to be reminded of trees and mountains and pink-footed geese. I want to be reminded of what I am — a hopeless, horrible human being. That's why every now and then I want to go back to Vegas and have a look at myself.

It's All Goa

Normally I'm as eager as the next man to find whither I am bound. In my time I have spent a fortune on guide books, potted histories, small and large scale maps and personal accounts by other intrepid explorers who live to tell the tale after a summer among the Basque people. The decision to spend a week on Goa was reached precipitously when a friend rang up and invited me to complete a party of four planning to spend a week mudlarking in the Arabian Sea. 'I am your man,' I told her, looked up my vaccination certificate (for we are now the last smallpox risk in the world) and boarded a jumbo that very evening for Bombay.

'From Bombay to Goa,' I enquired, over the complimentary champagne, 'how do you envisage the journey?'

'By plane,' she told me.

'But surely,' I argued, 'your son and his girlfriend travelling in the economy section will be anxious to see as much of India as possible. We must go by road.'

Sitting in the Taj Mahal Hotel that evening I made the necessary arrangements or, to be accurate, my friends had already made them but the gentleman from the travel agency had expressed a desire to meet me personally. It was apparently one of his lifelong ambitions to meet an actor whom he had admired for so long on the silver screen. I make no apology for simply repeating his words. Those of us who know our India will realize that all that has been written about the singular faithfulness of character ascribed in so many novels to the bearer boy, Sepoy, Pathan, servant and village headman still holds today. I don't say the travel wallah was actually waiting for his master's return on the tarmac but here he was with a glass of whisky in his hand, closely questioning me on the various roles I had played, with particular emphasis on a rather early work of mine, *The Final Test*, which dealt with the game so dear to the Indian heart.

He also was the director of an amateur group of players who frequently delighted Bombay with revivals of English drawing-room comedies, the presentation (or at least the casting) of which presented certain difficulties in that they did not lend themselves to the present trend for multi-racialism on the boards.

He was anxious for us to begin our travel as early as possible in the excellent motor he had secured, together with a driver fluent in the English tongue, and suggested we should assemble in the entrance hall at six, having not partaken of too much breakfast as a particularly fine one would be awaiting us at Poona.

'Now that is a place I have always wanted to see,' I told him as we bade him goodnight and fortified ourselves in the Golden Dragon with an elaborate Chinese Szechwan dinner, preparatory for our early morning fast. From the window of my bedroom I later gazed down on one of those unfinished office blocks whose state of uncertainty was emphasized by the squatters who had invaded the building. On the roof a family was putting the final touches to a hastily erected shack of rush matting by affixing an inverted U-bend lavatory pan to serve as a chimney.

Around the hotel, in a frieze of horror, beggars paraded armless children and mindless babies were laid out on the pavement and packaged in cellophane. The tourists cushion themselves from shock by telling each other that begging is a profession and a profitable one at that. On the whole, Bombay is a good place to be leaving at six in the morning or indeed at any other time.

The car seemed smaller than the occasion demanded but there is always a great advantage in being large for one's age; it means you can say, 'I'd better sit in front otherwise I might crowd you,' and no one argues. The idea of Poona, however, did not appeal to the driver who, if I understood correctly — and for the next sixteen hours I understood very little of what he said or indeed was trying to do—seemed to think lay in a different direction from Goa. On the other hand he gave very little indication that he knew in what direction Goa lay and none whatever that he could change gears without first stopping the car and starting from scratch or, perhaps more properly, from grind. At the rate of forty kilometres an hour we made slow progress but arrived at about twelve in the little town of Mahad, where our driver stopped the car in the main street, effectively blocking traffic in four directions, and departed in search of a repair kit for his gearbox.

The initial curiosity of the inhabitants gave way to irritation at the thoughtlessness of our behaviour in bringing life to a standstill; we thought it prudent to abandon the car and explore the market. Normally my companion is a keen shopper but she found little on the stalls to attract her. Suffering from a slight stomach upset, she went in search of a public convenience and was not to meet up with one for another ten hours, though I did persuade her later to seek out a private place by the side of the road while I stood by to repel Pathans and, of course, snakes. It was not for her, I am afraid, a happy situation, but as I pointed out we *were* seeing India and after a time the village grew comparatively silent as far as motor horns were concerned and we came upon our driver who, having mended the gearbox (at least to his satisfaction) was now parked in the square, exchanging wheel for wheel.

Another hour and we were on our way but relationships had subtly changed between us and him. He was now the master and realized he held the whip hand. For the rest of the interminable journey, whenever one of us was to question him too keenly as to our exact whereabouts and how much longer our journey might take, he invariably replied that we were now within a few miles of our destination. If we showed disbelief and remarked that a journey scheduled for nine hours had already taken twelve, he would stop the car abruptly, alight and inspect the tyres to remind us that we had no spare and only his goodwill to enable us to carry on.

Long after darkness fell, he continued to play on our nerves and although progress was slow along mountain passes, given a straight stretch of road or a village he accelerated, boldly contriving near-misses with laden ladies carrying vast bundles of water or food on their heads or buffalo attempting to cross his path. Eventually, and as it turned out only some fifteen kilometres from Fort Aguada Beach resort, whither we were bound, we found a taxicab stalled by the roadside. 'You are now under my protection,' I told the cabby kindly. 'Take your place beside our driver and direct him on the last stage of his journey. He is a stranger in these parts and has already made so many enemies on the road that no one but you can show the way. You will, of course, be handsomely rewarded.'

Half an hour later we were safe in the hotel lavatories and preparing to celebrate New Year around the swimming pool with the customary curry buffet and two bottles of champagne. I thought ordering the latter was a wise precaution as we had no reservations and would show an intention to push the boat out in the highly unlikely event of us being awarded accommodation. Finally, after the fireworks, we were all safely tucked up in one bedroom and the next morning allotted superior accommodation with patios and separate bedrooms.

All in all a most enjoyable holiday. It should perhaps be recommended only to·hardened travellers, who even proceeding by air from Bombay must expect a wait of an hour and a half before crossing the river by motor ferry. They must also not be put off the spectacle, glimpsed from the bus window, of young women ceaselessly toiling with iron bars to dislodge rust from the steel girders waiting to be erected when the new bridge is built.

'Conditions were almost as bad in Spain,' we tell each other, 'and look what we did for the place once the package tour industry got going.' But the Malabar Coast is not, alas, the Costa Brava.

Made in Hong Kong

Every now and again I take up my lute and wander off to sing for my supper. Often the expedition entails no more than a brief visit to St Albans, a banquet with the Worshipful Guild of Average Adjustors and half an hour on my feet cautiously admonishing the delegates on the folly of their calling.

Occasionally I grow bolder and accept an engagement further afield and for longer than one evening. Three weeks in the Harbour Room of the Mandarin Hotel in Hong Kong, for instance.

'But what do you do?' they ask before, and sometimes after, the performance. I have learnt not to commit myself. 'I get there,' I tell them, 'and again, about an hour later, I leave.' For one who neither sings, juggles or dances, the time passes pleasantly. I sip champagne, eat caviare and try not to talk with my mouth full. Sometimes my own enjoyment is shared by the guests and sometimes—when, for instance, they consist of a convention of Italian urologists—I don't go so well. Most of the urologists on that particular evening went quite early. 'I had hoped,' I told the manager later, 'that with the prices you charge here they would have been the doctors, not the patients.' He was unrepentant, and pointed out they had left separately and not in a body, which can happen with package tours, but not of course at the Mandarin. Elsewhere in Hong Kong it is not uncommon to be standing up to a full house when, at the blow of a whistle, the room empties—with the exception of two couples who have not paid the supplement for the midnight junk trip.

Say what you like about Hong Kong and up to a point I did, the world would be a duller place without it. For some, its peculiar blend of evangelical private enterprise points the way towards economical survival. For others it is a safari park where property developers, asset strippers and multi-national bankers can be observed from a safe distance grazing peacefully, apparently happily unmindful of the fate which has overtaken so many of their vanishing breed.

If, like me, you are lucky enough to be escorted by a game warden to one of their water holes, the Jardine Matheson Race Box on Saturday, for instance, and actually rub shoulders with these gentle creatures, you will be fascinated, as I was, by their exquisite manners. Mr and Mrs Newbiggins, a surprisingly young couple to be in charge of such a vast reserve, provide the browsing and sluicing every raceday for upwards of thirty different species collected by their social secretaries from near and far. There is much light banter over losing or gaining a fortune with the purchase of a five-dollar tote ticket. They listen to, laugh and commiserate with and compliment each other with effortless charm. A closed circle, a magic ring, a treasury of bankers holding hands and dancing to the tunes they call and the piper they pay.

Their hosts, observing the quadrilles, get advance warning of any hazards they are likely to encounter when further entertainment of a particular specimen has to be contemplated on the morrow.

For myself, I was fortunate to be bidden on the next day to lunch with a beautiful young barrister, Miss Chua, and later watch her conduct the defence of a client charged with arson and murder. The star of the courtroom is neither judge, nor counsel, nor prisoner, but the interpreter, who leans against the witness box and translates first the learned counsel to the prisoner and then the prisoner to learned counsel, judge and jury. The interpreter seems unable to believe his ears, there is a perceptible pause after counsel has posed his question. Then, with slightly raised eyebrows, the enquiry is repeated in Cantonese, and there is an even longer interval before the answer can be framed in English. Surely, the interpreter seems to imply, none of you can be serious? But of course we are, and so is the paraphernalia of the court, the wigs, the robes, the articled clerks, even the oath on the Bible, or the Kung Fu manual. Deadly serious.

There is no explanation for this particular crime. Why would a landlord burn down his own uninsured massage parlour, having first chopped off his patron's hands? A motiveless misdemeanour, committed by a man with such a remarkable photographic memory that he recalled the number of the badge of every single one of the dozens of police officers who had interrogated him. Commenting afterwards on the beauty of his face and his extreme pallor, both were accounted for by Miss Chua by his having spent his brief life underground and not exposed to daylight. 'Tell me,' I asked her later, 'will you ever become a Chinese judge?' 'Mr Morley,' she assured me, 'if I ever become a judge it is almost certain I shall be a Chinese judge.' A gentle rebuke, and, like Bassanio, I was lucky to escape so lightly. The pit pony was, not unnaturally, convicted.

Walking along inhospitable corridors glazed with lavatorial precision, we enter the sanctum of the Lord Chief Justice of Hong Kong, who, looking like a youthful Somerset Maugham, is concerned with the turmoil which will be occasioned by the construction of the new tube railway planned to pass directly beneath the courts. All the buildings on both sides of the street will have their overhanging structures demolished, some having to be entirely rebuilt, and four years and eighty million pounds from now the ferry which makes life in Hong Kong bearable for many, providing the occasional ten-minute interval to get their breath and suck an iced lolly on the China Sea, will be a thing of the past.

Meanwhile, back at the Mandarin, Mr Andreas Hofer, who, I read in the house magazine, holds a diploma in Hotel Restaurant Management and has recently taken over from my friend Peter Stafford (who I presume wished me upon him), is giving a farewell banquet for the retiring incumbent of the Harbour Room, Miss Millicent Martin. I am totally unprepared for the pigeon legs in my soup and the impossibility of cracking turtle shells with chopsticks. I complain loudly and am quietened by my host, who explains that the legs are there since I am the honoured guest, and if I wish I can crack the turtle in my teeth. How the Chinese can eat the nonsense they do continually surprises. It is not so much what one puts into the mouth as what one has subsequently to remove that embarrasses. In England, I remind the company, a country impoverished by Hong Kong standards, we put crumbs out for the birds and do not expect them to reciprocate by bequeathing us their discarded and apparently digested nests.

Although the weather is appalling I am persuaded to take the ferry to the Island of Lantau and visit the Trappist Monastery high on a mountain. The Smiling Golden Buddhas emerge suddenly through the swirling mists, and priests stand in front of them interminably praising the Gods with monotonous chants, which surely must get as much on the Almightys' nerves as on my own.

'Hold hard,' I tell my companions, 'these are supposed to be silent fellows. What's amiss?' We have, of course, come to the wrong monastery. We watch the drab preparations in the refectory kitchen for what must surely prove a terrible repast, and half-way down the narrow mountain road encounter trouble, not to say stalemate, in the form of another vehicle trying to get up it. This is apparently the exact spot where, only last year, a bus plunged over the side of the precipice killing its entire load of passengers. No one seems anxious to try again, but in the end a new driver is summoned, who spins the wheels expertly around the hairpin bend, breaking two windows against the rocks in the process, and we are off helter-skelter to the ferry.

Aboard, I suddenly realise what is wrong with my cabaret act, decide to change the format and finish munching the caviare, if not scoffing the champagne, earlier. What the audience has obviously been lacking up to now has been my undivided attention. By some miracle it works, and I am happy again and give a supper party after my triumph in Kowloon at the Golden Slipper where, though it is two in the morning, small children pursue each other around the tables and enormous parties of footballers, or just possibly jockeys, play 'Scissors Stone Paper' at the tops of their voices and get very drunk indeed. All very jolly, and I even enjoy the egg rolls and jumbo shrimps, up to a point. We walk from the Star Ferry in the rain while I hold forth on the extraordinary beauty, wonder and excitement of the Far East. The skyscraper in front of the Mandarin, a monster with circular windows, is called by the Chinese the Palace of a Thousand Arse Holes.

Invited to luncheon with the Governor, I take in the Botanical Gardens cleverly slotted into the hillside between the Peak Tram Station and Government House. A bewildering variety of parrots preen their extravagant plumage in the soft rain, while parties of school children clad in regulation blue serge, cluster, squawking, round the ice cream kiosk. An immensely sombre statue of George VI surveys the terraced beds of dripping azaleas. The luncheon party includes the Canadian Ambassador to Peking and the Deputy Prime Minister of New Zealand, both with their wives and aides. Having been repulsed earlier at the optimistically-named China Travel Office, I broached the subject of visiting China, perhaps even staying with His Excellency, but he seemed to think that both he and the Republic had enough on their hands already. It would seem there is a power struggle in progress and though I promised him that I wouldn't interfere, he politely refrained from issuing the invitation. About conditions in Peking he was reticent, and no one else at the table seemed remotely interested in drawing him out on the subject. If there is one thing never mentioned in Hong Kong it's the neighbours. At three o'clock the Governor bade us farewell. We shook hands and patted the labradors, without which no British Residence is considered properly equipped; my companions climbed into Rolls Royces for the quarter-mile trip down the hill, and I walked out of the gates and was disappointed to find no sentry to present arms.

The military presence of the British in Hong Kong is now reduced to a few hundred troops and enormous quantities of surplus barbed wire. Occasionally on the Island or towards the border past Kowloon, a notice-board announces a closed area and heavy penalties for anyone attempting to climb over the fence and investigate the deserted Nissen huts rotting among the dank grasses and crumbling cement. Charabancs convey the tourist daily to a small hill overlooking the railway line leading to China proper, where children hire out field-glasses and a mock excitement is engendered by the notices warning against taking another step towards the forbidden land on pain of imprisonment, an enormous fine, a bullet, or possibly all three. There are various mountain tracks, ostensibly forbidden to visitors, over which the residents propel their nervous guests to obtain a more panoramic view of a countryside which not unnaturally exactly resembles the land on which the reluctant explorer is already standing. Two parallel fences about four feet high and marking the supposed boundary are in no state to repel a rabbit, never mind the Mongol horde. The British expect at least a week's notice in writing before the invaders finally arrive, and if there is one thing we do really well, it's troop evacuation. In any event, the business community will presumably continue to look after itself.

I am told the one thing I should see in Hong Kong is a jade auction, which takes place every Wednesday in a mysterious Doss House in the Canton Road, and where allegedly millions of dollars are bid for quartz rocks, into each of which a small window has been opened to display its treasure. The problem facing the dealers is to decide the quantity and quality concealed in each lot. Bidding is by handshakes under a blanket; each bid is determined by the number and position of the fingers proffered. When the auctioneer is satisfied that all bids are in, he returns to his rostrum and consults the Lady President before deciding which dealer is entitled to the property. The winner is not necessarily the highest bidder, as questions of credit are also considered. Otherwise proceedings are comparatively straightforward. I never found the correct location, but Canton Road seethes with dealers unwrapping small tissue-paper packets of uncut jade, and their prospective customers, mostly old ladies, peering and poking and rubbing the stones between their fingers to ascertain the temperature. Good jade is cool. It is also a cushion against inflation.

At the Szu Chuen Restaurant in Lockhart Road the fried egg-plant with pepper and hot garlic and the smoked duck are delicious, but sear the palate. I cool off at Repulse Bay where hardier souls are bathing in the chill April sea and a few Garrison wives paddle their children by the water's edge. Above the beach the last of the memsahibs, in shady hats and with complexions of haughty porcelain, survey the scene from the verandah of the Repulse Bay Hotel and sip lemon tea. I come upon Frank Knight who, years ago, broke his parole after having been kidnapped on the border by Chinese guards and somehow found his way barefoot back into Hong Kong. Surprisingly he was not welcomed as a hero but admonished by his superiors for not keeping his word to his captors. He still smarts from the blow to his pride, and now is an Inspector in charge of the affluent tourist section, a larage exuberant bear who seems to know everybody and whom everybody certainly knows. His companions, two judges and a solicitor all originally from the UK, discuss the unwillingness of the rich Chinese to make a will, which they consider to be unlucky, and the endless difficulties occasioned to the surviving relatives by the concubines who habitually demand and are entitled—or were until recently—a share of the estate. Not that the solicitor was complaining. I asked one of the judges if he had tried any good cases lately. He seemed to think it depended on my definition of good. His last trial concerned the death of a policeman who, arriving a shade too promptly at the scene of the crime, was hacked to pieces in the elevator before he could leave it. A policeman's lot in Hong Kong is not altogether a happy one.

I bade them farewell and took a bus to the Peak, bathed for once in sunshine, and this week the scene of another cop killing. On the way down, two Englishmen in tuxedos rode the tram with all the aplomb of white-tied pilgrims to Glyndebourne embarking at Victoria Station long before tea-time. They left unexpectedly half way down the mountain and disappeared into the undergrowth. What formal occasion demanded their presence and dress at four-thirty in the afternoon I shall never know.

I have found Lamma, an island only thirty minutes by ferry boat but undisturbed by Europeans. A long pier stretches out from a quiet bay around which a little village has been lulled to slumber by television. Through the shutters one glimpses whole families motionless, spellbound in the darkness of high noon, the light excluded the better to enjoy the flickering magic of Chinese soap opera. There are no cars on the island, little water, great peace. In the evening the work in the market gardens resumes. The children, with a pair of enormous watering cans yolked to their shoulders, painstakingly, methodically and very slowly tend the rows of spinach. Mothers cut bean shoots with penknives, while fathers, now back in the cafés, bang down the Mah Jong pieces on the plastic tables and pick up the money. If I worked in Hong Kong I would wish to live nowhere else, but apparently the typhoons disrupt the ferry services. This year, for the first time, they are to be named after the weather men themselves and not their sweethearts. So much for male chauvinism.

A friend of a friend who teaches at the Chinese University turns up and we lunch at The Old Vic in Lambeth Walk and drink draught British bitter. He has the disconcerting habit of fixing his gaze at my waistcoat while he talks and convincing me that, as usual, I have spilled my food. While I search in vain for the gravy stains, I miss a lucid explanation of what the Chinese expect from life and what international business expects from educated Chinese. He contemplates pulling up chopsticks, and enquires the price of houses in the old country which, according to him, are likely to be cheaper than in the New Territories despite the fact that there are whole villages thereabouts denuded of menfolk who have gone to be waiters in Gerrard Street. After luncheon we watch construction workers scaling improbable heights on flimsy bamboo scaffolding to replace the tiles on the Palace of a Thousand Arse Holes.

I am entertained by Mr Hofer and his boss, Mr O'Connor, an expansive Irishman, at the Excelsior Roof Garden, where we appear to be the only guests. I am startled to hear plans to make the restaurant even more exclusive by turning it into a club, and Mr O'Connor wonders whether Mr Hofer would care to take home, or at any rate as far as the Mandarin, the elaborately-carved sweet trolley now surplus to requirements, as redecoration is to be the order of the day. The Excelsior is to be transformed into a vast convention complex in honour of the Miss Universe contest scheduled in the late summer, and meanwhile, in what will be the largest theatre restaurant in Hong Kong, they are readying some pigeons to provide a breath-taking finale on opening night. We accompany Mr O'Connor and his aides for a preview in an empty and gigantic ballroom where, after a few moments and some encouraging shouts from the staff, a flock of white doves flap languidly and with a notable lack of enthusiasm from the projection booth high up in the roof and descend on what will surely one day prove to be customers' pates. Like me they are either imperfectly rehearsed or just possibly suffering from jet lag. They will have to buck themselves up, says Mr Hofer, or they'll find themselves off the programme and on the menu. Mr O'Connor, an altogether softer character, picks up a straggler and deposits him tenderly centre stage. 'He'll learn,' he maintains stoutly.

Albert Smith, novelist, playwright, humorist, friend of Dickens and Barnum, and one of the greatest entertainers of the Victorian Age, besides being one of its most popular comic authors, left London and the Garrick Club in search of material for his autumn season of one-man shows to be staged as usual in the Egyptian Hall, and arrived in Hong Kong on August 21, 1858. His previous entertainment, entitled 'Mr Albert Smith's Ascent of Mont Blanc', besides delighting the Queen and Prince Albert, had chalked up over two thousand performances and earned him in excess of thirty thousand pounds. His account of the journey, *To China and Back,* was published on his return to advertise the opening of 'Mont Blanc to China' on November 14. The Egyptian Hall was decorated with Chinese curios and objets d'art, the foyer lit by Chinese lanterns, the walls hung with Chinese scrolls. 'Smith naturally did away with the Swiss chalet on the stage and replaced it by an exact copy of a flower garden as he had seen laid out by a former Hong Kong merchant, Howqua' (Wu Ch'ung-yueh). He also brought back with him two wooden crosses from the execution ground at Canton. The new entertainment was a howling success and people flocked to see Smith perform in his new Chinese setting, but he died suddenly after an attack of bronchitis on Derby Day, 1859.

He had been surprised on his arrival in Hong Kong that there were no hotels in those days, and confided to his diary that a well-conducted house would surely make a fortune, but he was made a member of the Hong Kong Club, and was given a bedroom commanding the harbour and the Bishop's palace. He found the service in the dining-room poor, as the waiters had been recalled by an Imperial edict, but the steadiness was agreeable after so much steamboat living. All in all he enjoyed himself hugely, as I did more than a hundred years later. He had his pocket picked, went over the prison—which he found clean and airy—and met the terrible young American pirate, Eli Boggs, and Jack Ketch, 'a mild looking man enough.' The convicts who had tried to escape were ironed, some who had tried twice were double ironed. Returning to the Club, he met Mr Gilbert of the Surprise, who had been in action with the pirates earlier in the day, and gave him a freshly-severed pigtail. Unlike me, Mr Smith was welcomed in Canton; he inspected the sacred pigs at Honan, thirteen or fourteen in number, enormous in size, blind with age, and was entertained to dinner on board a flower boat where the lady singers were all wonderfully like each other with wooden and perfectly inexpressive features. There were five or six Chinese guests but the rest were English, and he was more than ever impressed with what he had already noted several times before: the almost remarkable ignorance of every feature and phase of Chinese life peculiar to the 'commercials' out here. The almighty dollar in its relation to tea, silk, opium, was the only study of thought with them and what they could possibly do when left to themselves to get through the day, beyond smoking and tea-tasting, was to him a matter of the most marvellous incomprehensibility. A perspicacious busker, Mr Smith, and what was true a hundred years ago, still disquiets.

I had an English neighbour once who decided to sell his house and retire to a small riverside apartment. All his life he had dealt fairly but not over-generously with his staff, and when the time came to pay them off, he made as he thought adequate provision for each and bade them goodbye. Months later he was still brooding over his gardener's farewell speech. 'Then I'll say goodbye, sir, and leave it at that. I don't think I have anything to thank you for.'

'He never even shook my hand,' my neighbour told me, 'after all those years.'

We mustn't expect too much in Hong Kong when the time comes.

Russian Salad: 1
One Steppe at a Time

Over the years I have always extolled the Soviet; in countless arguments across countless dinner tables I have defended the Communist way of life. Believing the Tsars to be monsters of wickedness, I must of necessity champion those who overcame them. To me the issue was simple; it always is. Besides, I delight in talking about matters of which I know nothing. Always at some stage of the row, and having infuriated my opponents, they would ask if I had ever been to Moscow, and always I told them I had. Even if I was troubled by the lie on the first few occasions, I eventually came to believe it myself. The other day, seeking new pastures to explore, I attempted a visit to China, but was repulsed on the doorstep of the Consulate. 'Why not try Russia?' I asked myself. 'I've been to Russia,' I replied. 'No, you haven't,' I was told, and straight away went round to Intourist. The lady at the desk was my sort, affable and rotund.

'How will I manage for money?' I asked.

'You are an artist,' she told me. 'You will do an artistic wangle.'

From that moment I knew I should enjoy the Russians. But Russia is by no means the Utopia I have always claimed it to be. There are times when one finds oneself in a land dreamed up by Lewis Carroll and decorated by Emmett. The regime is defeated by the weight of numbers. Everything looks as if it would function perfectly until you add the customers. Nothing, in the final analysis, is equal to their insatiable demand. Everything is in short supply at one time or another, except the queues. The art of shopping must be to arrive at the precise moment when the goods turn up, and before the crowds gather. Standing idly in a department store beside an empty counter, I could, had I wished, have purchased a live carp which chose that exact moment to arrive, in company with hundreds of its fellows, in a huge tank which was suddenly wheeled forward. Like lightning a queue formed, and for once I was at the head of it. Splendid Russian ladies, their hands heavily bandaged – presumably from former fish bites – seized the carp and thrust them, still threshing wildly, into paper bags, weighed them and then handed a ticket to the lucky purchaser, who beetled off to queue by the cash desk, and then to descend once more to claim her prize, giving the ticket to the girl, and the carp a smart rap over the forehead to make it easier to carry away. If you found yourself at the end of the queue, the whole operation might have taken you half an hour, by which time of course the carp line might have snapped.

There are now very few Hotel Metropoles left in the world, but Moscow is still stuck with hers. It was the first hotel to which I was assigned in Russia, and far and away the most uncomfortable. A bedroom on the fifth floor, furnished with shabby simplicity, a dripping lavatory pan, and of the two lifts by which it could be reached, only one ever in service, and that usually stuck between the landings.

In the enormous dining-room every third light flickered in the chandeliers, and I encountered for the first time the Russian waiter's habitual determination not to serve his customer as long as he can avoid doing so. Until one grows accustomed to it, the hostility alarms. He will watch you alight at his table with smouldering fury in his eyes, and then with a violent wave of his hand, indicate that you are to take yourself off. I was reminded of bird scarers in Ceylon. If one is cowardly enough to move to another perch it will only be to encounter the same peremptory dismissal from another custodian. It is better just to sit it out. Once having decided he is not going to shift you merely by gestures, the waiter will adopt other tactics. Employing the technique of Russian schoolteachers in dealing with a recalcitrant, he will try to convince you that you do not exist. Passing rapidly by your table, he will stare through you at the wall beyond, and should you attempt to attract his attention, will studiously ignore your signal. However, after about ten minutes or so, there will be a sudden change of tactics. He is beside you, with a menu, even possibly a napkin, a knife, fork and a glass, and from now on it's just a question of time. He will continue to pass by your table on his way to and from the kitchens, once again ignoring your presence, and spending interminable periods behind the scenes; but now, in some curious way, your roles are reversed. He has become the bird and in time, with inordinate patience, and by remaining absolutely motionless, you will give him the courage to alight once more beside you, and this time take your order.

The traveller does well to remember at this stage that most

Russian menus are pure fantasy. Whether such dishes as baked hazel grouse or sturgeon roasted in silver paper ever actually existed, even in the days of the late Tsar, must surely be doubted, but they remain stubbornly on the menu, a constant trap for the unwary, and should one be tempted to order anything of this exotic nature, the waiter will instantly withdraw, without even bothering to write down such a flight of fancy, returning from the kitchen in due course, beaming with pride and happiness, to pronounce the magic word 'Niet'. The choice thereafter is almost invariably between boeuf Stroganoff, chicken Kiev or hamburger, and it is always a mistake to order borsch, or indeed a first course of any kind, as the waiter, now understandably exhausted and eager to close the joint, will bring all the dishes at once in order to get the whole painful business finished as soon as possible, and while you swallow your soup, the rest of the food congeals. Occasionally the traveller will find a restaurant at which he will be made almost welcome. In Samarkand I had a table fetched from the kitchen, and a place on it laid up for me, but such happenings are rare indeed.

I am not much of a one for museums, but not to have visited the Kremlin would have been unthinkable. I toured it in three hours, a good deal of the time panting to keep up with the guide for fear of becoming attached to one of the other delegations who, like us, scurried through throne-rooms and up and down staircases leading to Chapels and Water Towers, and of course more throne-rooms. How the Tsars would have hated us all, and how right they would have been to do so. For one thing we are far too many, and for another we look so apathetic. We must of necessity ration our rapture. We cannot swoon with ecstasy for fear of falling behind. Confronted with one showcase, we are forever asking ourselves what the next one holds. Inspecting eight Gauguins on one wall, we look around for the other four listed in the guide book. We are children opening the presents, but alas, we shall never have time to play with the toys or even, perhaps some of us, to see them again.

The treasures of all the Tsars, displayed before my popping eyes, consisted almost entirely of enormous gold platters. I don't see how anyone could have got most of them through a door, let alone on to a table, but the enthusiasm of the Russian rulers for such objects appears to have been unbounded. They were constantly receiving them from, or dispatching them to, their favourite relatives, or relative favourites. There was also a collection of coaches, and a golden train constructed by Fabergé to run round the Imperial nursery carpet on little golden rails, and to be wound up with a little golden key. The Romanovs were fond of gold — a family of magpies who suffered the fate of vermin with unwonted dignity.

Back in Red Square, we joined the crowds waiting to watch the changing of the guard. As the clock strikes the hour, the two soldiers on either side of Lenin's tomb are relieved in a curiously unnerving ceremony. The sentries, motionless as the corpse they guard, are replaced by two more of the elite in a manoevre so swift that the eye can scarcely follow it. Still not certain, indeed, whether they had actually changed places with their comrades, I watched them march off in solemn goose-step, commanded by a single officer, and finally disappear into the fortress. The crowd dispersed, in so far as the crowd ever disperses in Moscow.

The magnet to which all Russia is drawn, where all decisions are taken, the centre of the web, the seat of power, is in fact a hideously overcrowded provincial town. Without the beauty of Leningrad, the charm of Samarkand, the excitement of Siberia, there is little to catch the eye or enthuse the senses, once you have visited the Cathedral of Saint Basil and admired the Gauguins in the museum. Across the river, next to the largest open-air heated swimming pool in the world, is the permanent exhibition of Soviet achievement, containing all the enormous triumphal arches, golden fountains and outsize space rockets you would ever want to see. In vast farm buildings, enormous white bulls, huge pigs and the celebrated caracul sheep from Bukhara, bedded on wood shavings, their immaculate coats shampooed and curled, wait patiently for inspection, their stillness as unnatural as that of the sentries.

Most curious of all the phenomena in Moscow is the celebrated subway, the platforms of each station seemingly designed for a State reception. The one through which I was conducted happened to be decorated in the style of Louis XVI, the marble floors reflecting the glitter of a hundred chandeliers hanging from the ceiling, and here all the bulbs were for once alight. Was it possible, I asked myself, that the engine driver might be arrayed in white breeches with silver buckles on his shoes and a full-bottomed wig? But alas, when the train drew in I caught ne'er a glimpse of him, so great was the crush and so intense the struggle to climb aboard. Versailles was never like this, I reflected, as I made my way up the escalator and back into the street where, in the rain, a long queue waited patiently to buy matches. Whoever built Moscow subway had a great sense of humour.

Russia was full of water melons at the time. Though one doesn't see them much in the hotels, there seems a brisk demand for them at most street corners. Like ice-cream and some vegetables, these are sold on the free market. There are no supermarkets and as most shops specialise in one line of goods, it seems as if the housewife is kept pretty much on her toes, which is perhaps the reason why, although they are mostly about my weight, they are so incredibly spry. Even when they are quite elderly, the Russian women never seem to let up. An army of grandmothers and great-grandmothers are out in all weathers, sweeping the streets. They are warmly clad, immensely cheerful and apparently undaunted by the task of collecting the leaves as they fall, and carrying them away in small tin cannisters, and when the trees are bare there will be the snow.

As we ventured forth one evening on our way to see *My Fair Lady* at the Theatre, we came across a group of them sitting on a little bench under the plane trees. They were laughing and chattering to each other as if it was the pleasantest thing in the world to be sitting in the dusk in the cold and the rain, and waiting for Heaven knows what. More leaves to fall? Perhaps a bus to take them home to their fire-sides and their grandchildren? The trouble, one Russian explained to me, is that the old ladies are allowed to earn money on the side, besides drawing their pensions. Most of them prefer to sweep up the leaves than stay at home with the grandchildren — for one thing it's more profitable, and oddly enough they find it more amusing.

I do not understand the Russians, but then I'm not particularly anxious to do so. Admire them? That's a different matter altogether. It's easy to do that, especially perhaps in Leningrad, where through the centuries in countless struggles against tyranny they have suffered and died and prevailed. There is hardly a square in this most beautiful city without a statue commemorating some outrage against the citizens. Here they were mowed down by the Cossacks, there hanged by the Tsars, everywhere they were burnt alive by German bombs. For three years they endured the worst that Hitler's armies could do to them. In one year Nature herself took a hand. It was, they will tell you, as though she wanted to test us too. But they fought on, with the temperature forty degrees below freezing, with no heating or light, no water, no transport. They carried their relatives to communal graves and died on the way home, and when spring came, men, women and children volunteered for three hours every day to clear the streets of the dead bodies, and thus avert an epidemic which might have finally conquered them.

They ate glue and sawdust, but they never thought of surrendering. In Leningrad, where the revolution was born, it was a possibility not to be contemplated.

They have been forged in tremendous fires, and they have emerged triumphant, but what sort of people are they? Yesterday, because I was pushed for time and because to eat in a restaurant cannot be done under an hour, I resorted to the hotel cafeteria, and snatching my coffee and cakes, and finding all the chairs occupied, went and sat on a staircase. An old gentleman, coming upon me unexpectedly, was plainly horrified. He lectured me on the impropriety of my conduct, but I was determined to misunderstand him until I had finished my doughnut, then smiling and waving gaily, I returned to the counter for more coffee (the coffee in Russia is unvarying in its excellence). This time the lady serving me and the gentleman who had chided me, led me firmly over to a now vacant chair. The war, the struggle, was over, they seemed to be saying. Now for Heaven's sake let us all try to behave like civilised people.

Russian Salad: 2
The Trans-Siberian Express

I arrived in Irkutsk, the capital of Siberia, in two minds as to whether or not to pick up the Trans-Siberian Railway, or to drop the idea once and for all, and fly the rest of the way to Khabarovsk. For one thing, Intourist had given me a plane ticket instead of the rail one I had requested, but whether by accident or design I couldn't decide. For another, my friend the Flying Dutchman, whom I met earlier in Bukhara, had painted for me a gruesome picture of the jollity on the train. Drunken Russians climbing in and out at every station; enormous ladies being hoisted up onto the upper bunks and falling back on top of everyone; the smell of the food, the state of the lavatories, above all the incessant singing of the peasants. Admittedly I was only joining the train at the halfway stage, but it still left three days and nights of a rugged community life in which, so my friend assured me, I should really get to know the Russians. But did I want to?

It was the food that finally decided me. For some reason, all the Irkutsk restaurants seemed permanently reserved for private receptions; munching salami in a bar, I was harangued by a Russian soldier. 'He is trying to tell you,' a bystander explained helpfully, 'that he has a brother in Vietnam.' 'Tell him,' I replied, 'that I have an aunt in Czechoslovakia,' and drifted rapidly towards the door before he could get the message.

The next morning I caught the train, and found myself sharing a compartment with a retired fruit farmer from Adelaide, who drank nothing on the journey, and sang hardly at all. The sun was shining, the air as balmy as Bournemouth. The guide was almost affectionate when she saw me off. 'Shall I need snowboots when I come to England?' she asked. A lady came and made up the beds, hoovered the compartment and brought tea. In the restaurant there was champagne and caviare. All day we hugged the shore of Lake Baikal.

On the great plains, Russian cowboys and cowgirls in quilted dressing gowns herded the cattle. We stopped at little towns where for once there were no great blocks of workers' flats and the houses were built of wood. The children were skating or pushing themselves across the ice on sleds. On the platforms there were stalls selling preserved fruit in jam jars, and tripe in paper bags.

In the evening about seven, we are invaded by a Russian officer, his wife and daughter, not pleased to find they have to occupy separate compartments. If I surrendered my bunk there would be room for them, but my instinct of gallantry soon passes. He speaks only a little German. He thinks East Berlin is a fine city. In reply to my query as to whether Russia and Germany are now friends, he flings up his hands. 'How about the Chinese?' He laughs and shrugs. I get the idea he is going to Vietnam, and am resigned to having him with us for the rest of the journey, but in the morning he is gone. I wash in cold water. More of a lick and a promise, as my mother was always saying. How it used to annoy me, along with her other adage 'It is necessary that a door should be open or shut.' Mother always said this in French. Now, in the middle of Siberia, with a slight anxiety that I may have jammed the lavatory door and will have to stay until I am released, I find it comforting. I wonder whether my children will remember my reiterations with affectionate irritation. What are my pet sayings? I rattle the door again, and this time it gives. It was, after all, with mother that I saw *Shanghai Express* and longed ever afterwards to come on this train. But now, alas, there are no Chinese prostitutes, no bandits disguised as Russian officers, no Marlene Dietrich, no Anna May Wong, no Warner Oland, no suave Englishmen, only myself and a few Australian tourists.

What a poltroon I am, this constant anxiety that I shall lose my passport, or get left behind at the station. What would happen? Presumably one wouldn't be eaten. Still, on the platform I never take my eye off the guard, and am always the first to climb aboard. Siberia is looking a trifle more rugged. We manage to clean the windows. The radio from the next compartment blares a constant exhortation. Why am I so sure it's not just a cookery lesson?

For the rest of the journey we have the compartment to ourselves. My companion reads nothing but a travel guide to the hotels in Japan and pores over his itinerary. When he talks it is of remembering to retrieve his ticket, which he surrendered to the lady with the hoover. On the fourth day we are woken at five, and alight at Khabarovsk. Here the Trans-Siberian Express disembarks its casual passengers, and continues to the great submarine base at Vladivostok. For tourists this region is out of bounds, and they are funnelled down a shute to Nakhodka. The journey is made overnight in Russia's most up-to-date train — wide, comfortable beds, private bathrooms, and something that has been missing from our journey from Moscow — hot water.

The train had hardly started, when the Devil, in the shape of a Washington fruit farmer — I am destined apparently always to share compartments with fruiterers — introduced himself, and dismissed the entire Soviet system as corrupt, and impractical, arguing that nothing is ever achieved in the world by political leaders or even by generals. 'Wars are won,' he insisted, 'by the poor bloody foot soldier, not by the commanders at staff headquarters.' Which was what was wrong with Russia — too much staff work, not enough getting down to it. At Khabarovsk he had been watching the inevitable workmen digging the customary hole in the ground, and computing the wastage of man hours involved. Abruptly, or perhaps because I wasn't following him blow by blow, he was in his own back orchard in the state of Washington, and dealing with the problem of casual labour at picking time.

'I employ,' he reminded me several times, 'the unemployed unemployable.' Each time he used the phrase, he closed his eyes as if with the effort of getting it spot on, and after each triumph he opened them again, like a cat basking by the fire. The unemployed unemployable where he came from consisted of three main streams — the alcoholic (from his point of view the best), the tobacco addict (more reliable, but likely to develop lung cancer on the site — he regaled me with gruesome anecdotes of the plight of several he had employed on their way to the morgue), and finally the last class, transients. But they, he affirmed, were really a pain in the arse. They had money in their pockets, and they wanted to choose the row they were to pick.

'That's no good to me. They're worse than Mexicans and niggers. Not, mind you, that I ever hire either. Nothing against them, just won't hire them, mind. Any more than I hire a man with money in his pocket, unless I'm pressed.'

I left him to go to the dining car, and when I returned, he had climbed into the upper bunk.

I sat on the edge of mine and communed with myself, perhaps as Lucifer had intended I should.

Russia knows none of this nonsense. No hate hangs in the air. It is a country where religion is practised, but not preached, as opposed to the West, where it is preached, but not practised. Does the Russian really love his neighbour as himself, I wondered. Is there no lunatic fringe, no muggings in the streets? Is there no hatred, envy or malice? One phrase Lucifer had used kept coming back to me. 'If I see a dead body, man, I just step over it.' So this, then, was America, this perhaps what London will become: the ghouls not dancing on the graves, but stepping over them carefully. This was Vietnam and Chicago, Grosvenor Square and Salisbury, Colin Jordan and Enoch Powell. This was Hell, and the vast, gentle, lobotomised land I was leaving — Heaven? In the upstairs bunk I heard a snore, or just possibly a chuckle. No, I told myself, it's not as simple as that.

In the morning we reached Nakhodka and sailed for Japan. In the bar that evening, the Devil was still holding forth about the iniquities of the system. One of our fellow passengers had been interrogated by the police for taking pictures of railway platforms. Before letting him embark they had confiscated all his films and nearly frightened the life out of him into the bargain.

'Cruel, that's what they are, cruel. All that long, difficult journey, and now nothing to show for it.'

'Stupid, ignorant, clumsy, how can they expect people to come to their wretched country when they behave like that?'

'All the same,' I told them, 'it does say in the regulations that you mustn't photograph railway stations.'

'What regulations?' they demanded. 'We never read any regulations. They make up the rules as they go along.'

'But doesn't everyone?'

The sea was a dead calm, the fishing boats put on their lights to lure the sardines. The moon rose over Japan. There was a party in the lounge, but no one went. They sat drinking at the bar, still arguing about their hosts, for although everything had to be paid for now in dollars, the ship was still Russian. A month is a long time. Most of the tourists were bored with Communism. Czechoslovakia still nagged their conscience. 'Supposing,' I asked them, 'there hadn't been a Lenin or a Stalin or a war, what sort of civilisation would have been possible?'

'Free enterprise, that's all they needed,' said the Devil. 'They would be in fine shape by now.'

'Like the rest of us?'

'What's wrong with the rest of us? Bloody sight better places than Russia.'

'You can say that again,' they echoed.

'The trouble with Russia is, it's a poor country. It will always be a poor country.'

I thought of the old ladies, sweeping up the leaves in the cold of Leningrad; of the grey crowds queuing for tea cups in Moscow. I thought of the dusty, unmade roads in Bukhara, and the smell of the café in Irkutsk, and then I thought of the children.

'Not as poor as all that,' I told them, 'not by a long chalk.'

Traveller or Tourist?

We tourists are given to sudden enthusiasms, and just as well for the tour organisers that such is the case. We are content, nay eager, to sit in a bus for two or three hours and be trundled to, for instance, the Eureka Stockade. None of us has ever heard of Eureka, few can visualise a stockade, and are only mildly disappointed to arrive in Ballarat and discover that today it is a small green park containing a massive obelisk inscribed with the names of the fallen.

For a few days afterwards we are aware that here the gold miners and the army and possibly the police came to fisticuffs and worse in the middle of the last century, and that a half-hearted protest by the citizenry was whole-heartedly put down by the executive.

It happened all over the world; it still happens. No doubt before long a park will be laid out in Derry and a stone cross erected to mark Bloody Sunday. 'What was that, then?' the tourists will ask, and if they are on a conducted tour, they will be told.

I am a man who keeps close to the guide: I like to hear every word. I feel I am getting my money's worth. I don't remember what has been said, naturally, but I like to pretend that I am an instant historian or an instant zoologist, which brings me to the Fairy Penguins.

I have always had a horror of fairies, not human fairies, but the dreadful little creatures who dance at the bottom of the garden. I cannot abide fairy stories, I loathe Peter Pan, I am nauseated by pictures of the little people cobwebbing about on the grass.

Penguins do not fill me with the same feelings of abhorrence as fairies, but I am not fond of them either, or let us say I quickly tire of watching them. 'Next slide, please,' I tell Peter Scott. Penguins are so easy to photograph that naturalists always bring back more feet of them on film than any of us can reasonably digest.

Leaving Melbourne one morning on our pilgrimage to Phillip

Island, the shrine of fairy penguins, I was instantly in sympathy with the Japanese party who had preceded us the week before and in the same motor had infuriated our chauffeur by demanding to be driven home as soon as the first fairy penguin had emerged from the surf and made his way unsteadily up the beach. I defended their attitude and agreed with their verdict, delivered on the trip home. 'Once you have seen one fairy penguin, you have seen them all.' Not that we were expecting to see them all; at this time of the year a lot of them have departed with their chicks. I can no longer remember where they are headed for, possibly just the sea itself until summer returns, or just possibly spring, and then they are back to Phillip Island to burrow and breed.

To enjoy our excursion to the full and because we wanted to spend as long as possible in anticipation of the inevitable anti-climax induced by the spectacle of a cloud of penguins walking across the sand, we took the long way round to the Island.

We caught a ferry at a place called rather aptly, Stoney Point. The jetty was deserted when we arrived, save for a tramp steamer loading caravans. Like most jetties in Australia, it had fallen into disrepair and had to be negotiated with extreme caution. The coast of this land is littered with man's aspirations to reach the water on dry feet and always a fatal collapse of a pier or the splintering of boards has doomed the enterprise. Nothing is ever repaired; once it has collapsed it is, in the vernacular, 'given away'. When the ferry arrived we were the sole passengers. The Captain, unreasonably buoyant considering the weather, insisted that I steered and seemed hugely delighted by my efforts to collide with a tanker.

Cowes, when we reached it, turned out to be a small seaside town entirely dependent on the birds. A festival of penguins is not easy to sustain, the birds after all only appear briefly for about twenty minutes and the rest of the day must be spent viewing seals through a telescope or buying postcards and tea cloths. For us the time was brief, the penguins were due in ten minutes. We drove to the beach in an agony of fear that the creatures might have decided on an early night and we should be too late. We need not have worried. Right on the button they appeared in the rays of the searchlight sweeping the waves. They paused at the water's edge for what seemed an eternity, coyly retreated and then advanced again. Penguins can be quite a tease. The night was bitterly cold. I became convinced that I was about to catch pneumonia, but after coming all this way, I dared not retreat until the ceremony was over. I stayed while the penguins stumbled and rolled over and were assisted to their feet by kindly penguin concessionaires. I listened to the interminable commentary. I watched the confusion of a small child caught in the searchlight who didn't understand they were begging him to leave the enclosure reserved for the birds and allow them to proceed. When he finally grasped the enormity of his crime, he ran screaming into the darkness towards his mother or possibly the waves. At last it was over, the last smelly little bird safely holed up in the sand, save for the few stragglers who would be run over by the cars leaving the scene. I got back into mine, shivering, apprehensive and determined never again if I could possibly help it to look at a penguin, fairy or even king-size.

One day I shall publish the definitive guide on what not to see or do abroad. Avoid, for preference, any place connected with a legend. 'Here the simple fishermen threw themselves off the cliff.' They may have done, but it will involve a steep climb for the rest of us. Avoid towers for the same reason, and son et lumière, and plays acted in a foreign language and buildings entirely rebuilt since the war. Beware of government-sponsored stores and light operas. Limit yourself to one cathedral, one picture gallery and one giant Buddha a week. Remember, a tourist accepts, a traveller selects.

Down Under

Our driver came to an abrupt halt, surveyed the long line of stationary cars ahead, and turned into a side street. He wove his way through the little township of Cooma, only to be halted once again by the same procession.

'An accident?' I asked. 'A diversion?'

'A funeral,' he told me.

In Australia headlights are switched on for the dead. The dress is formal, the women and children in deep mourning. The whole town seemed to have turned out. The mayor, perhaps, a prince of the church, a grazier of renown? At the headquarters of the Snowy Mountain Authority we gave back the key which unlocked a gate guarding a private road through the mountain, and were told it was a Mrs. Bluett who had died, the wife of a local pilot, a young woman.

We had left Canberra till last; another week and I would be on my way. In the autumn sunshine we had explored the Snowy. The river below the Jindayne Dam is now a trickle. The little town dredged from the bottom of the lake and rebuilt on the bank. New motels and petrol stations, and roads bearing the warning 'Flooded' which disappear into the water. Are there, perhaps, elderly residents who venture back at night when the tourists are safely abed, to visit their old homes, to frequent a submarine bowling green or lay a watery wreath on a tombstone?

With the coming of nuclear power stations the whole tremendous enterprise lost face. Like the Apollo Space Missions, it's the spin-offs that count: Koscusto National Park, Thredbo Alpine Village, Smiggins Holes (smorgasbord lunch at Royal Coachman), the roads for the cars, the lakes for the fishing. It's the spin-offs too, of course, which have made this tour of mine so enjoyable ever since my daughter and I touched down at Sydney Airport far too early in the morning, with the bored photographers and television interviewers camped in the press lounge day after day, asking the ritual questions of the tired traveller, needling him into an admission he had never heard of Hobart, trying to get a new quote about the dreaded Opera House, the bane of travellers. The ground staff plugging their ears and the visitors what they have come to sell. 'We open in Melbourne, it's a beaut play, come and see it when we get there, you'll have a good laugh.' A single telegram from a single relative. 'Welcome to Australia, stop, Gloria.' The only Gloria in the family, a relict of a long dead uncle, the sort of man who always dressed for Randwick and never had the fare to get there. My Uncle Reggie whom I never met, whom the family seldom mentioned, the black sheep. But when Gloria came to tea she brought his passport and he looked so exactly like the rest of the family and wore pince nez. 'He was a good father,' she told me loyally, 'but gambled the remittance away in the first week.' It was paid monthly, so bread was scarce most of the time.

Australia has four proud daughters, Sydney, Melbourne, Adelaide and Perth, and one son, Canberra. I used to think Sydney the pick of the girls, a bit on the tarty side, but the easiest to talk to, the best dressed, perhaps simply the most theatrical. Melbourne I found a bit of a trial, reserved, a failed debutante. But not this time; this time there was a heat wave, over a hundred most days, and the inhabitants all looking as if they had been clothed in some gigantic relief operation carried out in the dark. They had grabbed a skimpy pair of shorts, a torn kaftan, and fled the earthquake. All over the town the young propped themselves against lamp posts and desired and devoured each other. The older women seemed to have agreed on no further competition as far as hair or clothes were concerned until the weather broke.

When an Australian woman lets herself go, she goes. The scrubbed face, the curlers which never seem to be taken out, at any rate in public. Do they ever let their hair down? Are they buried in curlers? What on earth does a curler do to a woman's hair, all those hours of looking like Medusa and a brief moment of what?

This time Melbourne was beaut. Business was good too; an actor measures his appreciation of the scene against the box office returns. I met old friends, made new ones – Francis Galbally, the most eminent criminal barrister in the land. I was overjoyed, when dining with him, to have him introduce the gentleman at the next table first as the most successful columnist in Melbourne and when that proved inaccurate, insist he was a Member of Parliament, which was also apparently wide of the mark. We never did discover what he really did, but it was comforting to discover that my host, who doesn't make many mistakes, could on occasions be even vaguer than I.

Sydney was sticky with the heat, but a friend lent us his harbour flat for a whole month. Would you lend your flat to an actor for a month? Of course you would! Long hours in the pool, and watching from the balcony the comings and goings of Captain Cook's Coffee Cruise. Did the Manley ferries really come out from England under their own steam? I couldn't decide about Sydney this time, they seem to have spoilt it, perhaps I had never seen the slums before, but this time we played in Newtown and drove each evening from the glitter to the gloom. Those awful Australian hotels still there, those awful Australian evenings with the drunk propped against the bar. One half of Sydney keeps up with the Joneses, the other half goes down with the Kalouris, and who, you may ask, are the Kalouris? Just a family of new Australians who are finding the sledding a bit rough. They'll make out, I suppose. I hope so. But meanwhile the skyscrapers cut off the harbour view and the Dutch Royal Family send out Prince Berhardt to preach conservation. Everyone interferes with Australia except the Australians.

Adelaide I hardly knew and this time I thought it the tops – until I got to Perth. Adelaide was brought up with a firm hand, a city a square mile in size and everything else counts as suburbs. Adelaide is the quiet one, the artistic child, the best listener, the best audience possibly in the world, so quick to get the point no one need shout. 'Let the audience do the work' has always been my creed. Here they do it without effort, they are used to theatre. I don't know why, I didn't ask, just went on gratefully every evening.

Adelaide is a family place, each vineyard producing its own wines and its own dynasty. The children go down to Melbourne to Geelong Grammar and then come home to learn the business. You might think that if your name wasn't Penfold or Hardy or Ayres it would be hard to start up, but such is not the case. You can still buy land for a song and a thousand sheep for a little more when times are bad and the rain holds off. Then suddenly the rains come and you are a millionaire if you've guessed it right. In the bush there may be no shower for five years and then ten inches of rain overnight, and you're in the flood, and what is even better, in the money.

'This,' said my younger son, who had joined us in Adelaide, 'is exactly how I pictured Australia.'

'It's not like this at all,' I told him. We were sitting on the beach, and might just possibly have been at Bognor. The children played on the sands, their parents bathed knee-deep in the waves.

'Why don't they go out further?' my son asked.

'Sharks,' I told him. In the summer, spotter planes patrol the ocean, searching out the munchies, but in the autumn it's each man for himself. Australians emphasize the drama of the bathe. Each beach has its life-savers, wearing the red hats of cardinals and arrayed in teams of four, complete with drum on which rope is coiled as we coil garden hoses. If a man or child is knocked down by the surf and carried away in the rip, they are down to the water's edge in record time, playing out the ropes to reach him. Much of the activity on the summer beaches consists of competition between the teams to see how fast they can launch each other into the waves. In Sydney they still remember with pride that the Queen Mother wore her pearls when she reviewed them. But in Adelaide the summer is spent, the life-savers have gone back to college and the munchies go unspotted.

All the same, Australia is not just beaches and bungalows, as I told my child. There is still Mrs. Ayres, thank goodness, who when she was a girl rode with her father, Kidman the cattle king, across Australia, more than fifteen hundred miles, eating breakfast before it was light and supper when the sun had gone down. In the heat of the day you didn't open your mouth unless you wore a veil. Her father owned properties galore, at one time more of the British Empire than anyone except the Crown. She remembers the ride with pleasure. Father never carried a compass, but found his way by the sun across the vast trackless bush, with thirty horses and a handful of cowboys and his two daughters. He made the damper and found the waterholes and never forgot a tree stump. He started droving at fourteen when he ran away from home after his own father had remarried, and all he took was his half blind horse.

He made fortunes in sheep and cattle and lost them in the droughts, and made them again. 'He never really liked sheep,' Mrs. Ayres told me, but he taught his children to run both. 'When sheep are bad in Australia, cattle are good' is as true today as it was then. Mrs. Ayres drove us to Victor Harbour. All her life she has wanted to see a whale out there in the bay, but the whales have gone. I kept asking her about the discomforts of her ride, but she had forgotten them. To her it had seemed a picnic, only the memory of the wild dogs still disturbed her. They had come across a bitch and her pups, set fire to the bush where they were hiding and, as they came out, the men had shot them. 'They had to do it, but it upset my sister and me.' There are no whales, no wild dogs, few kangaroos, even the rabbits are disappearing. In Victor Harbour down by the water's edge there is a monument to a tribe of Aborigines who once lived on the river bank. Mrs. Ayres remembered how on the ride they would collect the whycherly grubs and carry them in their shirts till it was time to feast. 'Did you ever eat one?' I asked, and she shuddered.

Sydney has its harbour, but also its slums, Melbourne its shops, but an uncertain climate, Adelaide its vineyards and beaches and a curious serenity. No probs, they'll tell you all through Australia. No probs, she'll be right. The dust in this happy-go-lucky land is not swept under the carpet, it just naturally collects there. In Australia nothing is ever mended until it lets in the rain. The coastline is littered with broken promises. Steps down to the beach, jetties leading to long-forgotten marinas perish and crumble away. There is no such thing as keeping up an appearance. There is no such thing as keeping up with the Joneses. There is a lunatic fringe around the Sydney Harbour where life is a society rat-race, and in Melbourne money counts, but Adelaide is a city of schools and bowling greens and uniforms; the short print dress, the dark flannels and grey blazer and then white ducks and white skirts and blue blazers when they grow up and change the school cap for the white panama and the correct club ribbon.

The temperature in Adelaide is around eighty, the water warm, the sands deserted, and the largest shark for a long time waits in the bay. Big Fred they call him, and only yesterday he savaged a fishing boat and ate a piece of the hull, or just possibly the prow. I am not a nautical man or a brave one: I shall go in just as far as my knee caps . . .

Emerging from the waves, I was confronted by two Madison Avenue-type Australians in bathing dresses, each wearing a single golden crucifix as an earring. For a moment I feared they were missionaries, but they explained they worked in the advertising department of a famous Australian store with branches throughout the continent.

'We were wondering,' they told me, 'if you were working?'

'Not at the moment,' I confessed, shaking the water out of what is left of my hair, 'but I expect to be doing so later in the day.'

'Would you consider taking on another assignment?' they askd, 'it's more or less of a temporary nature, but rewarding while it lasts.'

'That would depend,' I told them.

'We are seeking,' they explained, 'an Easter Bunny. It occurred to us you might fill the bill.'

Before we discussed money, I thought it wiser to withdraw. One can only take on a certain amount . . .

Perth had never heard of us, still hasn't. Perth is the tomboy, the most beautiful, most desirable. Here the British seem to outnumber the Aussies. On the beach I asked a fellow Pom what kept him. 'The bathing,' he told me. 'Here they have the last unpolluted ocean in the world.' I asked whether he had any desire to see the rest of the country. 'Not the slightest,' he replied, 'from all they tell me, Australia is much of a muchness . . .'

This is a dangerous country, or at least the inhabitants would have you and themselves believe so; sharks are constantly on the prowl along the beaches, the sea brings the dreaded sea wasps into the shallows to wrap themselves round the bathers. Here a man wades ashore, his shoulders covered by a curious mauve shawl, and dies on the sand; a child gets swept away in a rip and men are drowned like the late Prime Minister Holt in the surf, and their bodies never recovered. The insignificant number of such fatalities compared, say, to the toll which the traffic takes here as everywhere else, doesn't prevent the press playing each incident up for what it's worth, and a good deal more. The papers are incurably parochial, huge pictures of children off for a picnic on the shore, endless close-ups of cleavage, small rows between obscure politicians are blown up to mammoth proportions and crowd world events off front pages.

In public life the emphasis is on dullness and the spokesman inarticulate or verbose. This is a country of shirt sleeves. A man puts on a coat or turns a phrase only reluctantly. Australia seems determined not to make the best of herself, not yet anyway, the best is yet to come. No one doubts that, least of all the visitor like myself. It seems inconceivable folly that the British have deserted this huge, rich, beaut continent for the exhausted pastures of Europe. The ties are being broken, the special relationship which really existed here and never in America has almost vanished, the links that remain are become like old Christmas decorations which no one has had the time or the energy to take down for lack of a pair of steps. Australia Day, and the Governor and his Lady solemnly running up the Union Jack on the racecourse and inspecting the band as if it were a guard of honour. His Excellency speaks a few words, not bad words as it happens, but no one is listening, and why should they, when they have come to find the winner? Racing is still hugely important, betting the national pastime. Easy come, easy go, and an unemployment figure of less than one per cent. The taxi drivers here as elsewhere have tried it all before settling for a cab and a city. They have dug for gold and copper and opal; preached the Bible, rounded up the cattle; now most of them own their cabs and plan to buy another. 'Never buy a house,' one of them told me. 'A house is only somewhere for the wife to spend money. A house doesn't work for you, a second cab is different.'

Not that many of them are in the rat-race, which is run at a far slower pace here than elsewhere. This is a rich country all right; no probs. I am taken to a pub owned by the Brothers. The trade unions are very powerful and very rich. The bar was full of paid-up members and full-time officials. 'We don't go for the big strikes any more. Guerilla action is the thing, the other's too costly. Out for a couple of days, back for a week and out again. They get the message, brother.' Ask them about racial matters and they introduce me with pride to a solitary Aborigine boxer . . .

In the theatre I don't seem all that far from Shaftesbury Avenue, but I dream of adventure as I put on the slap each evening. They say in the opal mines a man still takes his life in his hands and the buyers sit in caves stashed with stones and dollars and guarded by ferocious hound dogs. Real John Wayne country, if I ever get there. I am planning to visit Ayres Rock, of course, and a fabulous dude ranch on the banks of Ross river. I am planning a trip to Hobart too, where they've opened their first casino, and then there's the Barrier Reef and surfers' paradise, and best of all Lassiter's Reef, the great gold field which Lassiter found and lost again, and which has never been relocated until . . .until . . .

I shall rename it, of course, Morley's Reef, and if by any unlikely chance I don't win the Sydney Derby Lottery, I'll be heading out west – or is it north? – pardner, for sure, with my little old pan and my little old billy can.

A Small Miracle in Quebec

'If the Queen came here they wouldn't dare open the door of her car.'

'In Quebec?'

'That's right.'

The speaker, as always with me, was the taxi driver. I am father confessor of all taxi drivers, to me they open their hearts. Driving round Toronto for a month, I have come to know my flock. There's the one who is married to a Japanese wife and thinks he's the luckiest man alive. There's the one who married the dame in Vegas and believes himself less fortunate. 'I'd wake up in the night and she'd be gone, with my bill fold. "Where the hell were you?" I'd ask when she got home at six in the morning. "Honey, I felt lucky and took the cab down to the Golden Horseshoe." That girl was so crazy she'd even try to sell my cab.' There's the taxi driver who is buying a house, and works days dealing with computers and nights dealing with drunks. There's the hack who has been in prison and can handle the muggers when they climb into his cab, and there's the one in Quebec who thinks they wouldn't dare open the door of Her Majesty's motor.

'Why ever not?' I asked, 'What have you got against the Monarch?'

'It's not personal, you understand. It's the money for one thing. Do you know how much she gets a year? A million and a half, and she wants a raise.'

'But you don't pay it, do you? I thought *we* paid it. Anyway, a lot of people think she pays it herself.'

'*We* pay it,' he told me, 'make no mistake, someone has to pay it, and it's us. What that dame has cost us!'

He stopped the cab outside the cyclorama of the Holy Land, a must for all good tourists. It is the largest picture in the world, was painted in 1860 in Munich and no one seems to know how it ever fetched up beside the sacred shrine of St. Anne de Beaupré. But fetch up it did, splendidly housed in a huge circular dome, and inspected hourly by hundreds upon hundreds of curious sightseers at a dollar fifty a throw. The explanation of the painting takes exactly nine minutes, and is repeated alternately in English and French, right through the day and, I imagine, far into the night. 'If you want to know who the figures are at the foot of the Cross, buy the guide book,' they tell you, 'not the Bible!'

Next door the sacred church and shrine of Our Lady was built by the traditional wrecked – or near-wrecked – sea captain who swore that if he ever got ashore again it would be to put up a church to the Virgin. There is a hospital adjacent for the cripples who come to be cured, and the enormous basement of the church is piled with crutches. I don't know what they do with them in the hospital. A very old priest was on hand to bless the faithful and selected unbelievers. I explained I had come only to shelter from the taxi driver and get a corn fixed, but he blessed me all the same. 'Did you hear,' he asked 'of the Catholic who was dying in mortal sin and when asked to say a prayer, told God he hadn't bothered him for twenty-five years and if he was allowed another twenty-five, wouldn't bother him again during that time?' I told him I hadn't, which wasn't strictly true, but as Kipling admonished us, be good to all poor parish priests.

Driving back to the city, the driver kept off the Queen and tried to get me to stop to try a piece of bread. The houses along the lake specialise in individual open air ovens and feeding the pilgrims. 'On bread?' I asked, 'just dry bread?' 'That's right.' 'No butter?' 'No butter.'

Perhaps it's the butter that is lacking in Quebec. While Toronto and Montreal forge ahead, Quebec drags her feet. She seems determined to preserve the past, to try and forget Wolfe and the final ignominy on the Heights of Abraham and remember all this was once going to be Nouveau Français, a vast continent reaching up north to Hudson Bay and down south to Carolina and the swamps of the Mississippi. In Quebec they never forget how near they were to conquering the New World. At the Laval Seminary, the largest in North America, a great map fresco on the wall reminds them of the huge, original, all-embracing parish of the Bishop of Quebec. Then we came along and spoilt everything for them, and now they only have the old town which we burnt down and the toboggan slide on the boardwalk around the citadel, and of course the Château Frontenac. The day will come, I suppose, when someone will have to start pulling that down and they will surely have to evacuate the city while he does so. It might even be cheaper and wiser to move Quebec and leave this great palace on the cliff to stand for ever as an example of what went on half way through the nineteenth century.

Few people realise that the Château is really not a hotel at all, but an ocean liner which no one dared to put into the water in case it didn't float. It would have done so, there can be no doubt of that, but courage failed at the last moment, and there it is high on the Heights of Abraham, looking as if a giant had assembled a do-it-yourself kit of a cabin cruiser in his back garden and found he would have to knock his house down to get it to the beach. Once inside, the illusion of being all at sea is complete; the decoration reminds one of the gay abandonment of the days when ladies and gentlemen promenaded, and Art Nouveau was indeed Nouveau. There were fishcakes for luncheon in the first class dining-room, and at tea an orchestra in powdered wigs and embroidered coats played Bach and selections from *South Pacific* in the Palm Court, while we gazed out through the stained glass portholes and tried not to notice that we were becalmed on the great waters of the St. Lawrence. Becalmed, that's the word for Quebec, and as if to drive home the point, that evening six hundred television sets in six hundred bedrooms were happily screening *Spring in Park Lane*. It was good to see Anna Neagle once more, and Tom Walls too, if it came to that.

At four in the morning I phoned the bell captain: my room had become a furnace; the radiators, long since turned off, were exploding with heat. An elderly plumber arrived and noted it was très chaud, leant out of the window and regretted there was pas de vent. Is this the evening it happens? I asked myself. Are we all to be roasted alive while the orchestra plays 'Nearer my God to Thee'? I was fairly near Him already on the very top deck of all. They gave me another stateroom and I slept fitfully, dreaming of icebergs. When I woke, the S.S. Château Frontenac appeared to be hoved to in thick fog.

Of my corn there was no trace.

FAMILY
ALBUM

Folkestone and Father

Anyone who has ever been stowed away in an ambulance will, while the operation is actually being carried out, have glimpsed on the faces of the spectators a look of shocked enjoyment. It is the same look as I experienced in my pram during the first few months of life. People peered at me as though I had been the victim of an accident, and so I had — the accident of birth.

I had a difficult birth, and after an anxious eight hours for all concerned, mistook the doctor for my father. I remember lying perfectly still with my eyes closed in a chill of terror. 'My God!,' I told myself, 'I've landed right in the middle of it.' My mother lay in a euphoric trance at having produced so splendid an infant, and I could not, even if I had wanted to, disturb her complacency and exhaustion. I could only lie there and shudder.

The doctor was not my idea of a father. I remember I particularly disliked his hands. I was not introduced to my real parent for some hours. It was not the fashion in those days for fathers to attend the birth of their children, and I approve of the modern attitude in this matter. The least a father can do is to welcome his offspring in person. I am all for coming out into the drive to greet my guests. I do not expect them to find their own way into my study.

In point of fact I was a singularly beautiful baby — all ten-and-a-half pounds of me. They don't come that size any more, and it was with justifiable pride that my mother handed me over to the nursery staff. Nineteen hundred and eight was a good year for my father, and we could afford a nursemaid as well as a nanny. I remember them both perfectly, although neither stayed with us for very long, my father's affairs calling, as they did so frequently, for sudden retrenchment. In those days we were always moving house. My sister claims it gave her a sense of insecurity; even now she is loth to move around;

travel, except local, is out of the question. Me, quite the reverse. I am always planning to go to China. One of us must have got it wrong. Our moving around was perhaps fortunate, as the farm where I was born was burnt to the ground soon after we left it. It had, after all, perfectly fulfilled its function. My father at the time dabbled in and dreamt of champion saddlebacks. How amply I was to compensate him for his early failures in that field, although he was not to discover until some years later that he had produced the greatest ham of all.

My father was the sort of father who upset treacle on the tablecloth to amuse his brood. Quite early in my life he had the disconcerting habit of lifting me high in the air. Babies do not on the whole like being lifted, and none of them care to be dropped. I don't say my father ever dropped me, but he came damned close to it. He lived until I was over thirty, a life of extraordinary crisis and financial adventure, full of alarums and excursions. He never understood money, but believed, like his son, that this was because he could never get his hands on enough of the stuff. He was in turn soldier, café proprietor, night-club impresario, club secretary, farmer and postal poet. He was often a bankrupt, always a gambler, and of all the excitement, happiness and occasional despair he brought me, I remember him best sitting pretending to be asleep, a handkerchief over his face, and four, sometimes even five chocolates arranged on his lap, while I, choking with pleasure and the effort of restraining my giggles, tiptoed towards him to seize a sweet while he feigned unconsciousness. Then he would wake, remove the handkerchief, look down with astonishment, count the remaining chocolates, and express bewilderment, rage or resignation before once more replacing the handkerchief and pretending to nod off. If there has ever been a better game, I certainly have never played it, and if I was honest I should say that the only acting I ever learnt was at my parent's knee.

But back to the nursery, the boredom of starting tea with bread and butter, and the delight of the patent medicine's which kept me and my sister fighting fit, or at any rate fighting. We fought with each other, with nanny, and later with a selection of governesses. We were apt to boast, the two of us, that we could get rid of any governess within a fortnight of her setting foot in our nursery. Later, my parents despairing, or possibly unable to afford the redundancy settlements, sent us to a dame-school at the end of the road. It was a long road, and halfway along it a dog barked menacingly at my approach. It was my ever-present terror that one day he would detach himself from the chain to which he was shackled, and tear into my ample and defenceless rump. I did everything I could to avoid alerting him. I walked in the ditch, I tiptoed along the road, I stooped beneath the hedge, I played truant. My mother poo-pooed, my sister jeered, my teacher scolded, and I grew up terrified of man's four-footed alleged friend.

Looking back on my first few years, I realise now they were ones of continuing anxiety. At six I craved chestnuts to bore through and thread on string. I hurled a stick one afternoon at a chestnut tree and brought down a couple attached to a small branch. Instantly at my elbow a lout appeared, threatening to tell the owner of the tree. He bluffed me out of sixpence and made me promise to meet him the next Saturday for a further contribution. I have forgotten now whether I did or not, but I remember the terror of my first experience with guilt and blackmail. As usual I overstate the case. What I experienced, I suppose, was being found out.

Nobody found out much about me when I was a child. There wasn't perhaps a great deal to learn. I survived to tell the tale, to hold my own grandchildren on my lap and to try to remember how my father looked when I play the chocolate game. I resist lifting them high in the air. I never tickle them. (God, how I hated being tickled!) On the rare occasions when I preside at tea-time, I give them cake first. There is no logical reason not to do so. When my grand-daughter is older I shall try and persuade her never to curtsy when shaking hands. I dislike 'manners'. I avoid finding things for them to do. I lived in an age when children were always being given simple tasks. I have never forgiven Mrs. Boddam Whettam who, when I was a child, once gave me seventeen invitations to a bridge tea, to be delivered personally by one who was frightened of dogs, who was shy of strangers, and who loathed exercise. Fortunately we were living in Folkestone at the time, and I climbed to a rocky pinnacle of The Leas and let the wind carry each invitation separately over the cliff and out to sea, and when Mrs. Boddam Whettam waited disconsolately at her bridge parlour, the cards set out on the green baize tables, a marker and a pencil arranged in every place, bravely blinking back her tears, I never gave her a thought. I was sitting in the Electric Cinema watching Charlie Chaplin playing the same scene far better on celluloid.

In Folkestone I still expect to be patted, to be recognised as the little boy who delighted them all in my sailor suit. I like to return whenever I feel the shadows beginning to lengthen, to ring the doorbells of the houses and explain to whoever opens the door that this was where I lived when I was a child. We were always moving round in Folkestone. We left The Leas and set ourselves up in Augusta Road. We had a house in Earls Avenue and another in Turketel Road, not at the same time, of course. We weren't rich by Folkestone standards. If there's one thing young people lack today, I am afraid it is Folkestone standards. It may well be what's wrong with the country. Who today rides in a Bath chair? 'I think,' the doctor would say, soon after the spots disappeared, the rash faded, the temperature subsided, 'I think he could go out for a little, in a Bath chair.' And in a Bath chair I went. The very best Folkestone Bath chairs had folding mahogany shutters with windows through which one looked out onto the patient back of the attendant, silently plodding ahead. With the shutters drawn one was insulated from the noise, a silent world with the delicious uncertainty that one might have suddenly become stone deaf. It was necessary sometimes to open the shutters and shout, just to reassure oneself. Mother steered from the back. Convalescence was achieved slowly, thoroughly, but achieved. Young people nowadays never get a chance to get better in Bath chairs. What's lacking is 'style'.

On Sundays the bands played on The Leas. The bandstands were situated at some distance from one another, but it was possible, by positioning one's Bath chair accurately, to listen to the Grenadiers with the right ear, while the Marines enchanted the left. No wonder I am not fond of discotheques. I was spoilt in my youth by the real thing.

What gave Folkestone, and in a sense myself, character, were the cliff-hangers, the lifts. I travelled in them on an average at least once a week, always my heart was in my mouth. It is this sense of danger that makes life sweet. I am numbed by the blaséness of astronauts, those laconic voices revealing their boredom. Even their names appear to me subnormal — Pete, Greg. My sister, who is called Margaret, and I, who was christened Adolf, used to scream loudly just before take off. Count-down was signalled by closing the sliding doors, and then there would be the terrifying surge of water. We would look up at the seagulls circling far, far overhead, at the tiny figures in the car which was about to crash down on our heads, and scream. Of course, it never really hit us. We used to pass the car halfway. Sometimes it would be quite full, whereas our lift would contain only my sister, myself and our governess. I always wondered whether they adjusted the weight of the water, how it was that we rose and they sank without unseemly haste, while the balance was so unequal. At the top, splash-down was always carried out without a hitch. The car was accurately positioned to enable us to step out of it and hurry home to tea.

Our governess was called Miss Faithful. She was called a lot of other things as well, by which I mean she didn't keep changing her name, it was we who changed our governess. My sister and I simply couldn't keep a governess. They came and went. We used to stick pins in them. What idiots they must have been to desert their posts, to cry halt. What trouble they caused my parents by deserting so frequently. But despite the incessant upheavals, the comings and goings, dismissals, resignations and engagements, my father and mother never lost hope, never surrendered to the modern and quite ridiculous assumption that parents can raise their own offspring.

What singles my generation out is this lack of coarseness so prevalent today. Young people are no longer refined. They never had a governess to show them how it should be done. For if our governesses had anything in common besides a deadly loathing for my sister and myself, it was this air of ineffable refinement, evinced in every action which they allowed us to observe, and which they encouraged us to emulate. The washing of hands, for instance, before every meal. They never held their fingers under the tap, or left a smudge on the towel. Soup spoons travelled outwards across the plate, bread was crumbled, toast was cut, butter was spread evenly. Tidiness was maintained, handkerchiefs were kept in sachets, pins arranged symmetrically in pincushions, bookmarkers placed between pages. Our governesses were always prepared for inspection, and they tried to keep us similarly at the ready. I wonder sometimes what was the reason behind the rule. Why did they insist on everything always being in its proper place? Was it only because when it was time for them to pack and go, they would know where everything was? And why did they go so often? There are pictures still in existence of my sister and me at various ages — dear, jolly little things we seemed — but not to our governesses.

When I undress at night I let all my clothes slide onto the floor — the big shelf, Miss Kipps used to call it — and there they stay until morning. My clothes seem to last as long as everyone else's. They may have to go to the cleaners more often, but I have saved hours of my life through defying Miss Kipps and not arranging them neatly on a chair, or hanging them in a cupboard. But what of the generation who never knew Miss Kipps? What pleasure would it be for them in middle age to let their clothes lie around? Or if it comes to that, to hold their hands under a tap, or not even to wash them at all? They will be simply doing what they have always done. They will never know the pleasure of not doing what they were brought up to do.

For in the tight little world in which I was hatched and reared, there was tremendous security, a security largely unknown today, and based I think on three great faiths — Keplers, Dr. Parrish and Syrup of Figs. These were the three great patent medicines which no household could afford to be without. Keplers was imbibed after breakfast. There was a special Keplers spoon kept in the medicine cupboard. A delicious treacly substance which wound itself out of the jar and down the gullet. Parrish's Chemical Food was taken through a glass tube, otherwise, legend had it, one's teeth turned black. The excitement of this ceremony could hardly be exaggerated. As the tube was clenched between the teeth, one entered the world of Jules Verne, H. G. Wells and R. L. Stevenson. The mixture thus assimilated, one handed the tube back and hurried to the glass to examine one's teeth. Syrup of Figs never quite managed the rapture of the others. It was always offered in a spoon overlarge for the mouth, had a tendency to spill and stain the pyjamas, and because one had already cleaned one's teeth, was seldom followed by a sweet. One had to content oneself with a throat pastille. Bath chairs, governesses, patent medicines made me what I am today. How sad that the younger generations would infinitely prefer to be without any of us.

I'll Try Anything Once

Somewhere in the archives of the British Museum there should be one of my father's poems. He may have written others but if so I never read them. I know this one arrived at the museum because I posted it myself. My father gave me the envelope which contained his masterpiece printed at his own expense on cardboard and there was a loop of silk attached to affix it in a prominent position. Mind you, in the case of the museum I don't think Father ever believed it would be hung up. By law, he explained to me, everthing published has to go to the museum.

'But is it really published?' I asked him.

'Of couse, boy, printed and published by me and incidentally advertised by me in the agony columns of *The Times* this very morning.'

He drew my attention to the insertion for which presumably he had also forked out: 'Is there a life hereafter? Send a shilling postal order to Major Morley, The Firs, Rolvenden, Kent.'

Intriguing, one must admit, particularly as the poem itself seemed to be the account of a wedding and subsequent funeral of a young lady who habitually wore a violet corsage. Father was fond of violets.

My father never published again. 'There is simply no money in literature,' he was wont to remark, 'I tried it myself once. People just aren't interested.' I inherited from my father a love of gambling, making the sweeping statement and never being afraid of having a go—although the last precept I had little opportunity of putting into effect until my schooldays were behind me. In the schools I went to there was little opportunity of having a go unless you wished to be soundly thrashed almost immediately afterwards.

My father liked to boast he had tried everything once and some things, like bankruptcy, a number of times. He opened tea shops and night clubs, bred polo ponies and racing pigeons, started militant

355

guerrilla bands in South Africa, held a commission in the Dragoon Guards and ever after retained his silver-plated helmet converted into a biscuit tin, another of his inventions which, alas, never caught on—and seemed to be perpetually clutching a hand of cards or a telephone connected to a bookmaker. It was his perpetual survival in fair health, and even better spirits, that heartened my own youth for the struggle to come.

Life for me really began, however, about thirty when most of the family were beginning to fear I had left it a bit late.

I had been an actor for nearly ten years and (as these were the days long before inflation) found it impossible, when I was not resting, as we called it, to get my weekly salary into double figures.

One morning I answered an advertisement not in *The Stage* but in the *Daily Telegraph* which invited applicants to call personally at an address in Bond Street which provided employment in an immensely attractive and lucrative field to willing lads with no previous experience of any kind. The first thing I saw when I entered the offices was a vacuum cleaner. 'Don't shy away from it,' the man sitting behind the desk advised. 'We pay while you train, give it a go.' I did just that, trudging the lanes and the avenues of Beaconsfield, ringing doorbells and trying to get my foot over the threshold. What you need in this game, I was told, is a good hat to take off and stout boots to act as a wedge.

The main trouble was that everyone already had a vacuum cleaner. My task was to get the customer to discard the one she had and go for novelty in the shape of what I learnt to describe as an entirely revolutionary domestic hygienic system. The revolution was in the plastic bubble in which the user could, if he wished, examine the dust atoms swirling around; they never actually went into the bag provided but gave at times a tolerable imitation of a paperweight being agitated to produce a snow storm. For the first few weeks I couldn't bring myself to believe anyone would be fool enough to fall for my foreplay and seldom got into the house, then one never-to-be-forgotten morning I sold two straight off and became a salesman, something I have remained ever since. Confidence is all—I went from strength to strength, was put in charge of a team, given a motor car and competed in inter-sales contests at monthly meetings. I even attended ceremonial prizegivings where hymns of praise were sung, admonishing the faithful. *Onward vacuum salesman, eager for the fray. Peal the bells and enter. Make the housewife pay.* Good stuff and in those days we had them more or less at our mercy and didn't have to state our business before the buzzer released the catch.

The money was good too, far better than that paid on yet another tour of *Charley's Aunt* which I found myself returning to with relief in due course. I had after all learnt my lesson in life, that there is what others less deeply in love than I with the common man might describe as the sucker element. The imponderable and unexpected rise of the fish to take the fly; how else to account for the fact that every now and again someone will answer their own front door and half an hour later have succumbed to the temptation offered by the sight of a new soap powder or a pair of panty hose. Big spenders may even sign up for *Encyclopaedia Britannica* and garden rollers. The truth once grasped, it seemed to me perfectly possible that a play I had written would be purchased straight or very nearly straight away by the leading comedy actress of her day. I more or less expected the phone to ring on the Monday morning summoning me to lunch and to discuss production after I had posted the script to her the previous Friday. So it proved. I was no longer surprised when given a star role, only astounded that it had previously been offered elsewhere.

To ensure such a state of affairs continuing I even became, with the help of trusted allies, an actor-manager. After three years my partners and I still had the prettiest offices in town, without a desk but with enormous sofas and an even larger dining table and the walls were hung with more than a dozen playbills as a reminder of our efforts and of the least complaining backers in the business. Like most managers we guessed it wrong three times out of four but those were heady days when in conference we would decide that Lord Olivier was too old for a part he would never have accepted anyway, and that I would be wise to play it myself.

It was the example of my own father which prompted me to say snap when the first offer was made, but it is to the housewives of Beaconsfield, who slammed the doors in my face and then one morning opened them unexpectedly, to whom I owe the deepest gratitude. They taught me, or just possibly I taught myself, that when pennies drop from heaven they fall into the lap of the faithful, the hopeful, the persevering. If you had told me all those years ago that behind the front doors of sensible villas lurk sensible matrons who can be persuaded every now and again in one single act of folly to get rid of a perfectly good cleaner and make a down payment on a new domestic hygienic system, so complicated that in my case at least I couldn't even demonstrate it efficiently, I wouldn't have believed you.

A Kensington Childhood

Long ago when smokeless fuel seemed as improbable as moon exploration, my town was known as The Smoke. Visitors came to London to experience the fogs. 'Is this,' they would ask each other, 'the genuine pea-souper?' Then, coughing enthusiastically, they would grope their way to Baker Street and the lodgings of Sherlock Holmes. But fog such as Dickens knew has gone the way of Derry and Toms, and if you ask who Derry and Toms were, I have forgotten. They were people who once kept a shop, people like Mr. Gunter who made brown bread ices, and the lady who sat outside Kensington Gardens, a hundred balloons above her head, the strings clutched in her hand, defying the winds to bear her away before she had disposed of her work load. Why didn't she take off and, floating just above our heads, crash into the Albert Memorial? I suppose because Albert would not have been amused.

No child brought up as I was in Folkestone and Kensington Gardens ever felt the need of a psychiatrist. Today adventure playgrounds have taken over, and children are expected to hang upside down like bats or tunnel like worms or swing like monkeys. We were expected to behave, to keep off the grass. There were occasional lapses on my part of course, like the morning I walked fully dressed, or rather fully uniformed, for I was wearing my first sailor suit, into the Serpentine, by permission of my father. Perhaps he hadn't really believed I would take him at his word; perhaps he was just tired of me whining that I wanted to paddle; perhaps he wasn't even listening. At any rate, with full parental approval I strode forward until the water encompassed my thighs and then, realising that all was not as it should be and that my trousers were clinging and impeding my further progress, I attempted to retrace my steps, lost my nerve and finally my footing, and started to scream. 'Come quickly,' the crowd told each other, 'they are drowning a child in the Serpentine!', and gathered at the water's edge to boo my parent and console me.

It was the first great drama of my life, but there were more to come. A few years later I was carried into the house we lived in in South Kensington on a stretcher. I have never forgotten the way onlookers regarded my recumbent form. There was still a vogue, at least in our drawing-room, for the picture that told the story, the physician comforting the parents of the dying child, the lonely colonial opening the mail with the postman on horseback retreating over the hill, the ruined spendthrift, head down on the kitchen table, a revolver within reach. Anyway, I wished there was an artist who could have captured that moment and titled it 'The Invalid, or Back from School'. For school it was that caused my health to crumple. I was always allowed home in mid-term with acute melancholia from horrific boarding-schools named after some saint, and where the sufferings of early Christian martyrs were cunningly reproduced — flagellation at St. Wilfrid's, starvation at St. Christopher's, conflict with dragon at St. George's. Do I exaggerate? I think not, but in London at least I never went to school. London was sanctuary. I ran home, I was carried home, I was sent home, and I was safe at least till next term.

Every now and then, when I have a spare hour to kill, I find myself again in South Kensington. I walk once more around Court-field Gardens and pause outside Number Seven, the earliest sanctuary of my childhood. Here my grandmother lived on seven floors, not that she ever climbed the stairs to the attics, but must often, I suppose, have descended the stone flags leading to the basement where the work was done. My grandmother ran a tight ship, with a first mate called Hinchley. When Grandmother lay in her huge bed, dressed for dying, she took formal leave of us all. One by one we were summoned by Hinchley, one by one kissed and admonished, and given our last sweetmeat from her hand, and then she would reach up and tug the great wide bell-rope behind her head, and Hinchley would usher us out. There was no reason to ask for whom the bell tolled, Grandmother tolled it for herself. When she did die, the whole of Courtfield Gardens was strewn deep with straw to muffle the sound of the horses' hooves and the carriage wheels. If, when I die, I crave anything, it is not a memorial service but the village street covered in straw.

We inherited Hinchley, but not for long. Ours was a different household altogether and my father, a Piccadilly gambler, couldn't keep a silver canteen, let alone a household. In our rough days we lived for a time at the Naval and Military Hotel in Carrington

Gardens, nearby. My mother hated above all one Christmas we spent there while she hunted among the small change in Father's pocket for enough to give the staff their Boxing Day tips. We were very poor that Christmas. We moved around a good deal, never further west than Gloucester Road, never, alas, further east than South Kensington Station. In Gloucester Road, Bailey's Hotel, a huge and rather splendid building with a glass portico and porters at the ready, reassured and comforted us when fortune was at its lowest ebb. Had not this great enterprise been named after my uncle, Sir James Bailey, who had in some mysterious way commanded it to be built? He was dead before I arrived on the scene, and his huge fortune gone astray, distributed piecemeal to what my father called the collateral side of the family. But then of course Sir James was only an uncle by marriage, having espoused my aunt Elizabeth rather late in his life, but comparatively early in hers. The match, so they said, was made at the behest of the curate of St. Jude's whom and where my aunt worshipped.

We would sometimes take tea at Bailey's, in which we still took a proprietorial interest, dreaming of the day perhaps when Father's ship would at last come home, along with the winner of the two-thirty, and we would simply repossess. We never, naturally, had the same *folie de grandeur* about Harrods, where my grandmother had shopped when it was still just a small fishmonger's shop and Mr. Harrod in the traditional straw hat would leave the sluice-board and come to the carriage to take the order. People stayed in their carriages in those days, even when they visited, or left cards, as the ceremony was called. Sometimes they didn't even bother to accompany the coachman on his rounds with the engraved slips of pasteboard. He just dismounted from the box, hastened up the steps, slipped the cards through the letter-box and was away before the horse got restive. If my grandmother was in the carriage, a footman came as well, but even so my grandmother never alighted, just gave her card to the fellow, with one corner turned down to indicate she had been prepared to descend, had the circumstances warranted it. The hostess would sit in her drawing-room in splendid isolation and the cards would be brought up for her inspection, and then scattered on the silver salver always standing in the hall. It saved on the tea-cakes and the washing-up, not that that was of course the object of the exercise. But what, then, was the object? I simply cannot tell you.

I only know that as I walk around, I miss Lady Gorringe's brougham in which we would travel on Saturdays to Whiteleys to buy chocolates. Her Ladyship never stopped in other departments, or imagined we would want to linger among the toys or even the tropical fish, although we had to walk through both departments before coming across the confectionery counter. Once arrived, we would buy three one-pound boxes of comfits and return to the security of the carriage. Bayswater, in Lady Gorringe's book, was no place to loiter. It just happened to have the best sweetmeats. When the boxes were empty there was a way of tearing the paper glued to the inside to simulate exactly the firing of a Maxim gun.

I miss, too, the smell of the Tube, as it was called, a hot, not very pleasant, but completely exciting smell; the threshold to pleasure, for we only took the Tube for an excursion away from the territory — to Brompton Road to shop, or to Down Street to watch a procession, both of which stations have vanished, although for a long time they remained ghost platforms at which no train stopped and no passenger alighted. In the war, Brompton Road Station was the headquarters of the London Air Defence Operations. From there orders were issued each night to haul down the barrage balloons and send up the night fighters, and a girl who is now my agent pushed model Spitfires across the maps and became General Pyle's Personal Plotter. For Down Street there was no such honourable retirement, or if there was I was never told.

But long before all this, when I was still governess-bound, I believed Piccadilly Circus meant what it said, and that in the centre of my town, in the centre of the world, was a perpetual display of acrobats and tigers, bareback riders and performing seals, and when I at last discovered quite late in life that this was not the case, the shock was traumatic. I was on a bus, an open bus with wooden seats and individual mackintosh covers which fixed with studs and straps to the sides of the seats. We circled the Circus and I asked if for once we could get down and inspect the menagerie, even if we couldn't see an actual performance.

'But this *is* the Circus,' they told me, 'don't you see, it goes round, a circus goes round!'

'But what about Oxford Circus?' I enquired, with panic gripping my heart.

'The same,' they told me, 'only you don't go round Oxford Circus, you cut across it.'

I knew then better than to ask about the others — Holborn, Cambridge. In a moment I had lost not one but four great pleasure domes.

I preferred the top of the bus whatever the weather, not because I was ever an open-air child, but because from there I could look down and read the names on the marquees outside the theatres and cinemas we passed. I would announce the attractions in an as uncommitted a voice as I could muster, not because I wasn't dying to alight and watch Ronald Colman in *The Garden of Allah,* but because I knew any request to do so was doomed to refusal, and I hoped passionately that my parent, guardian or whoever was accompanying me on whatever errand would abandon the plan of the day, or at any rate postpone it long enough for us both to alight and spend a few magic hours of excitement. Indeed I may claim, I think, to have been one of the pioneers of subliminal advertising.

I don't know what determined my father that it was time for me to know something of the world, nor can I remember at what age he guided my steps towards Chinatown, which he had reason to believe was situated in Limehouse. Had he waited a bit longer he would no doubt have settled for Gerrard Street, but it would have robbed us both of a long and exciting journey through the Docks and eventually reaching the Causeway which my parent was, I think, as surprised to discover as I was. He had only the shadowiest idea of how to pass the time until we could return the way we had come, and we wandered around aimlessly staring at the few Chinese who passed.

'I suppose as we're here,' my pater remarked suddenly, 'we might see if we can buy some snow', and then, since it was in the middle of summer, and sensing my surprise, he explained that by snow he had meant to indicate cocaine. 'This is where they sell it,' he told me, and taking my hand in a protective gesture which always embarrassed me, he entered the local friendly neighbourhood store. To his delight the old woman behind the counter was unmistakably oriental of countenance.

'Good afternoon, Mother,' he began, much to my astonishment, 'Mother, I wonder if you could tell me where I might find some snow?'

The old lady regarded him with the composure native to her race. 'Snow?' she asked, 'Did you say snow?'

'That's right,' my father leaned forward, hot on the trail.

'We had some last winter,' she told him.

'Ah, last winter. But not now? I wouldn't want much,' Father assured her.

'You won't get much this time of the year,' she told him patiently.

There was a long silence after that, while they stood staring at each other and then it was I who took Father out of the shop and led him away. 'I don't think,' I told him, 'she knew what you were talking about.'

'Nonsense,' said Father, 'she knew all right, but for some reason, she didn't want to sell. I expect she thought I was a plain-clothes Bobby.'

One adventure was enough for Father, besides it was time for cards. We took the bus home.

It mustn't be thought that my parent concentrated his efforts on educating me solely in vice. On the contrary, he was anxious that I should grow up an officer and gentleman and as unlike my aunt Sophie as possible. Aunt Sophie had once flung his *Ruff's Guide to the Turf* into the fire in an effort to stop him dissipating any further her sister's fortune. He never forgave nor forgot. My aunt was religious. 'How would she have liked it,' he would observe, when recalling the incident, 'if I had burnt *her* Bible?' To nurture my taste in horseflesh, Father would take me on Sundays to Tattersals Repository on Knightsbridge Green, which was in those days the Sotheby's of the Sporting World. Every Monday a sale took place in the vast Palladian Courtyard and the day before, Father would view the savage brutes. He was forever opening horse-boxes, entering and inducing the tethered creature to move over. I never knew what we were going to find — gigantic shire-horses, excitable hunters, clumsy mares in foal. All I knew and dreaded was the fact that sooner or later I would be menaced by their heels and have to take to mine. Father knew no fear. After all, had he not been a cavalry officer, if only for the briefest period? On Sundays he returned to the world of his military prowess. Clutching his catalogue and occasionally waving it to induce a horse to show its paces outside the box, led by a groom whom my father rewarded with a florin, he would estimate the price which 'Lot Seventy-Three, the property of a nobleman and regularly hunted with the Quorn and sold only because she is not up to the owner's weight' would fetch next day under the hammer.

He never, as far as I know, actually attended the sale, perhaps because he feared he might be tempted to buy a horse and hitch it to a lamp post outside the Naval and Military, to add to my mother's anxieties.

I learnt a lot from my father, but not perhaps the facts of life. Once and only once did he ever attempt to educate me in such matters. We were walking along Jermyn Street and my father suddenly choked on catching sight of a youth walking daintily on the opposite pavement.

'Bobbie,' he told me, when he had recovered composure, 'I am going to tell you something very dreadful, something you ought to know. There are men in this street who paint their faces.' I looked round eagerly in search of Red Indians and saw none. Oddly enough, I never walk down Jermyn Street without thinking of my father.

But each night before the curtain rises, while I am painting my face, I never think of him at all.

My Sister's Keeper

My sister was holding forth on the startling inefficiency of the Gas Board, who had delivered her new meter in an apparently otherwise empty pantechnicon, which had arrived on the wrong day and from the wrong direction. The man who had arranged to meet and install it meanwhile was down the village street knocking at doors enquiring whether the occupiers were harbouring an escaped appliance.

'But,' I pointed out, 'the meter was eventually installed successfully. You didn't have to pay for the petrol or the man-hours.'

'In the long run,' she told me, 'of course I have to pay.'

'In the long run,' I snapped, 'the people of this country are connected, disconnected, heated and encouraged to cook with a mysterious substance piped from the bottom of the North Sea into their individual homes with immense ingenuity and conspicuous safety. Except on rare occasions when the house tends to blow up, or they deliberately elect to finish their days head-down in the bottom of the oven, they are bloody lucky to get it.'

'The trouble,' I went on, raising my voice as my sister, like myself, is rather deaf, 'the trouble with this country is that it is full of people like you who criticise for the sake of criticism, who never believe anyone gets on with the job, who constantly complain of the ineptitude, inefficiency and downright bloody-mindedness of their fellow citizens, be they politicians or postmen. You ought to try fetching the gas yourself, old girl, in a bucket and you'd have some idea of the difficulties and danger involved.'

My sister, who is used to the give and take of family life, adjusted her ear-piece calmly. I was not sure whether she had heard a word. She certainly hadn't listened. At our combined ages of close on one hundred and forty years, we seldom listen to each other and never for long.

'The trouble with you, brother,' she condescended, 'is that you have never been near a gas ring.'

My sister and I are poles apart and when, as usually happens, we are wrongly connected to each other, we are liable to blow a fuse.

It is because I am so exactly like her that I find her particularly irritating at breakfast, like the shaving mirror which has just reflected the counter image of my double chins. Both of us firmly believe that what the country—what the world—needs most is our guidance. Because we are so seldom consulted on major issues, so infrequently bidden to walk the corridors of power, we have to exercise our inalienable right to advise and warn whenever and wherever opportunity knocks. We feel it our duty to instruct on each and every occasion. We may not have expert knowledge of the subject under discussion but, thank God, we have Common Sense.

'It is better, surely,' my sister will tell a chance acquaintance who has confided his intention of buying a second-hand car from a friend, 'it is better on these occasions to deal with a recognised second-hand car dealer and be sure you get the vehicle vetted by an independent expert. I believe the AA have just such a service available.'

Similarly, when anyone flourishes an airline ticket at me, I question first the wisdom of the proposed journey and then the destination to which he is bound. 'To go to Sorrento at this time of the year,' I remark, 'is asking for trouble. Why not Paxos?' There are, of course, many reasons, but I don't wish to be told them. What I wish to do is explain that once there, it is wiser to hire water goggles and fishing spears on the beach where the equipment is not only cheaper to rent but in better nick than that supplied by the hotel. In point of fact the fellow is going to Sorrento not to bathe but to bank, a fact which, if he is foolish enough to divulge it, will enable me to pass on some meaningful information on the state of the Italian economy not all that recently imparted to me in a conversation with an Australian handbag importer on a flight to Bahrein.

Both my sister and I absorb the minimum of information necessary to enable us to pass it on in depth. A cursory glance at St Peter's, a brief stroll around the Vatican, and I am able to explain not only the Catholic religion, but also the reason for sectarian strife.

My sister is an instant diagnostician. No one has to complain of a pain or feeling of discomfort in her hearing without being informed of the real nature of their trouble. 'Have you had your gall bladder examined lately?' she will question. 'I imagine that is where the seat of the trouble is likely to be.' Often she will prescribe a simple remedy such as a glass of hot water on rising, or a copper band for the wrist. We both know and will certainly try and verify, if anyone is really interested, the address of some quack in Nottingham who, at various times, has had a remarkable success in treating cases of suspected Dodd's Disease.

Neither of us are, I think, overtly concerned to know whether our advice has been followed or whether our patient has benefited thereby. Quite frankly we are too busy to follow up or even job back. We have only a limited time to spend with one group before hurrying away to attend our next surgery. If people don't get on and do as they are told, it's not our fault. On the rare occasions when our advice was not sought and there was no opportunity to proffer it, there is little for us to do but to visit the scene of the disaster, pausing, more often in my case than my sister's, to be snapped like Churchill amid the ruins.

This week, for instance, I was invited by the Northumberland and, I understood, Durham branch of the Royal Institute of Architects to their annual party in the Civic Centre to entertain them. The invitation specified this. 'Your brief,' it ran, 'is to amuse rather than instruct.' Alas, were it only possible, how happy I should be. It is true that my function on these occasions is really akin to that of a projectionist—that anonymous, sober stranger who walks up the garden path with his capacious black bag while the children are still munching the birthday cake, and sets up his apparatus in the sitting-room, so recently the venue of rough games and treasure hunting, preparing to exhibit Mickey Mouse or Charlie Chaplin for unenthusiastic tots who were hoping for television and *Dad's Army*.

The temptation for me, of course, is to include home movies in my programme, and like all home movies mine are in a pretty good muddle. A reel that commences with intimate shots of myself bathing on the Lido suddenly becomes an interminable picnic, the occasion for which, along with the names of the participants, has entirely escaped me.

For me, the after-dinner speeches hold no terrors as long as they are made by myself. I imagine my sister feels much the same, but I was glad she wasn't at Newcastle.

'How did it go by the way . . . that little junket of yours?' she asked, looking up from the newspaper behind which she had temporarily retired to regroup her forces.

'Marvellously,' I told her. 'Most enthusiastic. Afterwards I was invited up to the Lord Mayor's parlour for drinks and a free ashtray.'

'Did he agree with what you said?' she wondered.

'It's a she,' I told her. 'The Lord Mayor of Newcastle is a bonny wee lassie from Glasgow. Her friend is Lady Mayoress.'

'Is her friend a man?' asked my sister.

'No, of course not. The Lady Mayoress is a woman.'

'I believe sometimes their husbands take on the job,' she said.

'Not on this occasion. After the party the Lady Mayoress washed up the glasses.'

'I thought you told me there were five hundred guests,' my sister remarked. 'What time did you get away?'

'Quite early. The Lady Mayoress only washed up in the Lord Mayor's parlour. It was all quite informal. She's a Labour Lord Mayor.'

'Ah,' said my sister, a disciple of Mrs Thatcher's, 'I imagined she would be. What did you speak about?'

'This and that,' I told her. 'Theatrical reminiscences, the North as a cultural sounding board, my understanding of and fascination with the Geordie. The splendour of Seaton Delaval.'

'Who's he?' Margaret asked.

'Seaton Delaval,' I told her, 'is a Palladian mansion ascribed, for all I know correctly, to Vanbrugh. It's just outside the city.'

She went back to the paper. I was relieved not to have been further questioned. In point of fact the whole evening had been a bit of a disaster. To start with I had lost at the races and then, getting to the hotel, was told to present myself for the reception at six. When I got there at half past (I always make a point of arriving later than expected in order to transform the anxiety of the chairman into extravagant relief and enthusiasm when I do appear) , the vast Civic Centre was curiously deserted. Surely I had not come on the wrong evening? No, it was just that the proceedings were timed to start at eight.

I permitted myself to be shown around by the resident custodian. I was unprepared for the splendour and extragavance. The whole concept is that of a modern Vatican. It was late in the day to chide. I inspected the Grand Stair Hall, dipped reverent fingers in the ornamental pool, admired the galleries lined in random English oak, was baffled by the John Piper tapestry woven in Aubusson, abstract in concept and in colours drawn from the natural minerals and flora of Northumbria, crossed the Patricia Marble floor of the Council Chamber Lobby, entered the chamber and seated myself on one of the individual thrones upholstered in light green hide, designed with small individual tables serving not only as arm rests but (and I quote) 'allowing members to write on either side'. In point of fact there was little evidence of graffiti, and I lay back and contemplated the Rio Rosewood and Cedar of Lebanon and the jewel-like perspex brackets. I did not inspect the Rates Hall located in the East Block, floored in Fior di Pescho Arabescato Nuova and Perlato Isernia marble with a sycamore linenfold slatted ceiling and containing a public counter of American black walnut extending eighty feet on which, presumably, the ratepayers are expected to deposit their contributions towards the six million or so the project cost.

During a light dinner of foie gras, turtle soup, sea food in scallop shells, sorbets, chicken, cherries in brandy, I decided that the architects of Northumbria had never had it so good. I was also slightly miffed by having to surrender my chair after the foie gras to the Lord Mayor because it had a better back, and by one of my fellow guests warning me that Frank Muir made the mistake of having spoken for twenty-four minutes on the last occasion of the banquet. 'How long would you like?' I asked. 'As short as possible, old boy,' he urged me. Would that I had taken his advice and confined myself to a few humorous anecdotes and an expression of gratitude for the hospitality. Instead, and unaccountably, I started to enlarge on the hell that I had experienced during the last three days being driven around the cities of Cambridge, York, and Newcastle itself; of the endless frustration of being directed in a different direction from the one I wished to pursue; of the fury and rage engendered by having to sit for hours in a traffic jam with the bonnet pointing in the wrong direction; of the misery and confusion of Spaghetti Junctions and the peculiar horror of civic centres in general and this one in particular.

'The waste, the extravagance,' I told them. 'The sheer bloody-mindedness of the whole futile exercise. Who wants a building this size? Who would not prefer our towns and cities the way they used to be? The architect of today has hearkened to the greed and opportunism of the developer, and betrayed his own generation and the ones which have to follow, until the last concrete office block spills its blue asbestos and bleeds to death.'

My remarks were uncalled for, my criticisms ill-informed and my conduct inexcusable. It is permissible, possibly, to nip the hand that feeds, but not to make a meal of it. But sometimes that's how the bread roll crumbles.

Afterwards everyone was kindness itself. As I remarked earlier, the Lord Mayor gave me an ashtray and allowed me to examine the Northumberland plate. Someone even drove me home. Well, not home exactly, but to the Station Hotel. But home I was twenty-four hours later, even if not exactly dried, and my sister and I in a state of mutual contentment welcomed the next latecomer to the breakfast table who announced that he was never so tired as after a good night's sleep. 'Do you read at night?' asked my sister. 'I mean, just before turning out the light? I have always found it helpful before doing so to lie for a few moments consciously relaxing the lower vertebrae.'

'Nonsense,' I told her. 'The mistake people make is taking a book to bed in the first place. I never read in bed.'

'You never read at all,' said my sister. 'You only skim.

'You mean skip,' I told her.

'Skim. I said skim, and I meant skim.'

'I don't skim or skip. It's just that I happen to be rather quick at assimilating essentials and discarding trivialities such as relaxed lower vertebraes.'

I was determined to have the last word. I always am.

Dame Gladys Cooper

On the last evening of her life, my splendid and courageous mother-in-law, Gladys Cooper, rose from her bed and making her way, not without considerable effort, to her dressing-table, proceeded to brush her hair and make up her celebrated face. Then, gazing into the mirror for what was to prove the very last time, she remarked to her nurse, 'If this is what virus pneumonia does to one, I really don't think I shall bother to have it again.' She got back into bed and presently died in her sleep. Her looks were something she habitually shrugged off. People used to tell me, as no doubt they told her, that it was in her bones. 'If your bones are right, you can't go wrong. Look at Katharine Hepburn.' I go along with them to a certain extent, but believe that bones, just as clothes, must be worn with panache. A lot of women have good bones. Very few of them looked like Gladys.

Among all the letters the family received when she died was one from the secretary of The Postcard Club of Great Britain, assuring us that their historian had every card which featured Miss Cooper and that her beauty was thus preserved for posterity.

Most mornings of her life, Gladys received at least one letter returning one of these celebrated postcards. Occasionally they came in dozens, wrapped up in brown paper, announcing that they were from the collection of a deceased relative of the sender, and towards the end of her life she became increasingly suspicious of them. Like the late Maurice Utrillo, she would question their authenticity.

'I don't think that's me at all,' she would tell us. 'I'm sure there was another woman who used to pose as me at times.'

'But,' we would ask, 'who but you, dear, would dress up as a shepherdess and clutch a rake, a hoe and a besom while being photographed in Mr. Foulsham's or Mr. Banfield's back garden?'

Nothing would surprise me less than to hear that those two

gentlemen to whom my mother-in-law was in those days under exclusive contract, postcardwise, are alive and well and living in Leeds, producing that most favourite of all programmes, 'Stars on Sunday'. Anyone who has watched Anna Neagle or Louis Mountbatten undertake the chore, who has seen the choirs posed on on the Elizabethan staircase, James Mason reading the bible by the fire blazing on a hot summer day, must acknowledge how much the incongruity of the proceedings owe to these early pioneers of the absurd. Was it, I wonder, Mr. Banfield who worked the shutter and Mr. Foulsham who dreamed up the setting, or vice versa? Perhaps they collaborated in procuring the golf sticks and the tennis racquets, the artificial snowballs and the genuine dead trout. What was the significance of the teacup which so often appeared, half raised in salute? Was one of them perhaps a teetotaller? There was always something going on. Not a lot, perhaps, but something.

At times there was just the very faintest hint, the slightest trace of the erotic. One of my favourites shows Gladys with her hair in plaits and dressed in a brown peignoir over a pink wrap over a blue night-dress, about to open a bedroom door. But perhaps erotic is hardly the word. Saucy, that's what they were sometimes, saucy. When the children arrived and Gladys insisted on supplying these herself, life sobered up a good deal. Only the hats remained coquettish. There is one photograph of her sitting beside her first husband in a motorcar. She hadn't as yet taken the wheel, apparently. The expression is as always non-committal. 'Here I am,' she seems to be saying, 'what next?' And on this occasion of course, 'Where to?'

What did they do with all of these postcards, the great British public? And not only the British public. There must have been an enormous export market, hence the wording on the back: THIS IS A REAL PHOTOGRAPH OF A BRITISH BEAUTY. HAND-PAINTED ON RAJAH BROMIDE CARD. The insistence that the photographs were genuine gives a clue perhaps to the awe in which the sitter was held at any rate in later life. But who bought them, and for what purpose? Certainly not to send through the post. Very few of the ones in my collection are actually written on. The exceptions have a fascination all their own. 'As promised, here is the pretty baby. Those flowers you sent Mother were lovely. Things are in such an unsettled state I don't know when I wrote you. Haven't forgotten the headsquare, and shall send the prayerbook.' There is a sad little note from Geo. to Flo. 'I was watching for the post all day. Just a line hoping you are in the pink and still enjoying yourself.' At any rate nowadays the lovesick are put out of their misery a good deal quicker. Nothing in the morning delivery and you've had it, chum.

A good many of the cards were bought by soldiers in the last war but one to carry into battle. You couldn't be accused of being yellow if you put a thick wad of postcards in your breast pocket just over your heart. It was just that you happened to be a great womaniser and of course like everyone else, a fan.

To start life as a picture postcard and end as a Dame of the British Empire. After such a start it seems only natural that my mother-in-law's first job should have been in 'Bluebell in Fairyland'. Indeed about the whole of her early career in the theatre there seems an element of make-believe. The whole story of her success was almost too good to be true if she wasn't in a sort of fairyland, or at any rate a book written for children. This beautiful girl who went on the stage and in an incredibly short time became a star with all London at her feet. How it was done, the formula for this extravagant success, the lightning fame and fortune which in these days seems only to come to property developers, remains for me a mystery.

She never discussed past triumphs and when you asked her, all she would ever tell you was that she learnt her acting from Hawtrey. It was not that she was wilfully reticent, but when she recalled the past at all, it was to tell of the things that had amused her, the quirks of her managers, the practical jokes she used to play on her leading men. What leading men they were – Seymour Hicks, Hawtrey, Gerald Du Maurier, Ivor Novello, Owen Nares, and the one she married, Philip Merivale, and whose presence lived on in her life always, and whose family she adopted as she adopted us all.

Of all the performances I saw her give, my favourite was when she appeared in *The Indifferent Shepherd* and sat on the back of the sofa behind Francis Lister, or did he sit behind her? She had that unique gift of tugging at your heartstrings. Who can forget the curtain of *The Last of Mrs. Cheyney,* or her standing on the staircase in *Cynara,* or the curtain again of *The Letter?*

The pleasure of watching her on the stage before I ever dreamt I would be her son-in-law, and then the pleasure of being her son-in-law. Since she died I have thought about her often, always with a chuckle and always realising how much there was about her that I never found out. I never even discovered what she thought of me. I never even discovered if she knew towards the end of her life how ill she was. She had the most beautiful manners and about some things she never let on.

She could be very sharp at times. She was not good at feeling sorry for people, perhaps because she never felt sorry for herself. If you were in trouble, you got out of it, with her help of course, but it was up to you in the end. If you got ill, you got better. She was in her way something of a health fiend. She didn't eat much. She worshipped the sun. When we stayed with her in her Californian home she would come back from the studios at dusk and start cooking our dinner and then, when everything was in hand, she would disappear and a moment later sweep across the patio, wrapped in towelling, for her evening swim. Ten minutes later she would be back and five minutes after that she would reappear in the sort of shift dress of which she was so fond, gold bangles on her arms, her hair and her make-up immaculate, to mix a final round of daquiris before she took the lamb from the spit.

How is it done, I used to ask myself. How can she be so elegant? If she was vain about anything it was about her cooking. Two things you were never allowed to criticise — her marmalade and her driving. Both, I always felt privately, left a good deal to chance. But about everything else she was eminently reasonable. How good an actress she thought herself to be, how seriously she took her profession, I was never sure. She acted like she did everything else, naturally. But of one thing I am very certain. She was immensely proud of the affection and gratitude of her public. She answered every letter, she acknowledged every compliment and no day was too cold or too wet for her to pause as she came out of her stage door, or in later years the supermarket in Henley, to have a chat to a faithful patron who wished to compliment her on some past performance in the theatre or on the screen or on television, or on just being Gladys Cooper.

Laurence Olivier recalled her as hurdling the various fashions of the theatre, and if sometimes she knocked one over or it collapsed beneath her, she never faltered or shortened her stride. She raced ahead, and those who expected that one day she'd come back to her field were wrong. She was still in front at the finish.

Perhaps I've dwelt too much on her comparatively early triumphs, not mentioned her later ones, her films, but here again even the best of them didn't compare with the splendour and wonder of watching her in *The Bohemian Girl*. She loved television, was very proud of having done *The Rogues*. Asked once what she regretted in her life, she said, 'I was very sorry when *The Rogues* finished and when I just missed being the first woman to loop the loop. I was in the cockpit when the pilot's wife arrived, and I gave way. I didn't want to break up the marriage, but I've always regretted it. One should go on with things.'

She had a passion for all animals, the wilder the better. Ducks, cats, dogs, monkeys, parrots shared her houses with her, and she relished any opportunity of acting with lions or tigers or leopards or bears. Nothing scared her. Once on a beach at Acapulco a rifle bullet pinged past us. I turned and ran into the sea. Gladys turned and walked towards the firing. 'What happened to you, then?' she asked when I rejoined her. 'I had a sudden absurd desire to paddle. Was there a shot?' 'The gardener,' she told me. 'The owners of the house are away and he's been left in charge. Natural, really, he couldn't have been more than ten.' Natural, it's the word I most associate with Gladys herself; she was a natural woman.

At Home

Glancing back over the years, I think now that at the age of eight I seriously over-reacted to the death of Lord Kitchener. 'Kitchener Drowned,' I exulted loudly as I sped from room to room of the house in Wellington College grounds where I was living. In shocked tones it was pointed out to me that Kitchener was one of ours. 'The child is not pro-German,' my mother was obliged to explain to an outraged cook, 'just over excited. Besides, he has just learnt to read.' I was a slow starter where school was concerned. I used to walk there crouching down in the ditch because of a dog which barked whenever he set eyes on me. Later, as a pupil at the College itself, I adopted much the same tactics, but dogs and schoolmasters continued to bark and bite.

In early life I cannot pretend Berkshire was my favourite county. I had a peculiar horror of Reading. It was there one changed trains and took the branch line to Blackwater, Ash and Wellington. But now that I have lived more than half of my life in these parts, I have grown accustomed to the place and cannot imagine ever being happy elsewhere.

For more than thirty-five years I have lived where I live now in the village of Crazies Hill, in what was once the Keeper's Cottage on the Hennerton Estate, where the Rhodes family farmed in the nineteenth century and from where young Master Cecil set out to conquer Africa. In those days there was nothing they couldn't grow in Crazies Hill, even tobacco and flax.

I came to the house one morning and found the builder still laying red tiles in the hall. He named a price, I lopped off fifty pounds, and he solemnly rose from his knees and shook my hand without another word. Later I thought I'd better try and buy the wood at the back of the garden. The timber merchant came to tea.

'It's no use to me,' he told me, 'I've had the oak out of it.' 'It's very useful to me,' I told him, 'and there's nine acres of it.' He looked thoughtful. 'Give me two hundred and fifty pounds,' he told me, 'and we shan't quarrel.' He could have asked a lot more and I would have paid it if I could. It didn't occur to him to hold me to ransom.

The house in the grounds of Wellington was called Underwoods. I cannot imagine what induced my father to buy it. In the war he commanded the soldiers who guarded the railway bridges on the Southern Line. He was propelled along the rails manually by his staff and, according to him, was not signalled from box to box. 'I take my life in my hands, dear,' he told my mother, 'but am glad to do it for you and the children and, of course, the country.' I never quite understood the duties of soldiers deployed in the tunnels, but then, I imagine, nor did he. Before moving into our house, we lived in the Wellington College Hotel opposite the polo field. I don't think Father still played polo, but he was very keen on kite flying. When the wind wouldn't blow, he would drive round and round the grass in an open motor with the kite up and away triumphantly behind. All I can remember of the First World War was the kite, and an entire box of greengages he brought home as a peace offering for my mother, and Kitchener's death.

In the Second World War I was still in Berkshire. The summer of Dunkirk was nearly over, and one day we went swimming at the Yacht Club. Normally we were not encouraged to swim there for fear we should impede the dinghies. On that afternoon there were few competitors—a dozen children, the elderly commandant, and ourselves. After tea he took himself off sculling quietly down stream. The club steward hailed him just before he disappeared round the bend. 'Commandant,' he called 'are you going ashore? Because if so, I must lower your pennant.'

Berkshire is the county that takes things in its stride. The first time the Russians came to the Henley Regatta after many years, an old thatcher on my side of the river paused in his task to gaze at one of them trailing in a preliminary heat of the Diamond Sculls. 'Watch it, Popski!' he shouted from the roof. 'They'll shoot you when you get home.'

When the Chief Test Pilot of Britain took a house in the village, he was received with cautious acclaim. 'I have his account,' the grocer told me, 'for as long as it lasts, of course.'

My friendly neighbourhood road-man dealt me a lasting blow by bearing off our cook and marrying her. We still meet in the pub and I ask after her health and whether she cooks as well as ever. 'I imagine so,' he tells me, and then, with a twist of the knife, 'mind you, I don't let her try anything fancy on me.' As a boy he watched his father plant two oak trees on either side of the road which leads down to Wargrave. 'You won't live long enough to see these two shake hands,' he was told, but father was wrong as fathers often are.

When we moved in, an old gentleman came to lay a brick path and seemed surprised to learn I was an actor by trade. He too, it seemed, had once been to a theatre, the Drury Lane, to see *Decameron Nights*. They had charged him fifteen shillings for his seat and although he had enjoyed it after a fashion, it hadn't been worth the money. He was not, he assured me, contemplating another visit to the Smoke.

There are people in our village who have been to London only once or twice in their lives, and some who have never been at all. They read about what goes on there but, except for those rare occasions when Londoners drive down and leave a motor car or a mattress in the ditch and the villagers have to move fast if they don't want another left the following weekend, they are incurious and uninvolved.

Driving home after a performance I am aware that my neighbours are already in bed and asleep. 'There goes that fool Morley,' they tell each other as I pass. 'Why doesn't he pack it in?' When I finally decide to do so, I hope it's in Berkshire.